ABANDONED SACRED PLACES

ABANDONED SACRED PLACES

LAWRENCE JOFFE

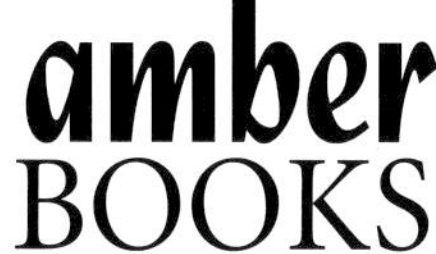

First published in 2019

Published by Amber Books Ltd
United House
North Road
London N7 9DP
United Kingdom
www.amberbooks.co.uk
Instagram: amberbooksltd
Facebook: www.facebook.com/amberbooks
Twitter: @amberbooks

ISBN: 978-1-78274-769-7

Project Editor: Kieron Connolly
Design: Gary Webb
Picture Research: Terry Forshaw and Kieron Connolly

Printed in China

Contents

Introduction

Inspired by a ruined pedestal of pharaoh Ramses II, poet Percy Shelley wrote these lines: 'My name is Ozymandias, King of Kings; Look on my Works, ye Mighty, and despair!' A giant statue of Ramses II still 'stands in the desert', part covered in sand, near Egypt's Abu Simbel Temple. What better symbol of the fragility of power – or, as the Bible says: 'How hath the mighty fallen.' Yet what a tribute, too, to memories of past glory.

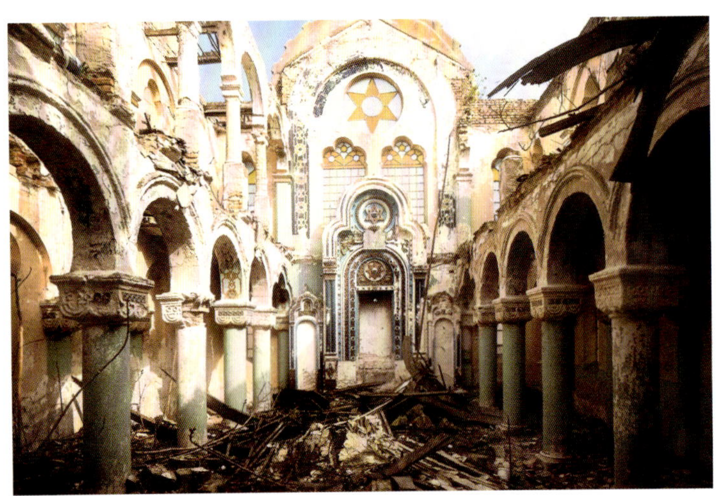

These themes apply to all abandoned sacred places, though reasons for desertion vary: foreign conquest, mass migration, ethnic cleansing, shifting faiths or declining religiosity. More prosaically, causes include changing trade routes, failed crops, natural disasters, even overambitious construction, unpaid bills and bureaucratic mismanagement.

Lastly, a quandary: why do holy sites survive when residences do not? Perhaps because they were built for something greater than our mere daily lives. For as the playwright Peter Shaffer put it: 'Without worship you shrink.'

ABOVE:
Great Synagogue, Constanta, Romania
Completed in 1914, Constanta's Ashkenazi synagogue survived the Nazi mass murder of Romanian Jews. It was abandoned during the 1990s.

OPPOSITE:
Sacred Valley, Cusco Region, Peru
Maize was grown by the Incas on the terraces of the Sacred Valley. The crop was an ingredient in *chicha*, a fermented drink used in religious ceremonies.

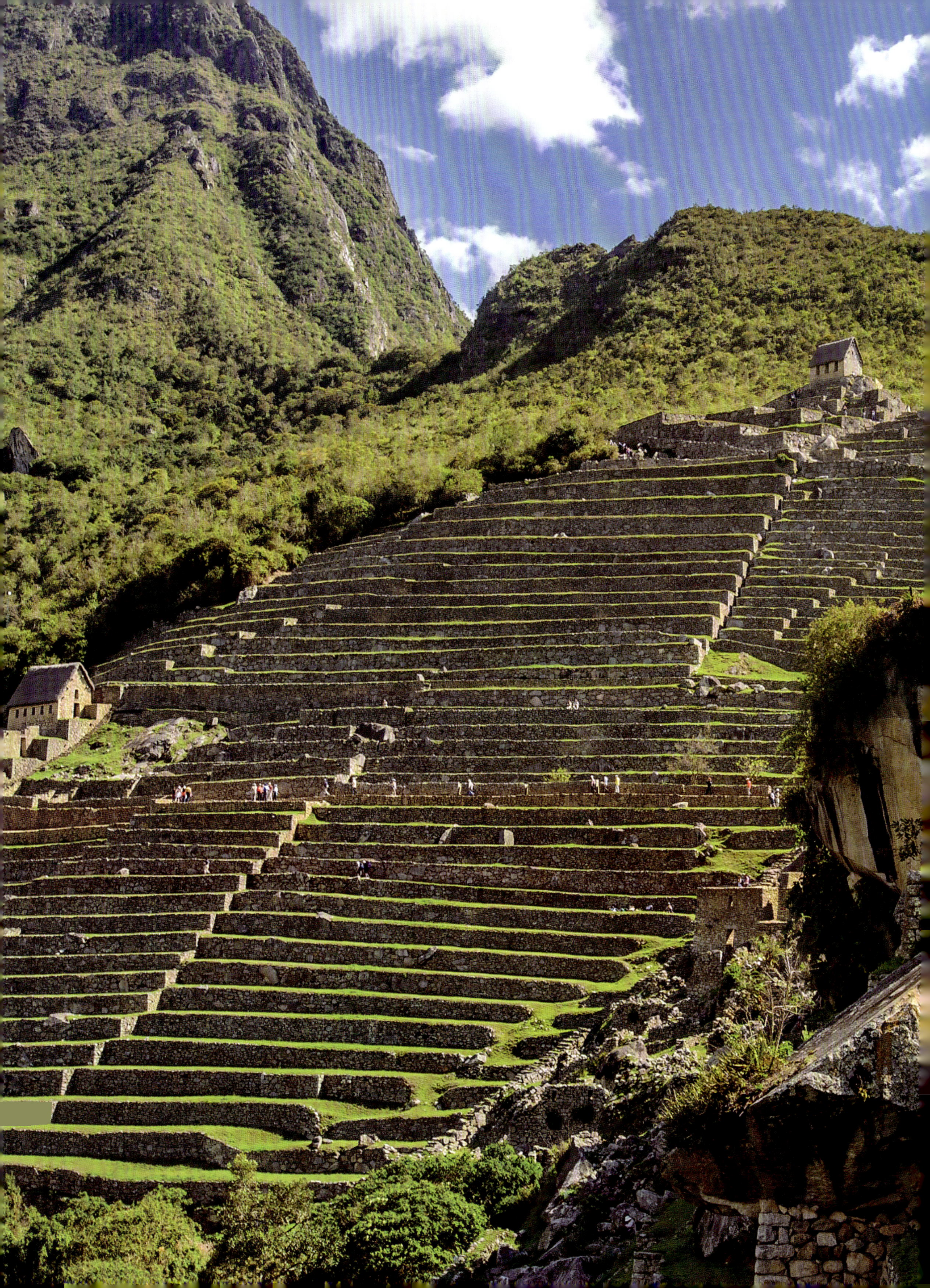

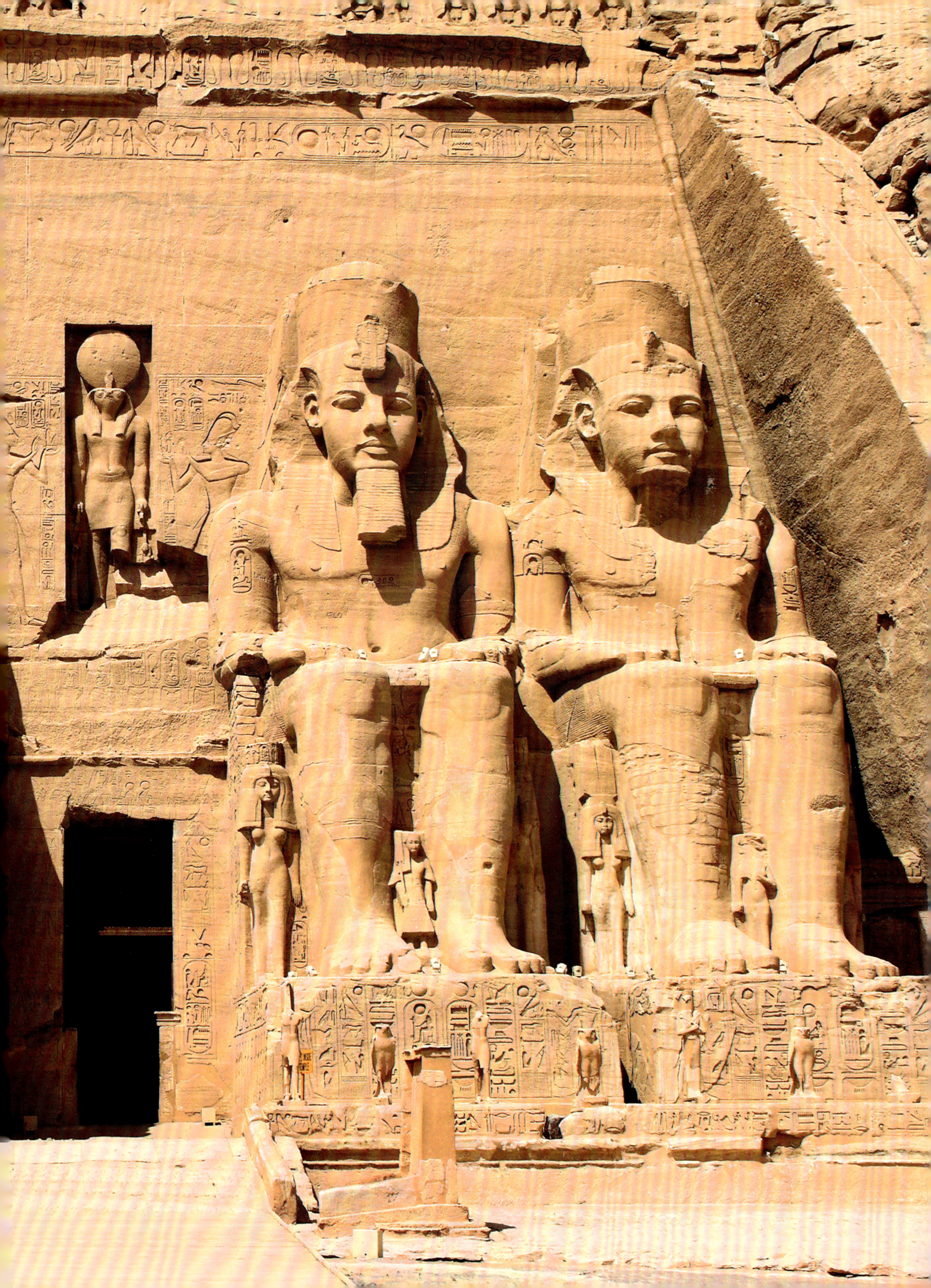

Africa

Mankind most likely originated in Africa, so the continent should tell us much about our earliest beliefs. Today's 1.3 billion Africans, however, are overwhelmingly either Christian or Muslim. Some 100 million Africans still follow traditional religions, although these are mainly conveyed orally and have left little material evidence. One exception is Great Zimbabwe, which gave its name to an independent nation.

North of the Equator, magnificent ruins in Egypt give a clearer sense of ancient faith. Intricate pantheons of deities and portraits of pharaohs as god-kings at Luxor remind us of the former closeness between politics, nature and religion. Meanwhile, Abu Simbel offers a modern lesson: when the Egyptian government removed temples to preserve them from the waters of the Aswan Dam, they revolutionized the world's approach to safeguarding heritage. As the Ancient Roman historian Pliny the Elder wrote: 'There's always something new out of Africa.'

Above all, the continent has absorbed imported faiths. Consider Roman ruins at Sbeitla in Tunisia, or later African-Arab blends in Kiswa Mosque in Tanzania. Lastly, European colonialists once held sway over all of sub-Saharan Africa, leaving their own legacy in the form of now often abandoned churches.

OPPOSITE:
Great Temple, Abu Simbel, Egypt
A colossal 33-metre-tall (108ft) statue of Pharaoh Ramses II the Great (reigned 1279–1213 BCE) is seated for eternity next to his consort, Queen Nefertari, at Abu Simbel. The king was considered an ally of the god Amun. Thus his temple complex, built in 1244 BCE near modern Egypt's southern border with Sudan, was as much a sacred place as a locus of political authority.

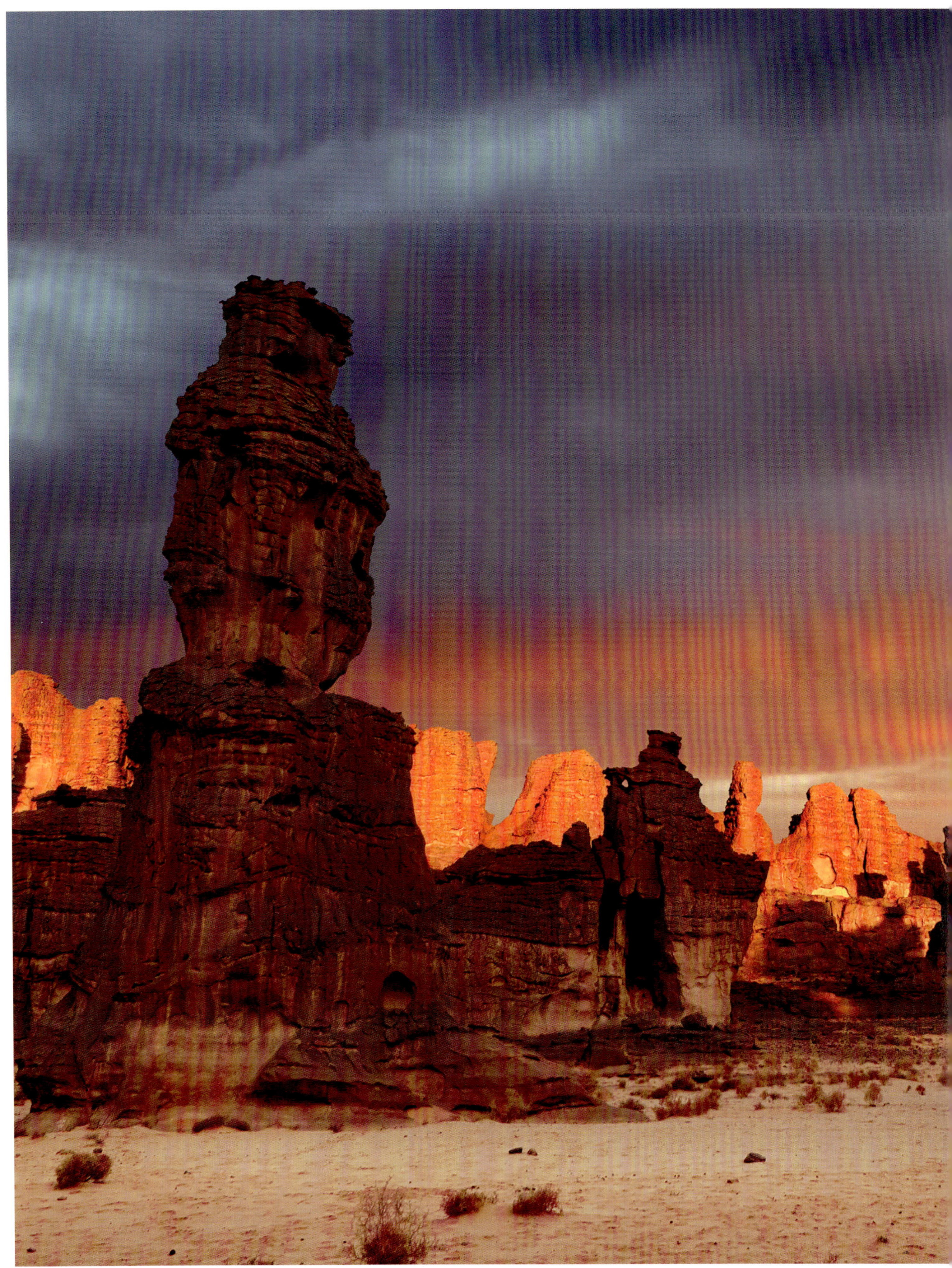

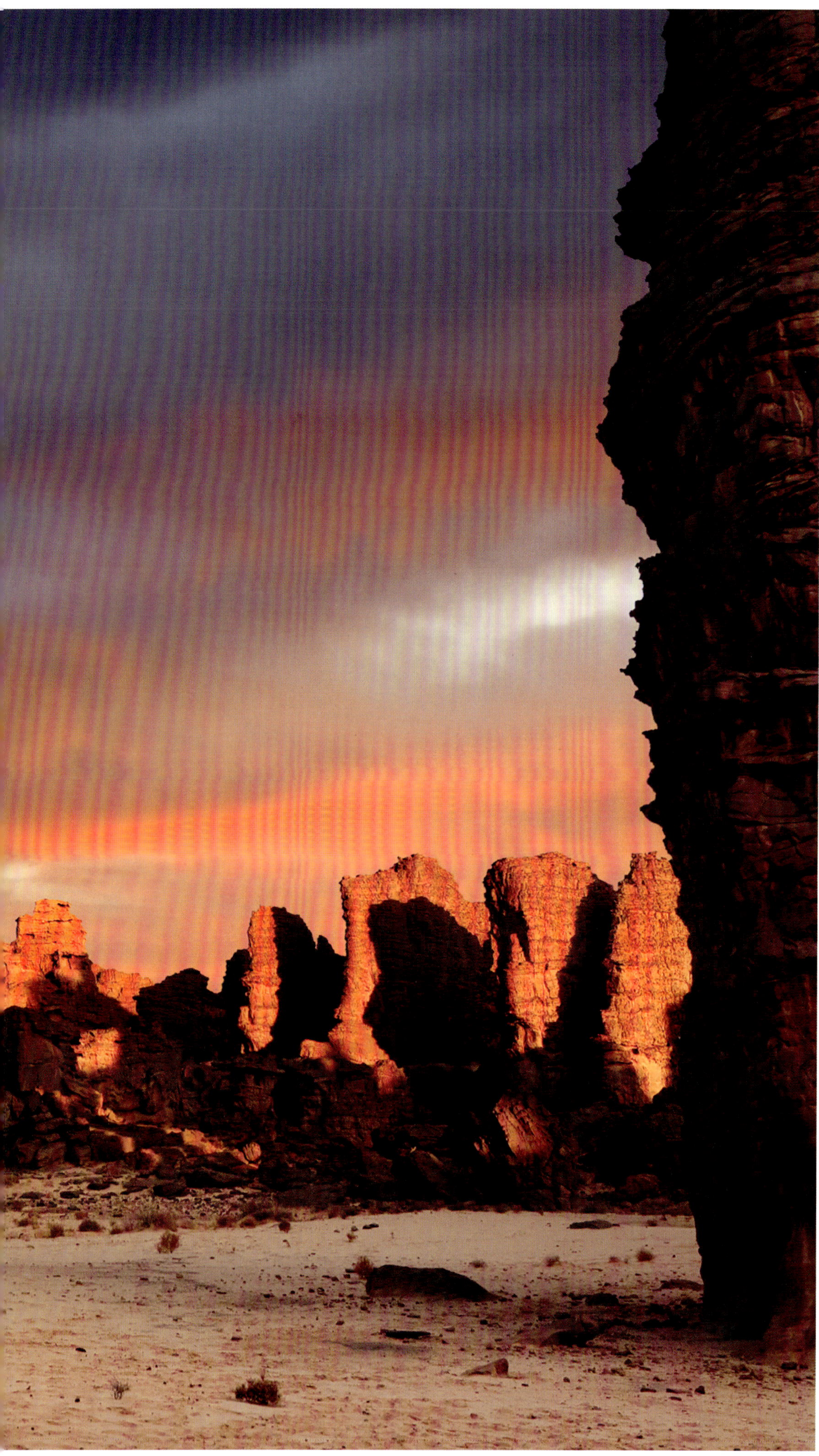

Tassili, Algeria
Lit by a Sahara sundown, these extraordinary eroded sandstone outcrops at Tassili still have the power to awe. Little wonder that early prehistoric nomads gravitated to the Tassili n'Ajjer plain, whose 72,000 square kilometre (27,800 square mile) footprint extends over present-day Algeria, Libya, Niger and Mali. Visitors or residents also left behind some 15,000 remarkable rock art drawings and engravings. The earliest date to c.6000 BCE and some suggest magic-religious rites involving shamanic masked dancers from the Round Heads Period, c.8000 BCE. One school says celebrants are holding magic mushrooms to represent drug-fuelled devotional trances. More prosaically, other etchings show daily social life, the taming of animals and teeming wildlife (the Sahara was not always a bone-dry desert).

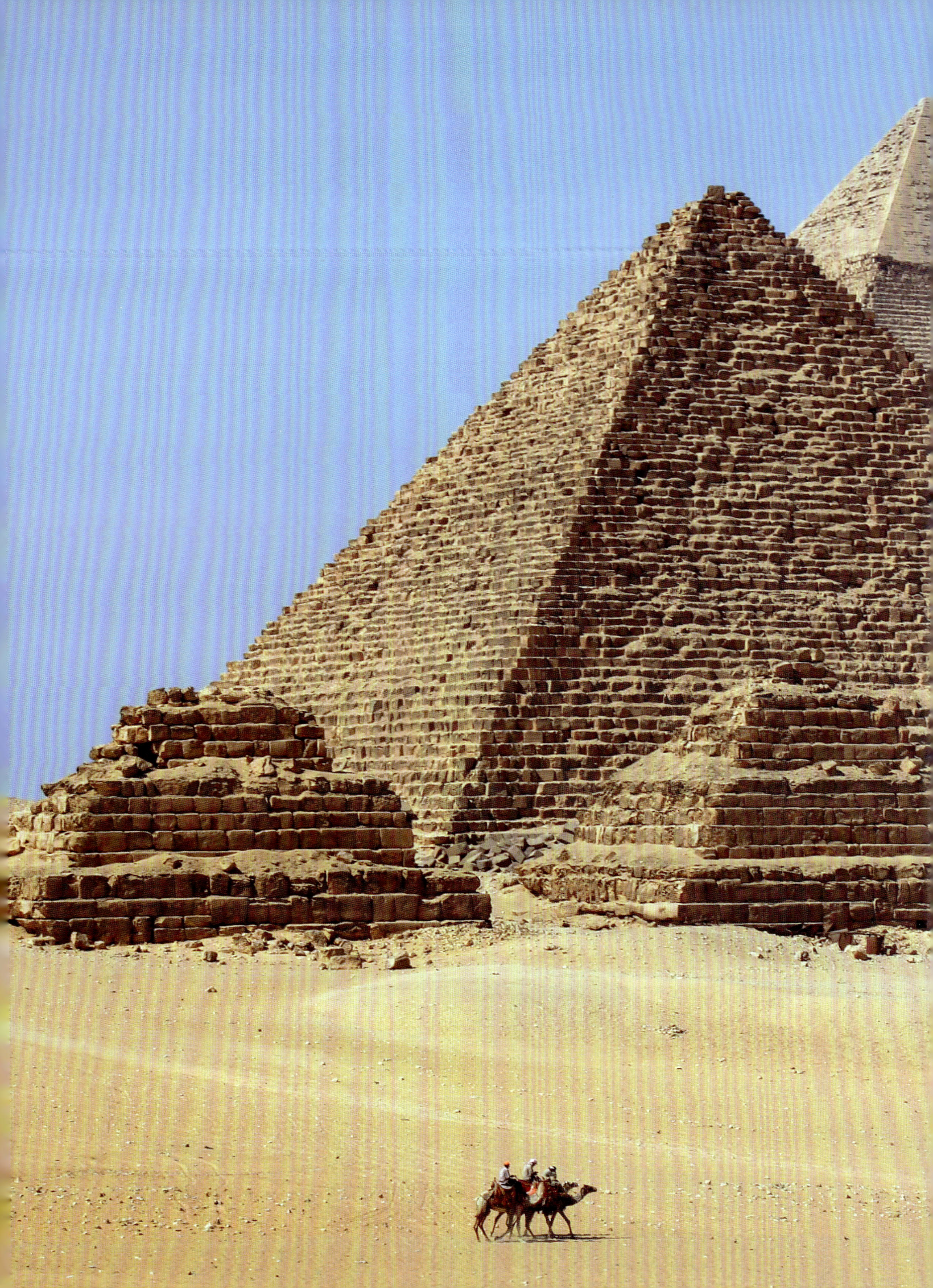

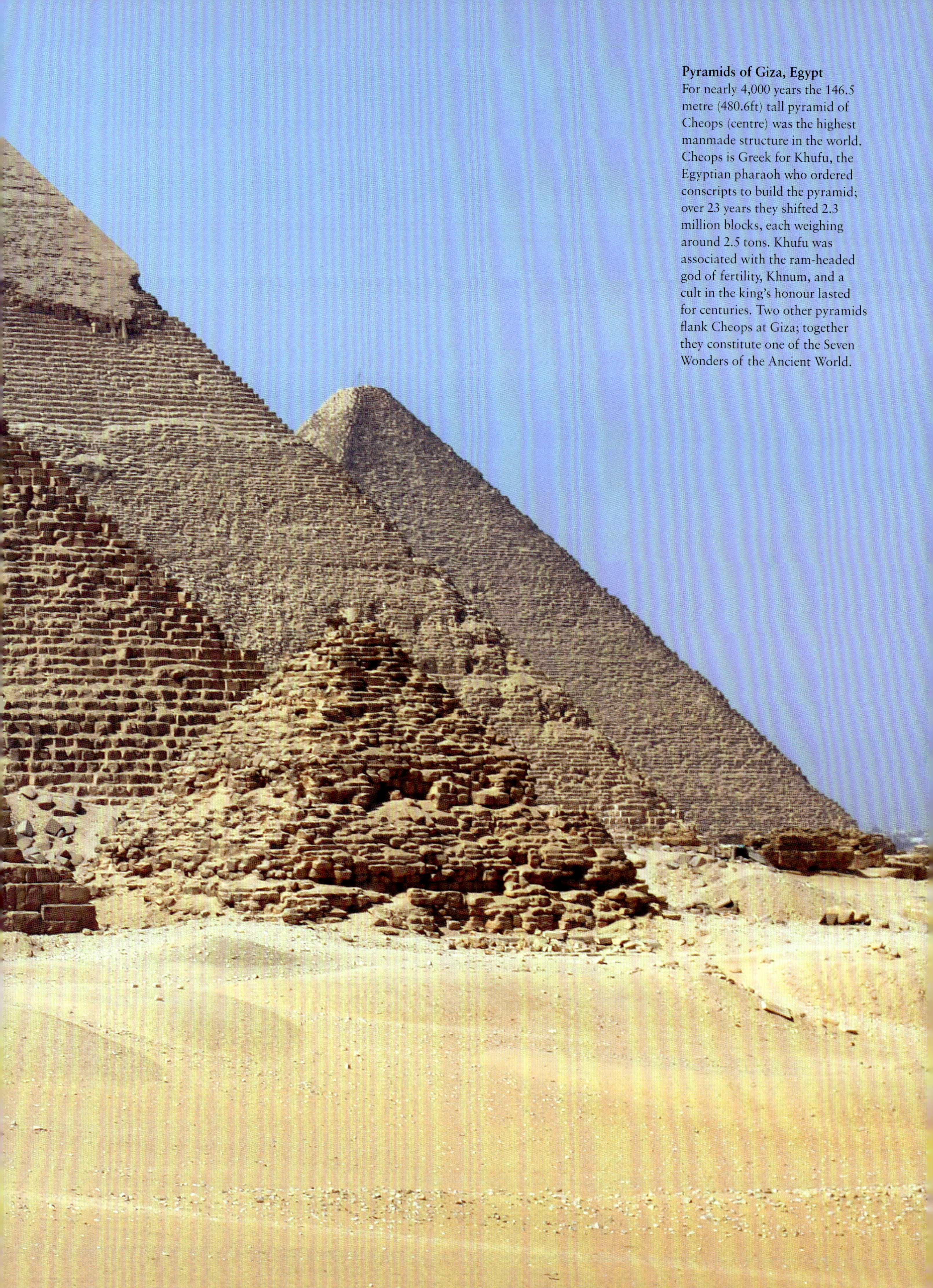

Pyramids of Giza, Egypt
For nearly 4,000 years the 146.5 metre (480.6ft) tall pyramid of Cheops (centre) was the highest manmade structure in the world. Cheops is Greek for Khufu, the Egyptian pharaoh who ordered conscripts to build the pyramid; over 23 years they shifted 2.3 million blocks, each weighing around 2.5 tons. Khufu was associated with the ram-headed god of fertility, Khnum, and a cult in the king's honour lasted for centuries. Two other pyramids flank Cheops at Giza; together they constitute one of the Seven Wonders of the Ancient World.

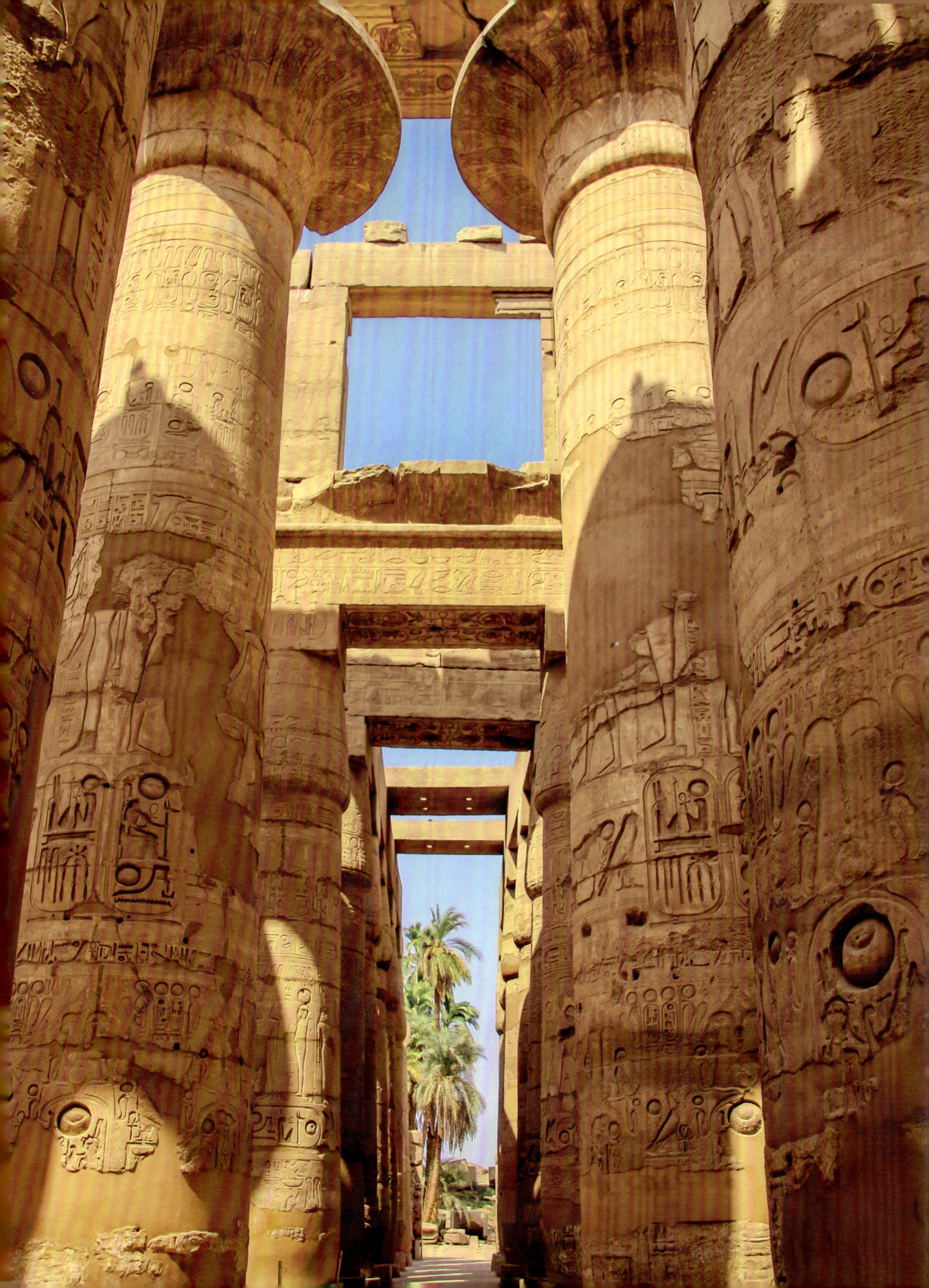

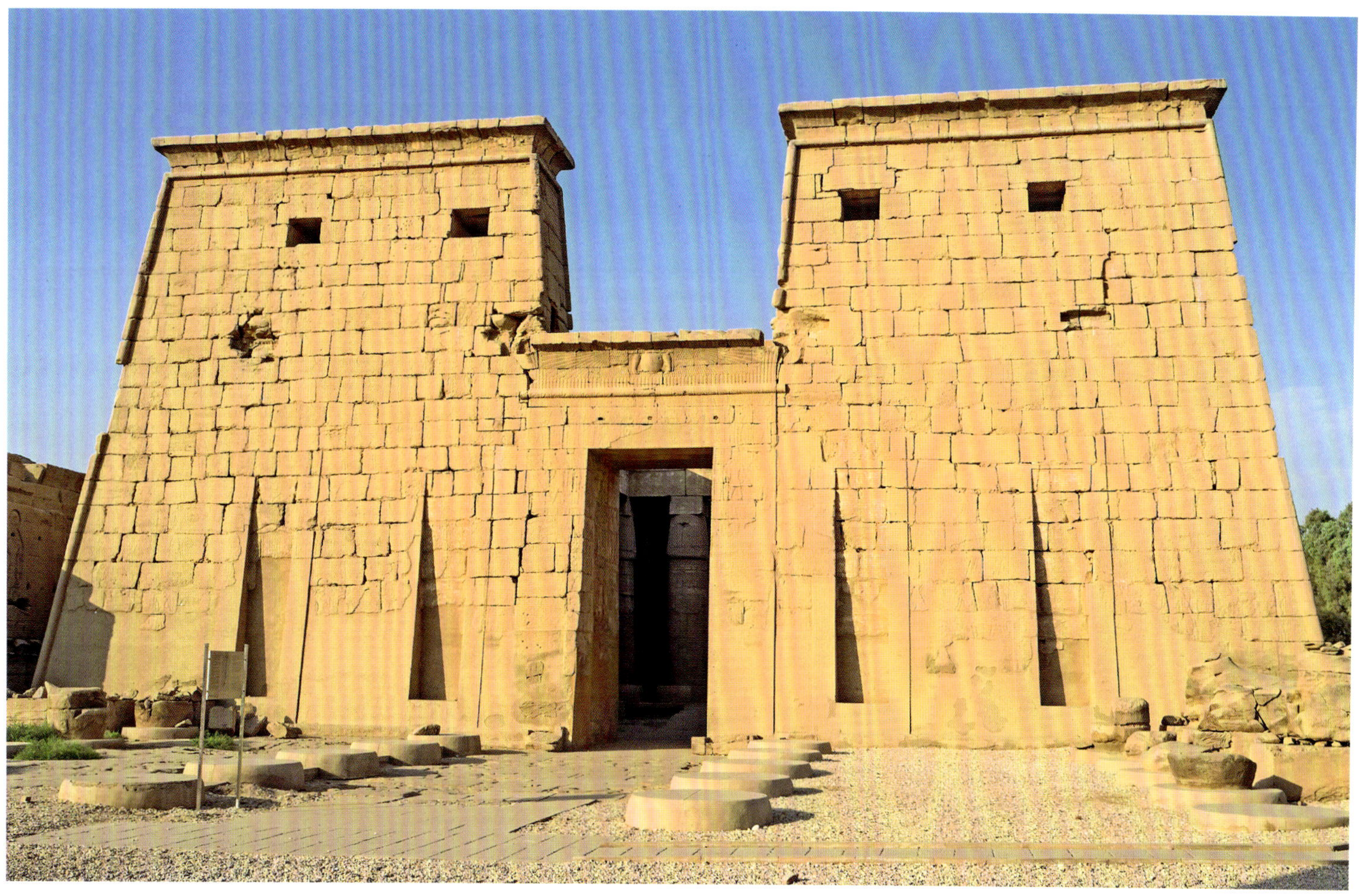

OPPOSITE:

Karnak Temple, Luxor, Egypt

The Great Hypostyle Hall of Karnak Temple remains the largest single religious room in the world. It boasts 12 central 21-metre (69ft) tall stone columns (pictured) and, around them, another 122 supporting columns, even if their roof has gone. Encircling hieroglyphs relate victories by Seti I, creator of the 4,645 square metre (50,000 sq ft) hall, and peace treaties forged by his son Ramses II. The site dominates Luxor's Amun-Re precinct, named after the Egyptian deity whom Greeks later called Zeus Ammon.

ABOVE:

Temple of Khonsu, Karnak, Luxor, Egypt

As faiths change, so older sacred sites are often replaced by structures dedicated to more politically favoured deities. Such was the case with the Temple of Khonsu, built by Pharaoh Ramses III on the site of a former temple in Karnak. Khonsu was a falcon-headed Egyptian god of the moon; his name meant 'traveller', reflecting the lunar passage through the night sky. A rearing cobra formed his crown, and cobras also adorn the New Kingdom era temple entrance.

Small Temple, Abu Simbel, Luxor, Egypt

Four statues of Pharaoah Ramses III and two of his wife, Queen Nefertari, emerge out of living rock at the entrance to the Small Temple at Abu Simbel. All six reach the same height of 10 metres (33ft), suggesting that Ramses admired his wife and that she wielded tremendous power in her own right. Likewise the princesses playing by their feet seem to be taller than their brothers, the princes.

Interior temple reliefs show the goddesses Hathor and Isis crowning Nefertari. The queen wears the same solar disc with cow-horn headgear as the deities. Meanwhile in the Great Temple, Ramses is seen vanquishing the Hittites and consorting with the gods Ra-Harakhty, Ptah and Amun – proof that Ancient Egyptians considered their rulers divine.

Located in present-day Luxor, Abu Simbel was sited near Waset, capital of New Kingdom Egypt (c.1550–c.1077 BCE). Its temples and colossi disappeared under desert sand by the sixth century BCE until rediscovered in 1813. Between 1964 and 1968 Egyptian and Sudanese authorities, helped by UNESCO, moved almost the entire complex 65 metres (213ft) higher and 200 metres (656ft) back to make way for the Aswan Dam.

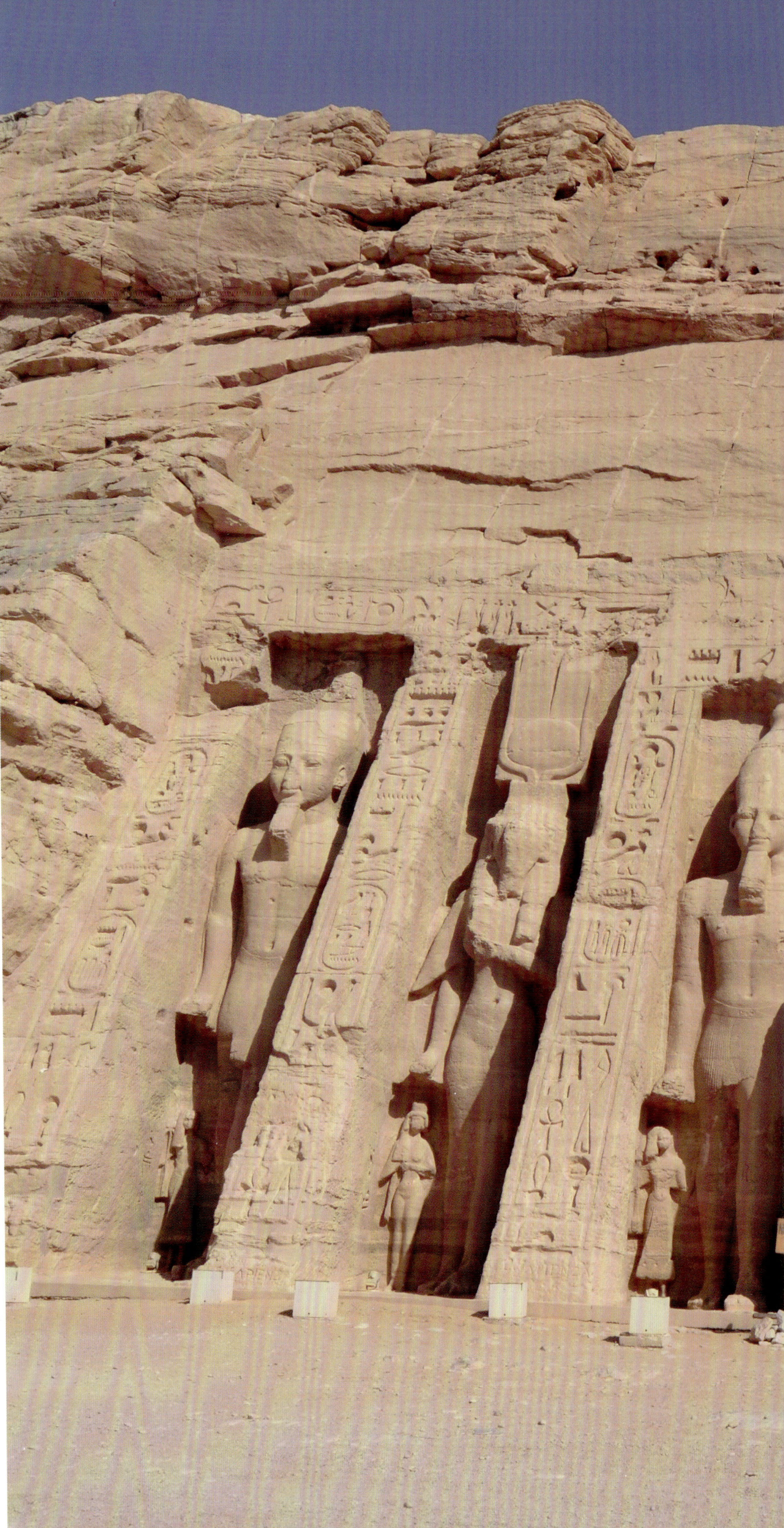

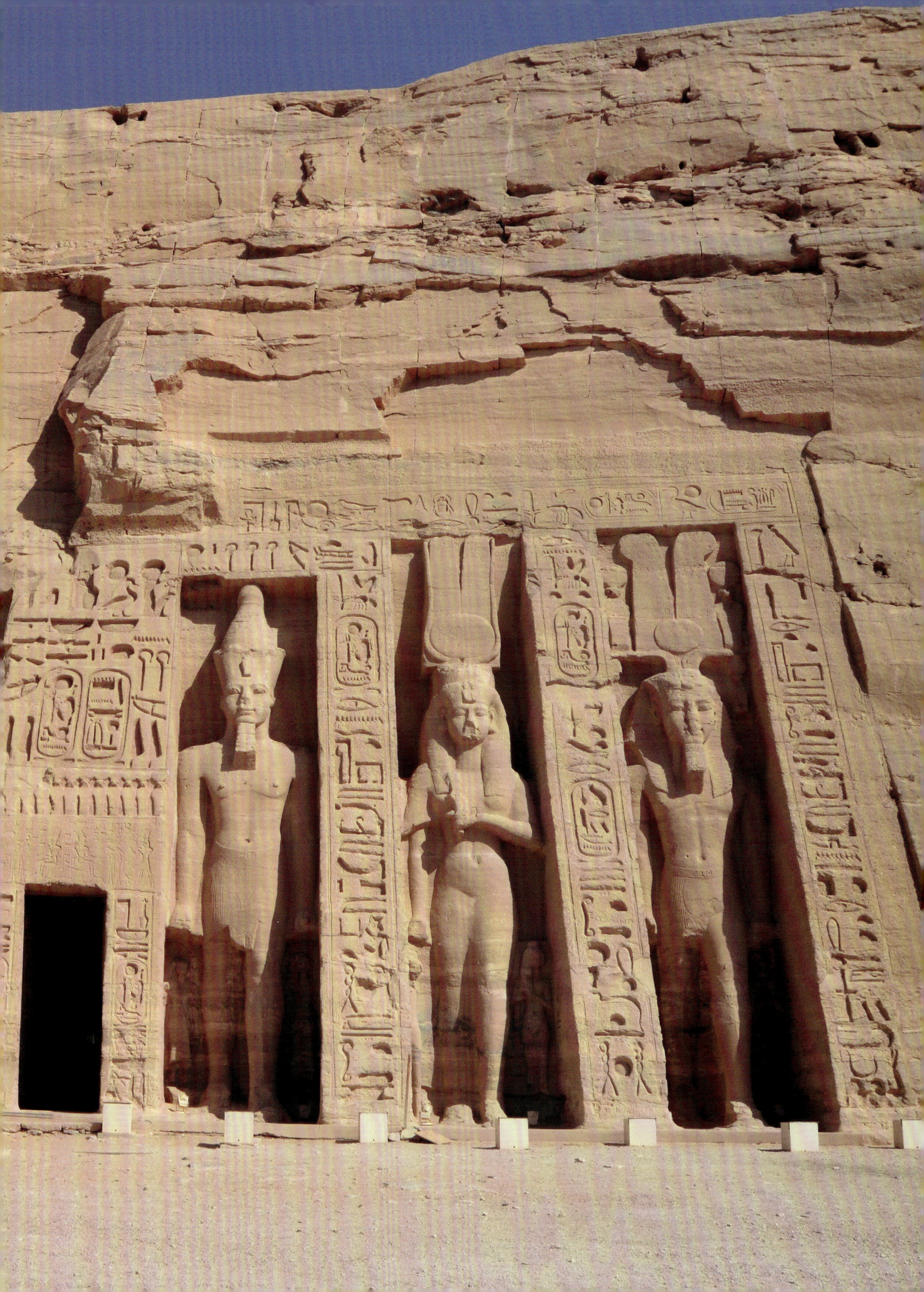

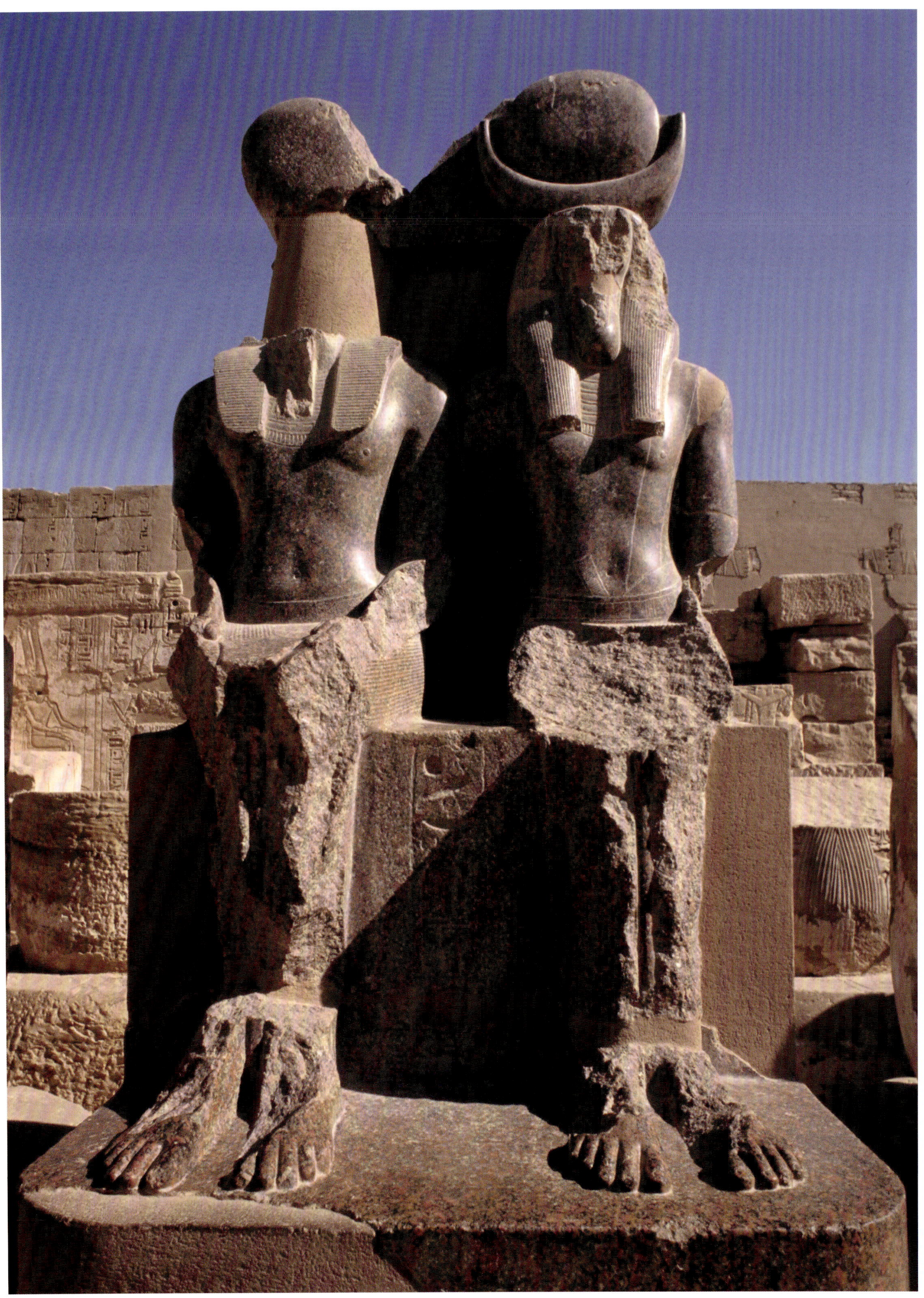

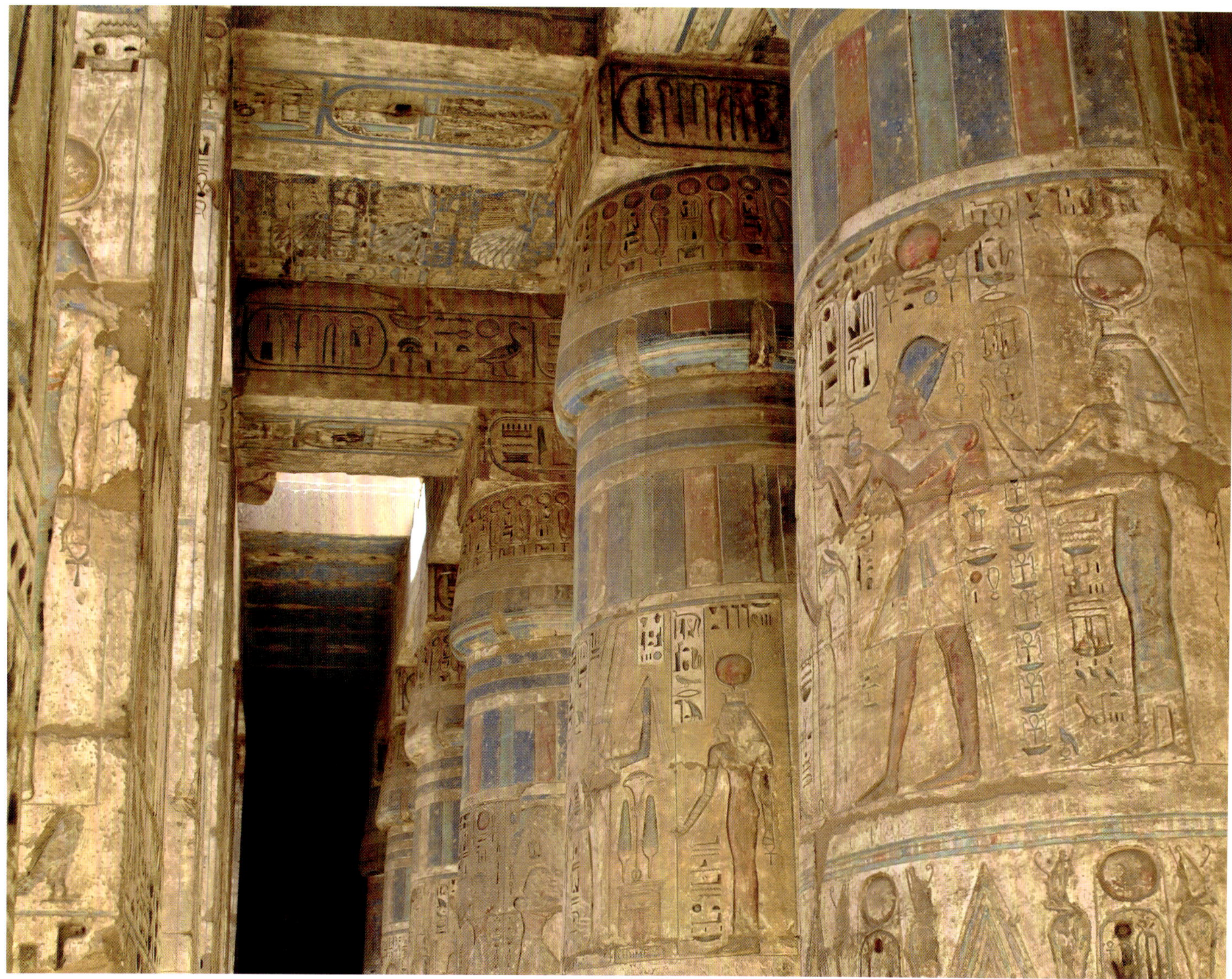

OPPOSITE:

Medinet Habu, Luxor, Egypt

Political power and faith blend seamlessly at Medinet Habu, a huge mortuary temple honouring Ramses III (reigned 1186–1155 BCE). The original building, however, was started by Queen Hapshepsut and her son Tuthmose III in the 15th century BCE. The statues here depict Ramses III (far left) and the baboon-headed god Thoth (near left).

ABOVE:

Medinet Habu, Luxor, Egypt

These courtyard columns show Ramses alongside Hathor, a sky goddess and avatar of Ra. Tower reliefs illustrate the king smiting his foes and leading an ox hunt from his chariot.

Located on the Nile's west bank, the complex includes a sacred lake, a Syrian-style entrance and chapels to the Theban Triad of gods: Khunsu, Mut and Amon Ra.

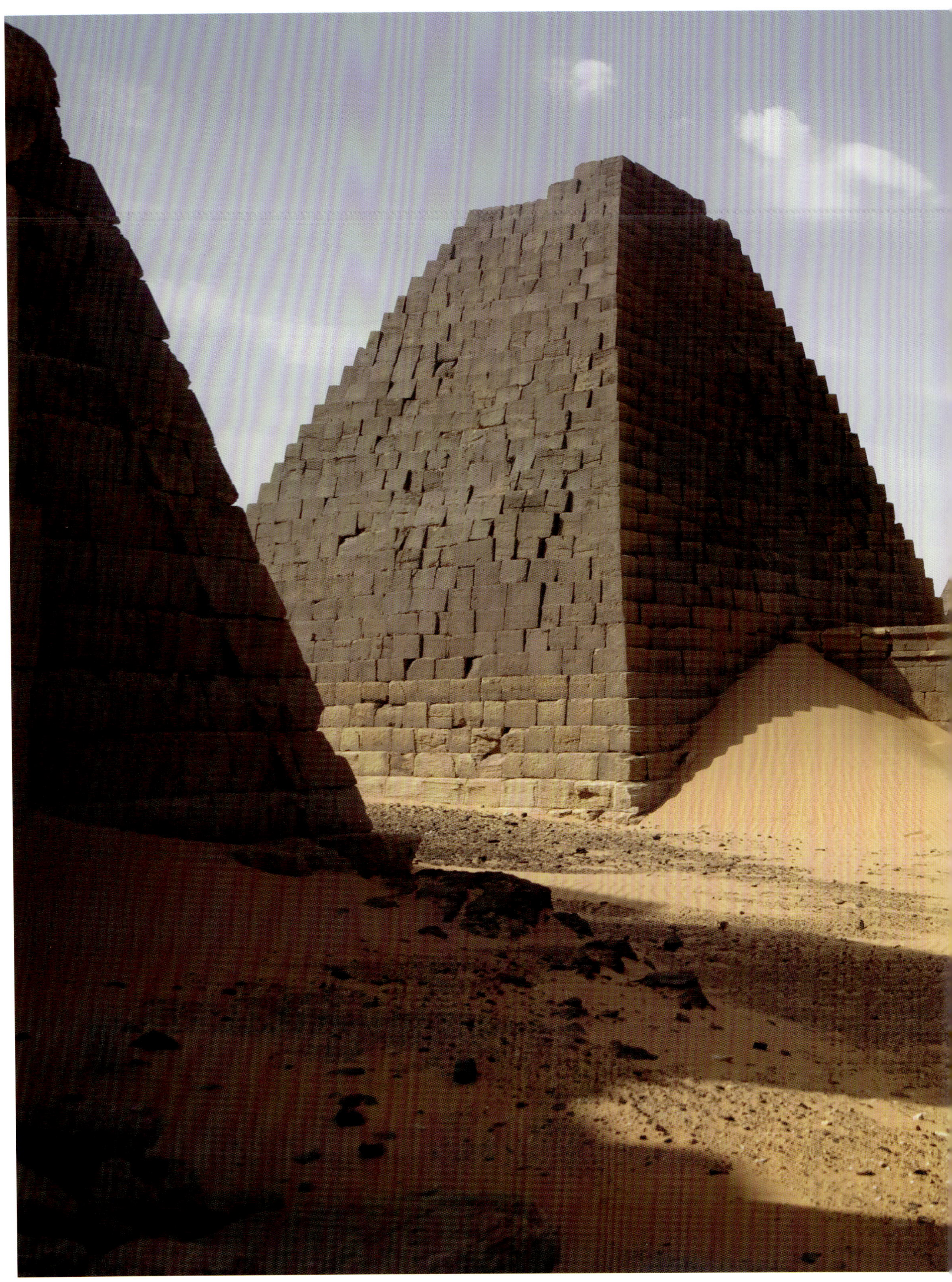

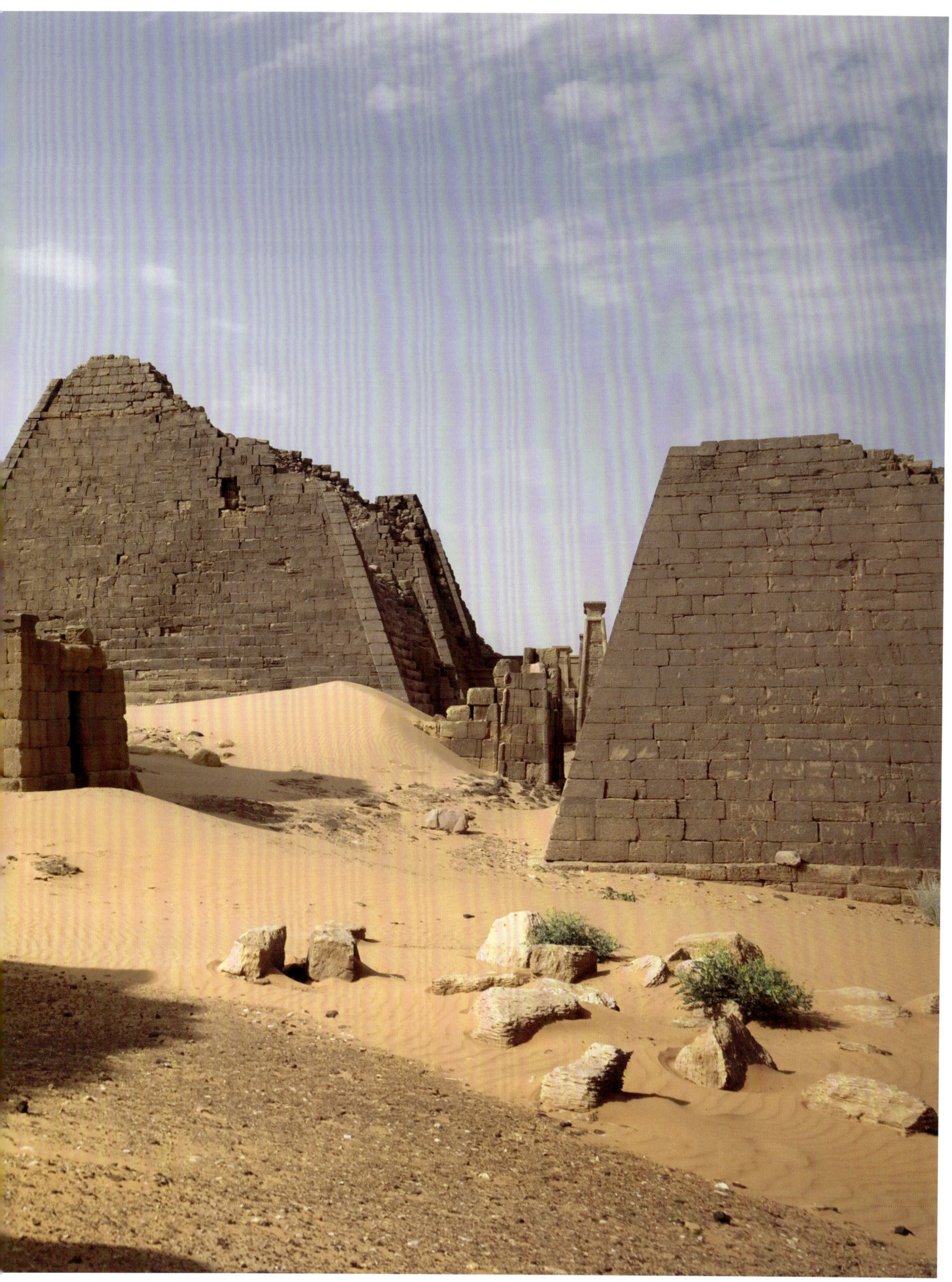

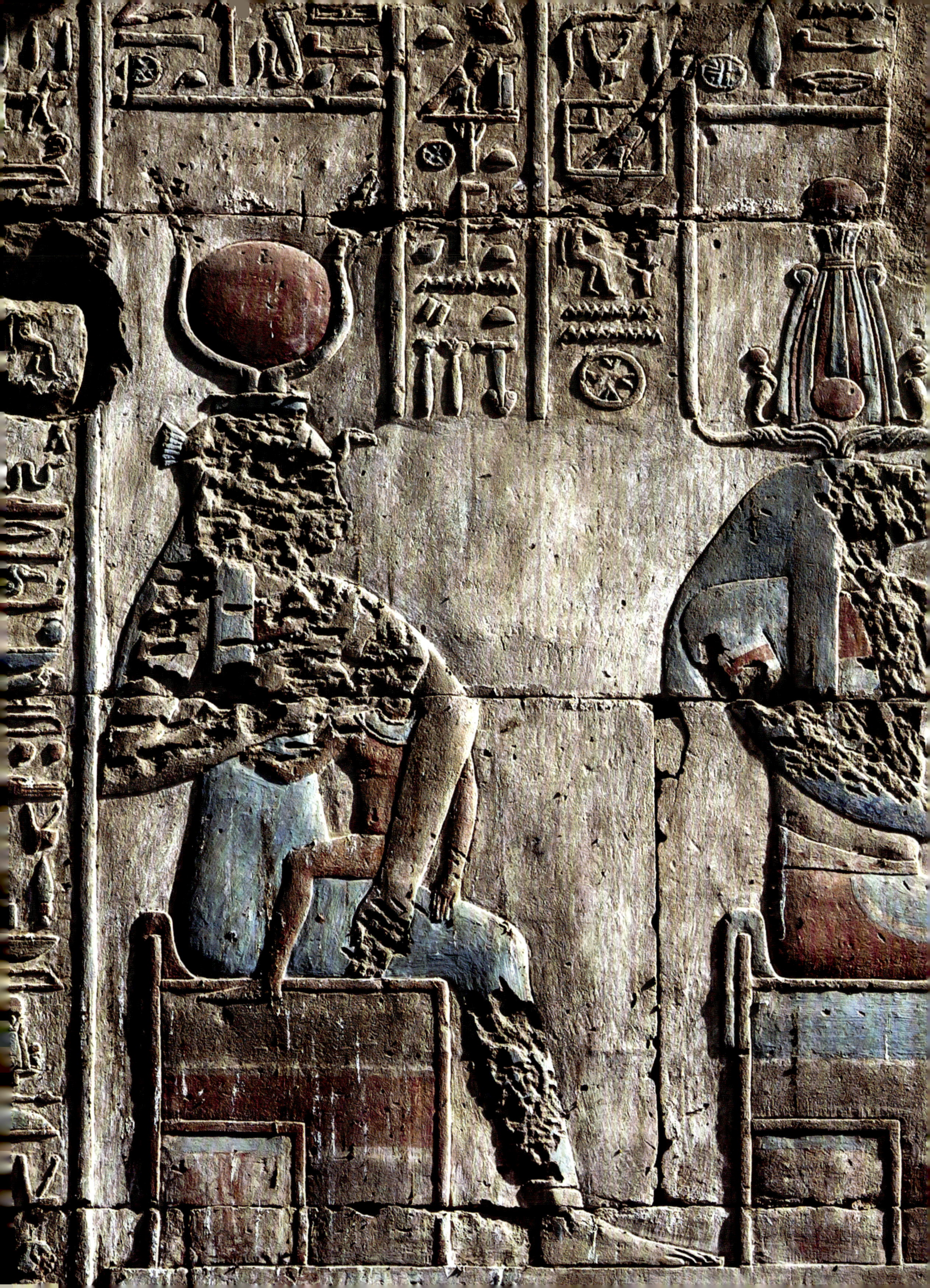

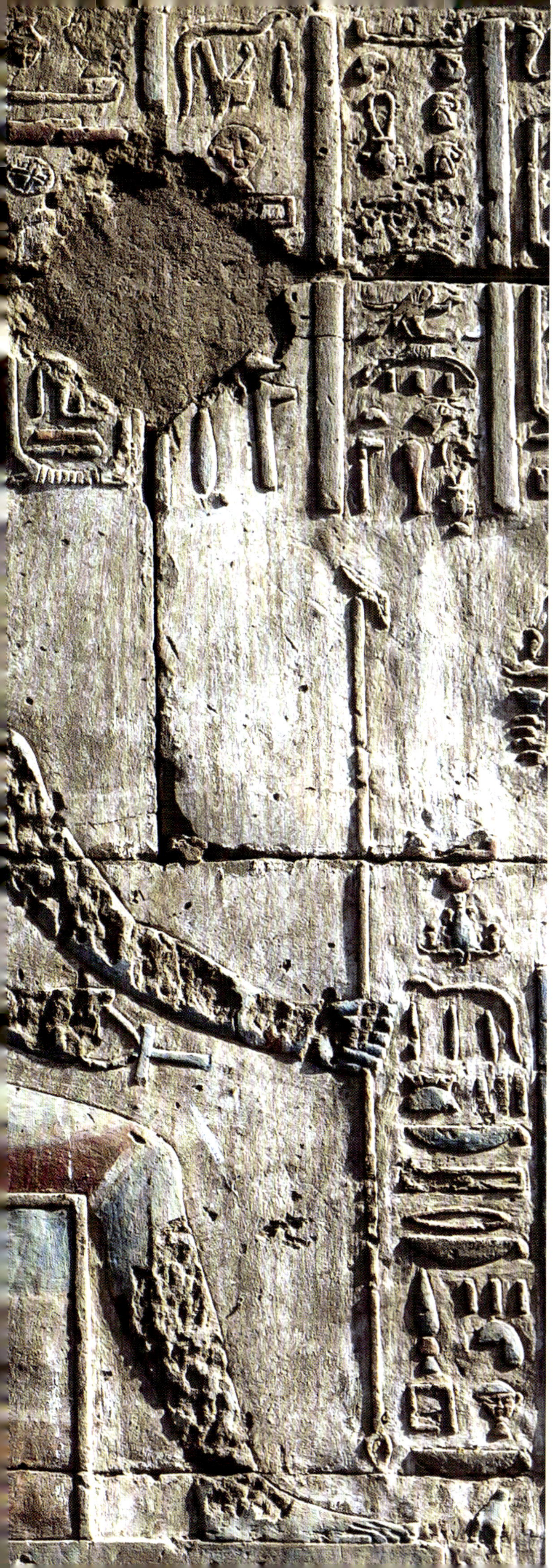

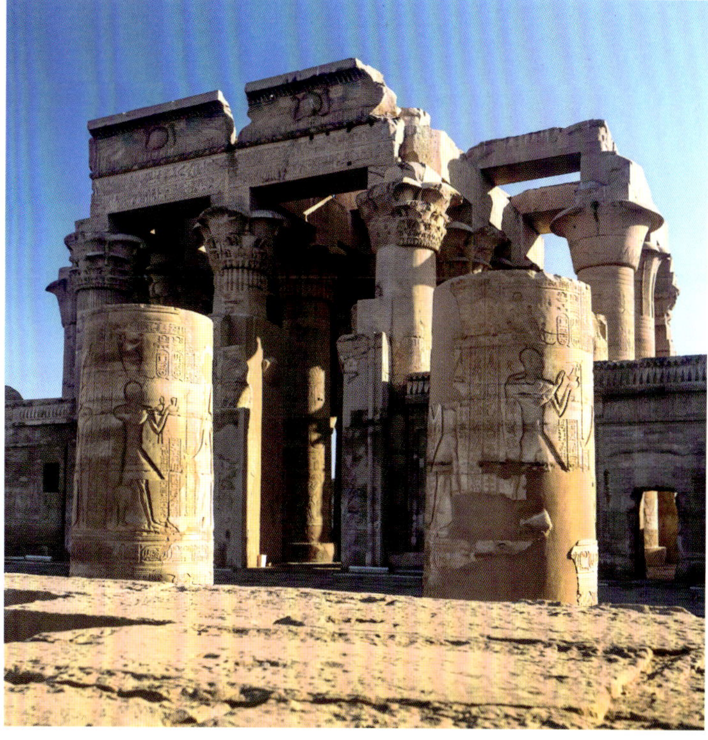

PREVIOUS PAGE:

Nubian Pyramids, Meroë, Sudan
Three black-stoned pyramids poke out of the desert, symbolising the former power of Nubia. Also called Kush in the Bible, Nubia at times ruled over its great rival, Egypt. These edifices are some of 177 pyramids found in Meroë. They were largely built from the 4th century BCE to 4th century CE. Steeper than their Egyptian cousins, many were decapitated by European fortune-seekers. And most have at their base offering temples for the deceased.

LEFT:

Temple of Edfu, Aswan, Egypt
A relief shows the goddess Hathor (left) and god Osiris (right) from a sanctuary devoted to Horus, the falcon-headed personification of living pharaohs. Built during the Ptolemaic Kingdom, 247–57 BCE, the Temple at Edfu abuts a sacred site predating 3100 BCE. Each year Edfu hosted the 'sacred marriage' of Hathor to Horus, until in 391 CE the Christian Eastern Roman Empire banned paganism and the temple fell into disuse. Only after 1860 was it unearthed from beneath 12 metres (39ft) of rubble.

ABOVE:

Temple of Kom Ombo, Aswan, Egypt
Kom Ombo, north of Aswan, shows a uniquely mixed heritage. The perfectly symmetrical Nile-side temple was dedicated to Sobek, the crocodile god, and the falcon-headed Horus – strangely so, as they were considered mythological enemies. It was built during Hellenistic dynastic times, c.180–47 BCE, and added to during Egypt's Greco-Roman period, 332–395 CE. Priests looked after captive crocodiles until the spread of Christianity and then Islam eradicated this last trace of Ancient Egyptian beliefs.

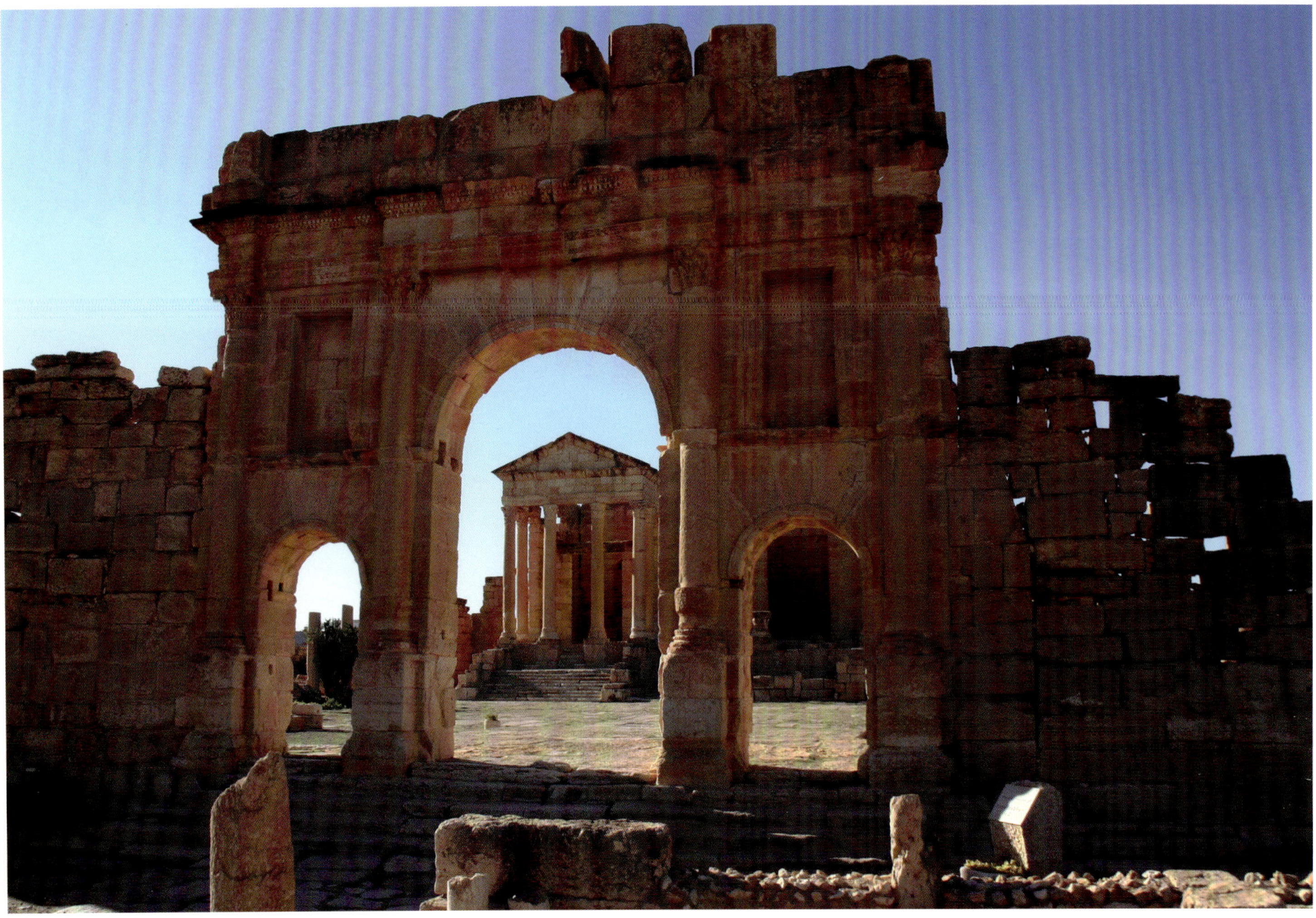

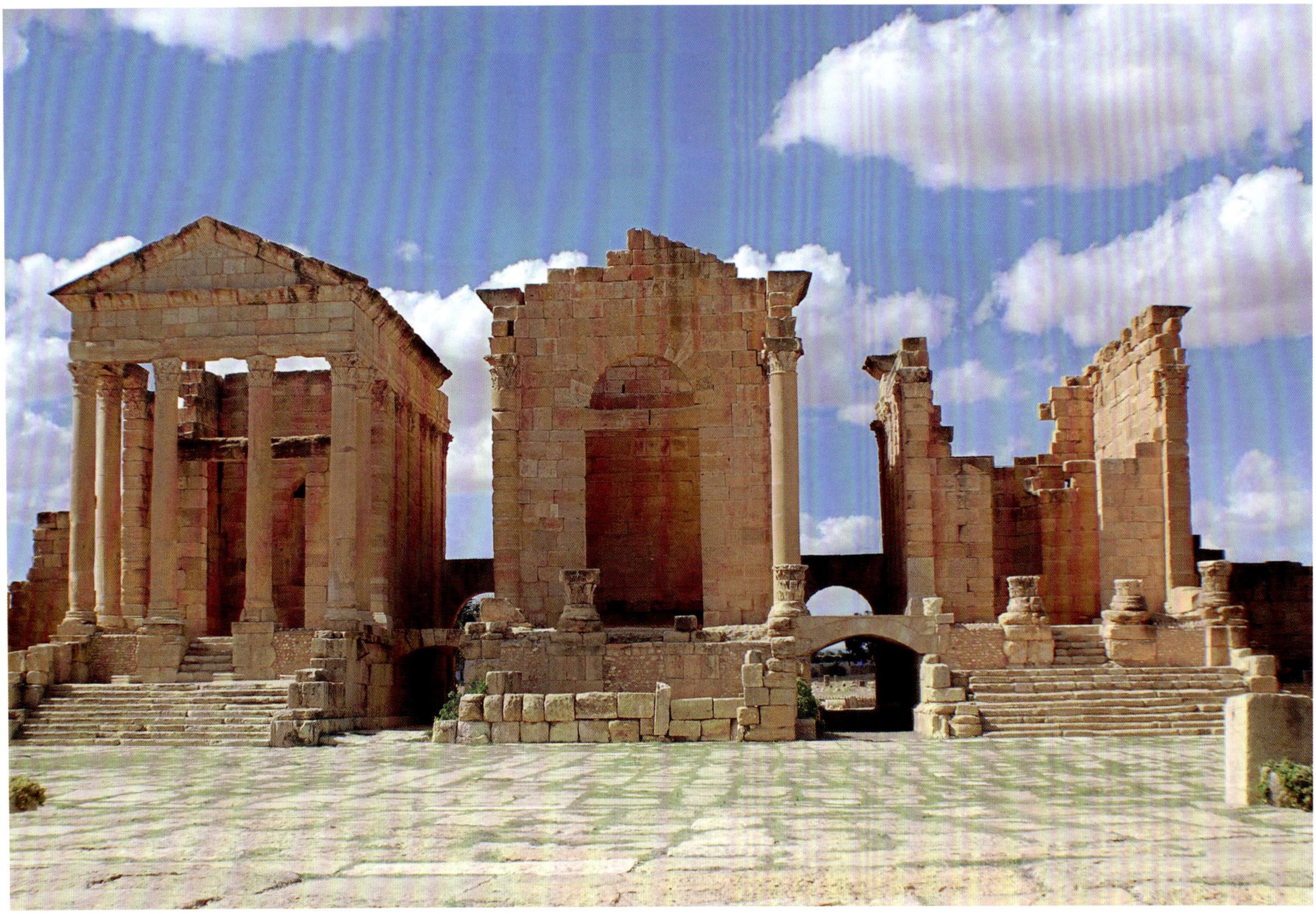

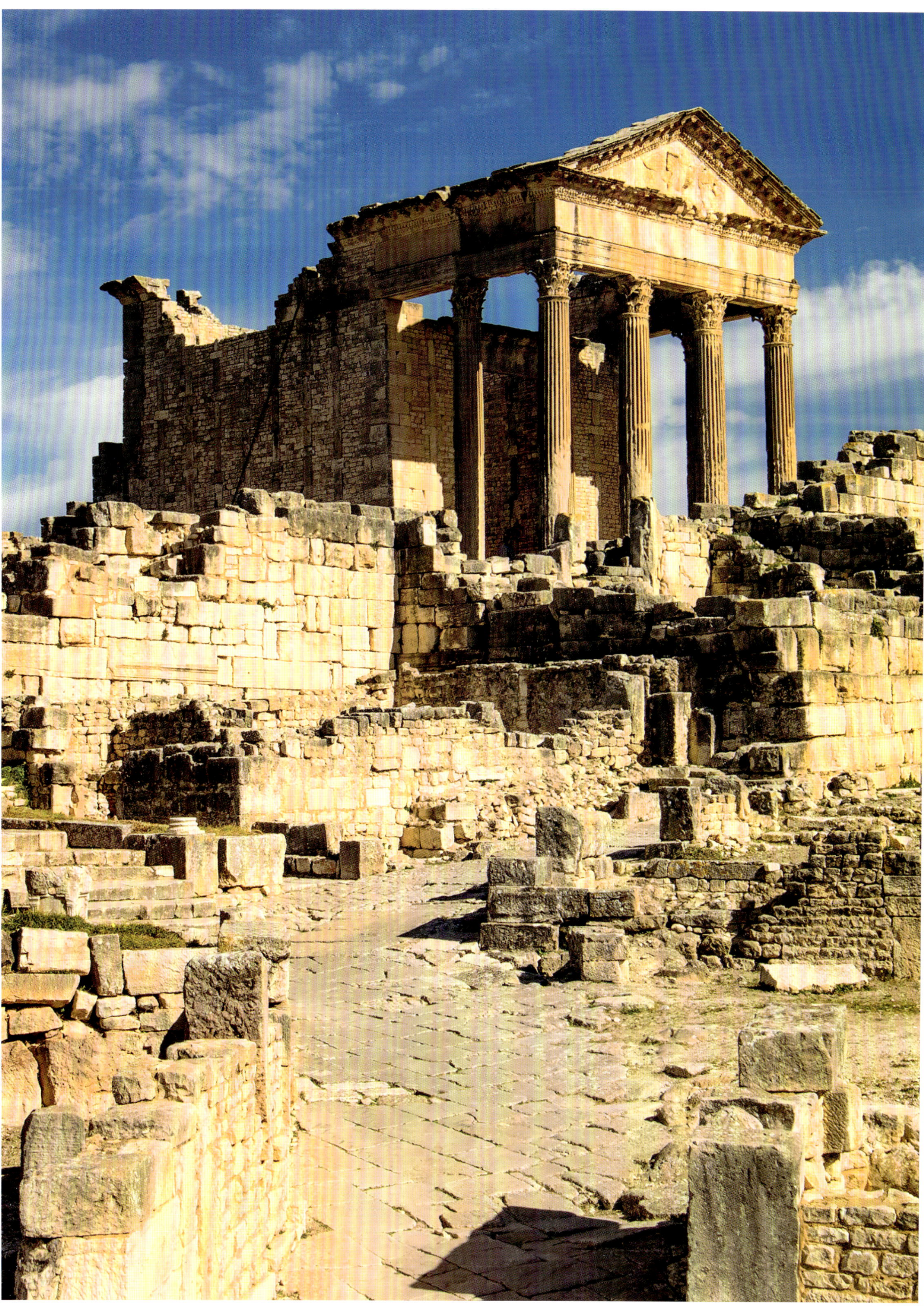

PREVIOUS PAGE: LEFT (TOP):

Sbeitla, Tunisia

This mid-2nd century CE Arch of Antoninus Pius illustrates the sway Ancient Rome once held over North Africa. It formed part of Sbeitla's complex of temples, baths, theatres, public spaces and a triumphal arch – plus three churches after Rome adopted Christianity. Emperor Vespasian (reigned 69–79 CE) turned the central Tunisian town into an administrative centre whose olive groves supplied Roman garrisons. In 647 CE, however, Arabs decisively defeated Byzantine troops at the Battle of Sufetula and Muslim rule swept the entire region.

PREVIOUS PAGE: LEFT (BOTTOM):

Sbeitla, Tunisia

Why do three temples to three separate deities sit together at Sbeitla's Capitol? Rather than suggesting religious confusion, this grouping of sanctuaries to Minerva, Jupiter and Juno really shows Roman self-assurance. The trio were Rome's guardians and this architecture cedes little to local aesthetics! Moreover, the grander central Jupiter temple lacks entry steps, thus forcing worshippers to enter via the lesser temples – a sign, perhaps, of Jupiter's supremacy?

PREVIOUS PAGE: RIGHT

Capitol, Dougga, Tunisia

This Capitol's pediment relief shows Emperor Antoninus Pius being elevated to godhood on the back of an eagle. Completed in 167–68 CE, the building probably served as a Roman Temple of Jupiter. Dougga was previously capital of a Libyco-Punic state in Numidia – even its temple to Juno Caelestis honoured the Romanized version of the Punic war goddess Tanit.

RIGHT:

Tombs of Al-Bagawat, Egypt

Near to the Kharga Oasis in the Sahara Desert lies Al-Bagawat, one of the world's earliest Christian cemeteries. Hundreds of tombs date from the 4th to 7th centuries CE. Frescoes of Adam and Eve, Noah's Ark and St John adorn Bagawat's Church of Exodus and Chapel of Peace. While Coptic Christians make up about 10 per cent of Egypt's current population, Bagawat last saw activity in the 11th century CE.

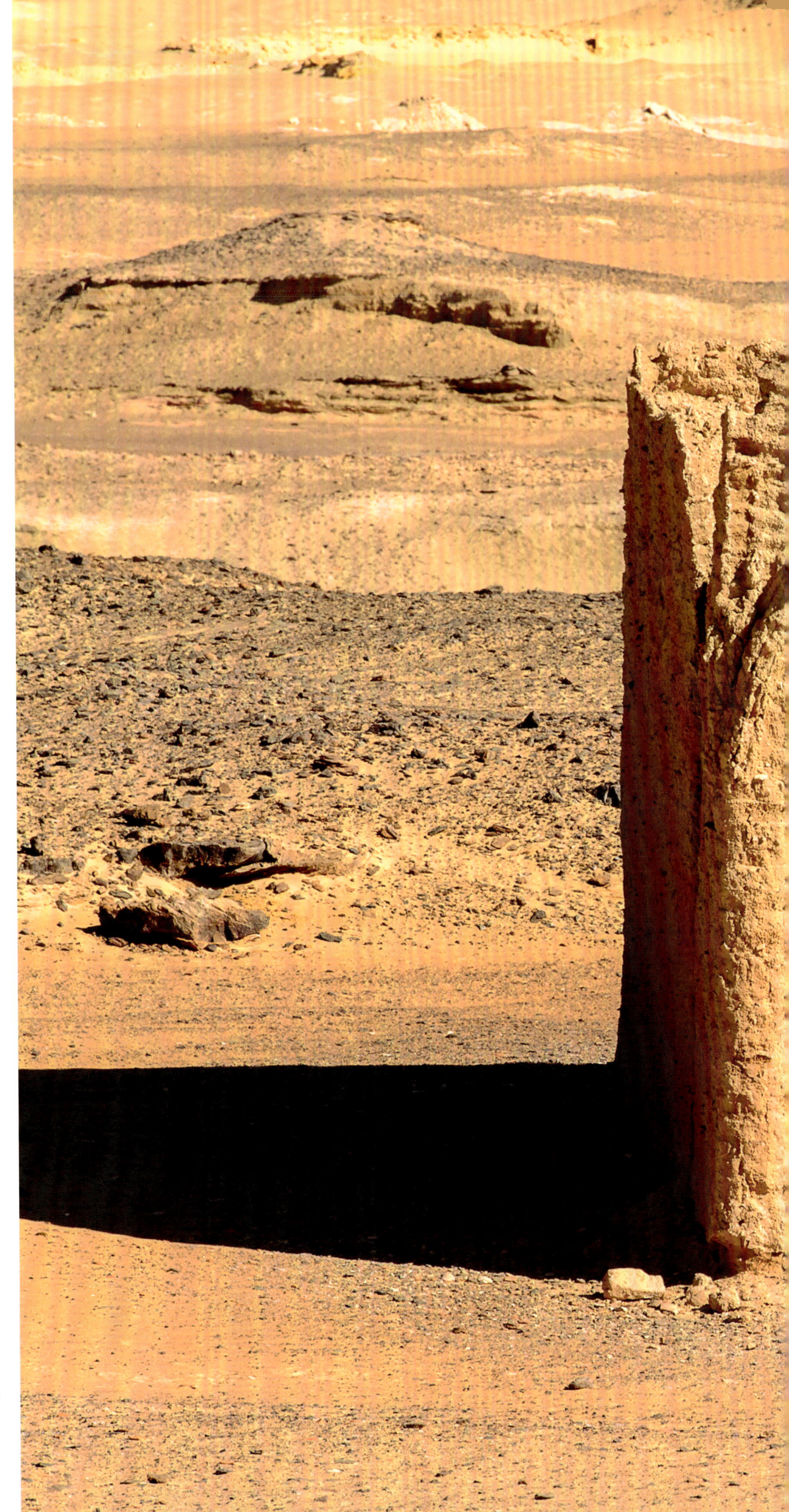

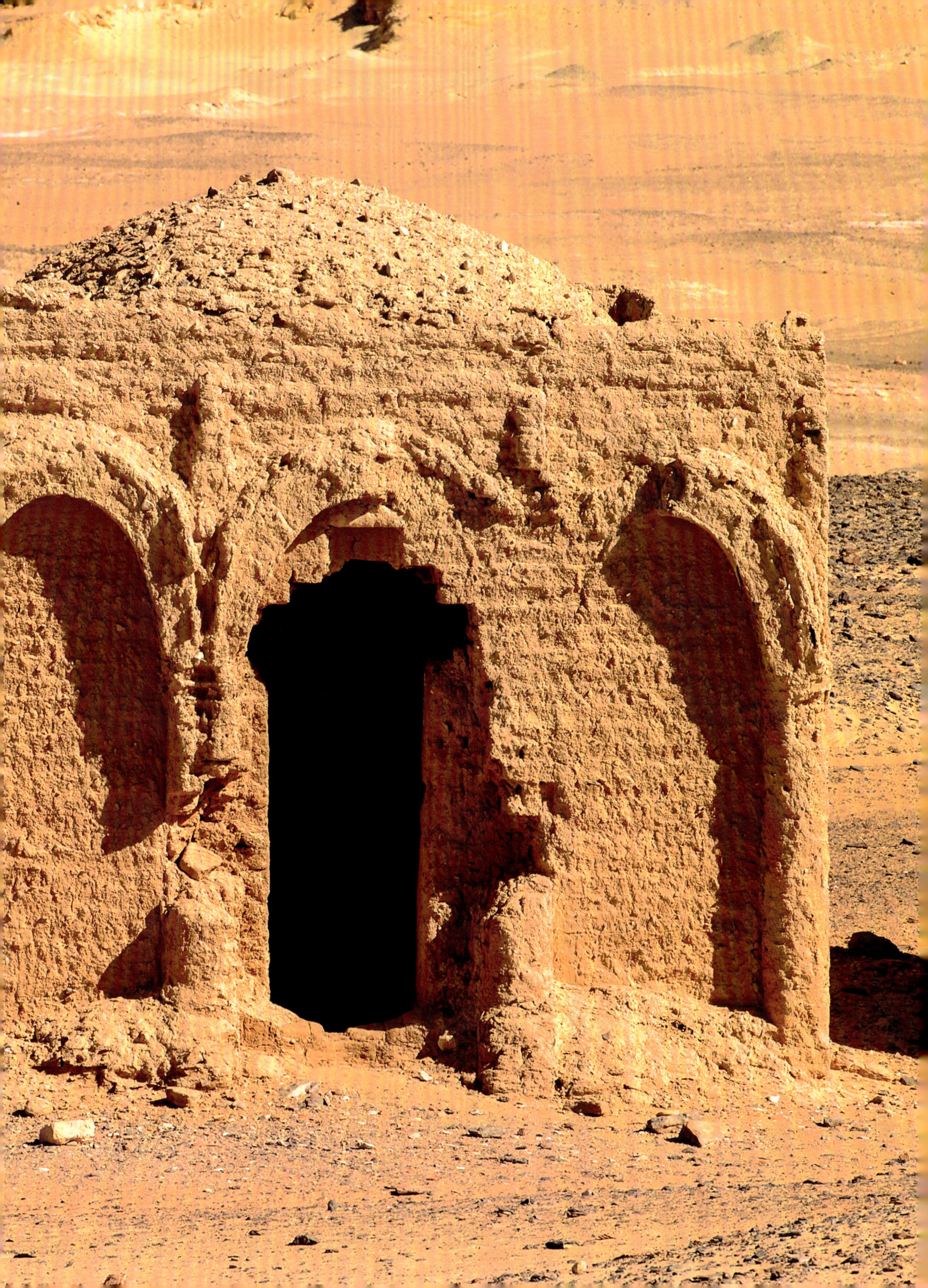

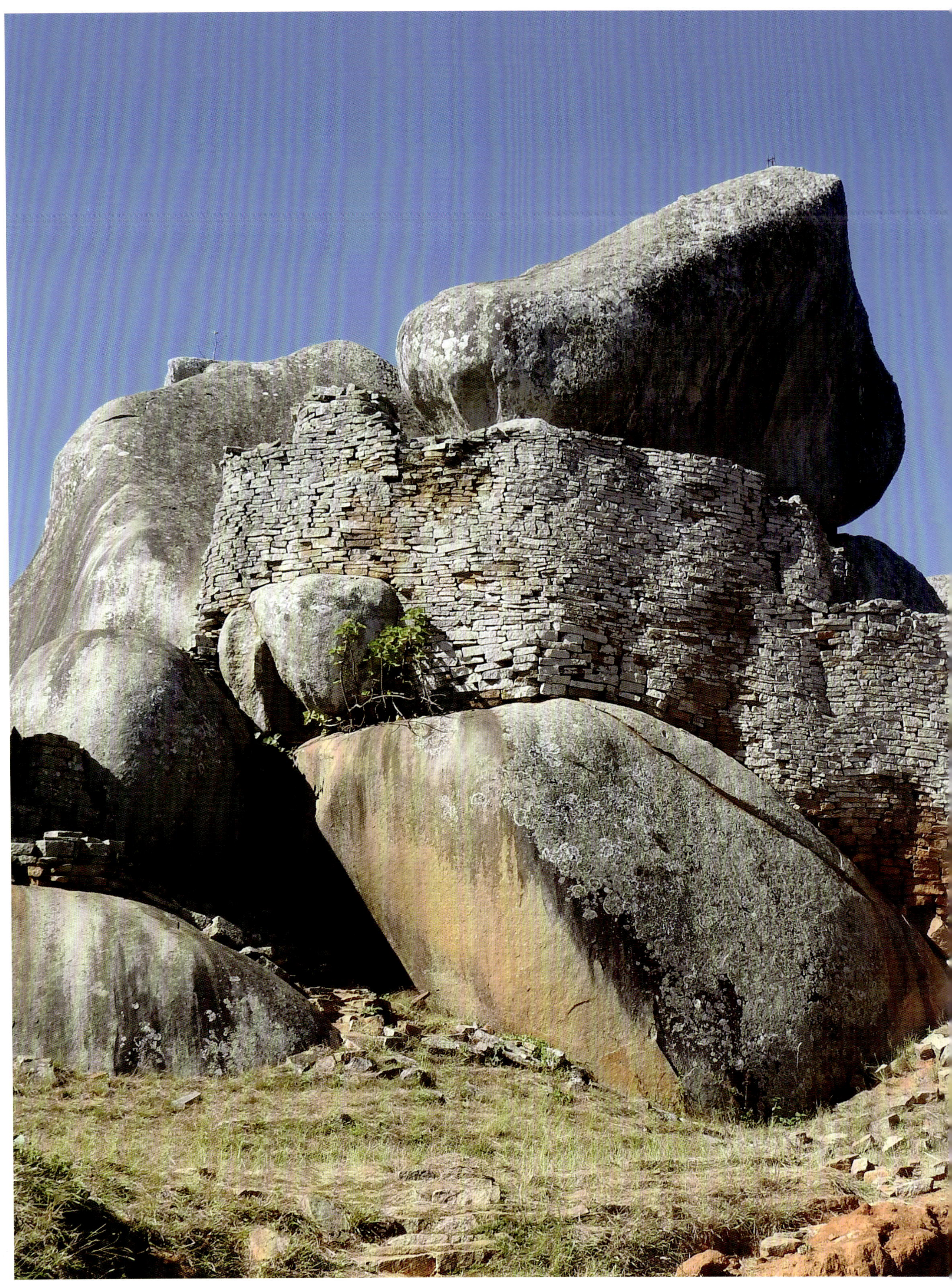

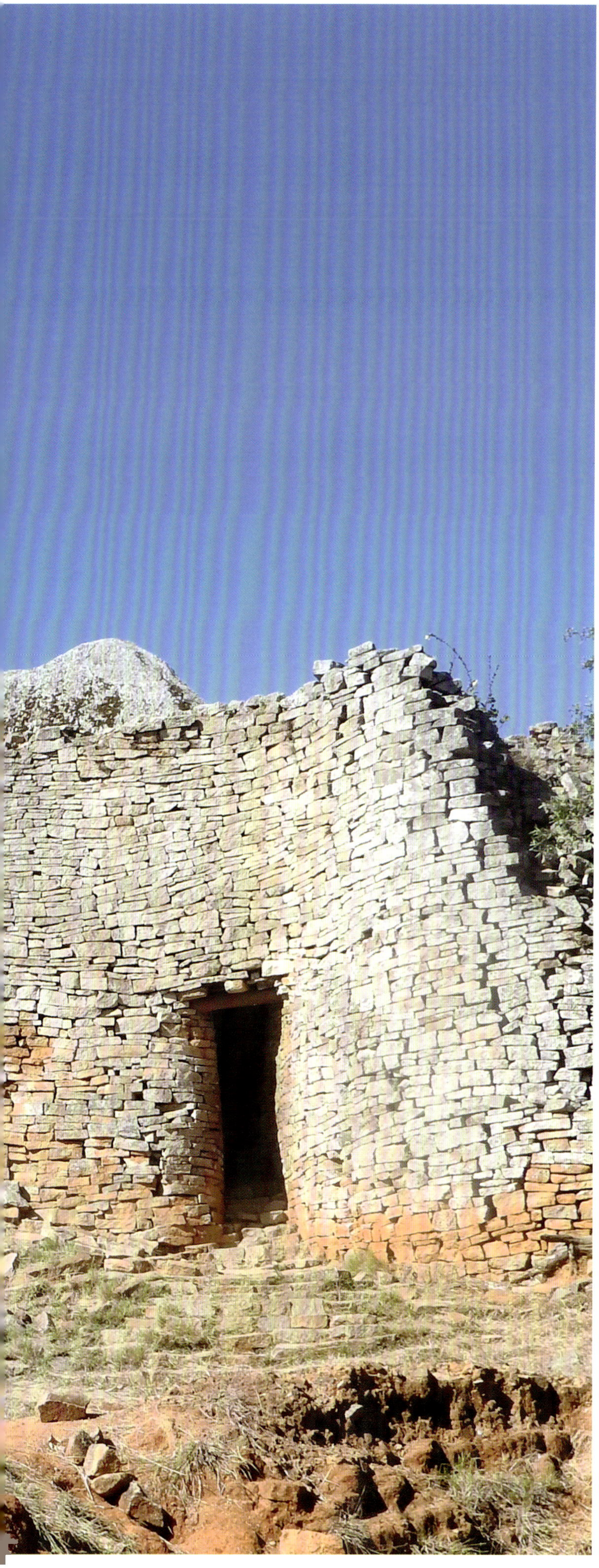

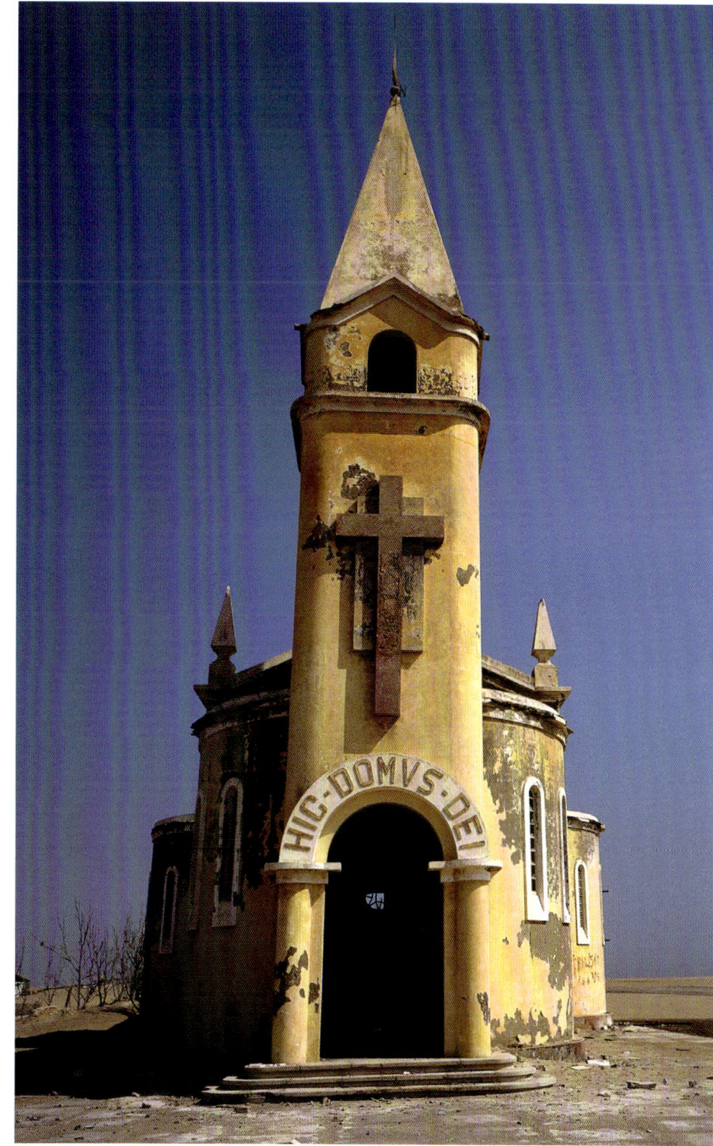

LEFT:
Great Zimbabwe, Masvingo, Zimbabwe
An expertly crafted undulating wall-tower marks the spiritual centre of Great Zimbabwe. Here it is thought people honoured Mwari, creator sky-god to the ancestors of modern Zimbabwe's Shona ethnicity. The Gomokere built this Hill Complex against an 80-metre-high (262ft) granite outcrop during the 9th–13th centuries. The 730-hectare (1,800 acre) compound was a trading hub, gold-mining centre and royal capital. It declined after 1430, gained new structures under the Rozwi and Mwenye, and finally crumbled in the early 19th century.

ABOVE:
Church, Baia dos Tigres, Angola
'This is God's House', proclaims the church plaque, but Baia dos Tigres' Catholic congregants left long ago. In 1960, 1500 residents, including 300 Portuguese, benefitted from Baia's thriving fishing and canning industry. Two years later a sea-storm severed a vital freshwater pipeline and turned the remote isthmus into an isolated 98 square km (38 square mile) island. The final blow came when Portugal abandoned Angola in 1974, leaving civil war in its wake.

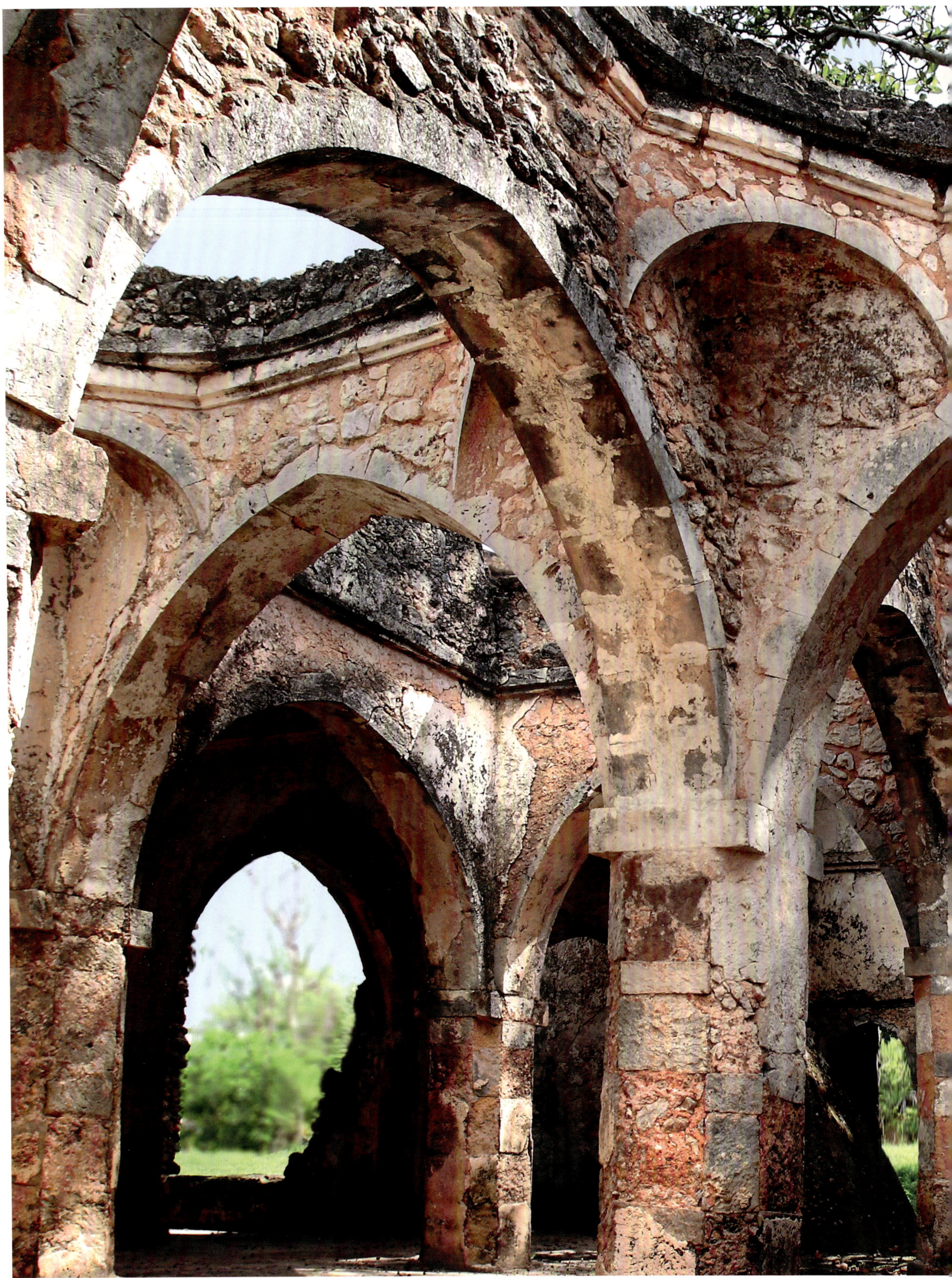

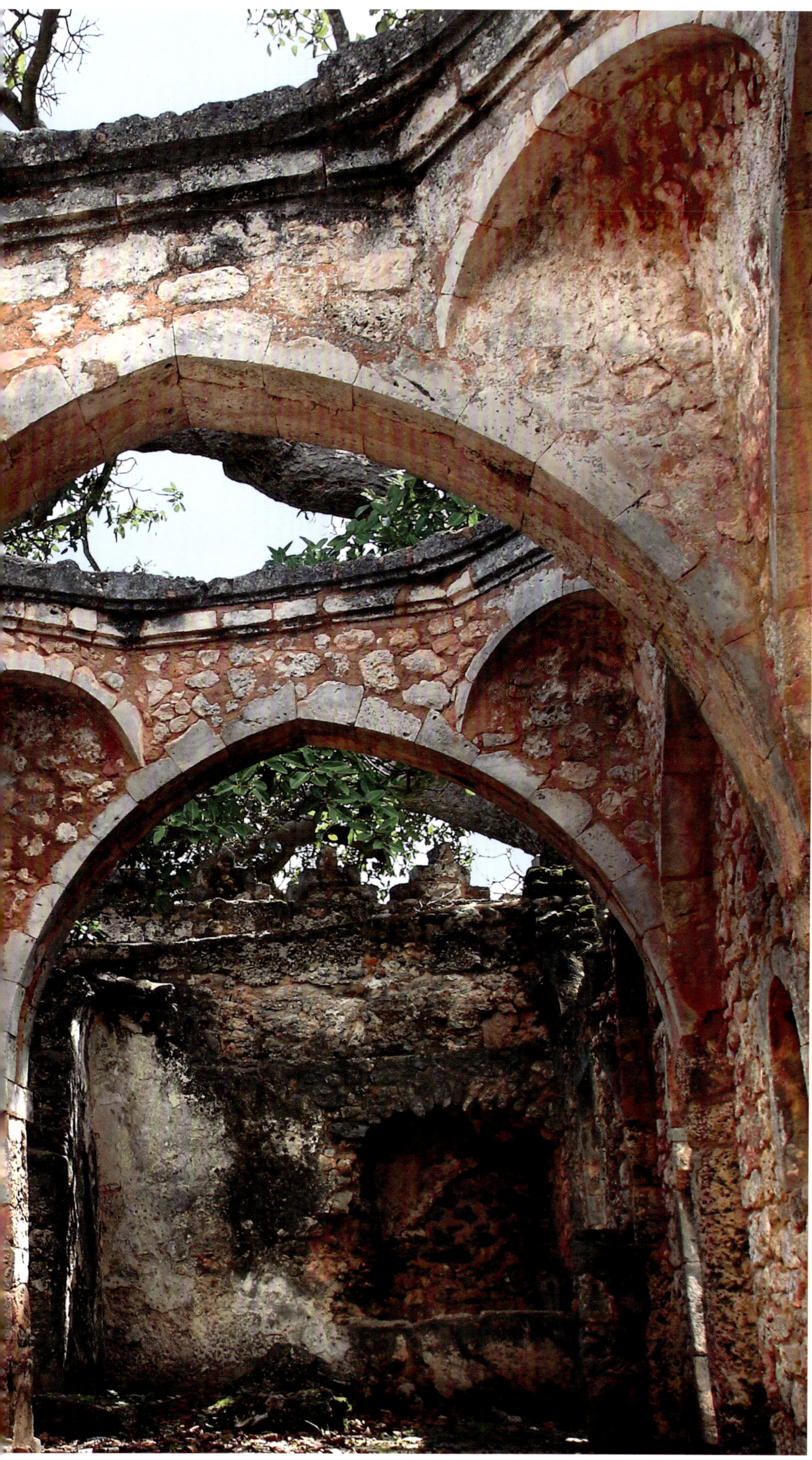

Great Mosque, Kilwa Kisiwani Island, Tanzania
The Swahili Muslim port of Kilwa Kisiwani was founded in the 9th century CE and flourished during the 11th and 13th centuries by trading in gold, silver, ivory, perfumes, Persian and Chinese porcelain. Situated on an island off Tanzania, the port declined after Portuguese occupation in the 16th century and faded out altogether during the 19th century. Begun in the 11th century, the Great Mosque was constructed of lime and mortar, and topped by dozens of domes and vaults.

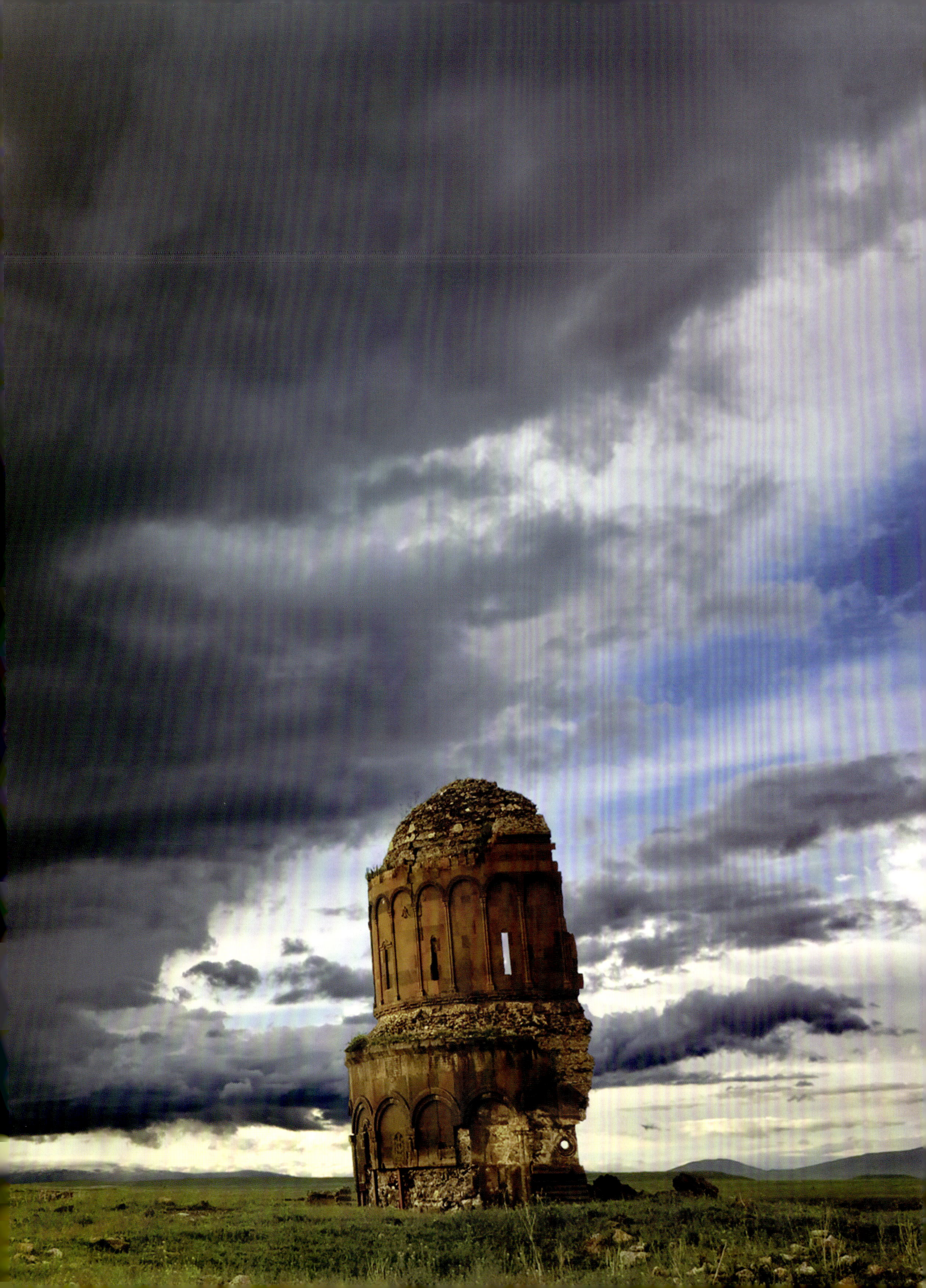

The Middle East

Fertile Crescent, Holy Land, birthplace of the three Abrahamic faiths, Judaism, Christianity and Islam – such descriptions remind us how central worship is to the Middle East, and how intertwined are religion and culture. Sadly, images of recent wartime destruction have become equally familiar. Think of shattered Palmyra in eastern Syria, or ISIS's blasting of an Armenian Church in Mosul, Iraq, in 2014. Or the Temple of Ain Dara, northern Syria, where Hittites worshipped 3000 years ago, now smashed by aerial bombing in 2018.

Another apt metaphor for the Middle East is crossroads of civilizations, and regional holy structures certainly display amazingly hybrid cultural clues. Consider Jewish tombs in Jerusalem topped by Egyptian pyramids, Roman-style columns in Petra, or hints of European Gothic in a church at Ani, eastern Turkey.

Often places of worship, such as the Greek Orthodox Church in Kayaköy, Turkey, were abandoned after forced population transfers. Even a simple change of trading routes could doom sites, like the oasis necropolis of Mada'in Salah in present-day Saudi Arabia. Here, however, religion provides its own explanation: local tradition associated Mada'in Nabateans with the Thamud nation, who were later described in the Koran as greedy idolaters – hence their divine punishment!

OPPOSITE:
Church of the Holy Redeemer, Ani, Turkey
Sliced in half by a storm in 1955, and already deserted by the 18th century CE, the Church of the Holy Redeemer in Ani tells a fascinating story. It was built in 1035 CE when Ani was the capital of an Armenian Christian kingdom. However, both church and city changed hands repeatedly over the ages.

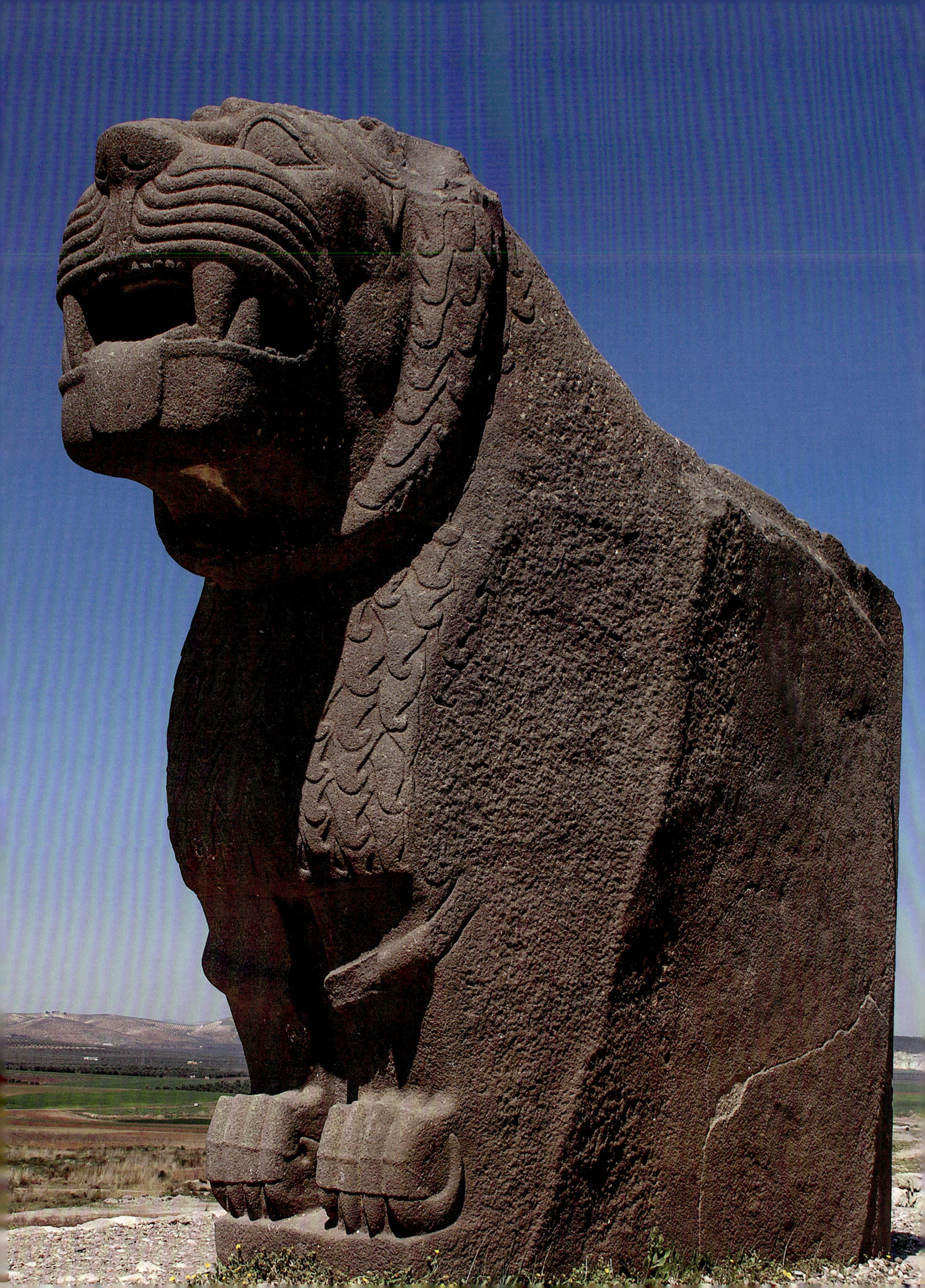

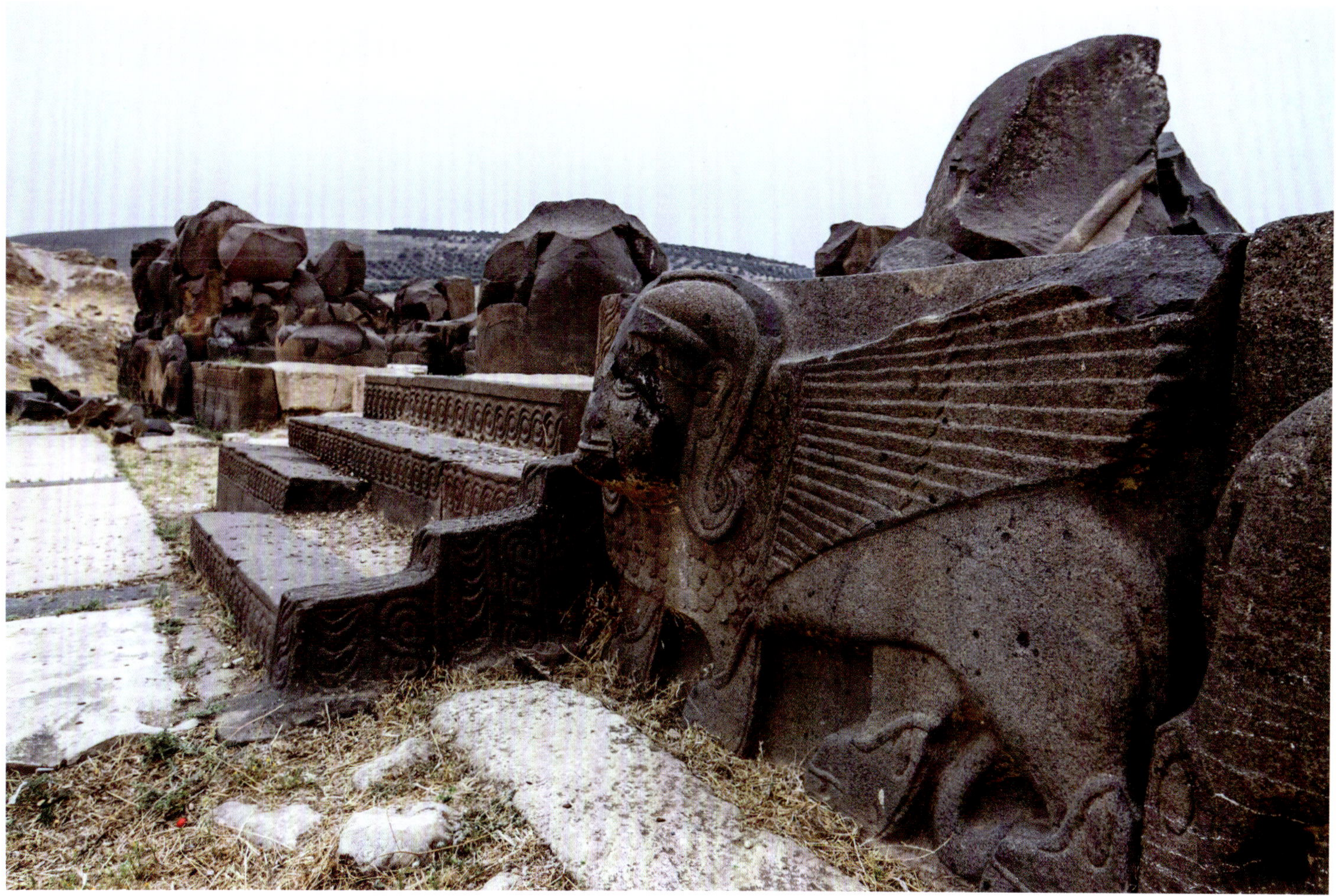

BOTH PHOTOGRAPHS:
Ain Dara, Syria
Modern warfare has damaged Ain Dara more than 3000 years of past battles have. In January 2018, this Iron Age temple was caught in the crossfire when Turkish planes bombed Kurdish targets in northern Syria. The site is – or was – renowned for its architectural blocks decorated with abstract designs and animal depictions, like this snarling basalt lion (left). Some say the lions would judge the dead and decide if they could ascend to heaven. The temple was built following the collapse of the Hittite Empire in c.1130 BCE when Neo or Syro-Hittite mini-kingdoms were spawned south of Anatolia.

Scholars compare Ain Dara's lions and winged sphinxes (above) to the cherubim that reportedly decorated Solomon's Temple in Jerusalem. Even the layouts of both shrines appear similar, sharing 33 of 65 architectural elements. One difference is that Ain Dara's Aramean-speaking creators engraved mysterious giant footprints on the temple floor. But which deity did they belong to? Candidates include Ishtar (Astarte), the goddesses of fertility and war, and Ba'al Hadad, lord of storms.

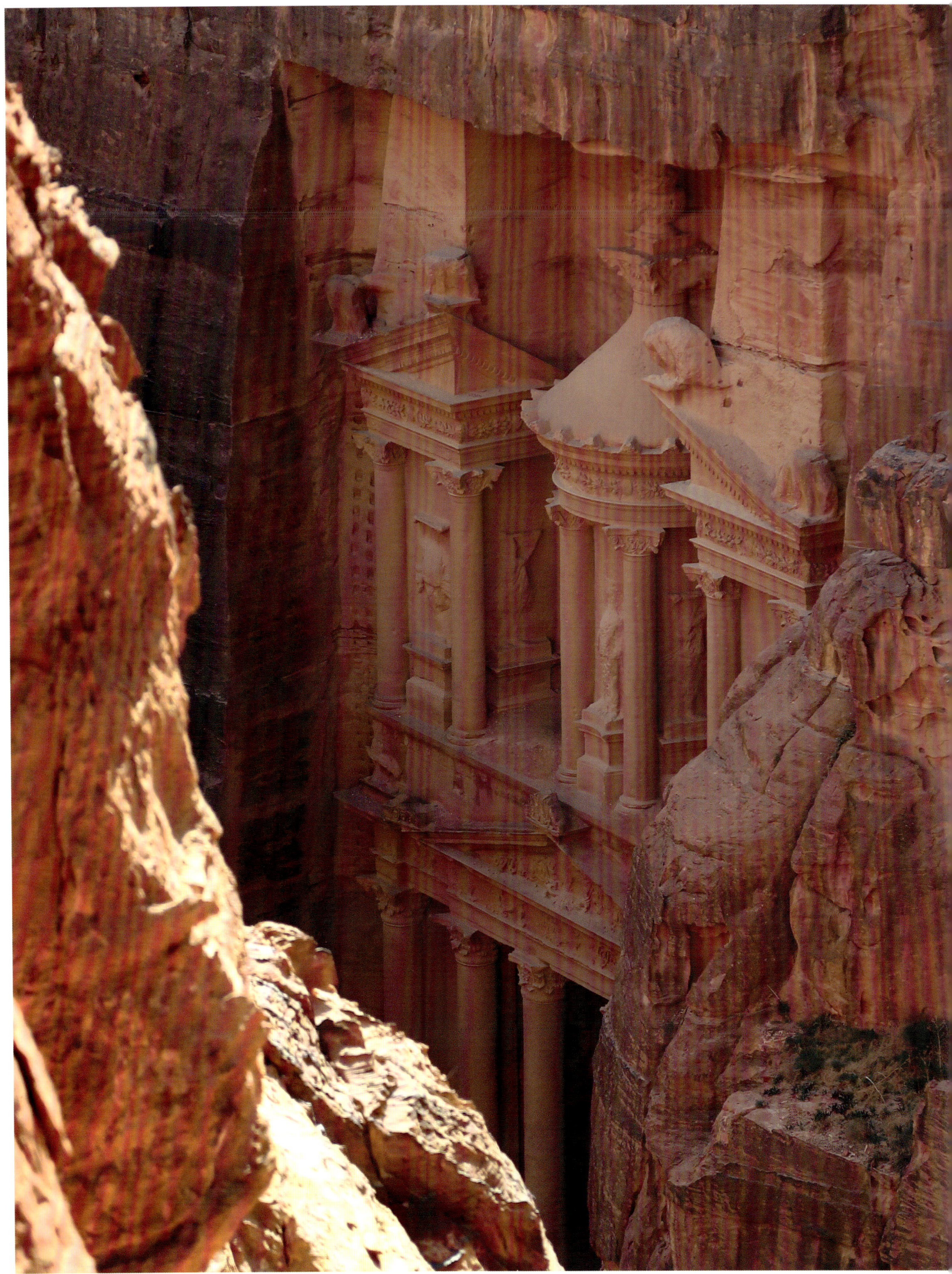

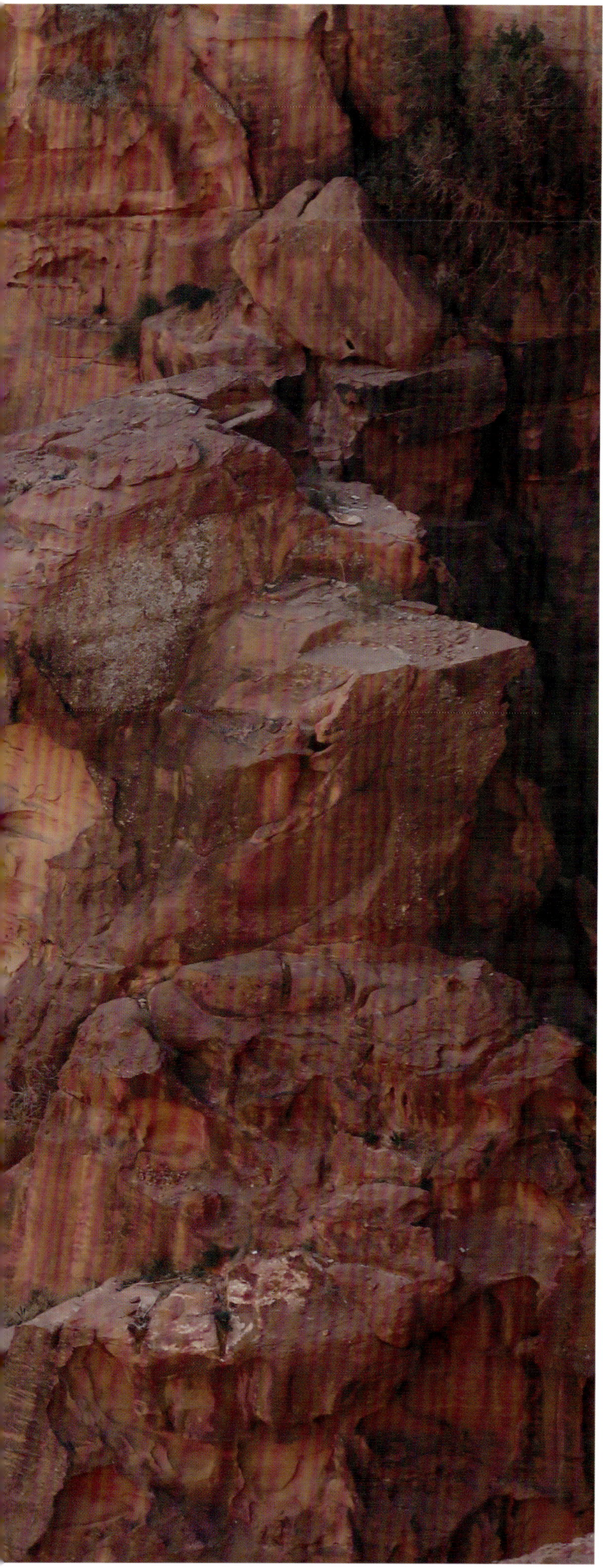

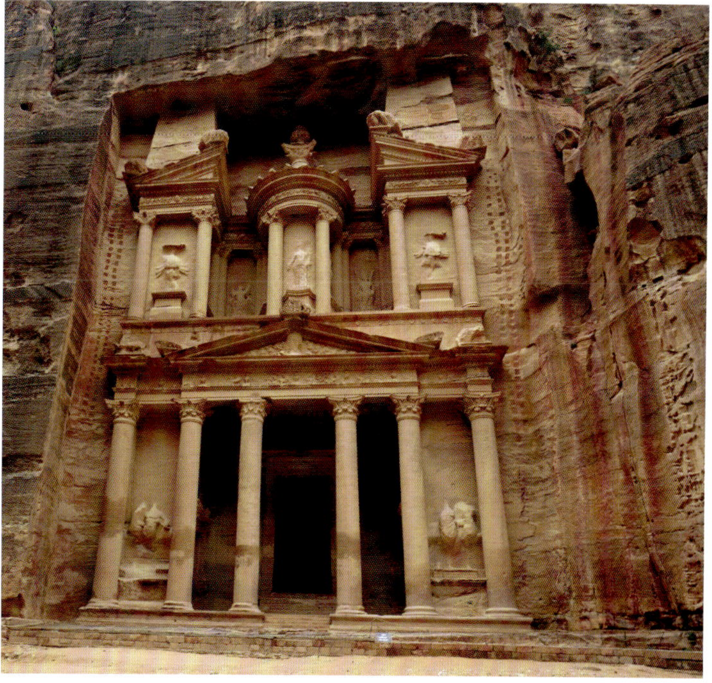

BOTH PHOTOGRAPHS:

'Treasury', Petra, Jordan

Emerging from the Siq, a narrow mile-long canyon carved out of rock, visitors at Petra suddenly behold the miraculous sight of the pink-hued 'Treasury'. Yet 'Treasury', or Al-Khazneh in Arabic, is a misnomer; it was really a mausoleum. Decorations show images probably of Al Uzza, a local Nabatean goddess of stars, who was associated with the Egyptian Isis, Roman Venus and Greek Aphrodite.

Petra was Nabatea's capital from the 3rd century BCE until the Romans annexed it in 106 CE. The city flourished at the crossroads of trade between the Mediterranean and Arabia. Nabateans practiced an early Arab form of polytheism, as evidenced by the many small temples and tombs with niches for 'block gods' throughout Petra.

BOTH PHOTOGRAPHS:

Mausoleums, Mada'in Saleh, Saudi Arabia

Cross-Arabian camel-borne commerce in frankincense, myrrh and spices turned Mada'in Saleh into a thriving metropolis. But it became a desert ghost town after Rome conquered the region in 104 CE and switched trade routes. Located today in south-western Saudi Arabia, Mada'in was the second great Nabatean city after Petra.

The city's 131 giant tombs were carved out of sandstone around the first century CE, blending Arabian, Hellenistic, Phoenician, Assyrian and Egyptian aesthetics. But how did the Nabateans manage to build on such a scale? They certainly knew how to source and store water; Mada'in survived its arid surroundings because of man-made, underground wells.

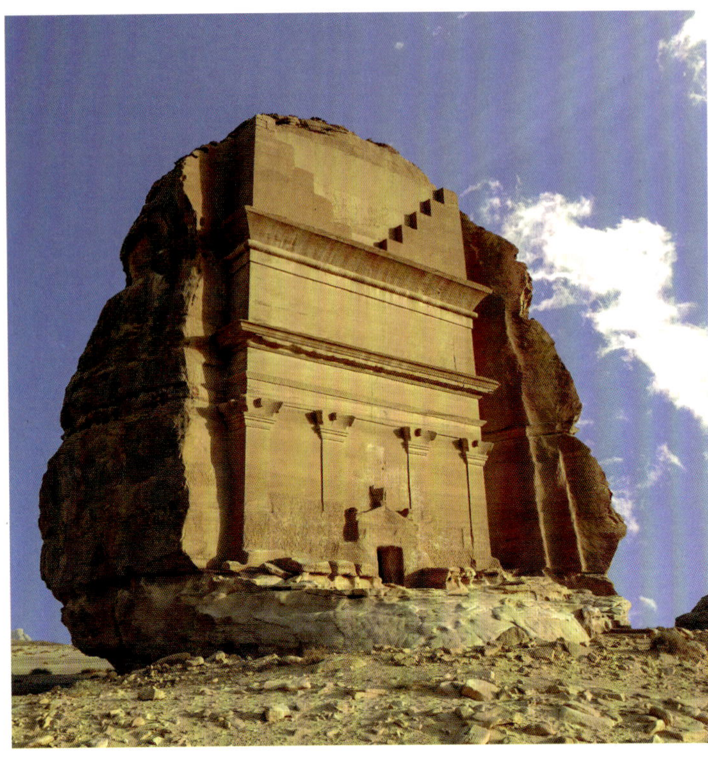

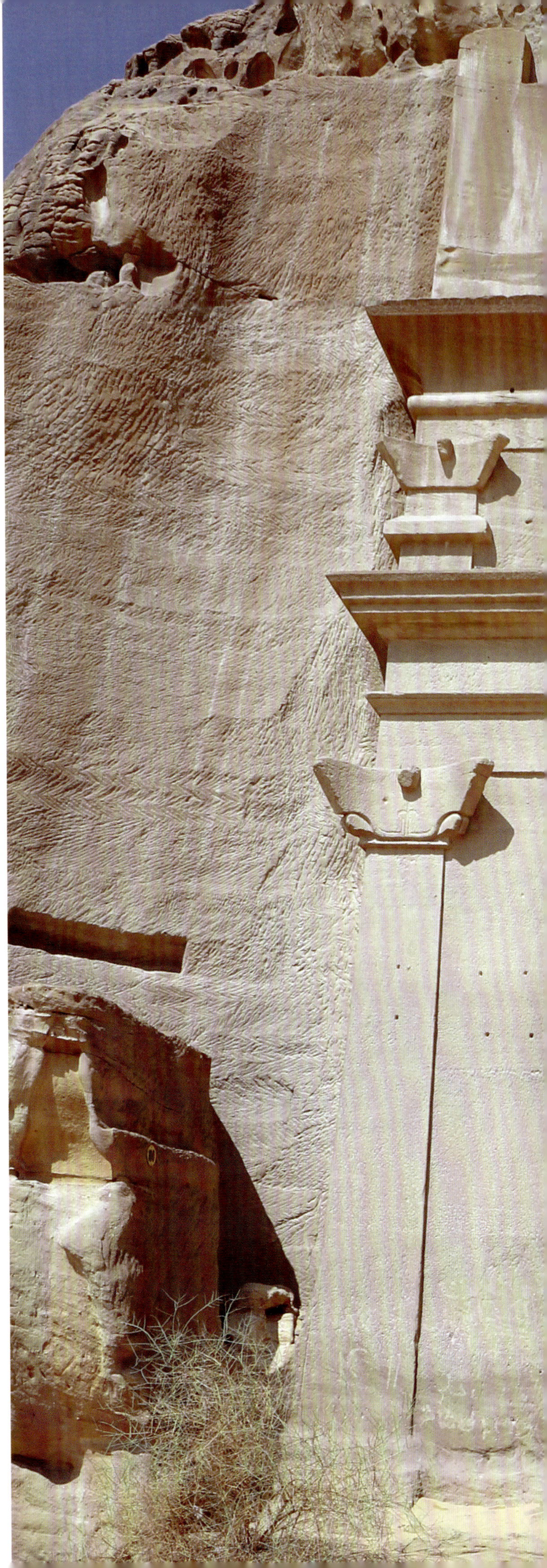

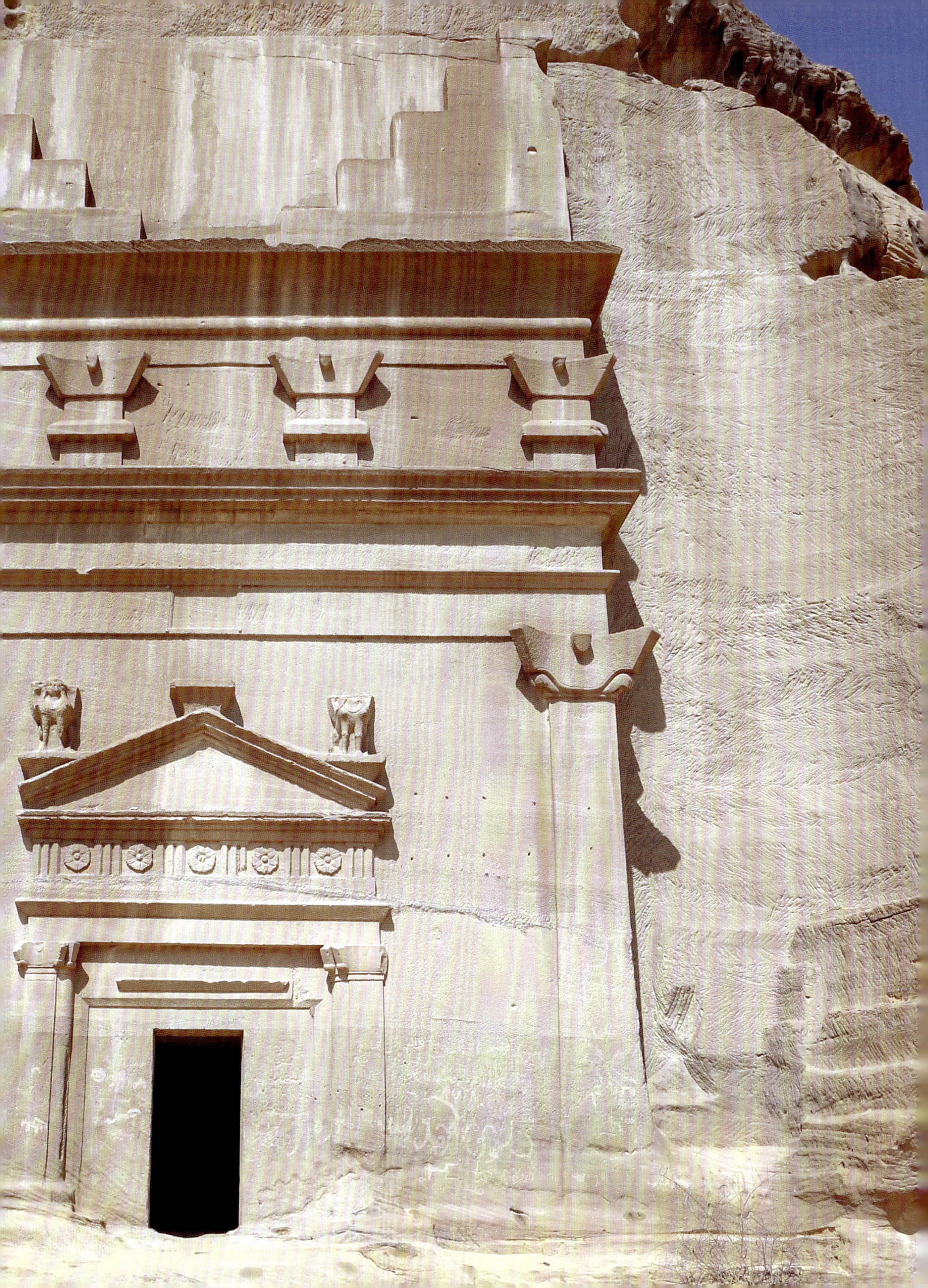

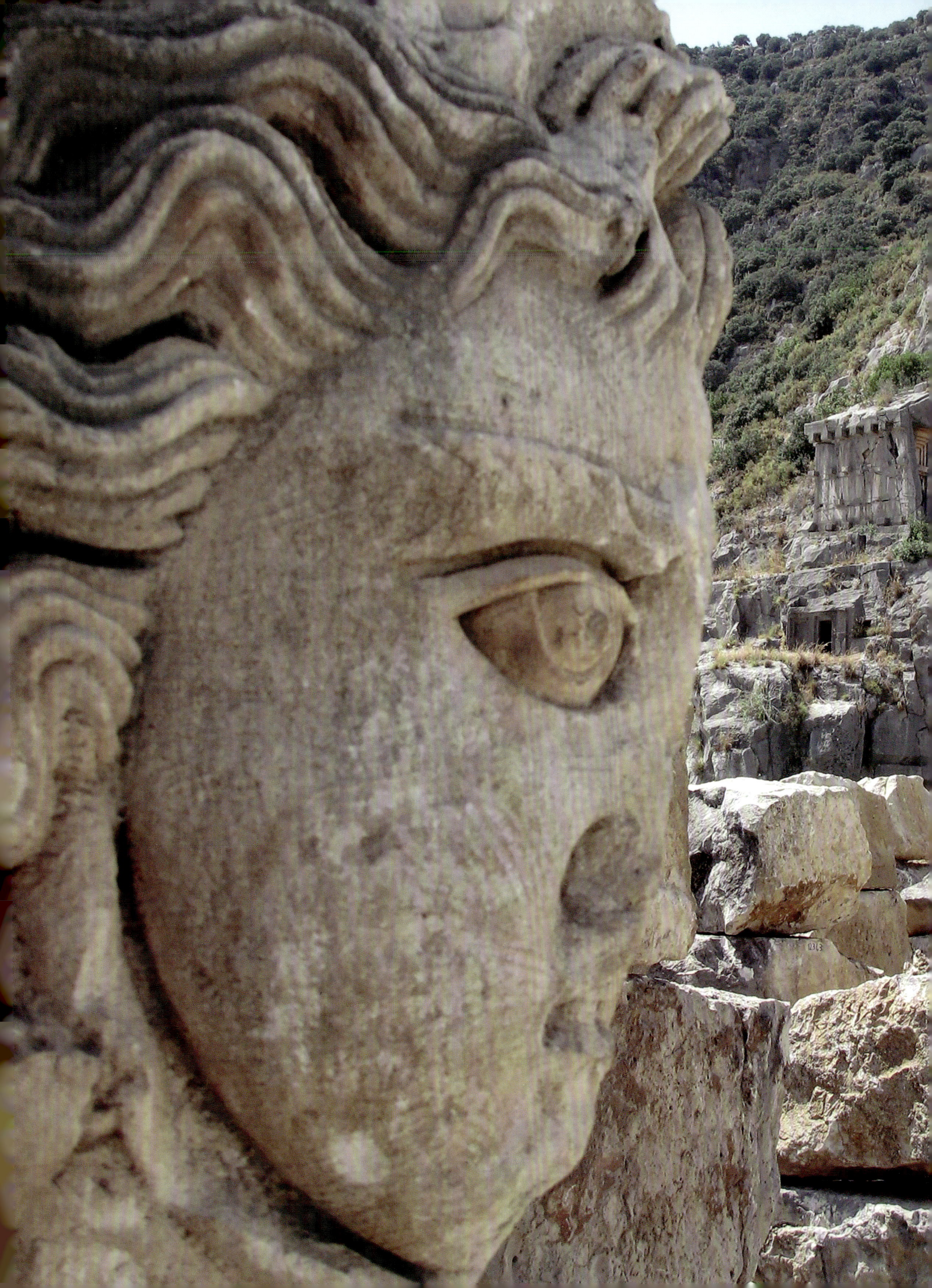

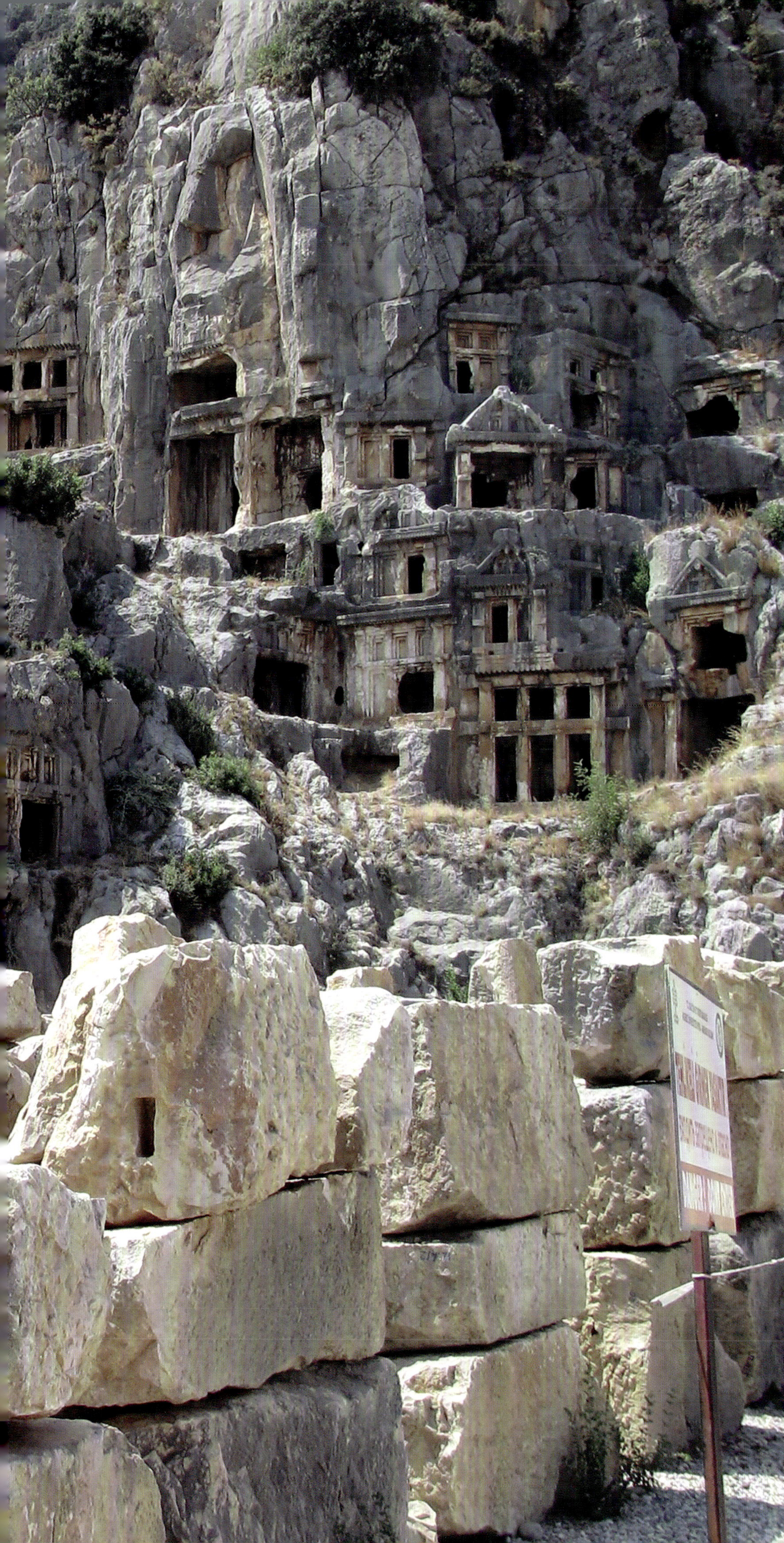

Necropolis, Myra, Turkey
Frozen in time, a bust of a youth stares past a 4th century BCE Lycian necropolis of Myra. Its tombs were excavated out of the mountainside above a Greco-Roman amphitheatre near modern Demre on Turkey's southern coast. Many distinctive house-type tombs contain entire families. Elaborate reliefs show mythical, banqueting and hunting scenes, or visual snapshots of the lives of the deceased.

Lycians lived on the seam-line between the Greek and Persian worlds, and their vivid art reflects hybrid influences. Myra cherished its democratic freedoms within the Lycian Federation, though seldom challenged stronger powers, whether Greek or Persian, Roman or Byzantine. St Nicholas – the original Santa Claus and bishop of Myra – demolished Myra's Temple of Artemis and inspired a still standing 6th century CE church in his name. Arab and Seljuk Turk conquests, as well as bubonic plague in 542–543, reduced the city, which was finally abandoned in the 11th century.

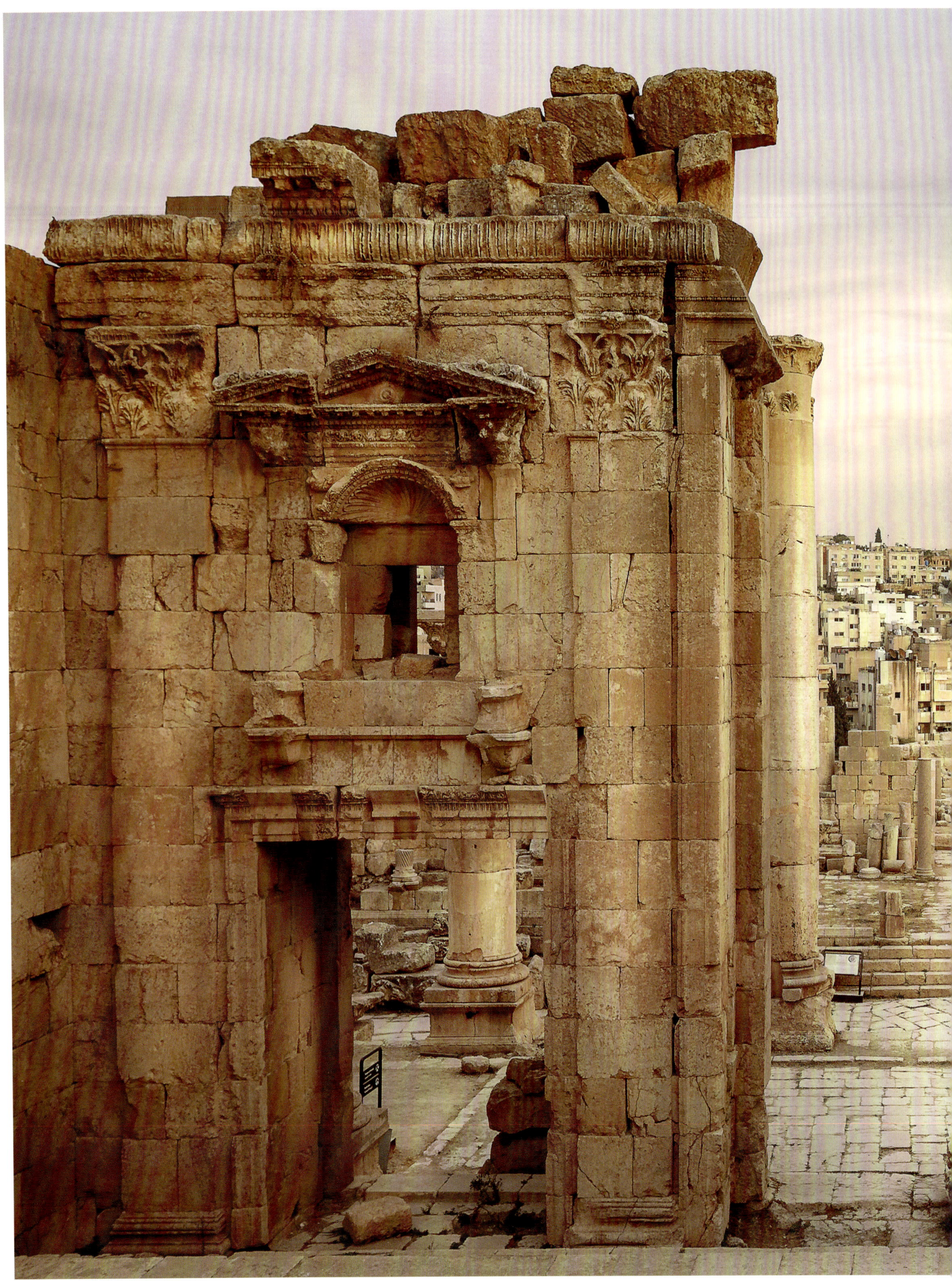

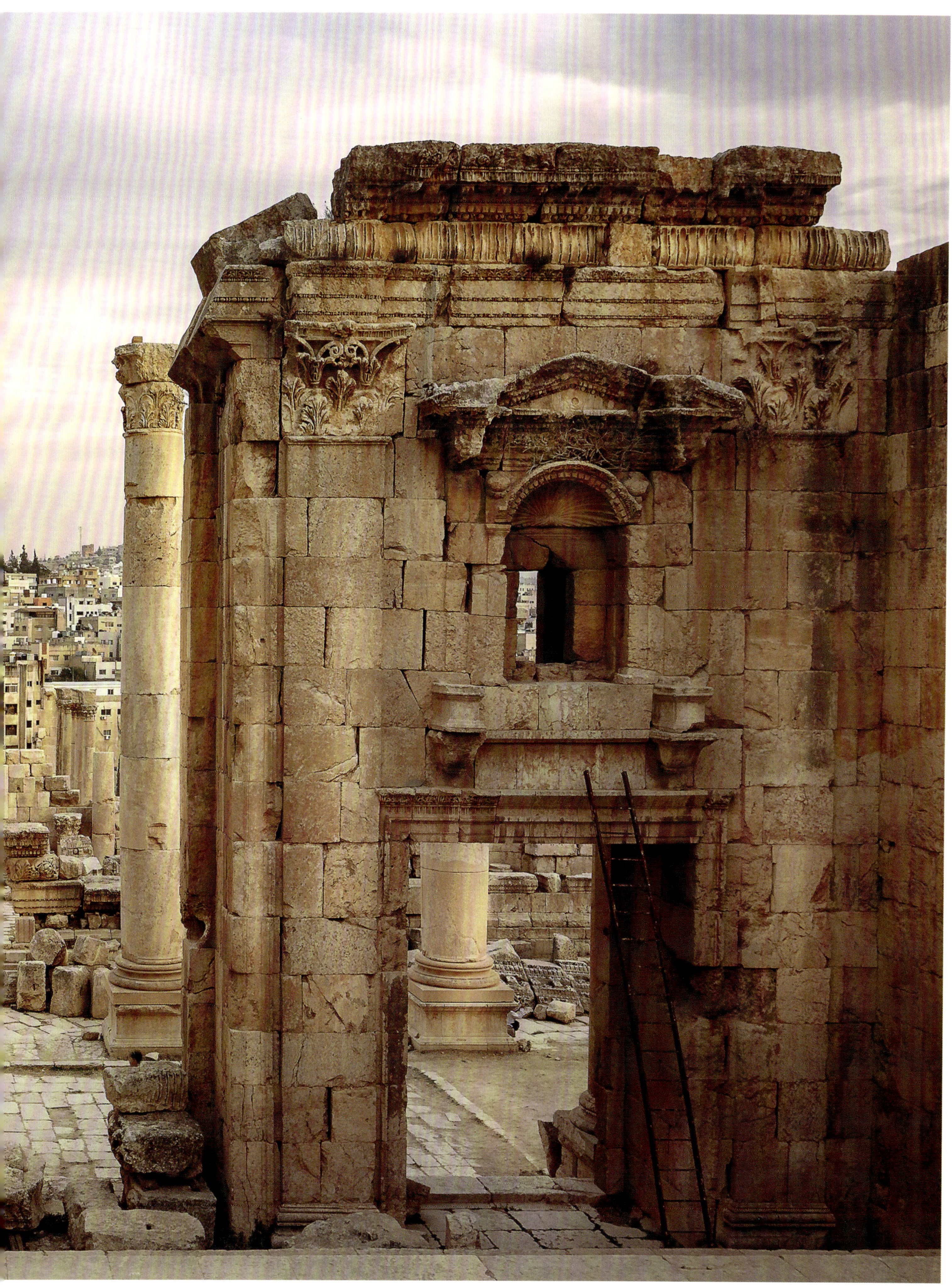

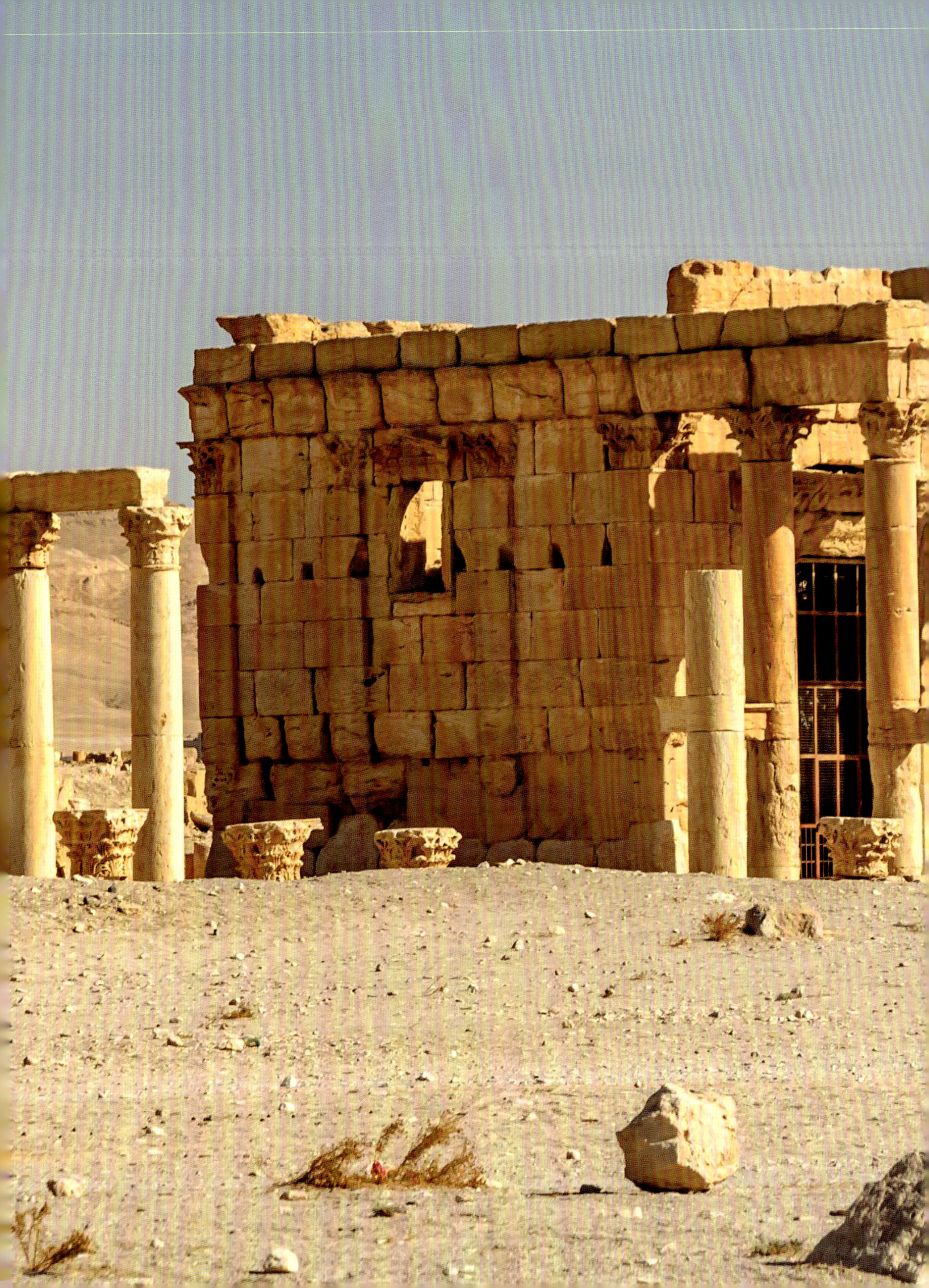

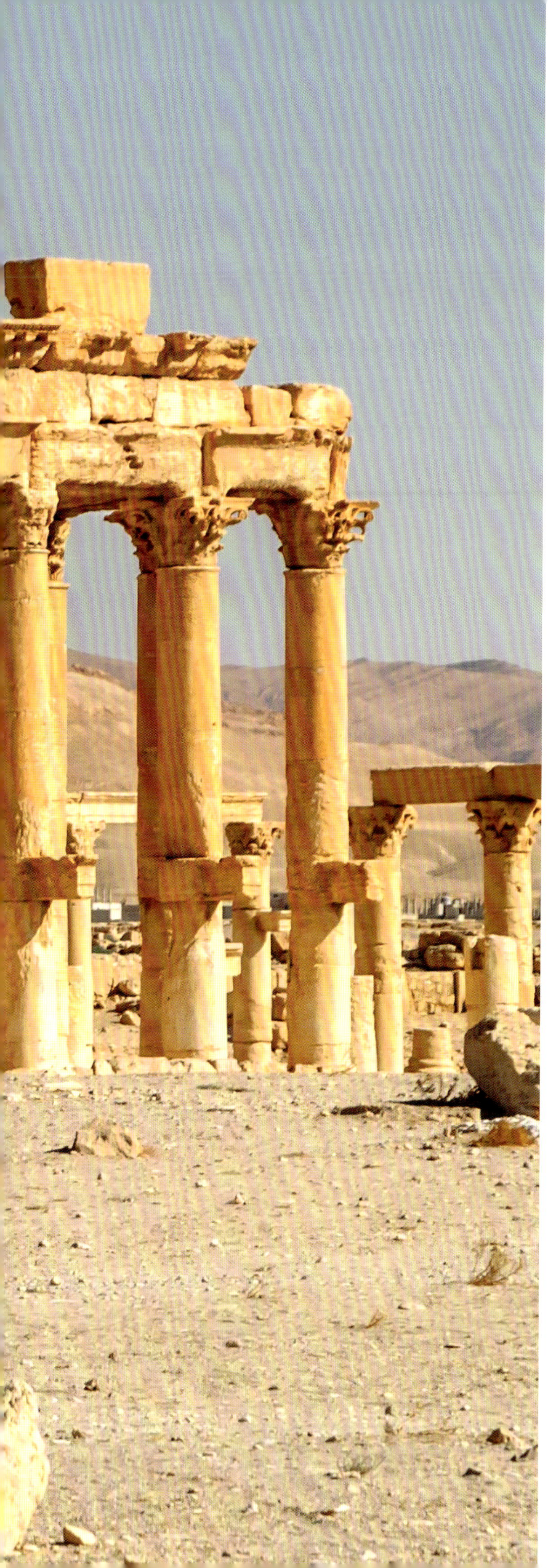

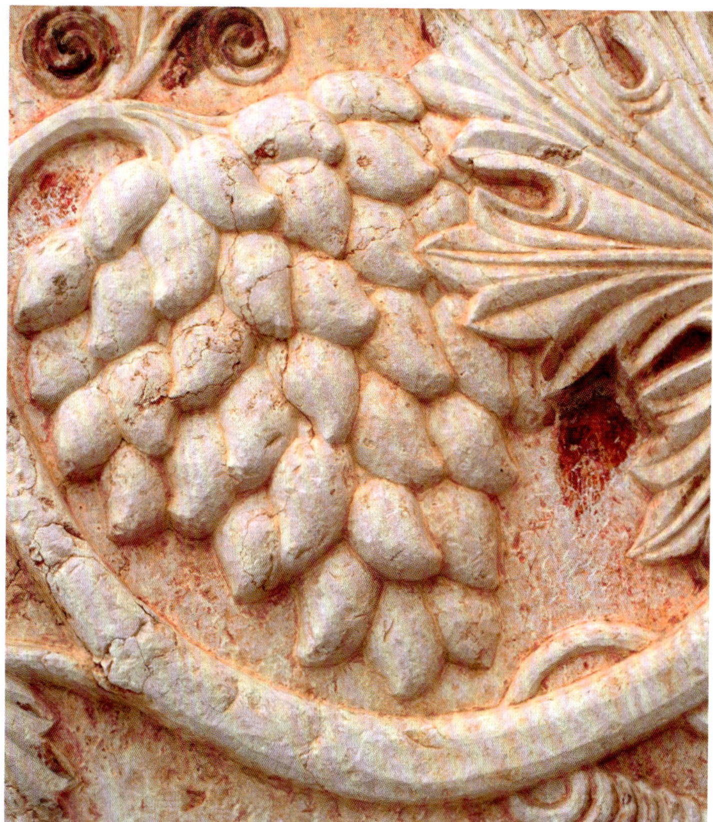

PREVIOUS PAGES:

Temple of Artemis, Jerash, Jordan

A majestic Greco-Roman Temple of Artemis, finished c.150 CE, still dominates the skyline of modern Jerash. It forms part of what some call the largest Roman complex outside Italy. Jerash's ruins include a unique oval-shaped forum, hippodrome, theatres and baths, Arch of Hadrian and several other temples. One is to Zeus, favoured by locals, though Roman settlers preferred the Artemis cult of chastity and the hunt.

LEFT:

Temple of Baal-Shamin, Palmyra, Syria

Preserved by the desert's arid climate, this Syrian temple to the Canaanite Lord of Heavens, Baal-Shamin, beautifully shows the Hellenistic and Aramean artistic fusion that makes Palmyra so renowned. It was rebuilt from an original in 131 CE, complete with altar and six-columned forecourt, but was shut when Romans persecuted pagans in the Middle East from 385–388 CE. By the mid-5th century CE, it had become a church. Sadly ISIS (Islamic State) extremists demolished the building in 2015.

Palmyra, called Tadmor in the Bible, was first settled c.1500 BCE. By the 3rd century CE it was a thriving Arabic-speaking trading hub squeezed between two mighty powers: Parthia (Persia) and Rome, which had made it a vassal state in c.18 CE. Queen Zenobia defied Rome in 269 CE and briefly created a Palmyrene Empire stretching from Turkey to Egypt, until Emperor Aurelian sacked the city three years later.

ABOVE:

Temple of Baal-Shamin, Palmyra, Syria

Syrian architecture historian, Nasser Rabat, calls Palmyra 'Arab in origin but classical in influence, temperament and inclination – a mark of how cultures can come together creatively' – as seen in the charming acanthus relief, which displays a strong Egyptian aesthetic.

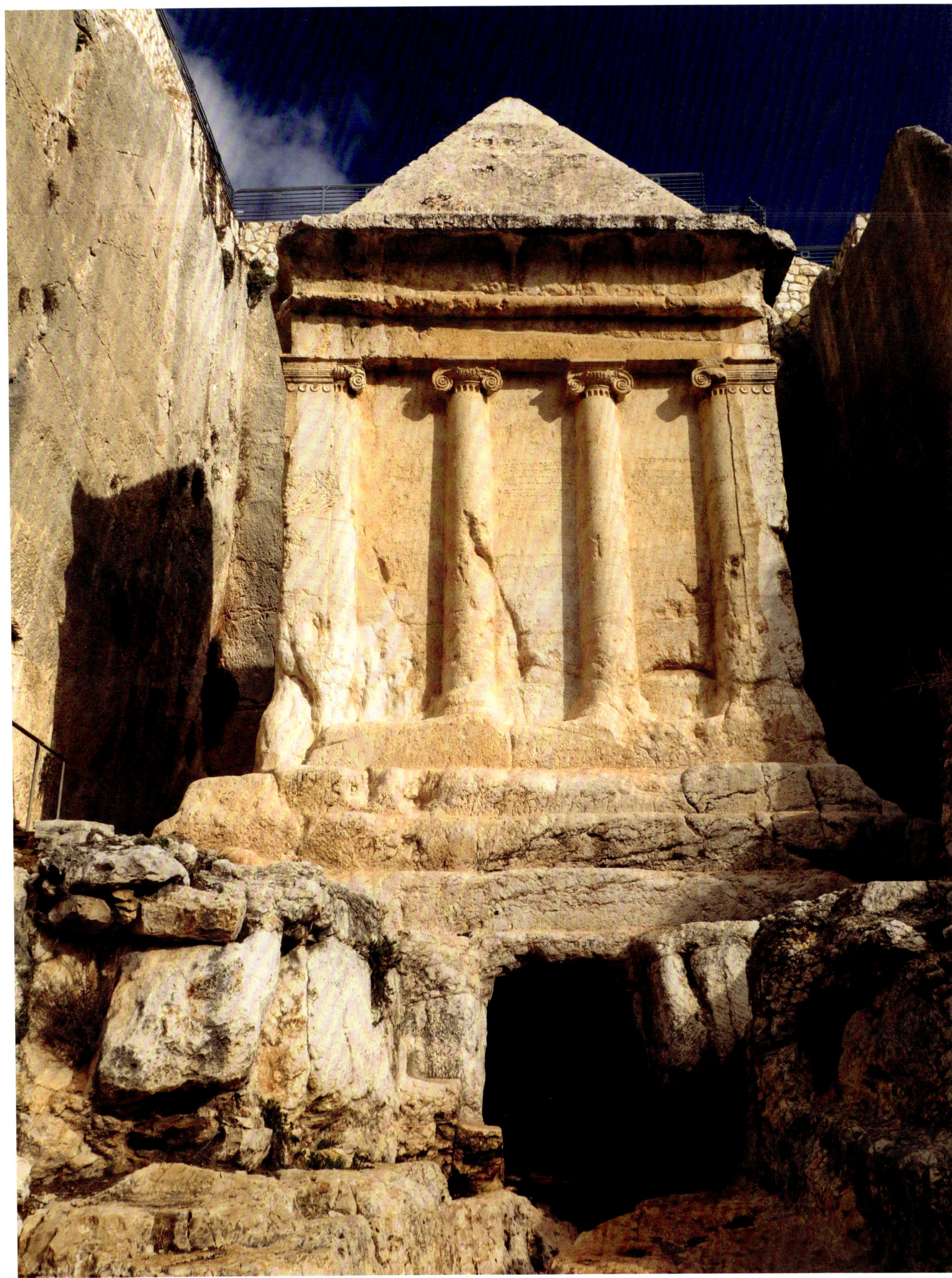

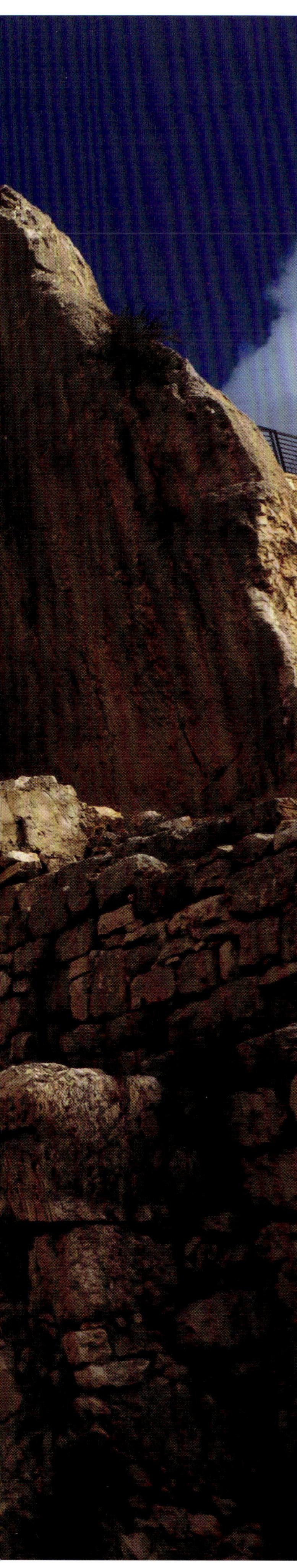

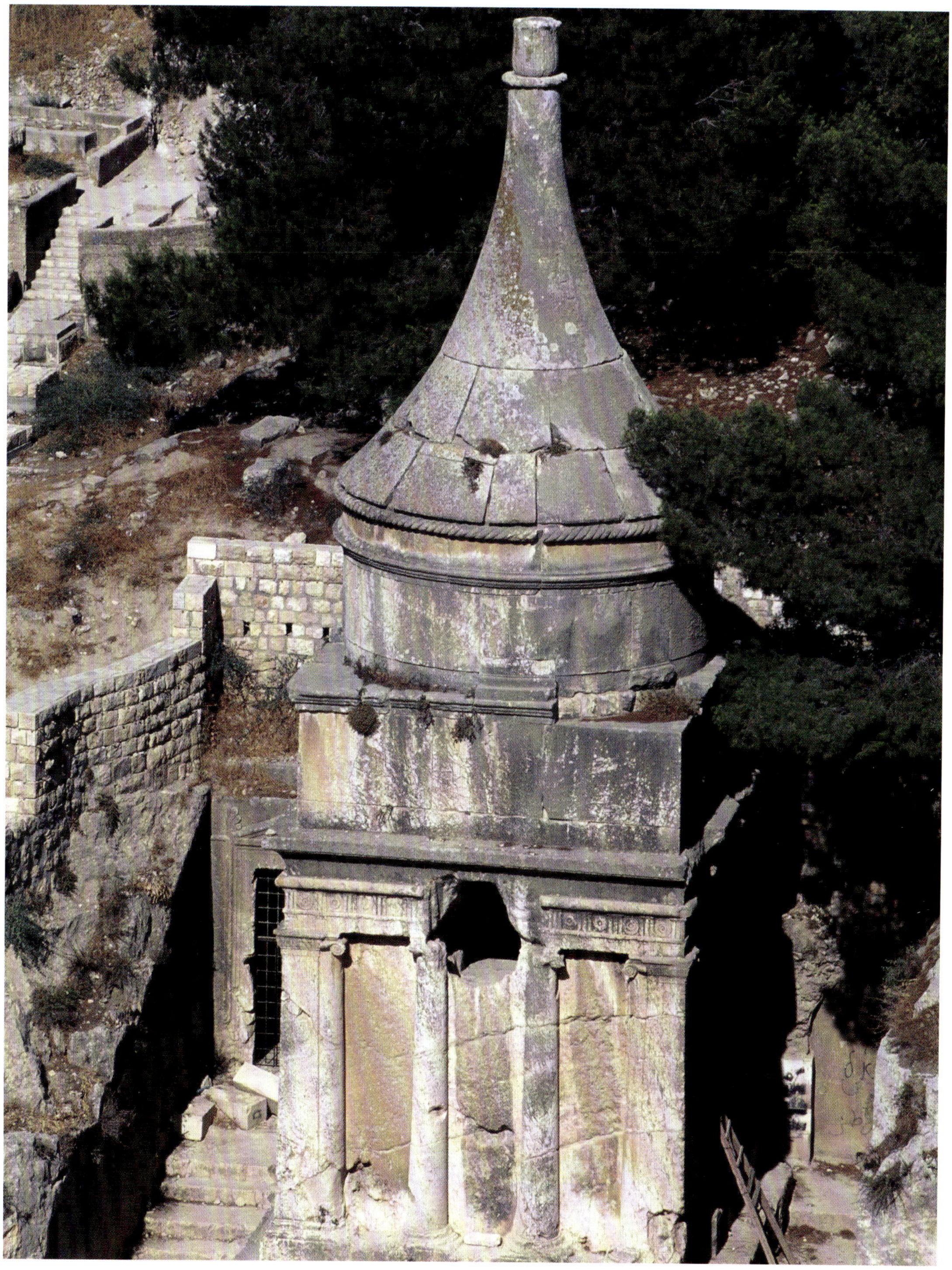

LEFT:

Tomb of Zechariah, Jerusalem, Israel

Carved out of a single stone, topped by a miniature Egyptian-style pyramid and decorated with Grecian Ionic columns, the Tomb of Zechariah presents a perfect example of cross-cultural creativity. It stands in Jerusalem's Kidron Valley and was probably built just before the nearby Jewish Second Temple was destroyed in 70 CE. Fancifully attributed to the 6th century BCE Biblical prophet Zechariah, it was more likely a Jewish funeral monument associated with the adjoining Tomb of Benei (sons of) Hezir.

ABOVE:

Tomb of Absalom, Jerusalem, Israel

Noted for its concaved cone roof and other Egyptian features, the 18-metre-tall (60ft) Tomb of Absalom is one of four mausoleums in Jerusalem's Kidron Valley. All face the Temple Mount – known to Muslims as Haram al-Sharif – and lie at the foothills of the Mount of Olives, a cherished Jewish cemetery with thousands of graves. The Bible says that King David's son Absalom was caught in a tree by his long hair, and killed, after rebelling in c.969 BCE. The current tomb was built in the 1st century CE.

Sumatar, Urfa, Turkey
A 50-metre-long (164ft) slab shows probable carvings of sun and moon gods at Sumatar. Nearby ruined buildings, altars and sacred stones may represent planets. They surround a mountaintop temple built in c.165 CE. After c.300 CE, Christianity and later Islam began eclipsing this Sabean lunar cult. Yet clandestine worship continued until possibly the 13th century at remote Sumatar.

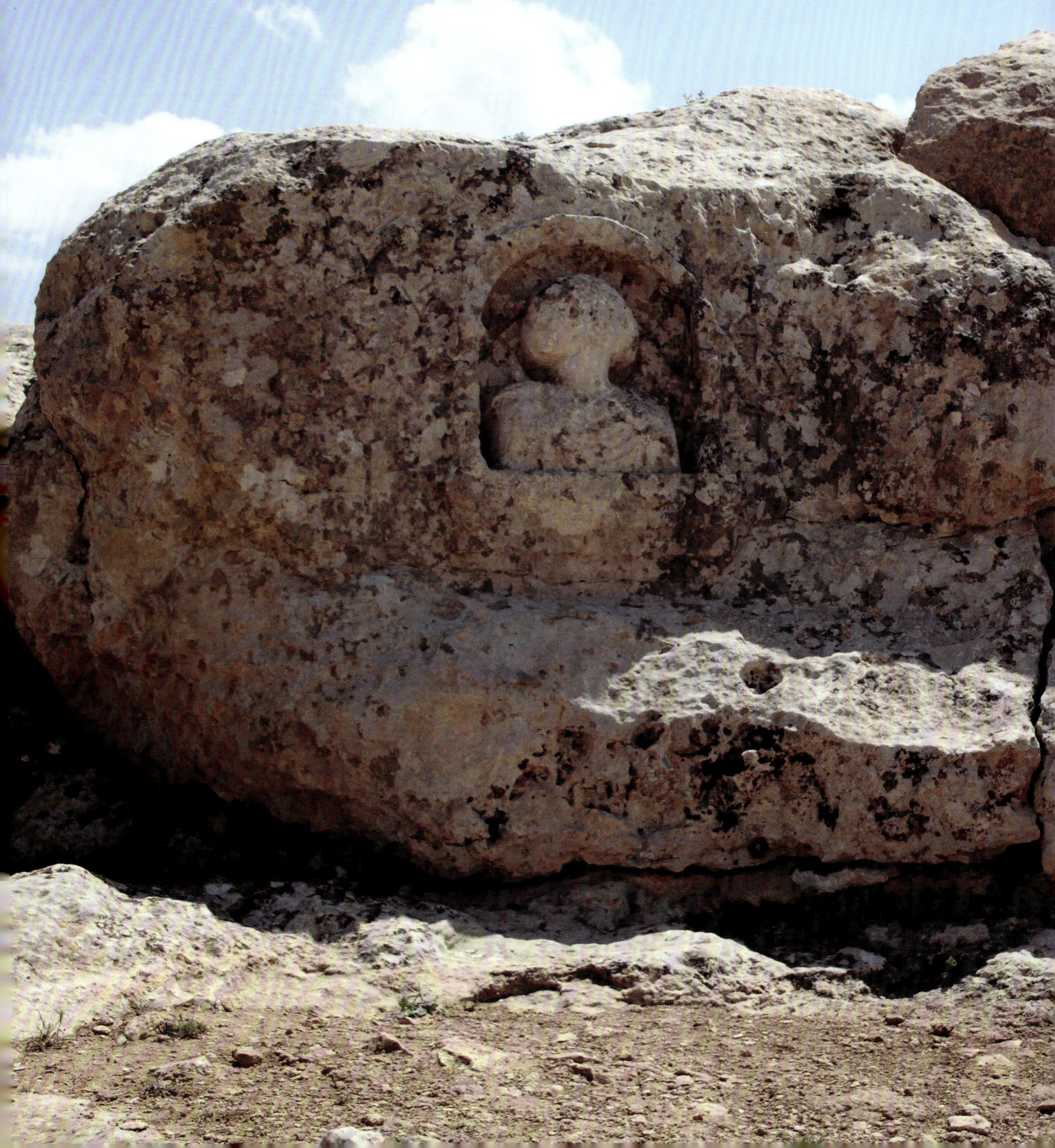

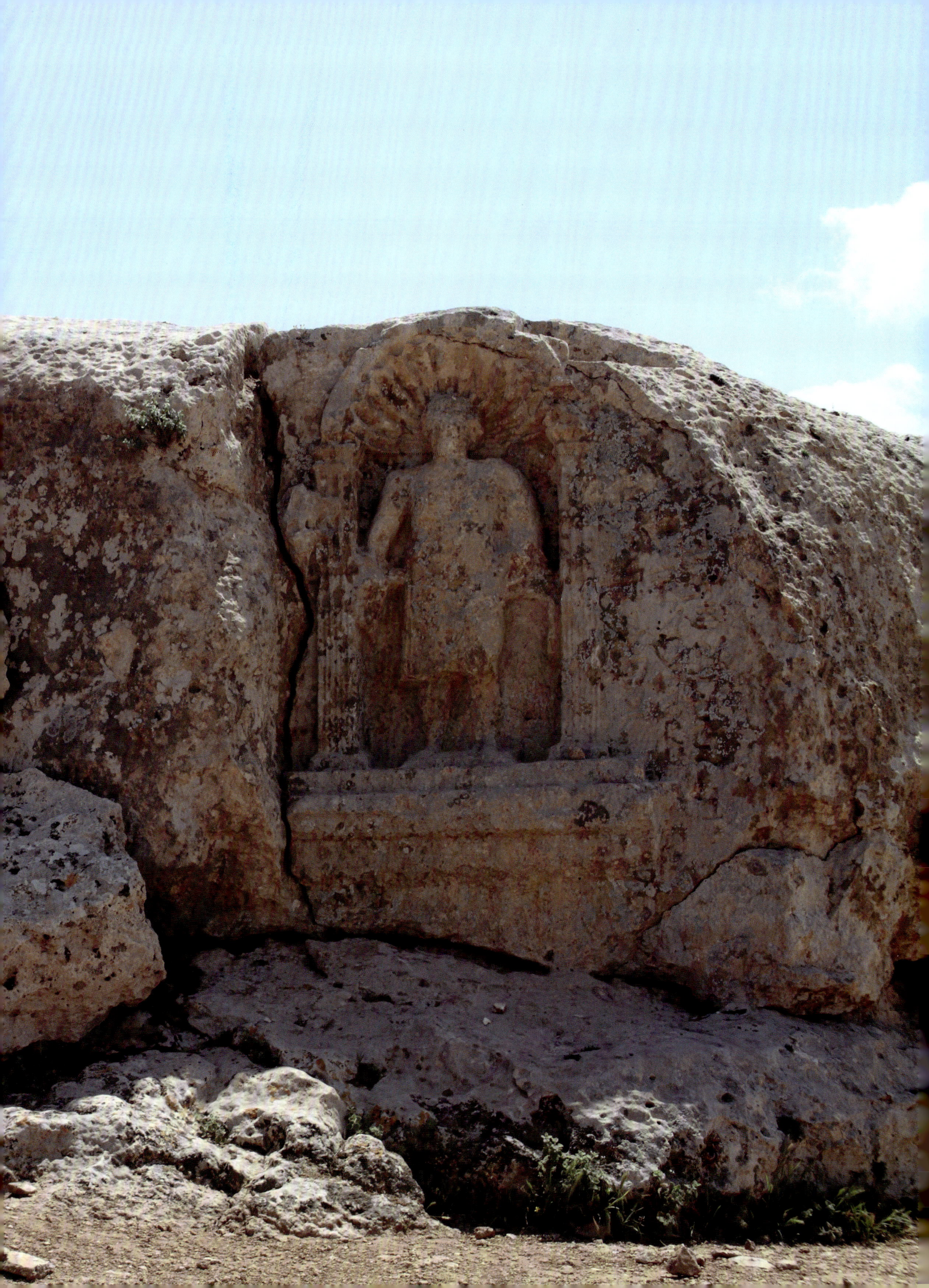

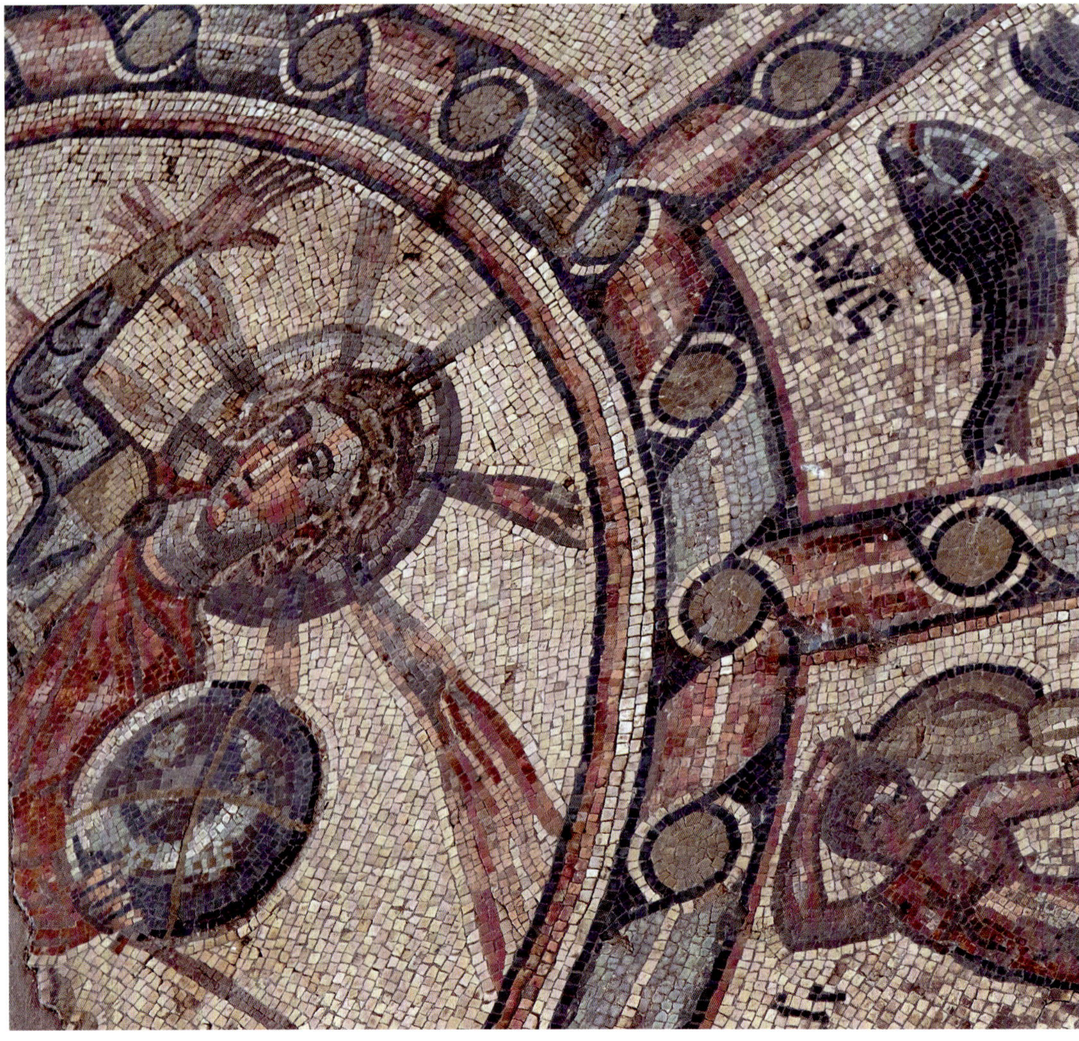

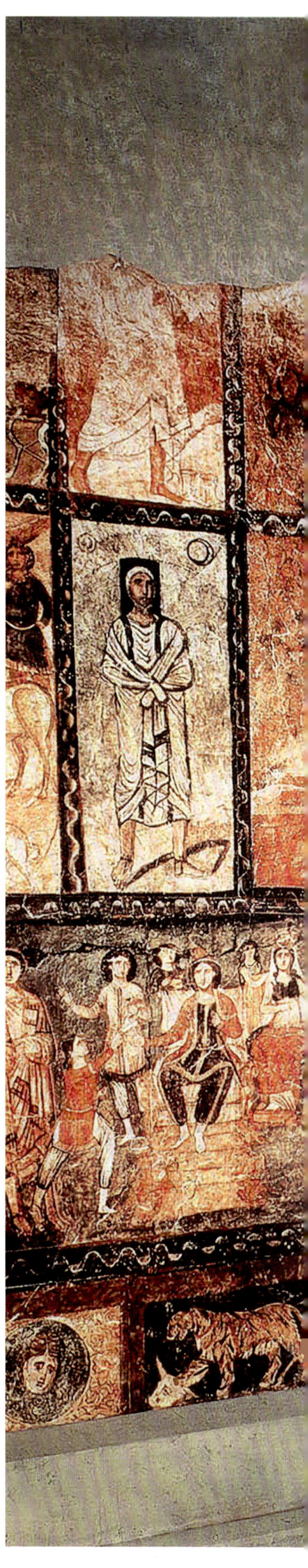

ABOVE:

Synagogue, Hamat, Tiberias, Israel

Formally the Torah and early rabbis disapproved of astrology as gentile superstition. However, later Jewish mystical texts suggest that the 12 zodiac signs could represent the Twelve Tribes of Israel, or 12 Hebrew months. Found in one of the earliest synagogues yet discovered – from the 3rd century CE – this charming zodiac mosaic shows Pisces with the Hebrew term *Dagim* (literally, 'fishes'). Foreign gods and graven images are also taboo in Orthodox Judaism, yet the central image shows the sun-god Helios. Some scholars say that he was added to appease the Roman rulers of Judea.

After the 4th century CE, the community gradually fell into decline. The synagogue was rediscovered during excavations in the 1960s.

RIGHT:

Synagogue, Dura-Europos, Syria

Built in c.244 CE and rediscovered in northern Syria in 1932, the Dura-Europos Synagogue offers a rare peek into a period of Judeo-Grecian fusion that ultimately evaporated. Extraordinarily, it displays human images – the Torah bans such use in sacred practice – and also employs Greek instead of Hebrew in its inscriptions.

The Jewish prayer-house was probably only used for 12 years, before Sassanid Persians overwhelmed the surrounding Roman garrison town in 256 CE. It consists of one room painted from floor to ceiling with tempera on plaster, which has been perfectly preserved after lying under layers of sand and rubble for centuries. Scenes include Moses in the bull-rushes, episodes from the Book of Esther, and a depiction of the Temple.

Today the entire synagogue room is housed within the Syrian National Museum, Damascus, which reopened in December 2018 after seven years of civil war.

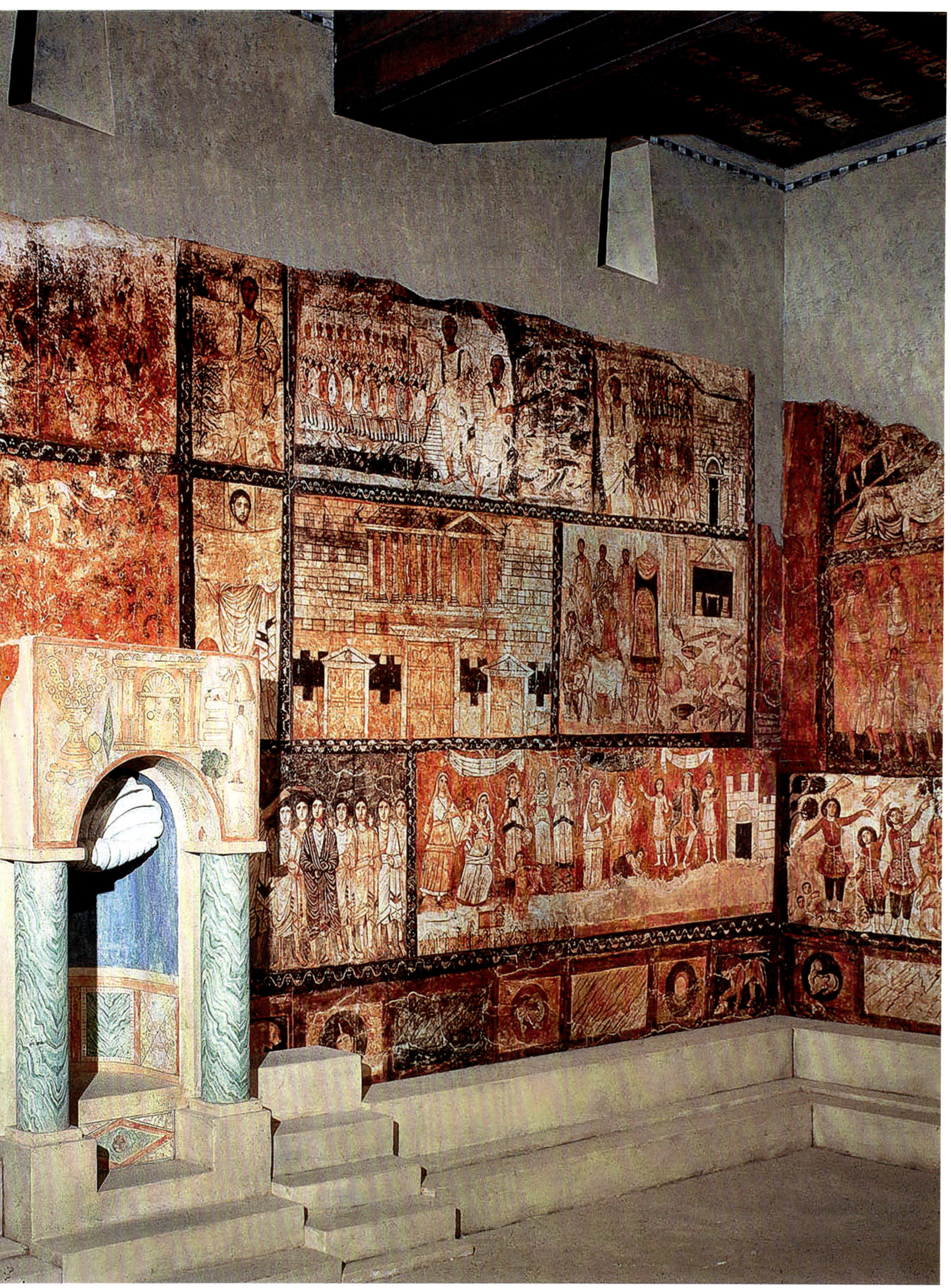

Mushabbak Basilica, Dead Cities of Syria

Today bereft of congregants, this imposing stone-built Basilica at Mushabbak, west of Aleppo, was a centre of Christian worship for nearly 1000 years. It was constructed c.480 CE, making it among the earliest still extant Byzantine churches. Mushabbak is one of Syria's 780 so-called Dead Cities. Once they fed ancient metropolises with wine, olive oil and food. After the 6th century, religious upheaval, as well as shifting trade routes, earthquakes and wars, including the Crusades, destabilized the larger cities. The towns lost their raison d'etre and slowly emptied.

Paradoxically, the Dead Cities gained UNESCO status in 2011, just before the Syrian Civil War erupted. Now refugees shelter in caves under the cities' ruins; and some fear that bombs or fortune-seeking looters may have damaged the monuments.

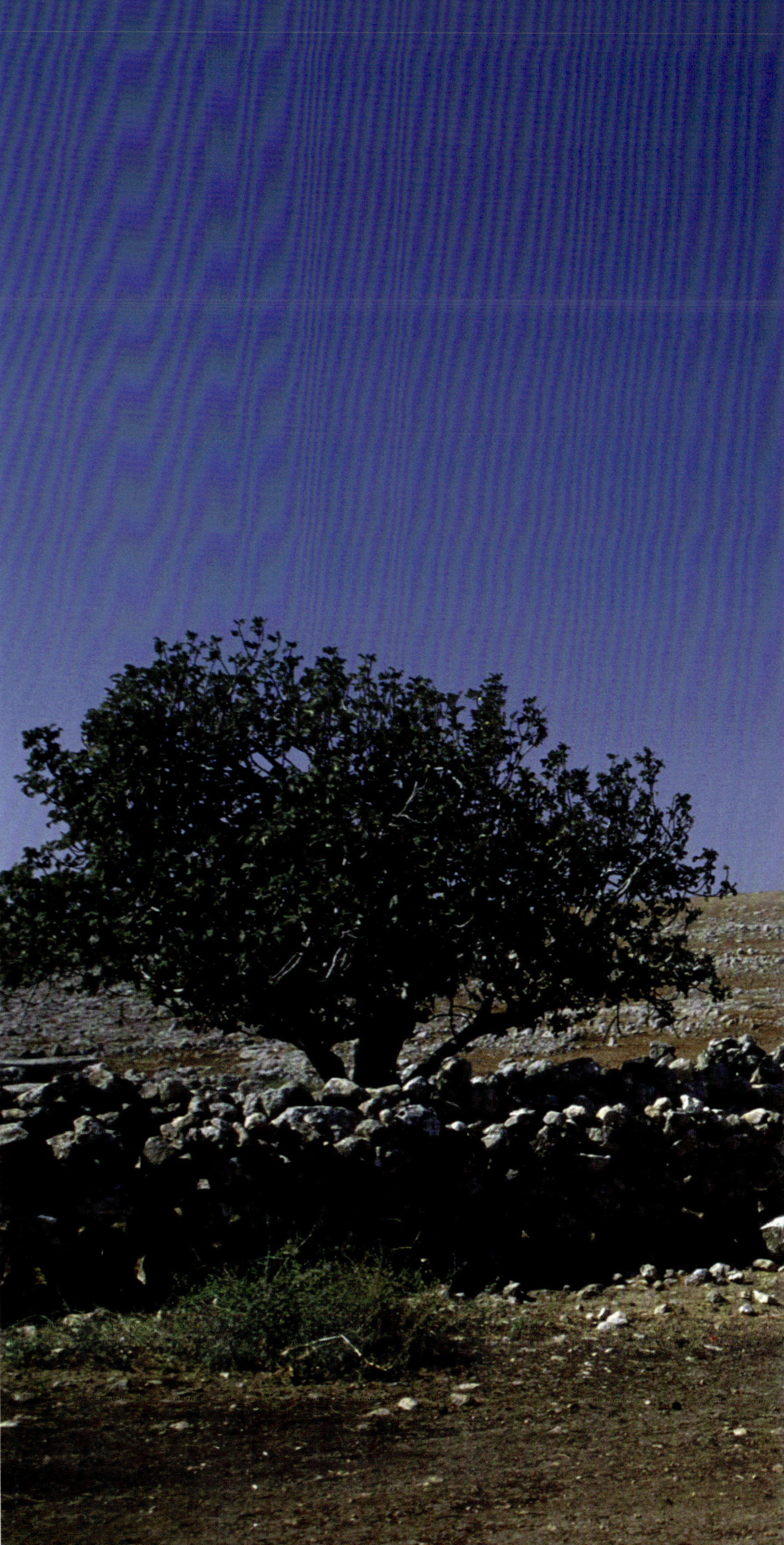

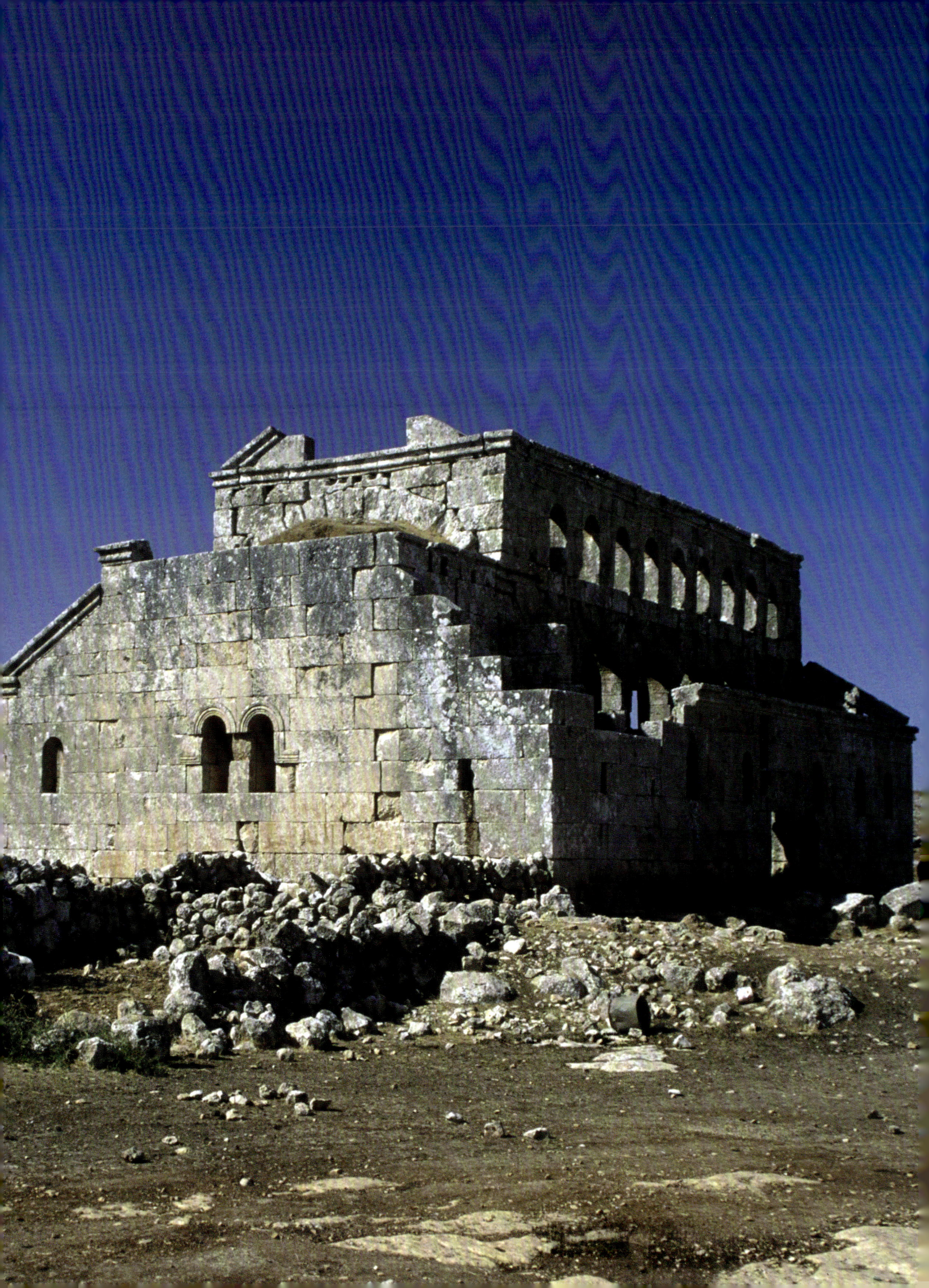

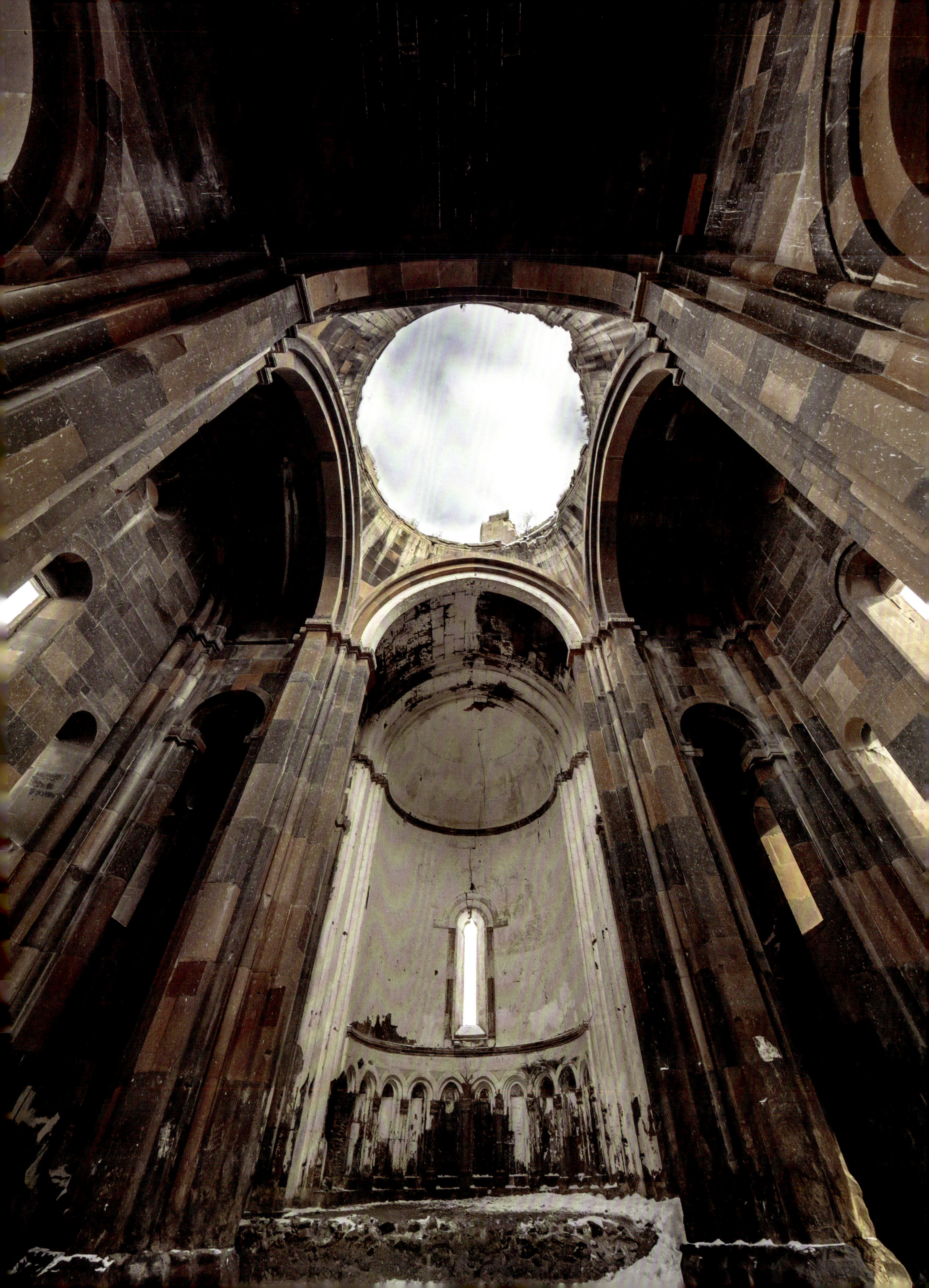

RIGHT:

Church of the Holy Redeemer, Ani, Turkey

In 961 CE, the Bagratid dynasty declared Ani the capital of their new Christian Armenian kingdom. Some 74 years later, Prince Abigharib Pahlavid completed the Church of the Holy Redeemer, or Surp Amenap'rkitch, to house supposed splinters of the True Cross. Abandoned in the 18th century, the church now lies on Turkey's border with modern Armenia. A storm in 1955 and earthquake in 1988 nearly destroyed the edifice.

OPPOSITE AND BELOW:

Cathedral/Fethiye Mosque, Ani, Turkey

Ani was known as 'the city of 1001 churches', and none was grander than its still half-standing cathedral constructed from 989–1001 CE. In 1064, Seljuk Turks conquered the city, after which it passed hands between Georgians, Byzantines and Armenians, Kurds, Persians, Mongols, Ottomans and Russians.

The Seljuks repurposed Ani's cathedral as the Fethiye ('conquest') Mosque. An earthquake in 1319 destroyed the dome. The town's last monks left in 1735.

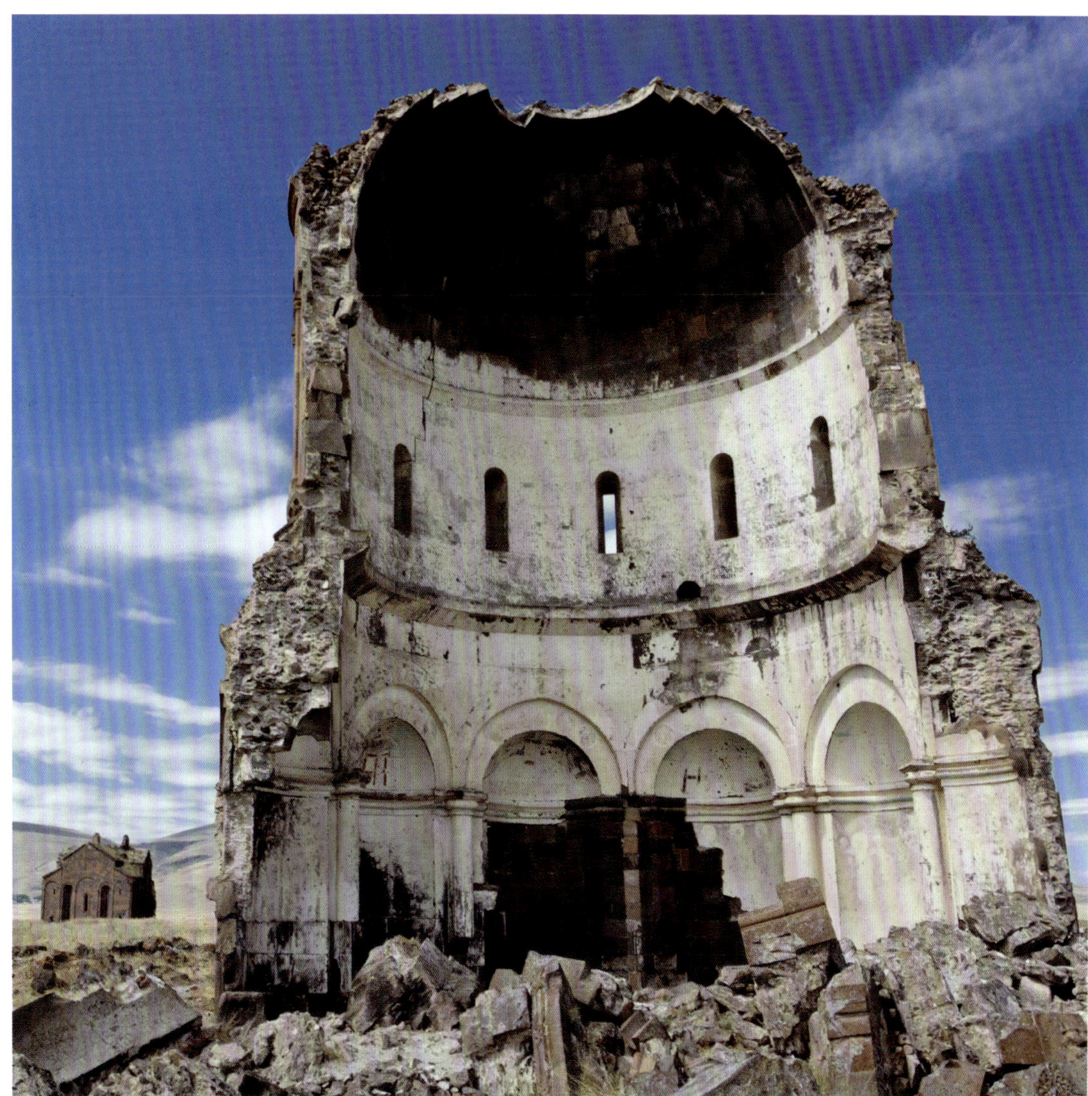

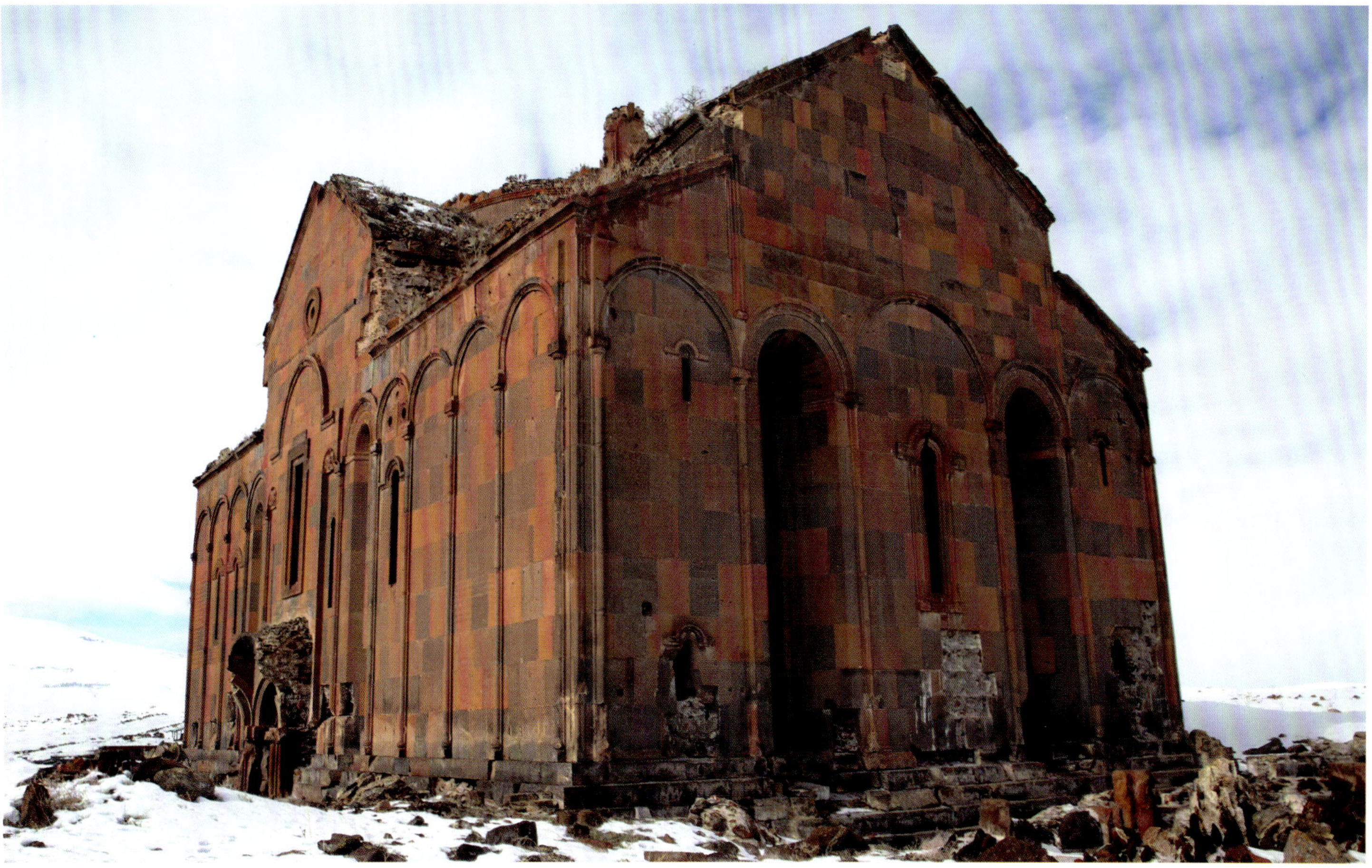

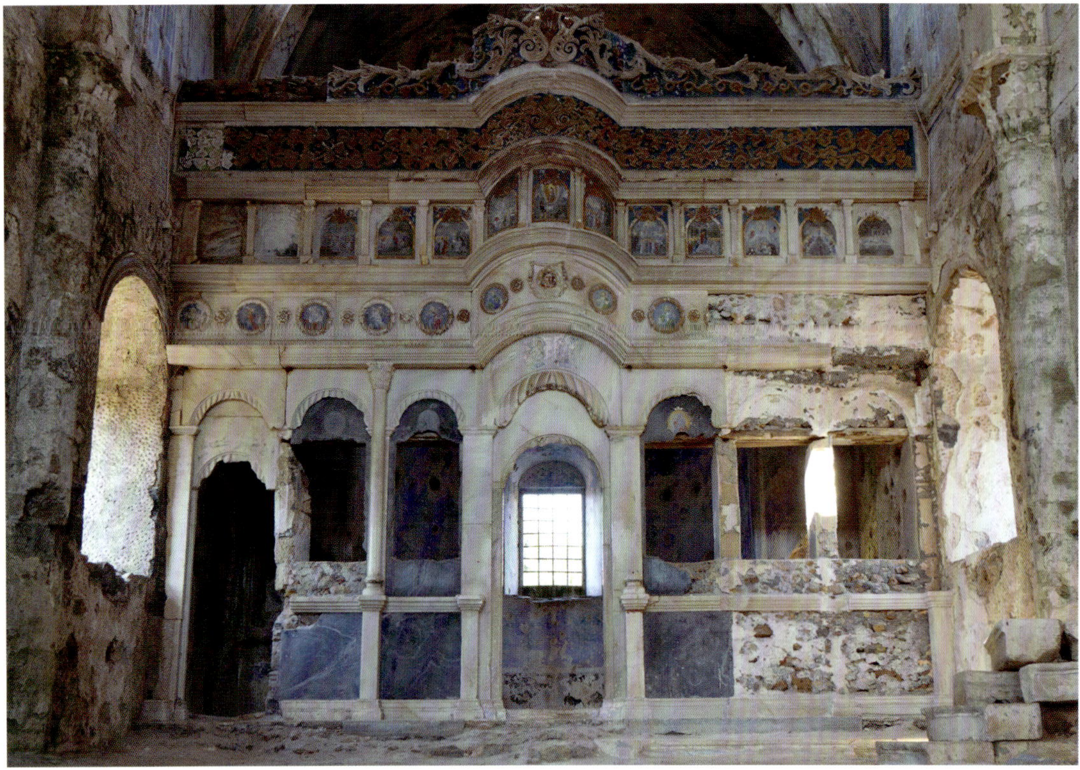

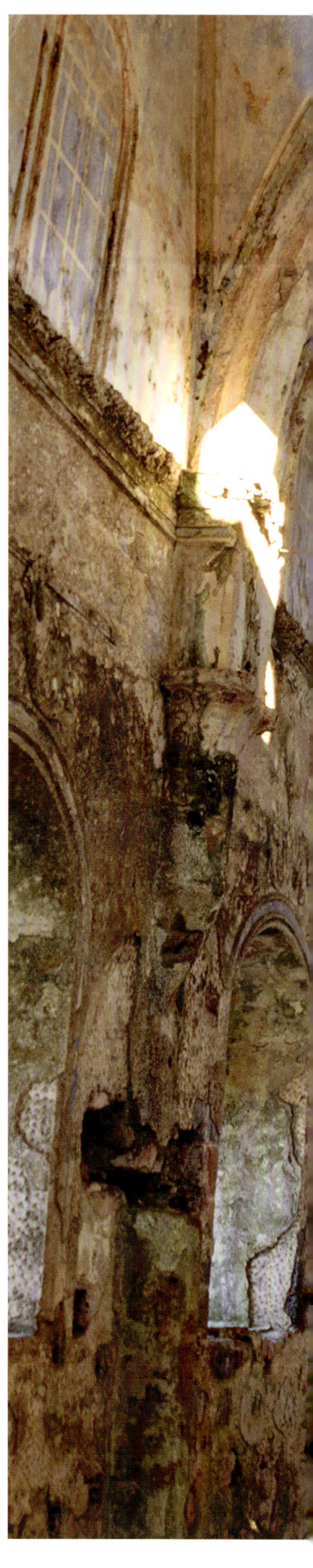

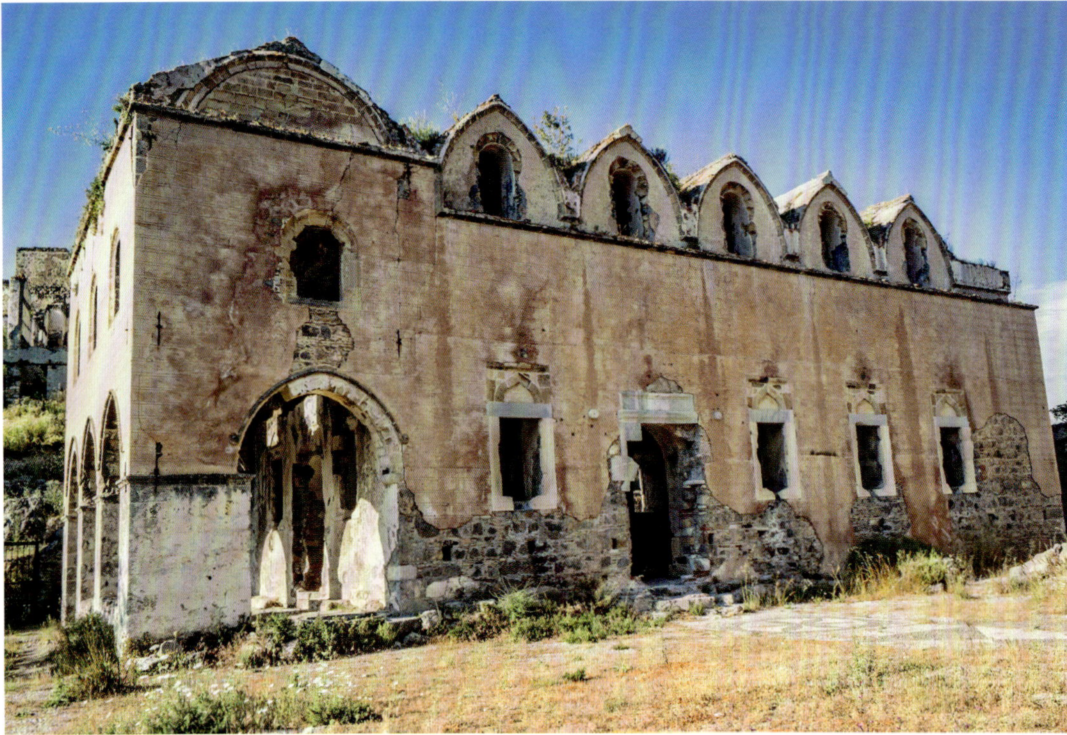

ALL PHOTOGRAPHS:

Kayaköy, Turkey

For seven centuries the town of Levissi in Turkey – now called Kayaköy – enjoyed harmonious relations between its minority Anatolian Muslim and majority Greek Orthodox populations. The latter prayed at places like the Lower Church (top and right) and 17th century Orthodox High Church (above). Yet all 6500 Christian inhabitants were removed during World War I and the subsequent Greco–Turkish War (1919–22). Many of their descendants now live in an Athens suburb dubbed Nea Levissi (New Levissi). Between 1914 and 1922, 1.5 million Anatolian Greeks were forcibly resettled, with 500,000 Muslims in Greece suffering the same fate.

Along with Kayaköy's abandoned churches, 2000 stone homes lie deserted. Once 'cleansed' of its majority Greek population, the town lost its economic cornerstone, so many Muslim Turks left, too. In the 1980s, Ankara mooted plans to redevelop the houses as tourist attractions, but artists and intellectuals vetoed the scheme as tasteless and a threat to Kayaköy's heritage.

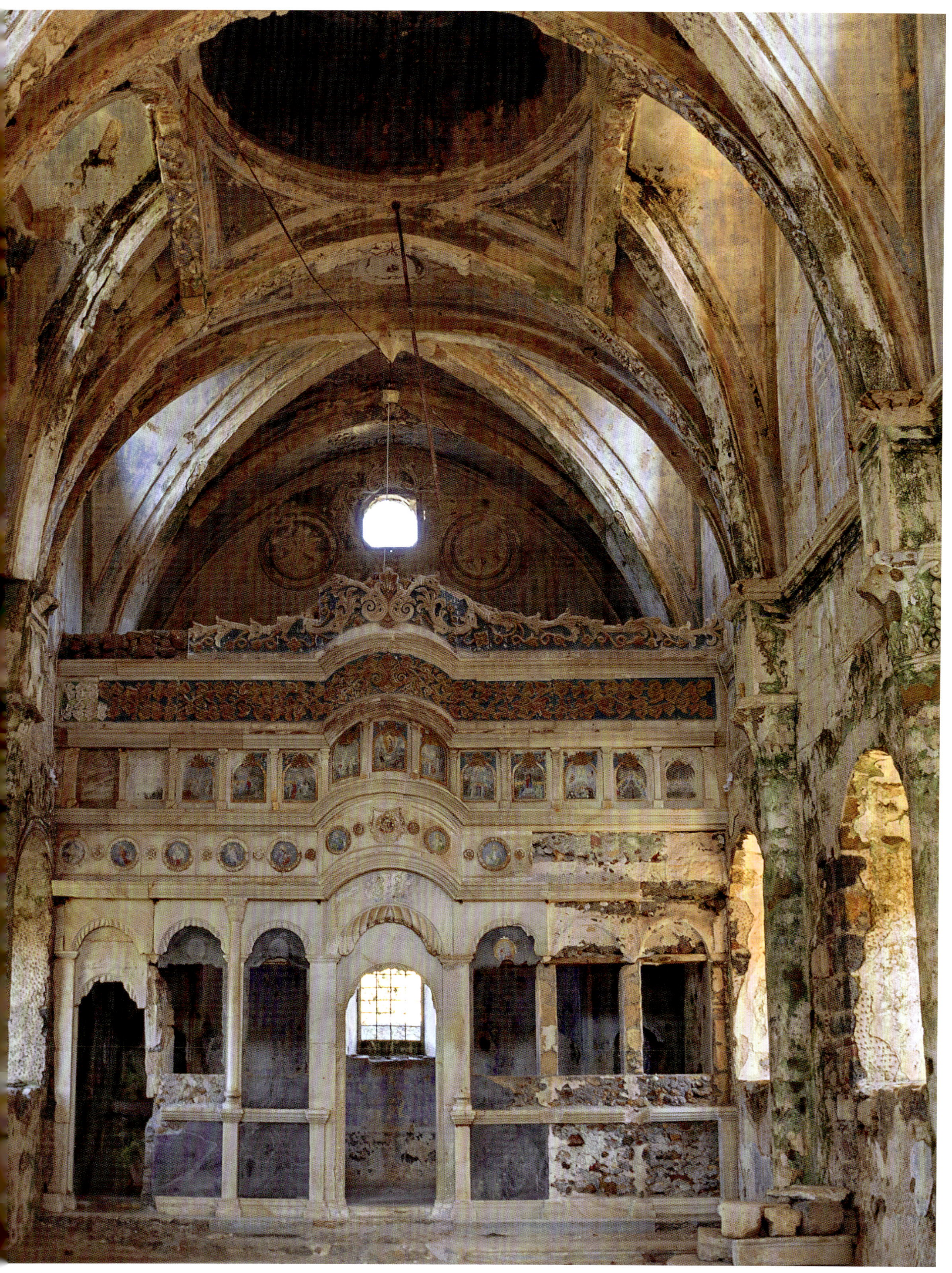

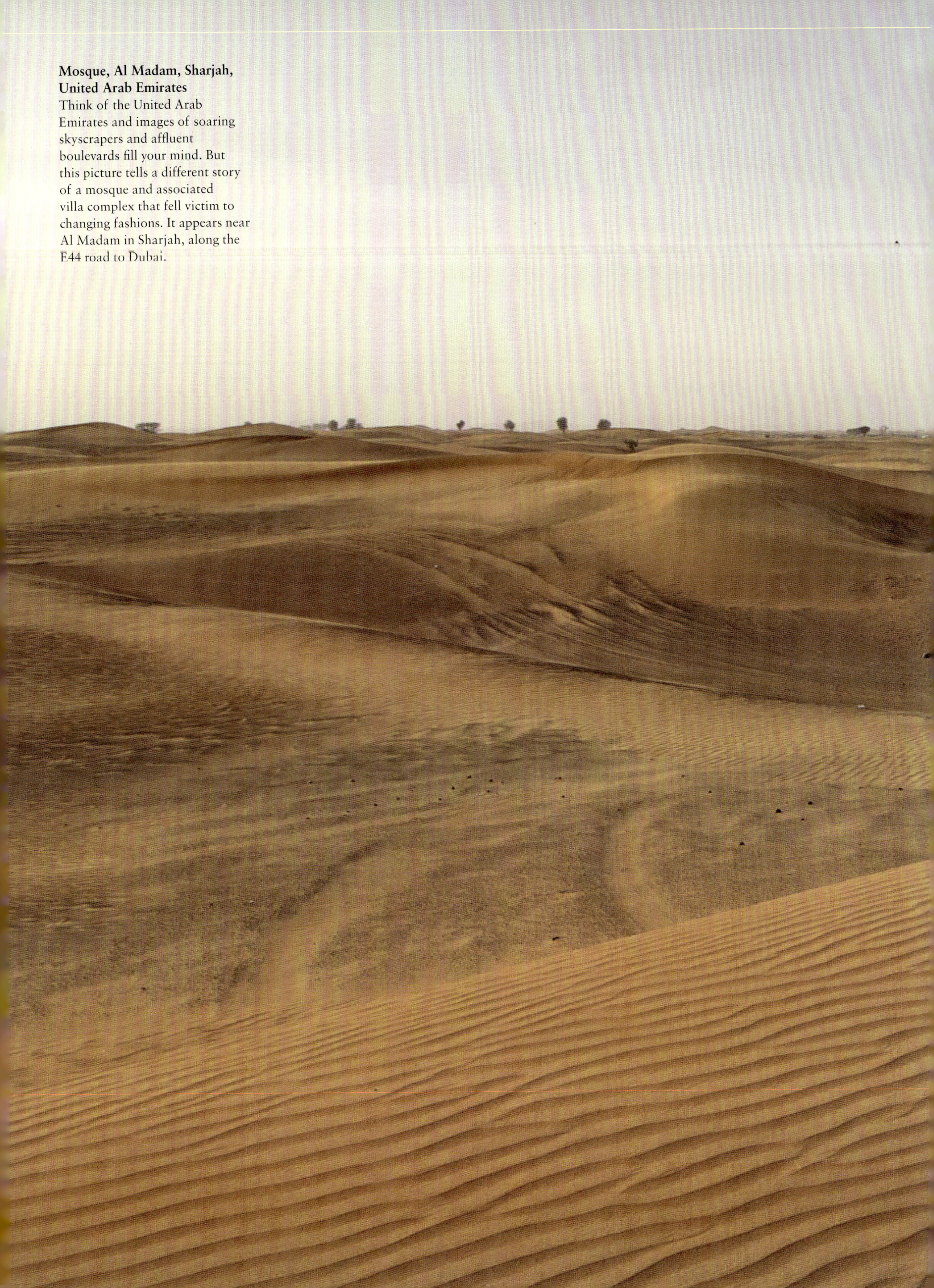

Mosque, Al Madam, Sharjah, United Arab Emirates
Think of the United Arab Emirates and images of soaring skyscrapers and affluent boulevards fill your mind. But this picture tells a different story of a mosque and associated villa complex that fell victim to changing fashions. It appears near Al Madam in Sharjah, along the E44 road to Dubai.

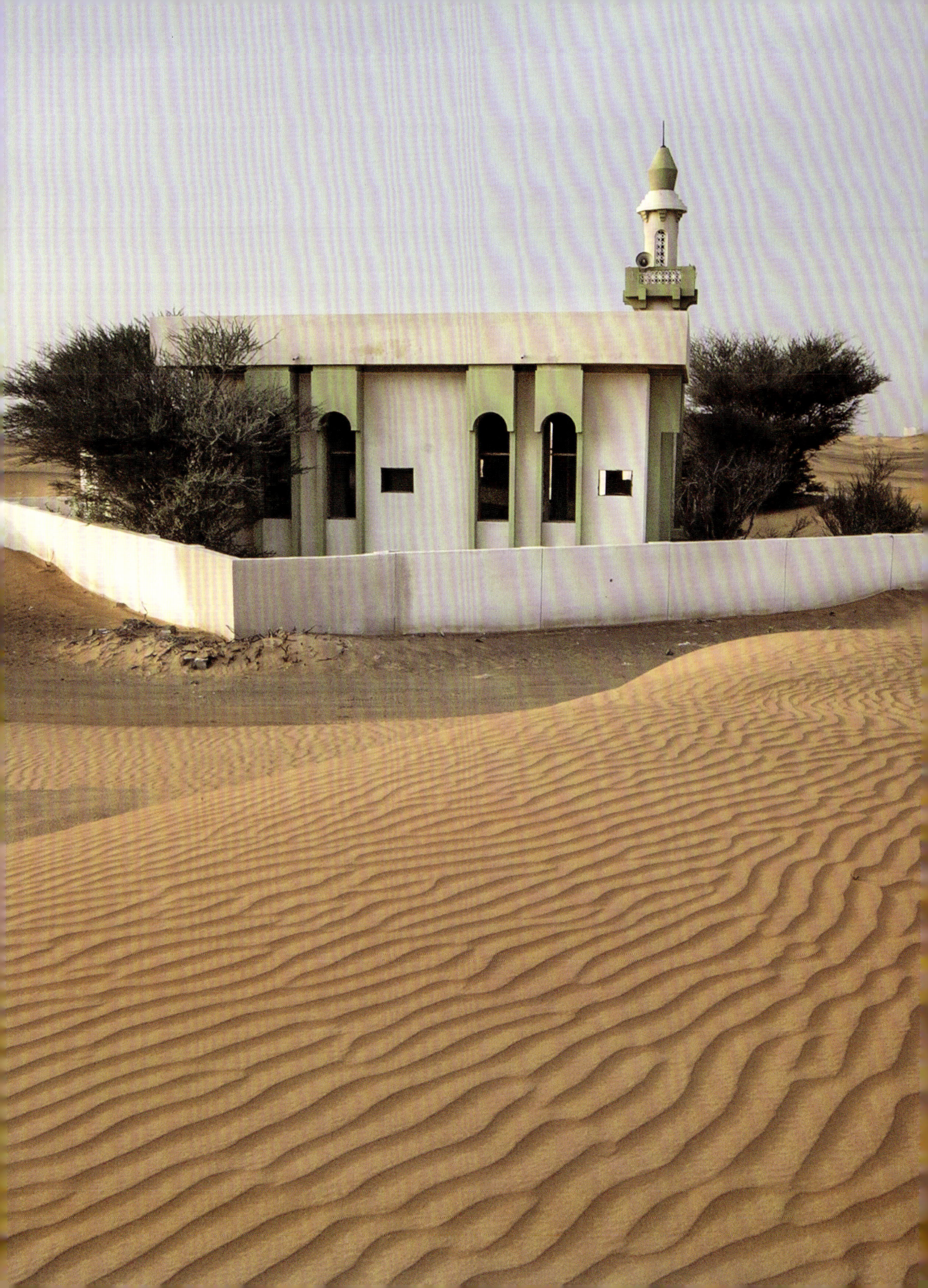

Armenian Church, Mosul, Iraq
This church used to symbolize the security felt by an Armenian minority in a largely Sunni Muslim and Arab city. Armenians call themselves the first nation to adopt Christianity. They have lived in what is now Iraq since late Babylonian times and began settling in Mosul in the 14th century CE. Many others fled there from Turkey after 1915, when about one million Armenians died in a state-directed killing spree.

A century later, the fanatic jihadist group ISIS (Islamic State) conquered Mosul. They occupied, damaged or destroyed all 45 of the city's Christian institutions. Some sites ISIS turned into mosques, others, such as this modern church, they blew up. Kurdish and Iraqi forces eventually liberated Mosul in 2017, but now only 10 Armenians remain.

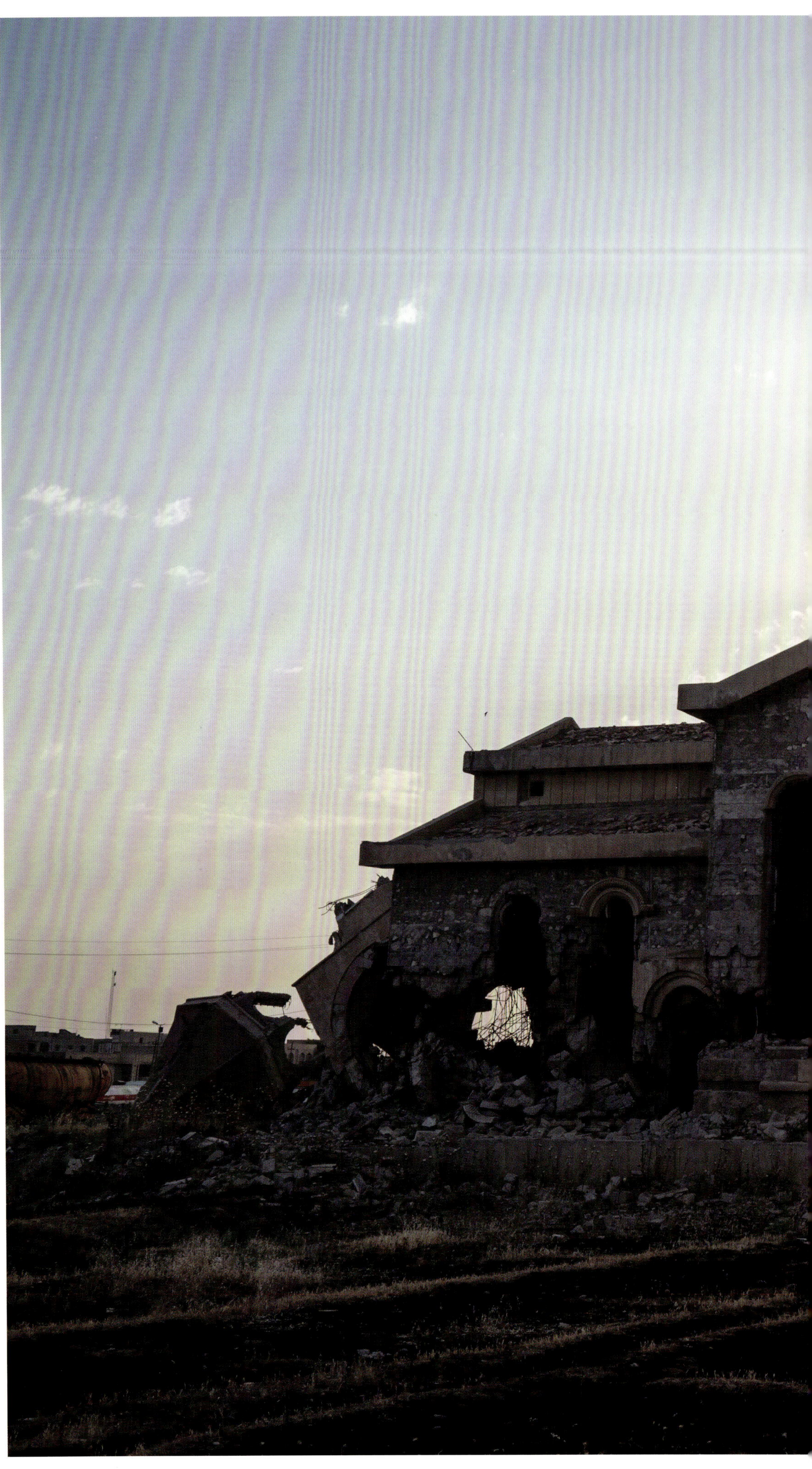

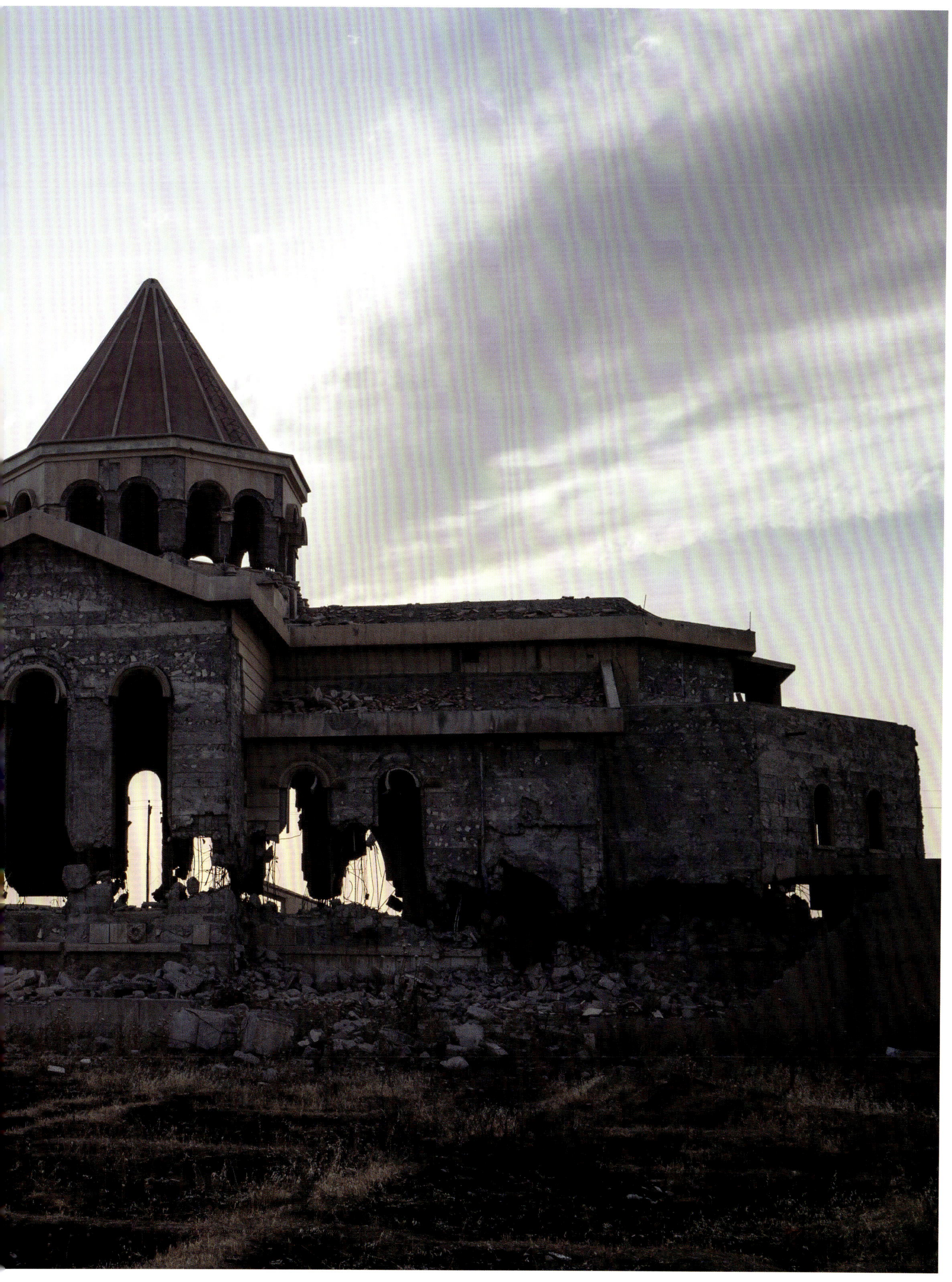

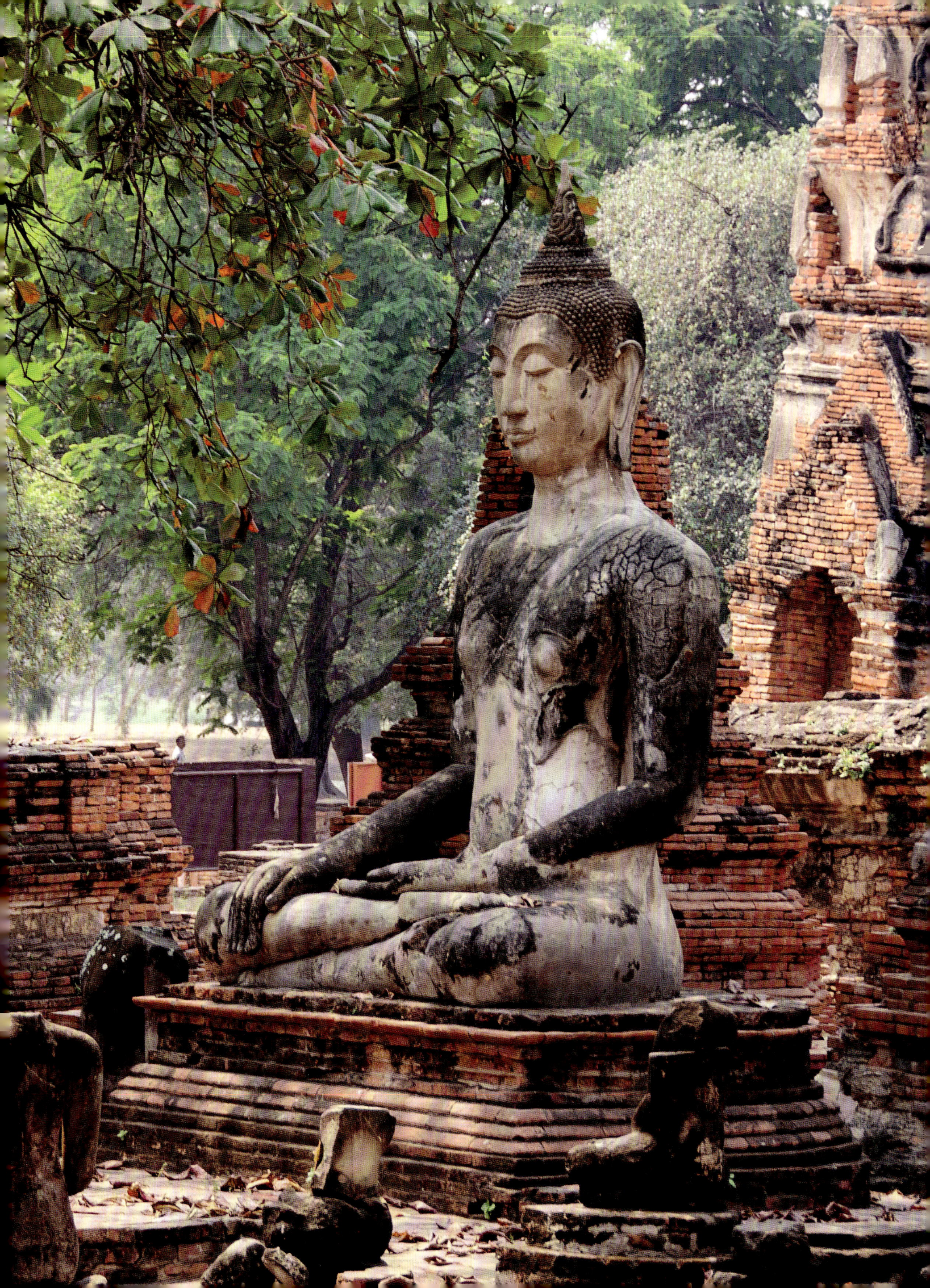

Asia

Birth, death and rebirth – the cycle of life symbolizes Asia's religions as well as its history. Abandoned sacred places across this vast continent evoke both past suffering and grandeur. Warfare destroyed many realms at their peak: Buddhist Ayutthaya in Thailand, sacked by the Burmese in 1767; Hindu temples in Hampi, south India, overwhelmed by Muslim neighbours; Bagan's sea of pagodas in Myanmar, overrun by a Mongol invasion.

Changes in faith, politics and demography had their effect too: Mogao in China and Ajanta in India were beautifully adorned cave complexes deserted after Buddhism fell from favour. The Jain flight from Pakistan after 1947 left Bodhesar Temple in ruins. More recent battles spoiled already abandoned sites: in the 1960s, US bombing destroyed most of Vietnamese My Son's remaining temples; and the fundamentalist Taliban notoriously demolished two massive Buddhas at Bamiyan, Afghanistan, in 2001.

Today Asia has become a global economic dynamo. Paradoxically, past mercantile trade often brought foreign faiths to new sites, such as Borobudur in Indonesia, the world's largest Buddhist compound, yet far from the faith's Indian birthplace. Twenty minutes away is 'Chicken Church', begun in 1992, abandoned, and now apparently reviving – an individualistic structure whose crazy creativity attracts thousands in a social media age.

OPPOSITE:
Wat Mahathat, Ayutthaya, Thailand
A Buddha sits in the esplanade of a 14th century temple, part of the spiritual hub of Ayutthaya, the former capital of the Siamese Kingdom. In its heyday, Ayutthaya was reputedly one of the world's largest cities. In 1767, however, a Burmese army burned it to the ground. Today only ruined buildings remain in the 289-hectare (714-acre) site.

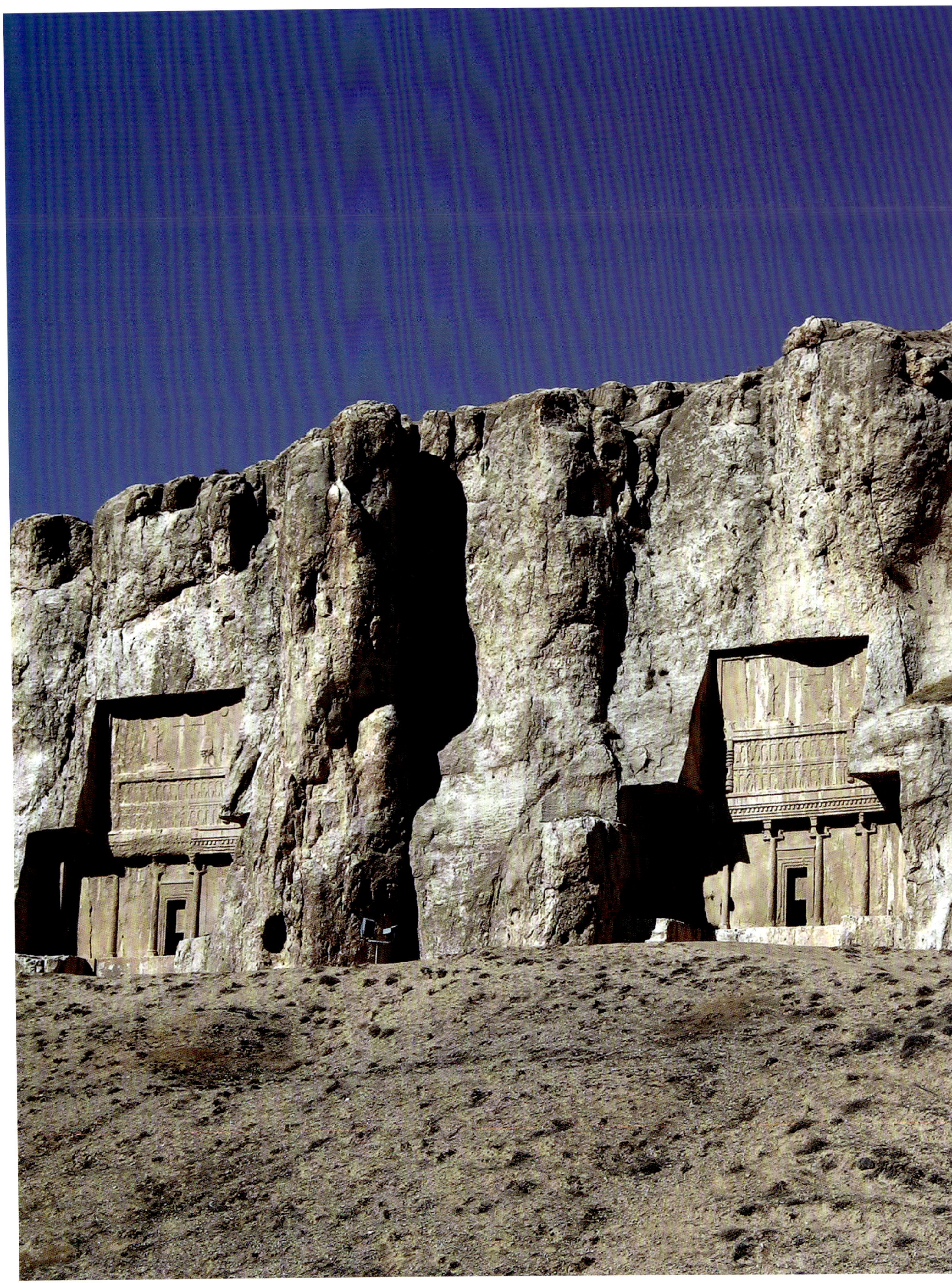

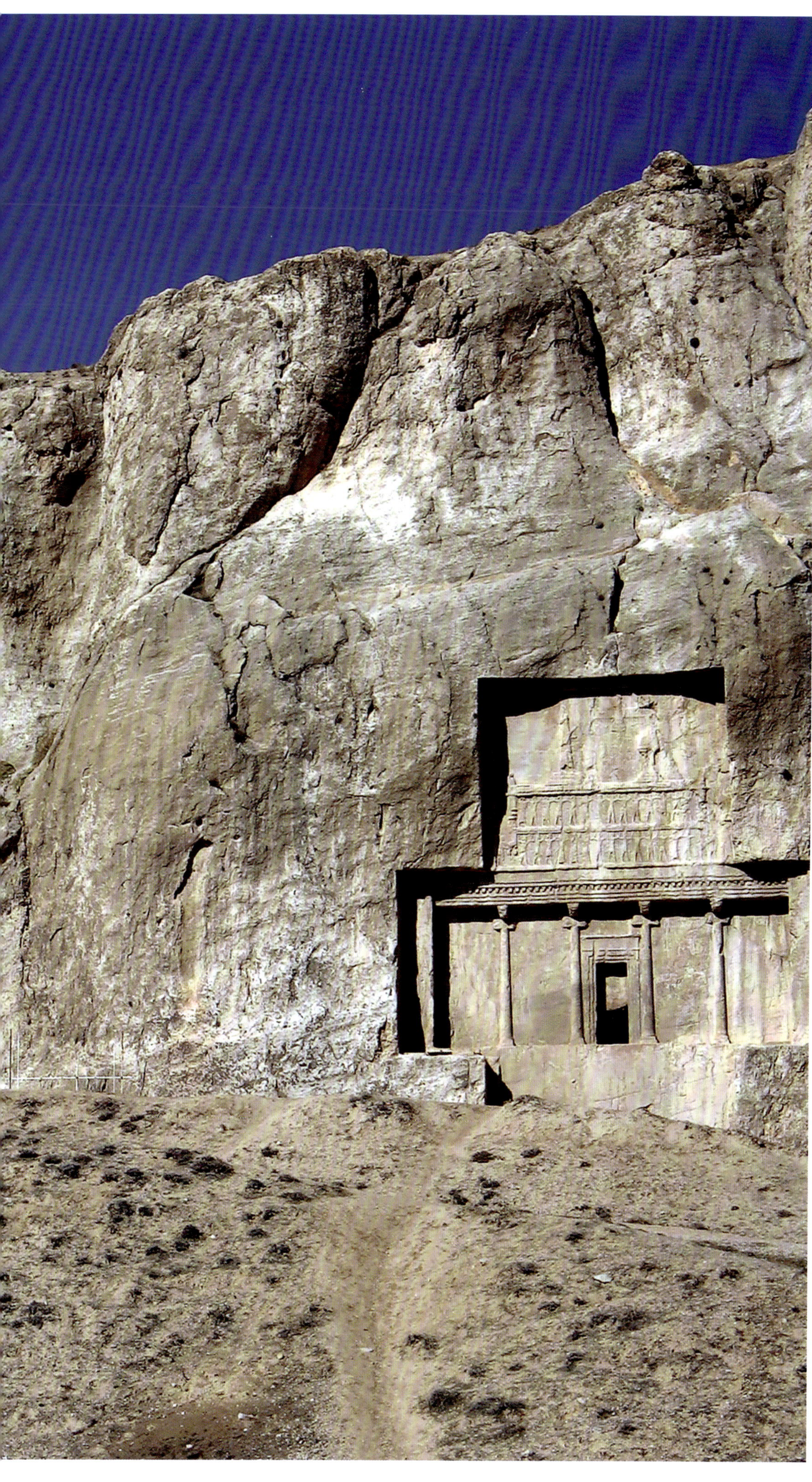

Naqsh-e-Rustam, Fars, Iran
Persia's greatest ruler Darius I (d. 486 BCE) is buried with three successors at Naqsh-e-Rustam. Here, above cross-shaped openings to the rock-hewn tombs, bas-reliefs show gods consorting with late royals, while nearby Zoroastrian priests would have conducted fire rituals. The kings belonged to the Achaemenid dynasty (550–330 BCE) and this complex stood 5km (3 miles) north of their capital, Persepolis.

Around 330 BCE, Alexander the Great vanquished the Achaemenids, yet the later Sassanian dynasty (205–651 CE) held ceremonies at Naqsh-e-Rustam up to the 7th century, until the Muslim conquest of Persia abruptly ended both the dynasty and their faith.

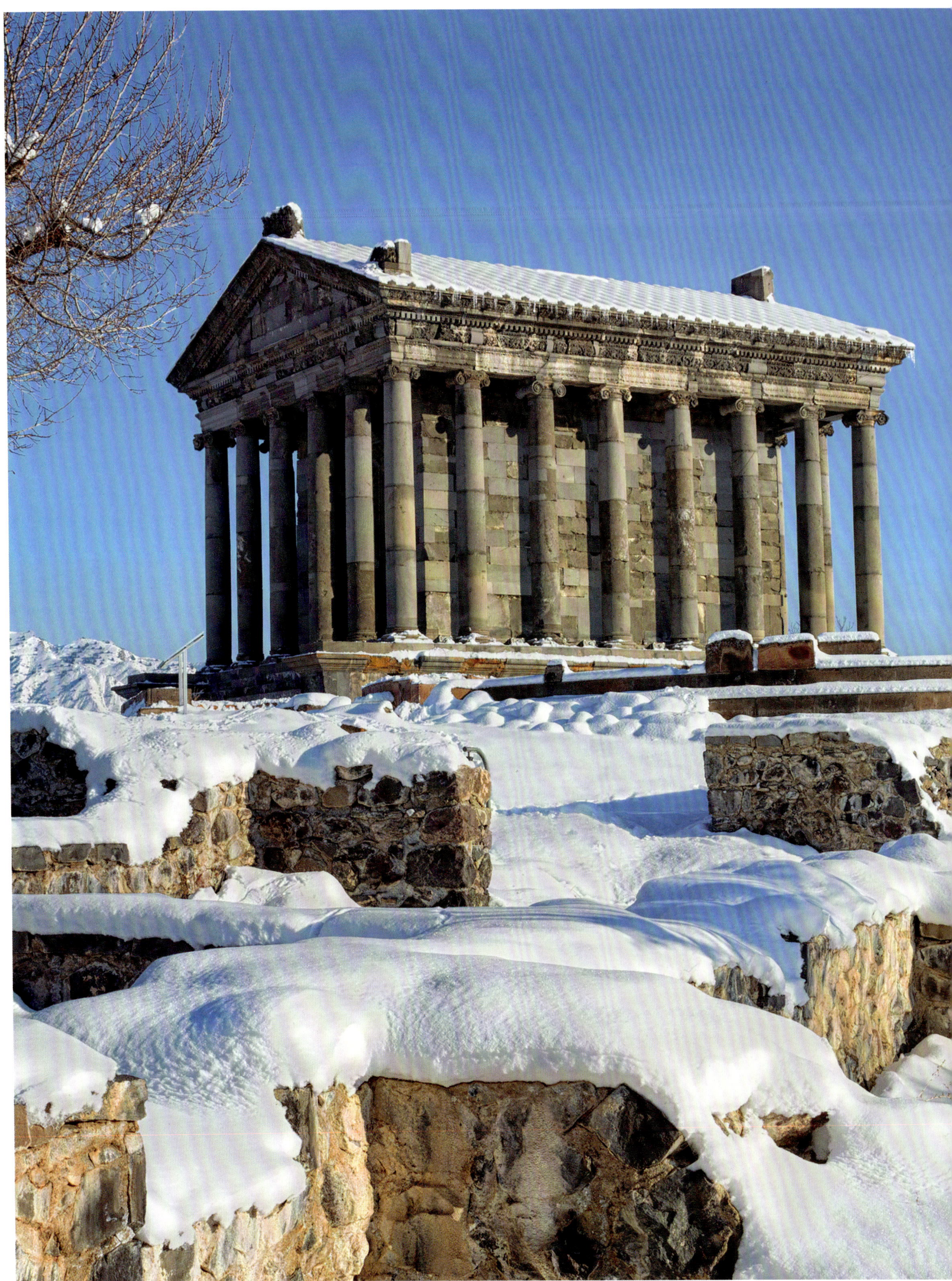

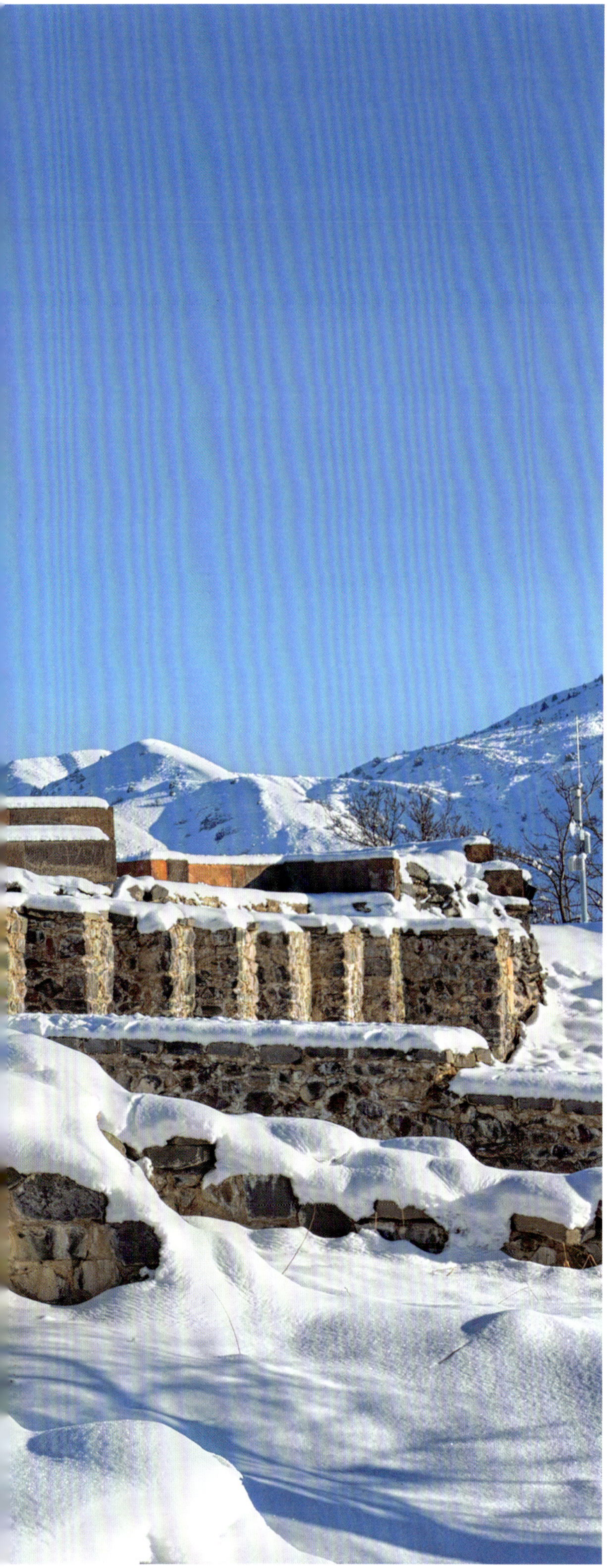

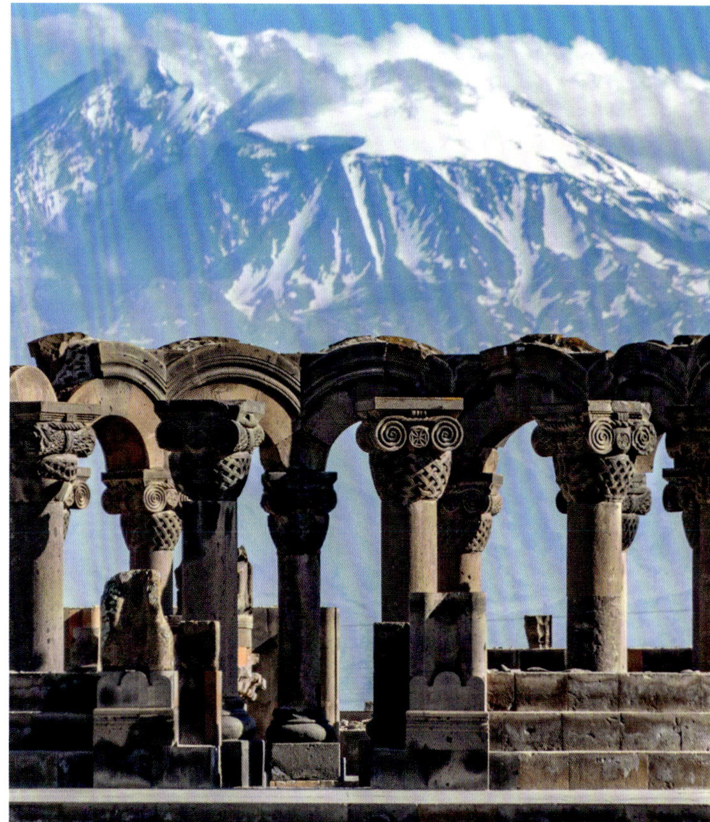

LEFT:

Temple of Garni, Kotayk, Armenia

Ancient Armenians often mimicked the aesthetics of their rivals, as in the Greco-Roman style of this shrine to the sun god Mihr, probably built c.70–80 CE. When Armenia adopted Christianity in the 4th century, Princess Khosrovdoukht spared the temple. Later invasions by Persians, Arabs, Byzantines, Turks and Mongols, as well as an earthquake in 1638, all damaged the structure, but it remains the only surviving self-standing classical structure in Armenia.

Between the 1969 and 1975, the then-Soviet Republic of Armenia restored the national treasure.

ABOVE:

Zvartnots Cathedral, Armenia

The decision to build Zvartnots Cathedral in the mid-7th century was a daring act of faith. At the time, Byzantines and Muslim Arabs were fighting throughout Armenia, yet Catholicos Nerses III, Armenia's spiritual potentate, was determined to protect his nation's Christian identity.

Zvartnots was abandoned in the 10th century, most likely after an earthquake, and reconstructed in 1905.

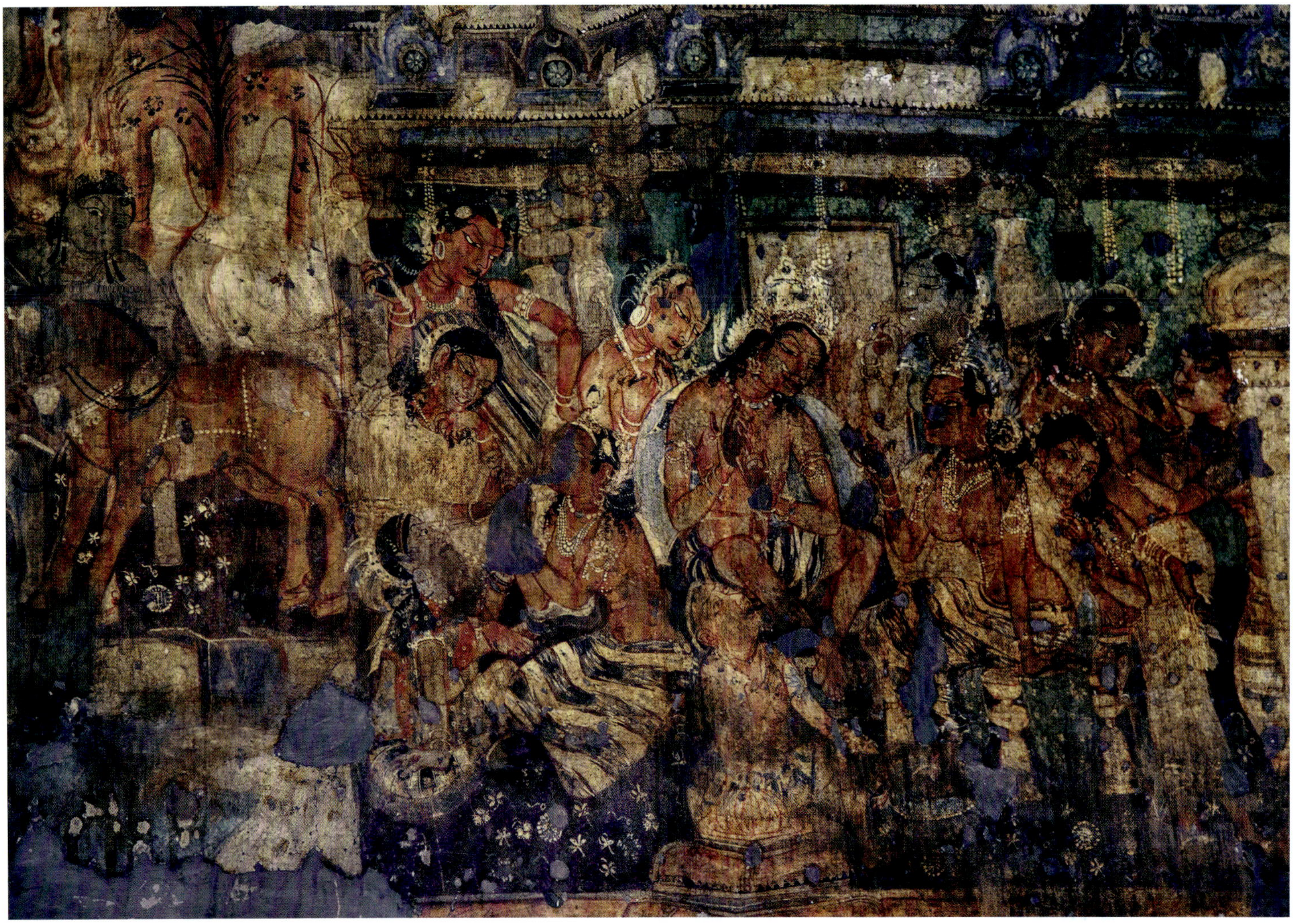

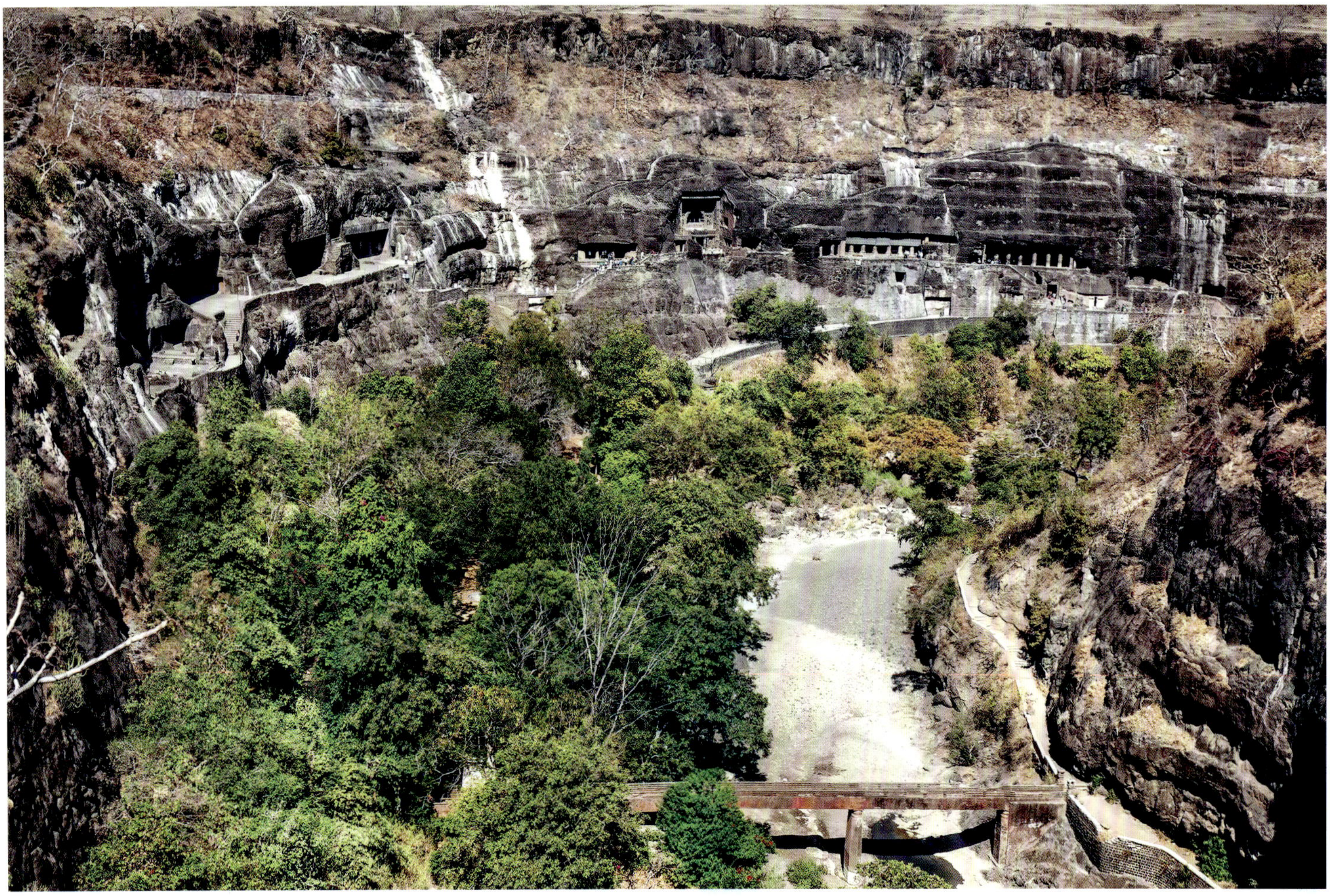

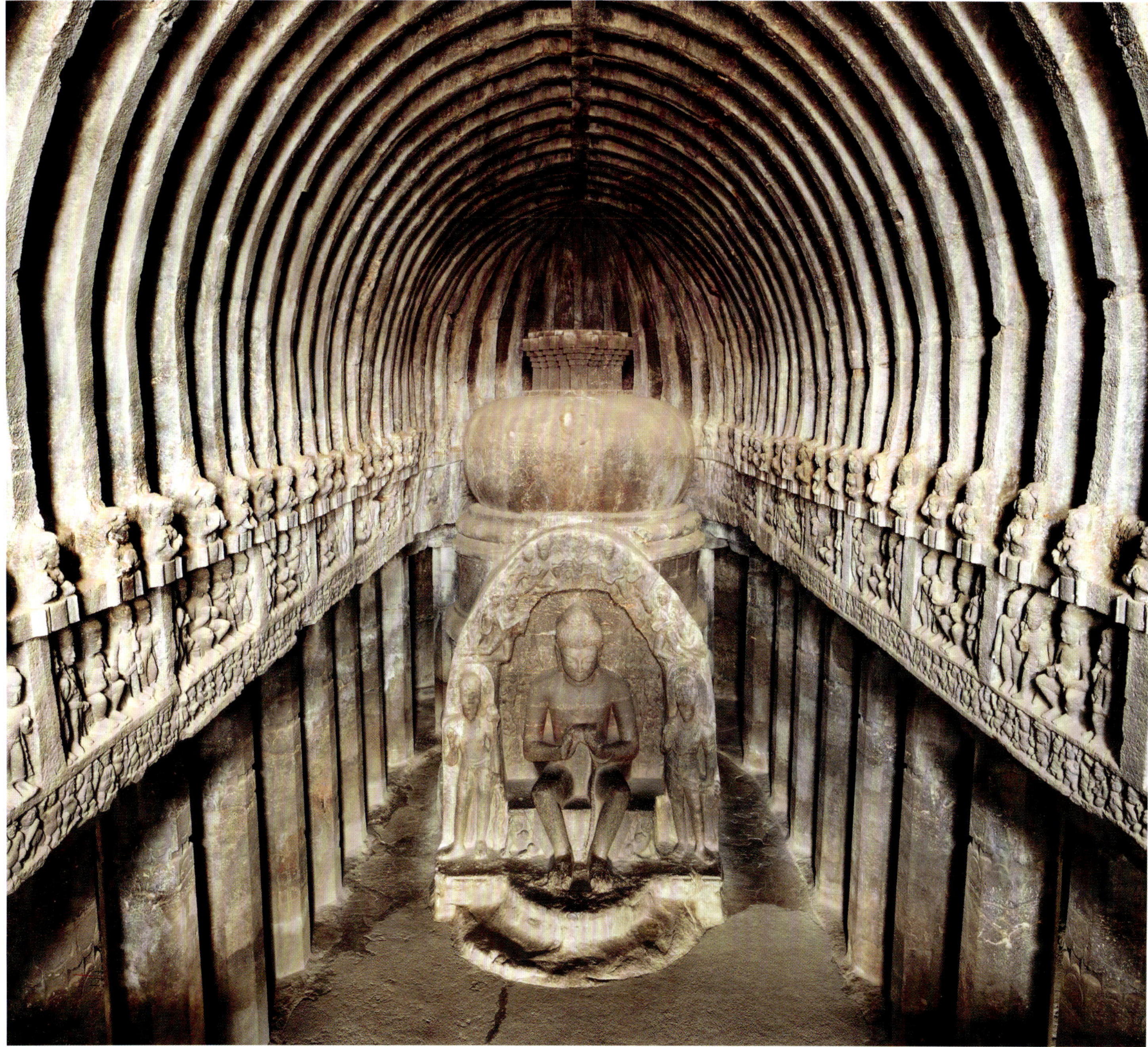

ALL PHOTOGRAPHS:

Ajanta Caves, Maharashtra, India

(Opposite top) In this masterpiece of early Buddhist Indian art, Queen Sivali tries to divert her husband from his meditations. She would far rather Mahajanaka enjoyed the swirling dancers, servants, horses and other paraphernalia of royal life. His reluctant expression speaks volumes!

(Opposite bottom) The Ajanta Caves, dug out in horseshoe formation above the Waghora River, were probably created in two phases: from the 2nd century BCE and then c.400–650 CE. Devotees left the caverns around 650 CE for unknown reasons. A British tiger-hunting party 'rediscovered' them in 1819.

(Above) Probably hollowed out in the 7th century CE, the 21-metre-long (68ft) sanctuary houses a seated statue of Buddha. Behind it, monks chant while circling a *stupa* – the hemispherical top symbolising the dome of heaven. The ribbed ceiling and ornate columns echo the wooden pillars and beams of India's earliest jungle shrines.

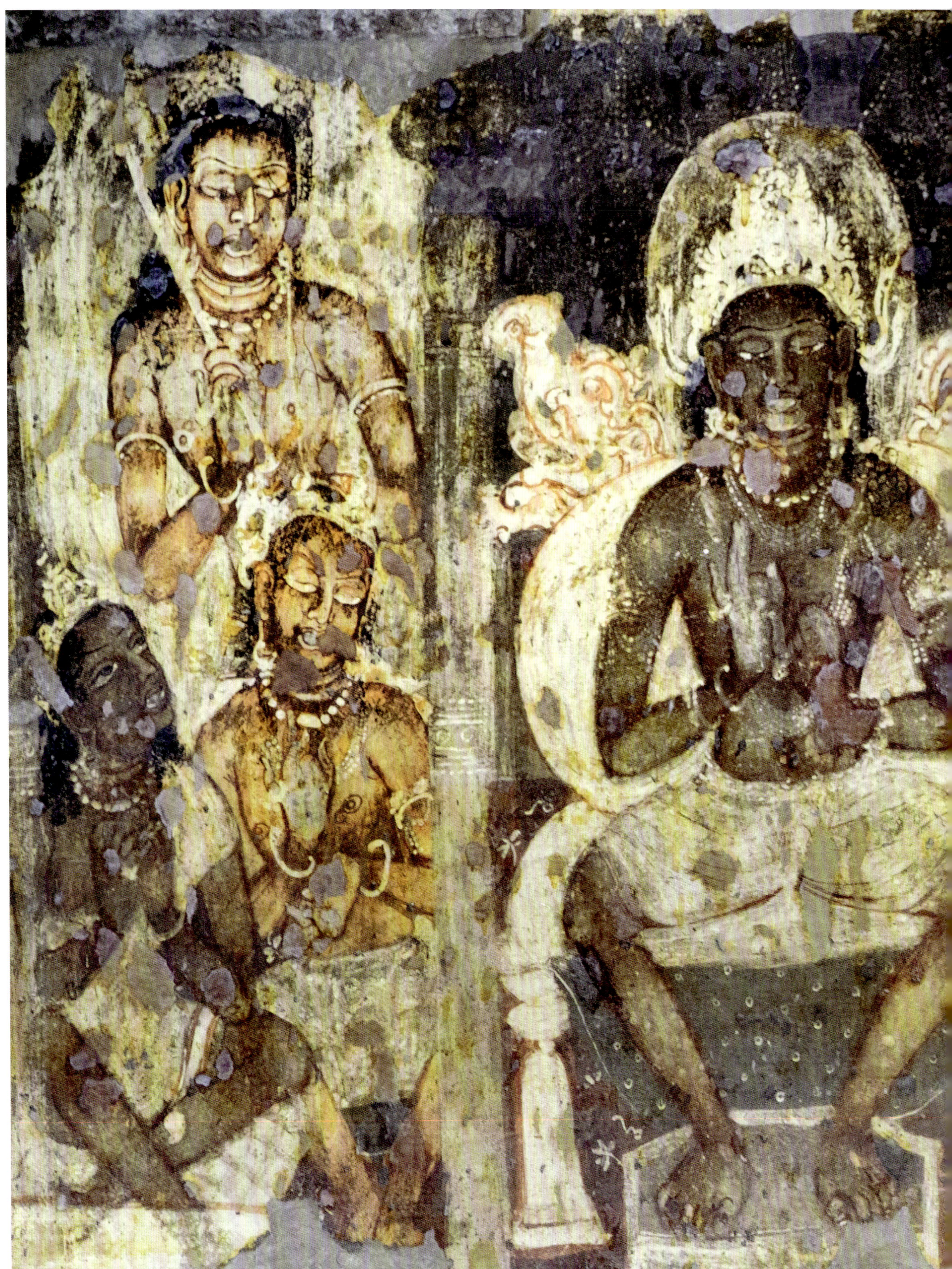

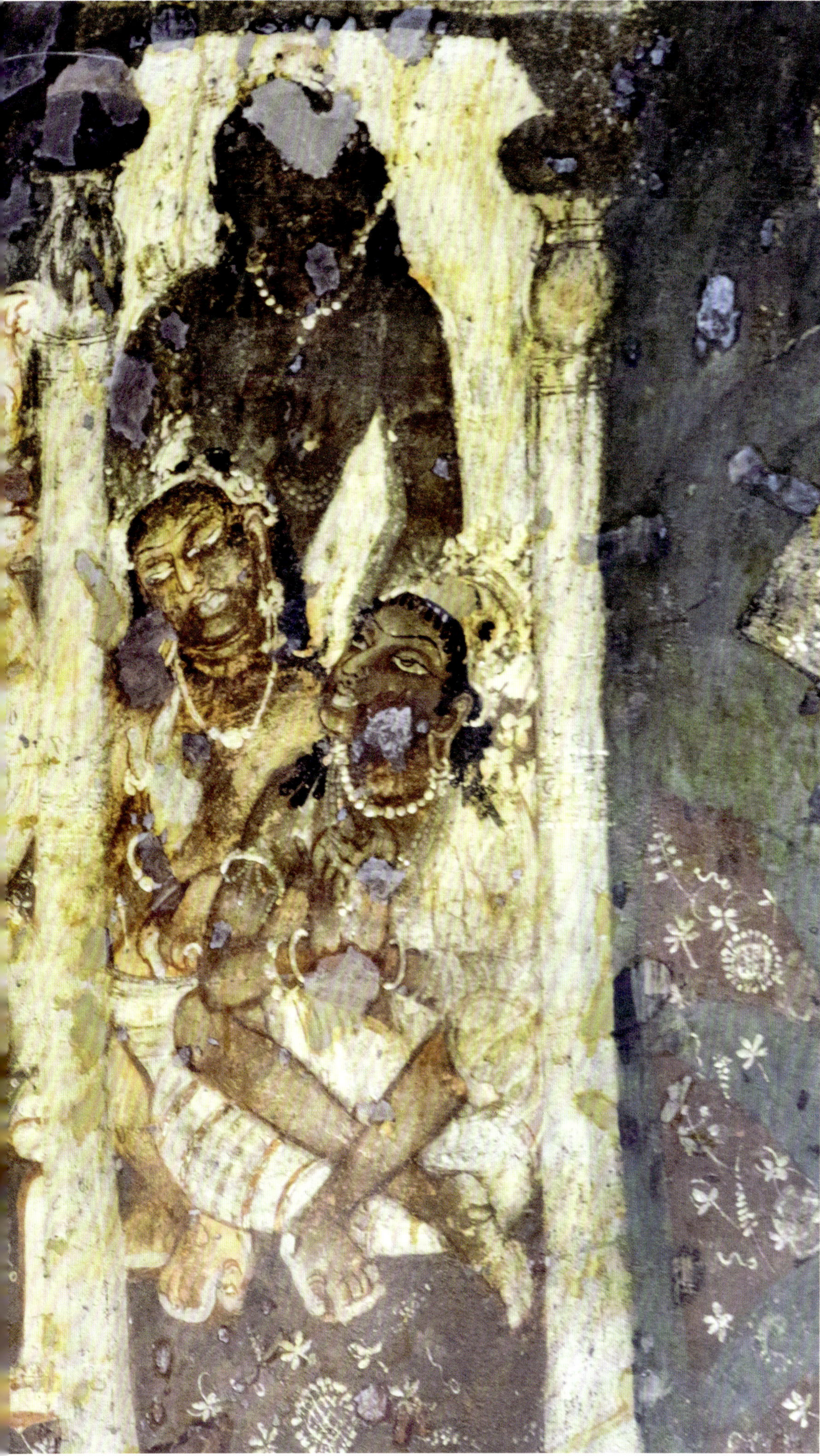

Cave 16, Ajanta Caves, Maharashtra, India
The Ajanta Caves house the oldest Buddhist paintings in existence. These frescoes also graphically explained the complexities of Buddhist theology to illiterate believers. Consider this majestic late 5th century portrayal of a bodhisattva – an individual on the path to Buddhahood – about to descend from Tushita's 'realm of contentment' before being reborn as a Buddha.

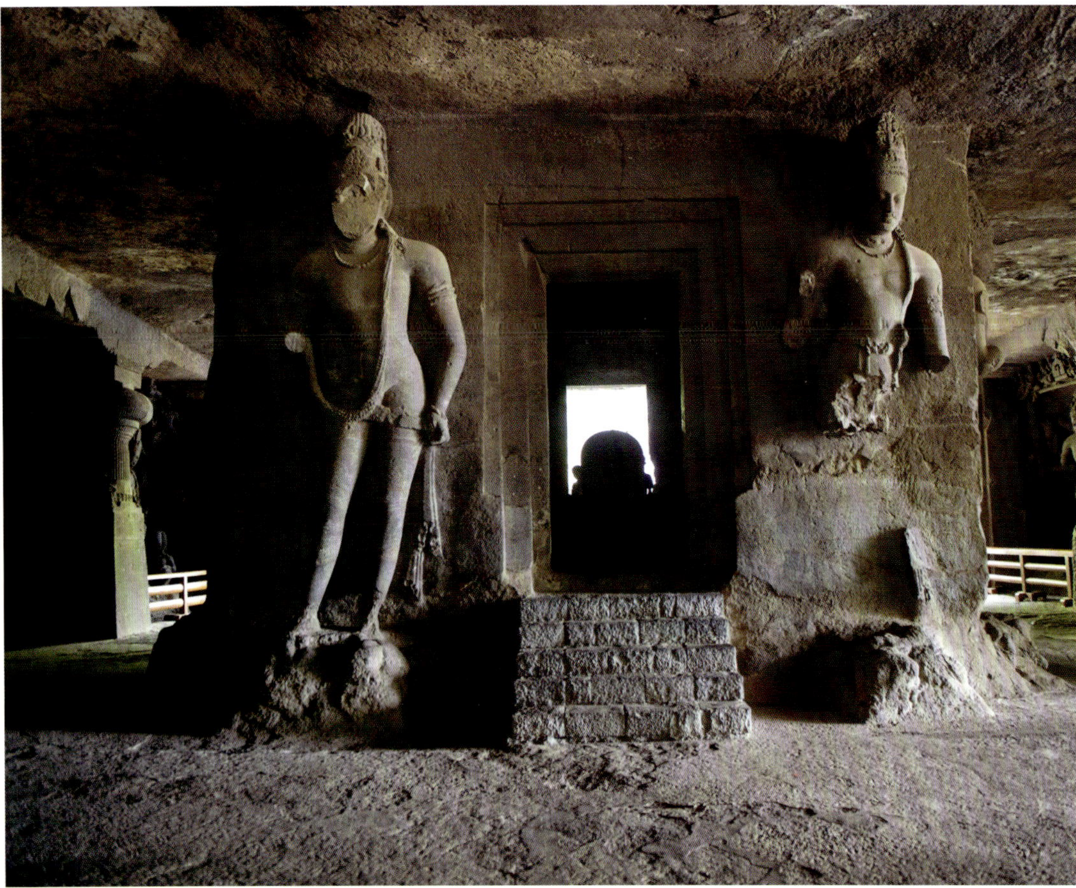

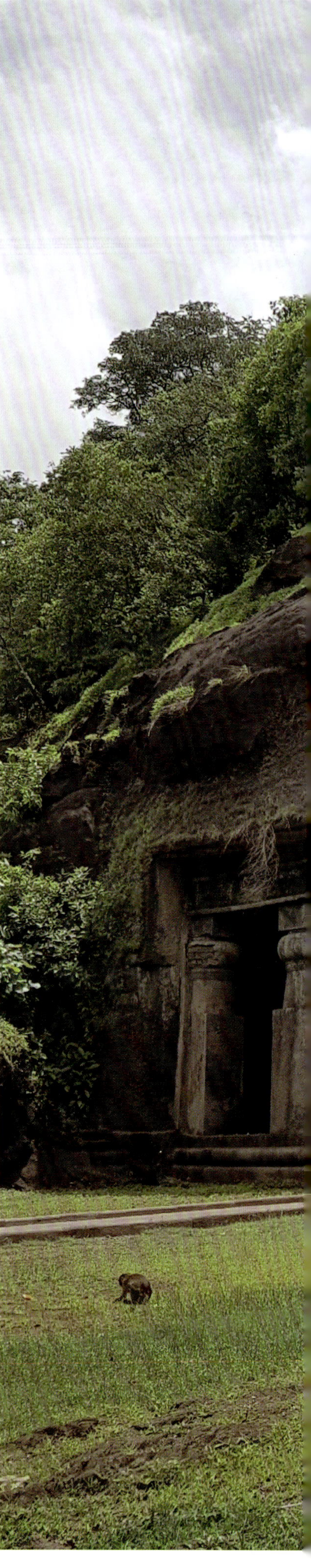

BOTH PHOTOGRAPHS:

Elephanta Caves, Maharashtra, India

Some of the most exquisite sculptures honouring the Hindu deity Shiva are found in a cluster of caves on Elephanta Island, 10km (6 miles) off the coast of Mumbai (Bombay). Pictured above are two statues of guardians at the Central Shiva Shrine. In addition to depictions of Shiva, bas-reliefs show mounted gods, including Indra on his cloud-elephant, Brahma on a lotus and Vishnu on his winged manservant Garuda.

Artwork on Elephanta coincides with the decline of Buddhism and revival of Brahmanic Hinduism in the period from around 450–750 CE. Scholars believe that the sculptures were mostly funded by merchant guilds, Mumbai being a major ancient trading gateway.

All chambers at Elephanta show signs of looting and defacement by soldiers from Portugal – which ruled Bombay from 1534 to 1661 – and later by British explorers.

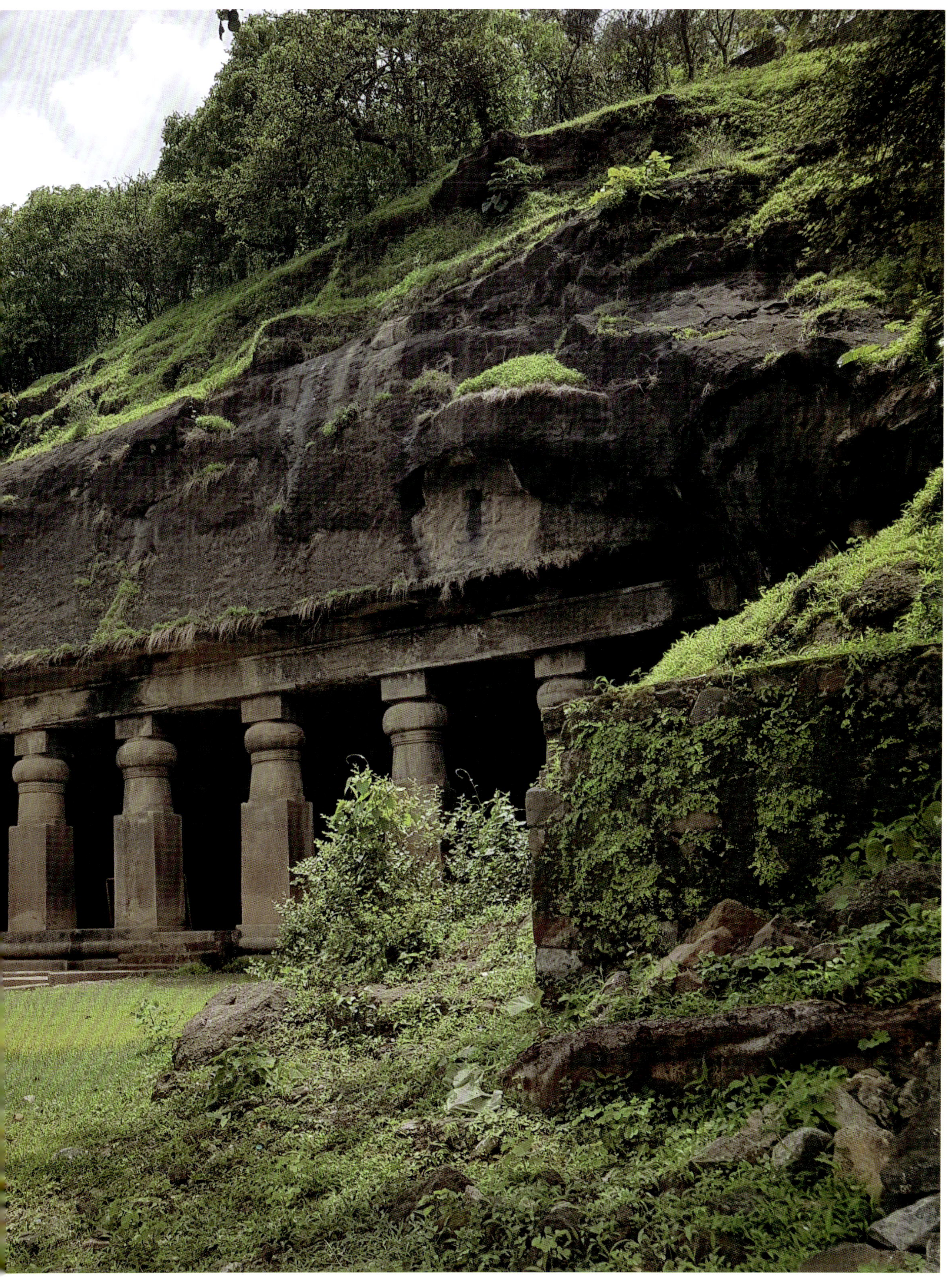

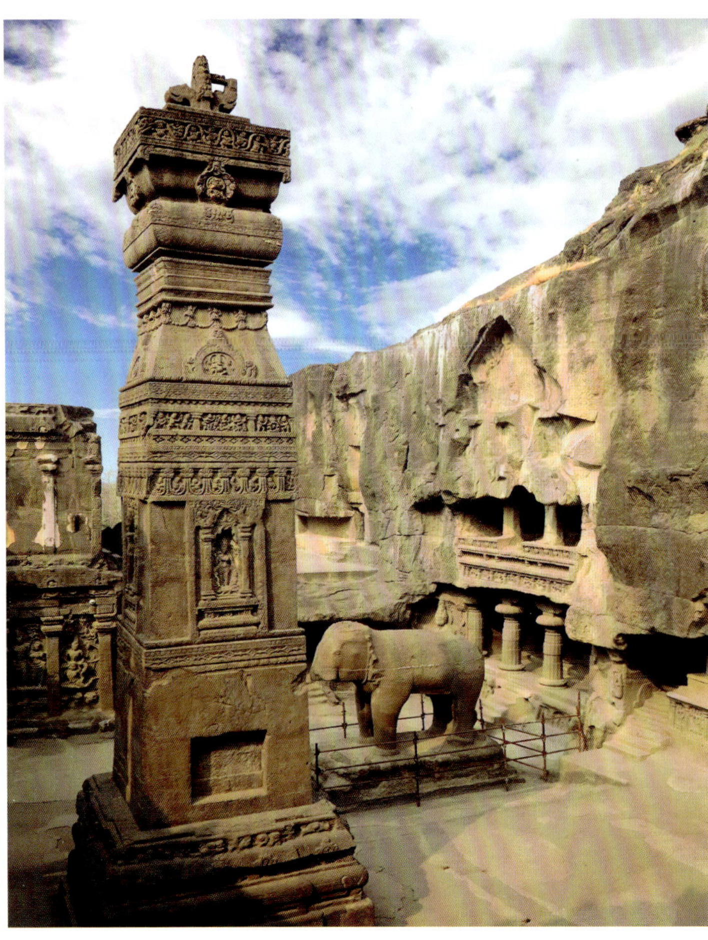

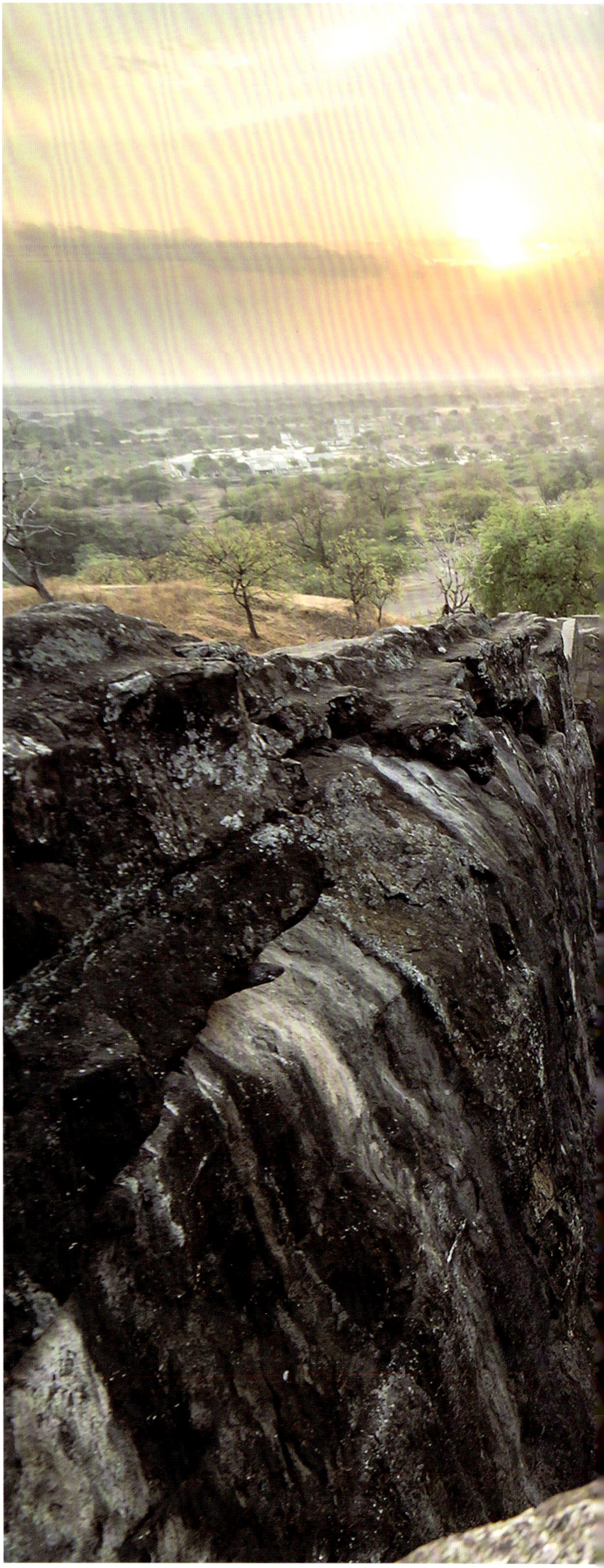

BOTH PHOTOGRAPHS:

Kailasa Temple, Ellora Caves, Maharashtra, India

(Above) A stupendous column and life-size stone elephants surround Kailasa Temple's courtyard. King Krishna I built the temple in around 760 CE to emulate Mount Kailash, the Himalayan abode of the Hindu deity Shiva. Pillars support carved chambers once used by Hindu, Jain and Buddhist worshippers.

Cut from a single rock, the three-storey temple is a marvel of engineering. It covers twice the area of the Parthenon in Athens and is 50 per cent higher. Over 100 years some 200,000 tons of rock were moved by hammer and chisel to accommodate the edifice and craft its lavish decorations. Scenes from the Hindu epic the Ramayana adorn its surface; inside are panels evoking the Mahabharata saga and adventures of Krishna.

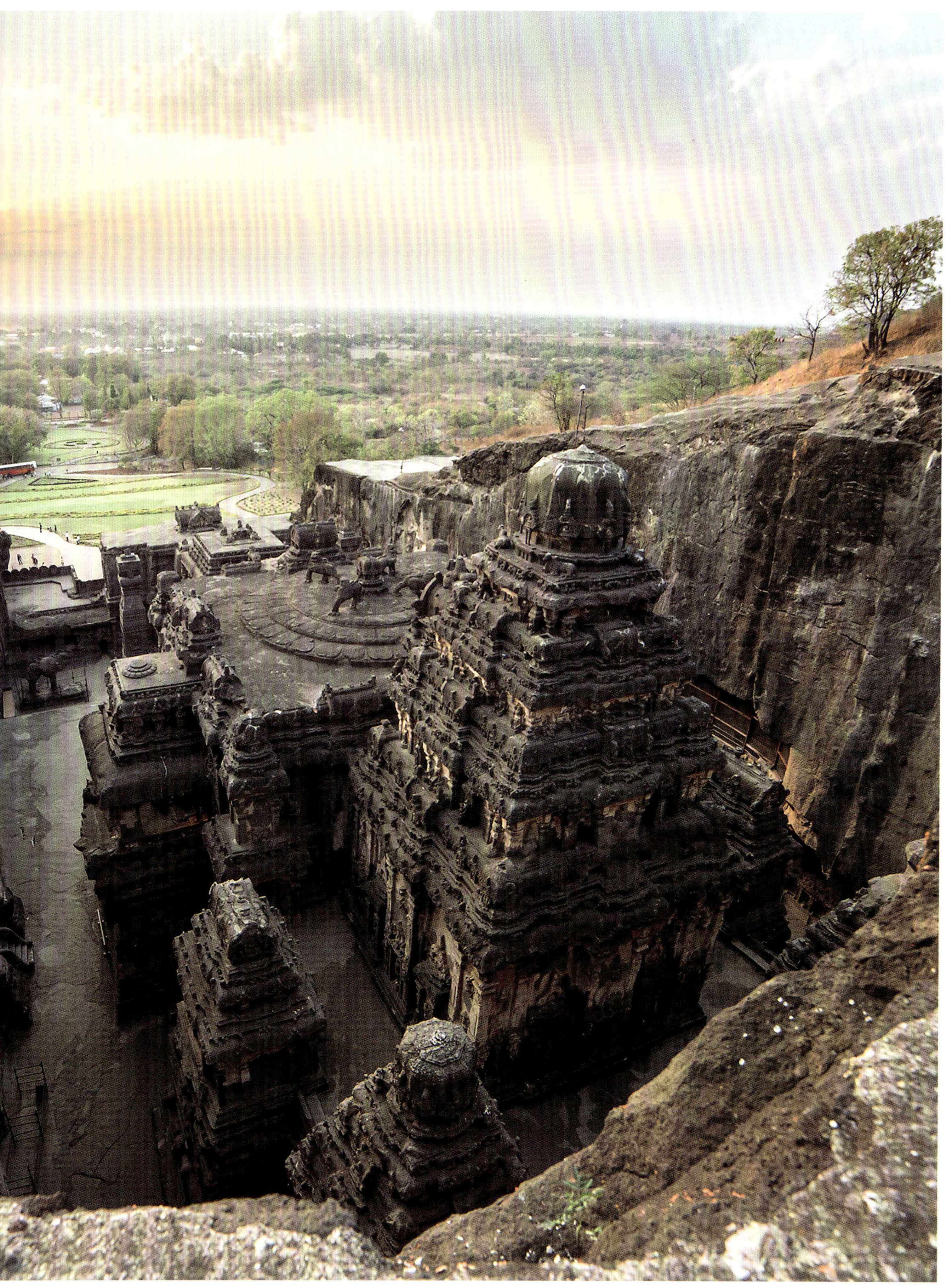

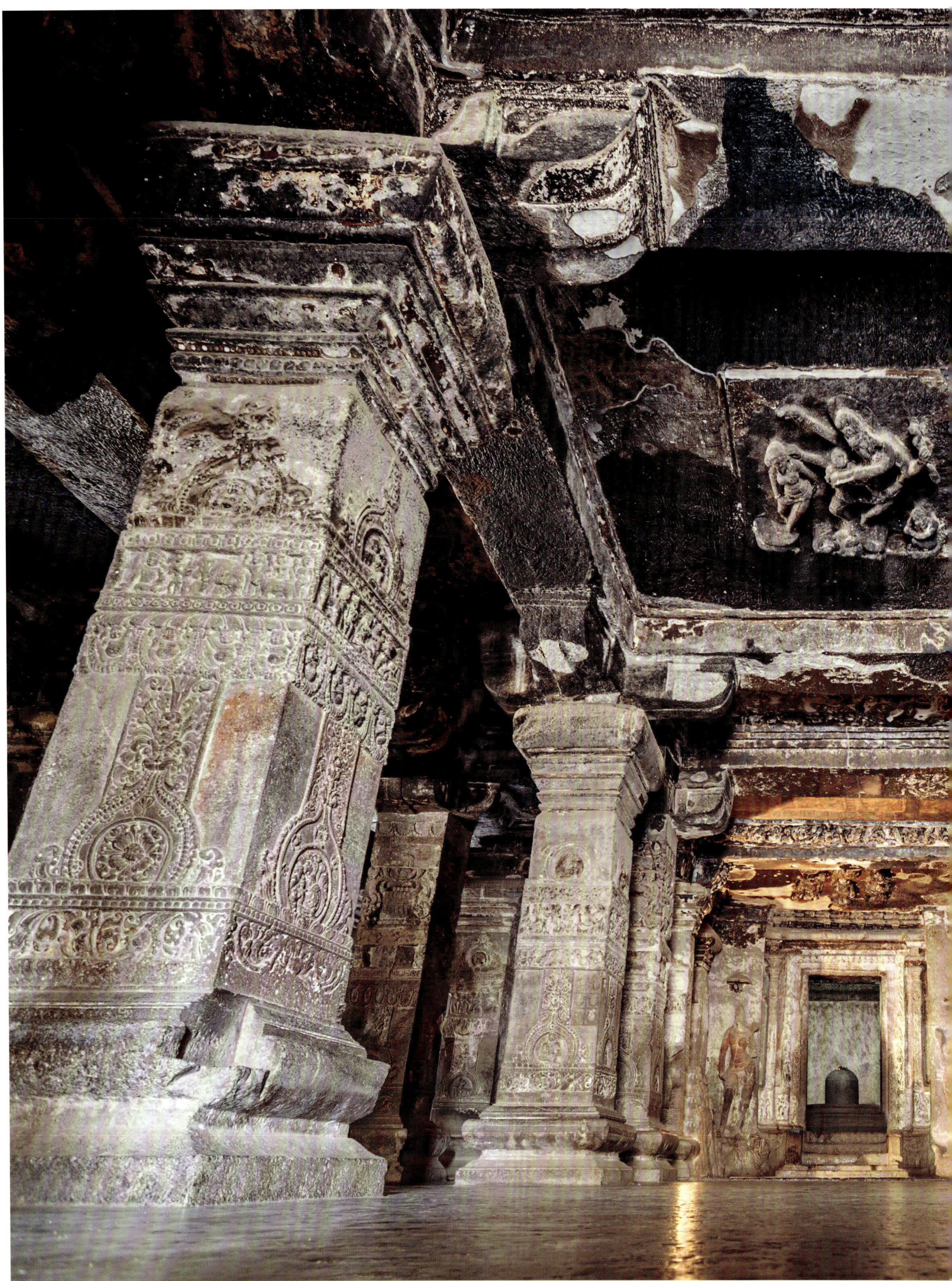

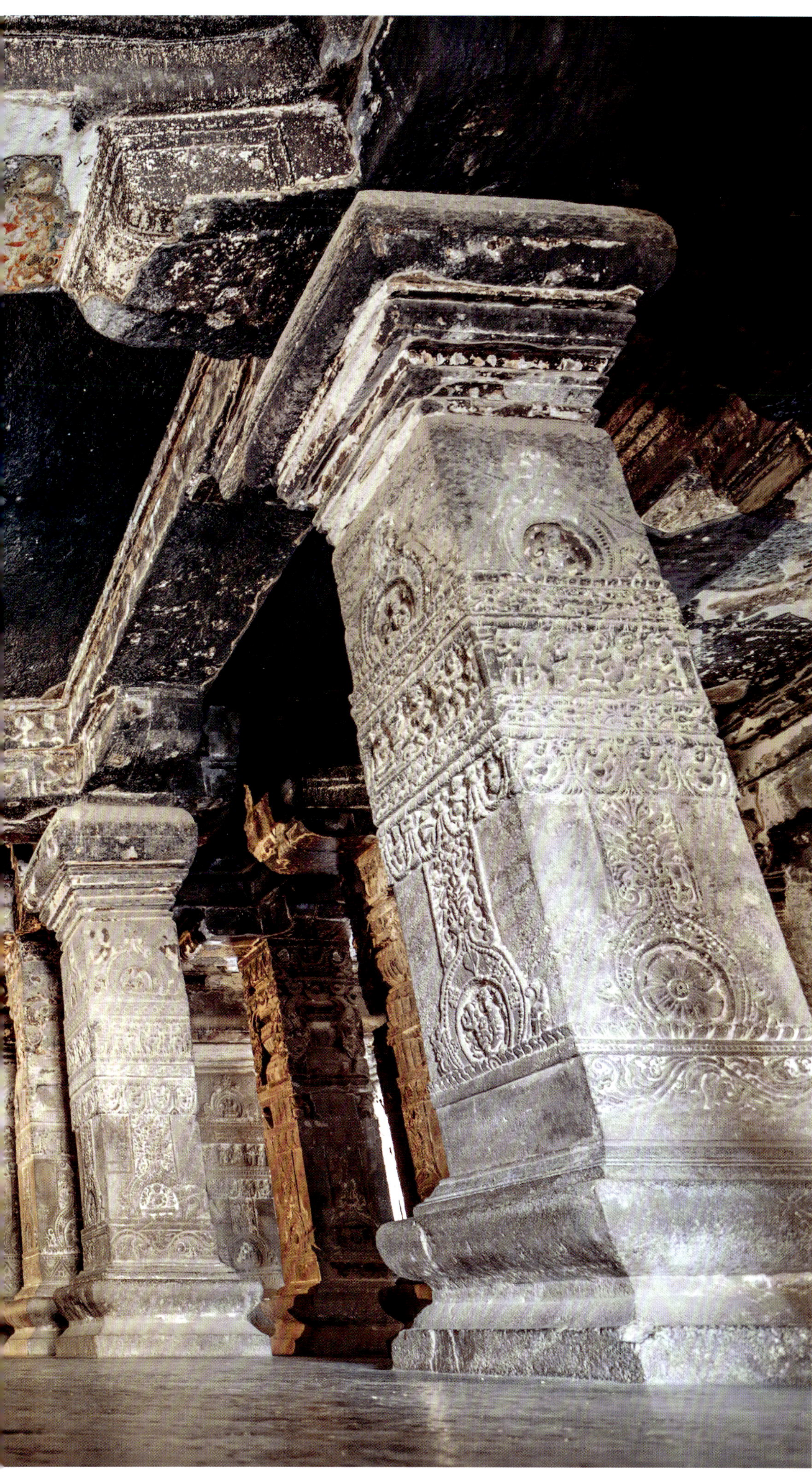

Kailasa Temple, Ellora Caves, Maharashtra, India

The design of the Kailasa Temple aimed to unite different branches of Hinduism: deities to the left appealed to followers of Shiva, while those to the right were favoured by followers of Vishnu.

Unusually, Kailasa was carved from the top down. It resembles Indra Sabha, a 9th century Jain shrine at Ellora. Both complexes have elephant sculptures, a freestanding courtyard temple and a huge Dravidian gate. Again, this suggests a unifying message: Ellora is in central India while Dravidians inhabit the south.

The multi-faith site at Ellora flourished as the exclusively Buddhist Ajanta caves were deserted – many monks from Ajanta relocated to Ellora. But by the 11th century, Ellora itself had fallen into decline.

Buddhas, Bamiyan, Afghanistan
The Taliban's destruction of Bamiyan's two giant Buddhas in March 2001 created a defining symbol of fundamentalist barbarity only surpassed by images of the September 11 attacks six months later. In fact, by the 13th century Buddhist worship had mostly ceased in Muslim majority Afghanistan. So what explains this act of nihilism? Taliban fanatics saw pre-Islamic history as 'a time of ignorance'. Worse, the rock-cut statues seemed like idols, which are forbidden in Islam. Yet historically, most Muslim rulers have tolerated, and even protected, non-Muslim sacred sites.

Afghan Buddhism thrived under the Kushan Empire (200 BCE – 200 CE). At Bamiyan Valley on the Silk Road, Buddhists sculpted the world's tallest standing Buddhas between, depending on accounts, either 200–400 CE or 500–600 CE. An early Chinese report described the statues as covered in stucco, metal, gems and pigment, but how they were constructed remains a mystery. In addition, around Bamiyan nearly 1000 Buddhist caves were carved along a cliff face.

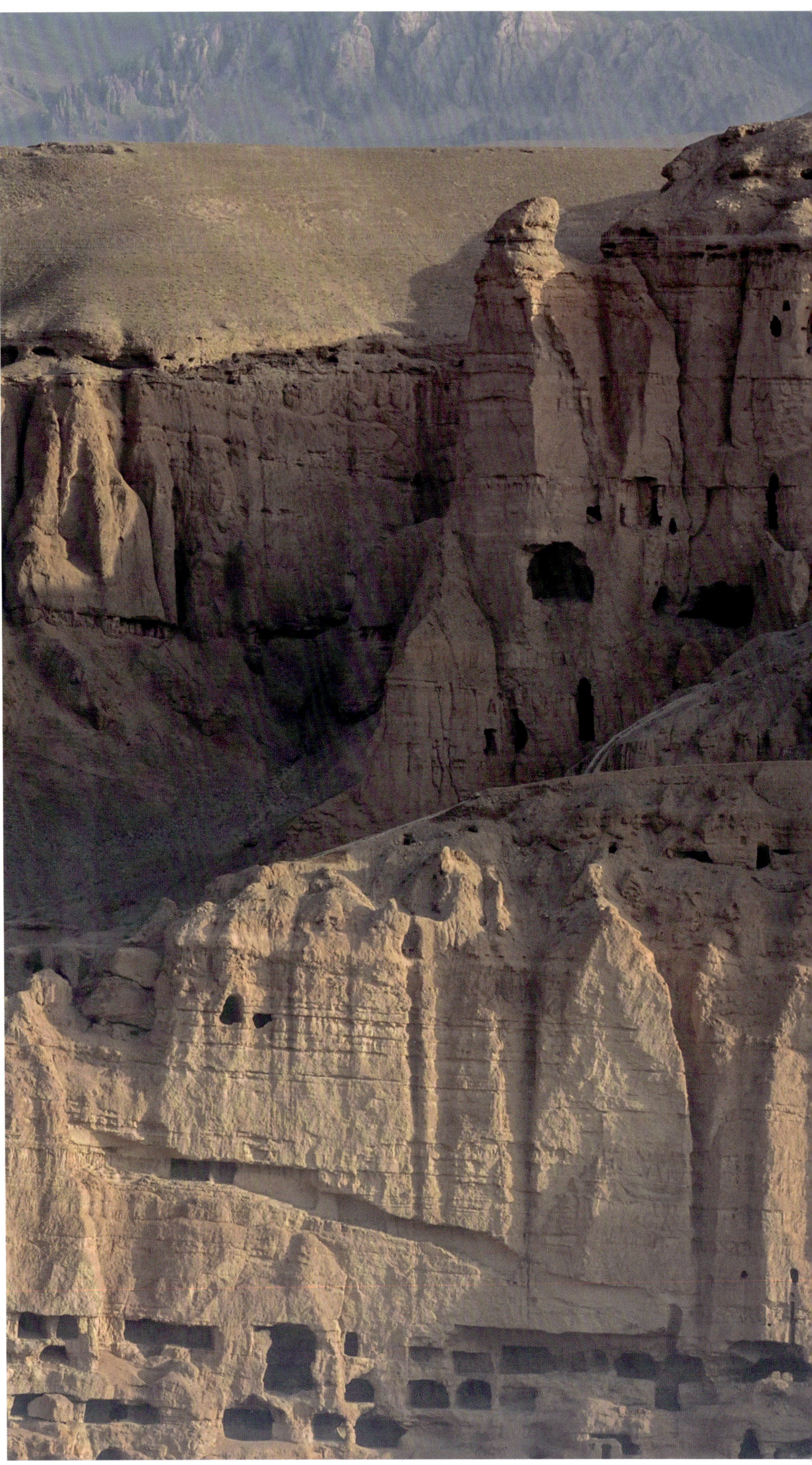

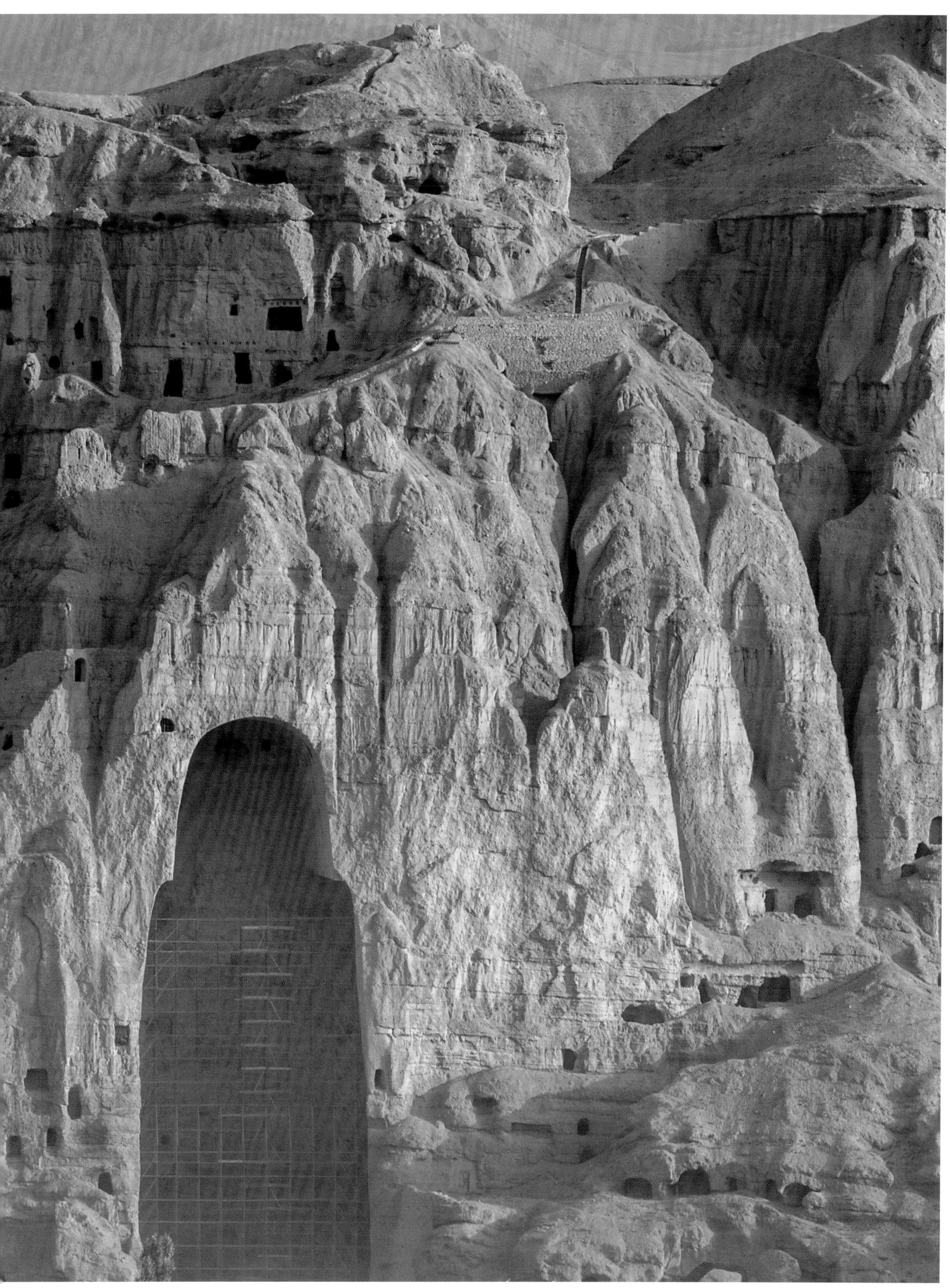

Kandariya Mahadeva Temple, Khajuraho, Madhya Pradesh, India

Kandariya Mahadeva Temple conveys soaring height despite its relatively small size. Builders achieved this effect by raising it on a 6-metre (20ft) terrace, then compressing five halls and pavilions into a compact shape, and clustering domed spires around a graceful 31-metre-high (102ft) tower. The result replicates a Himalayan peak where Hindus believed the gods lived. A 10th century CE king constructed Kandariya, dedicated to Shiva, as one of 20 temples he built at Khajuraho.

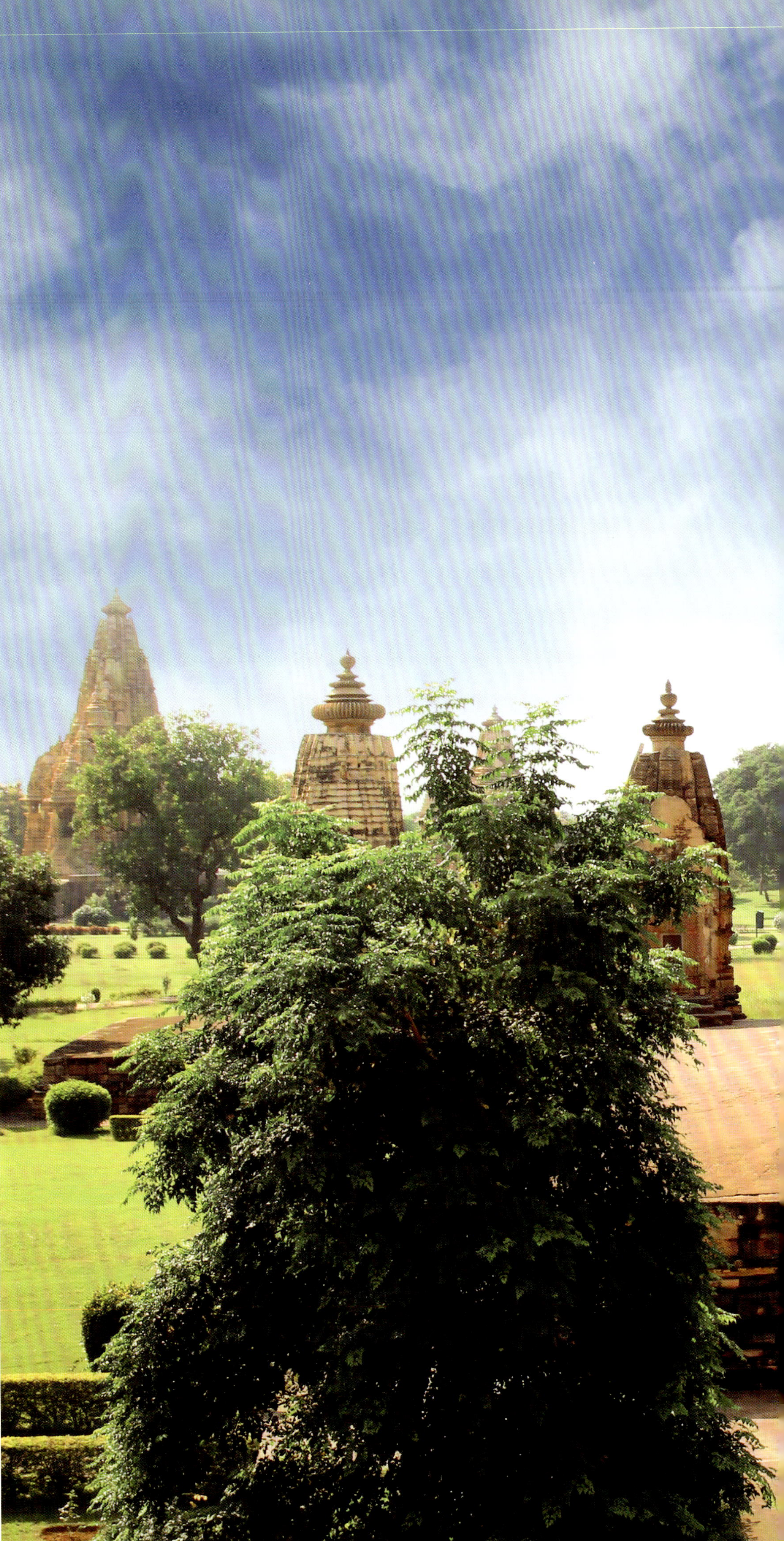

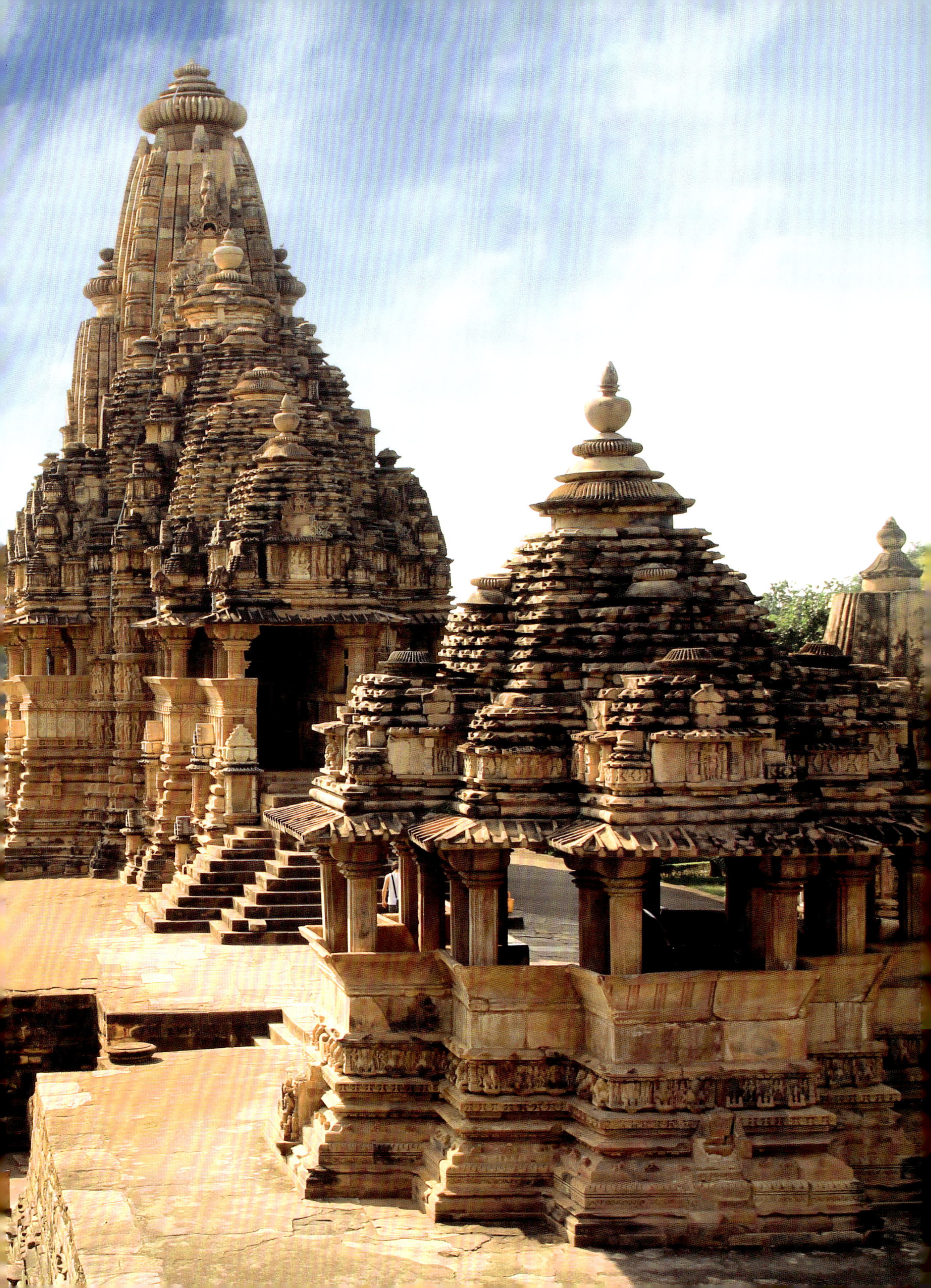

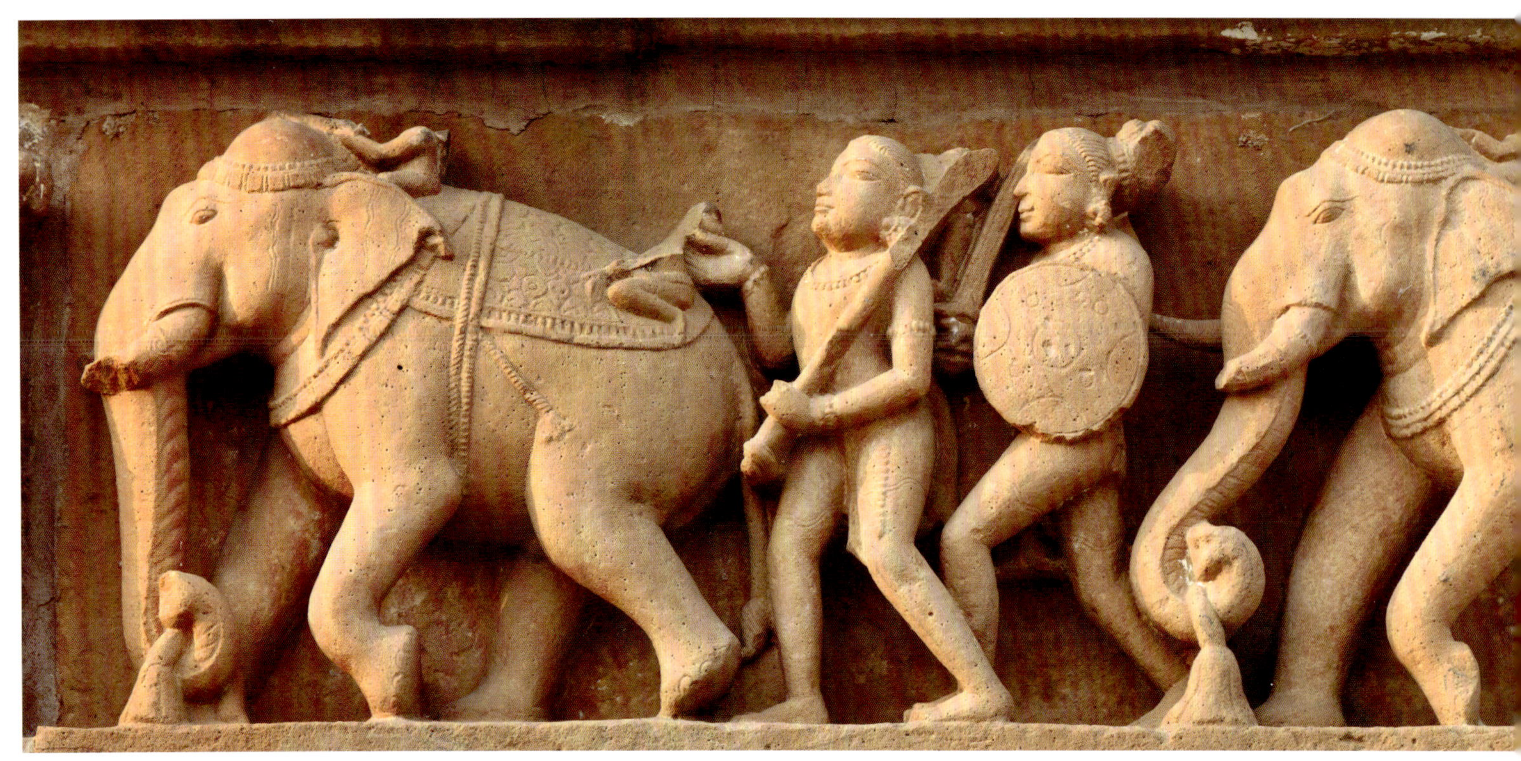

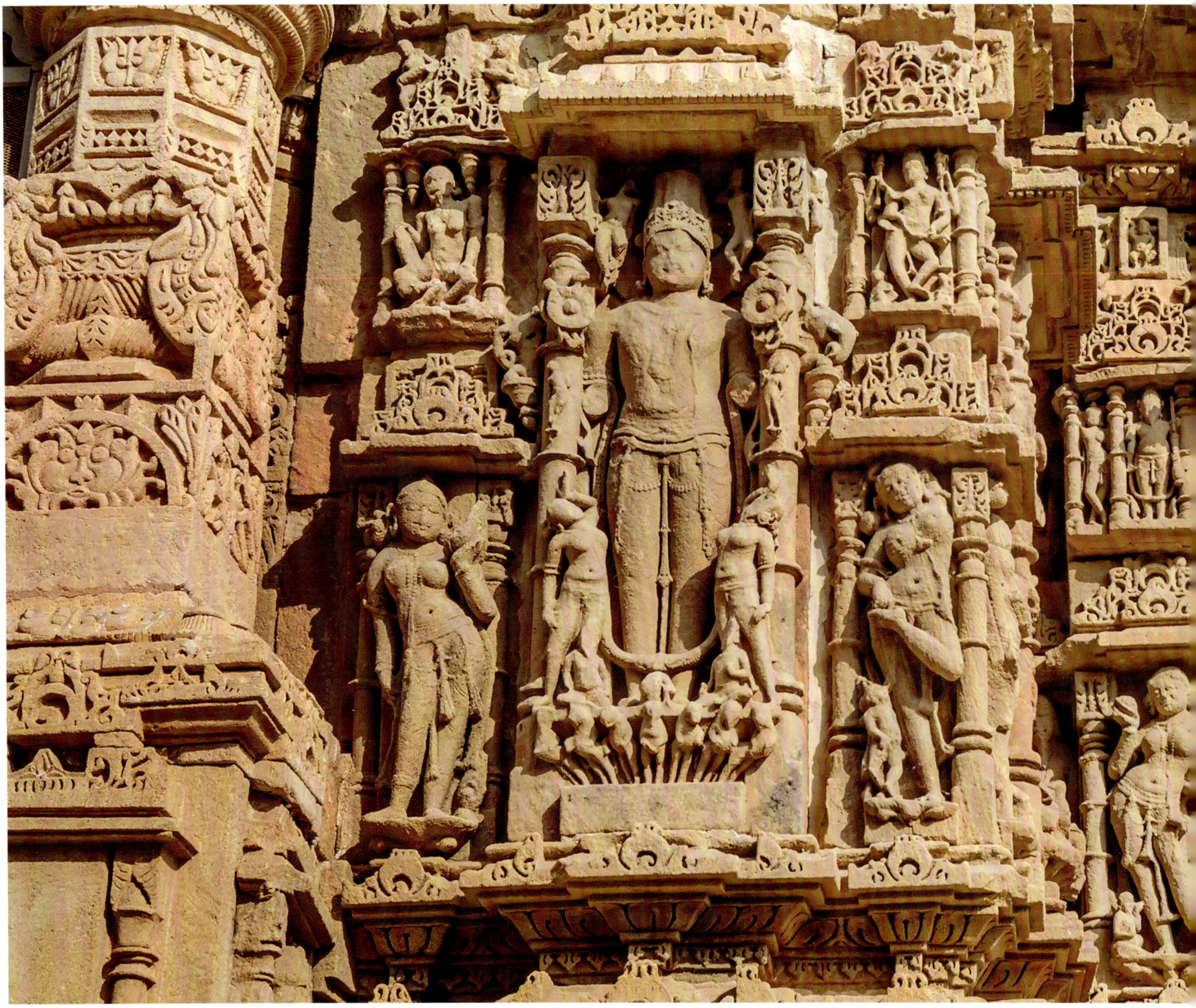

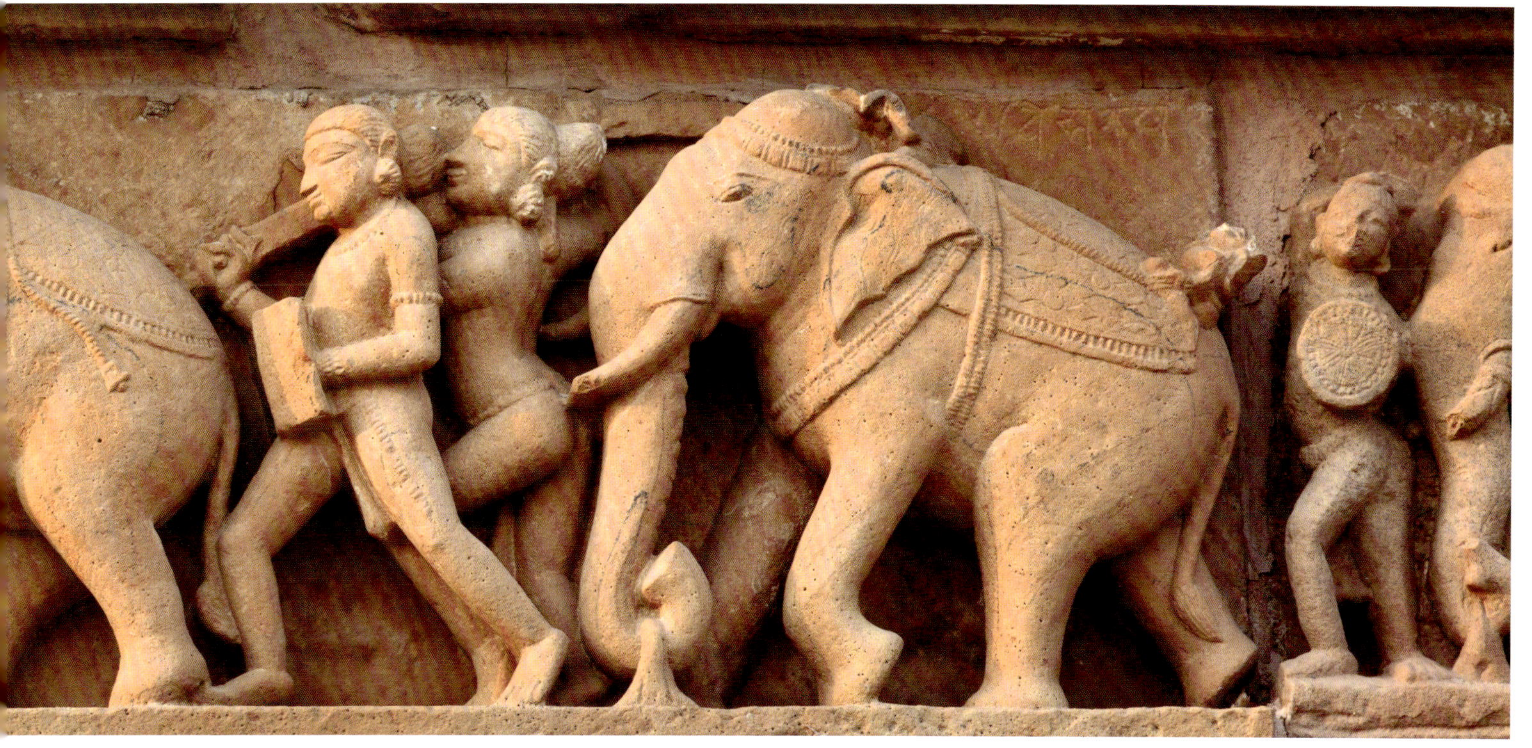

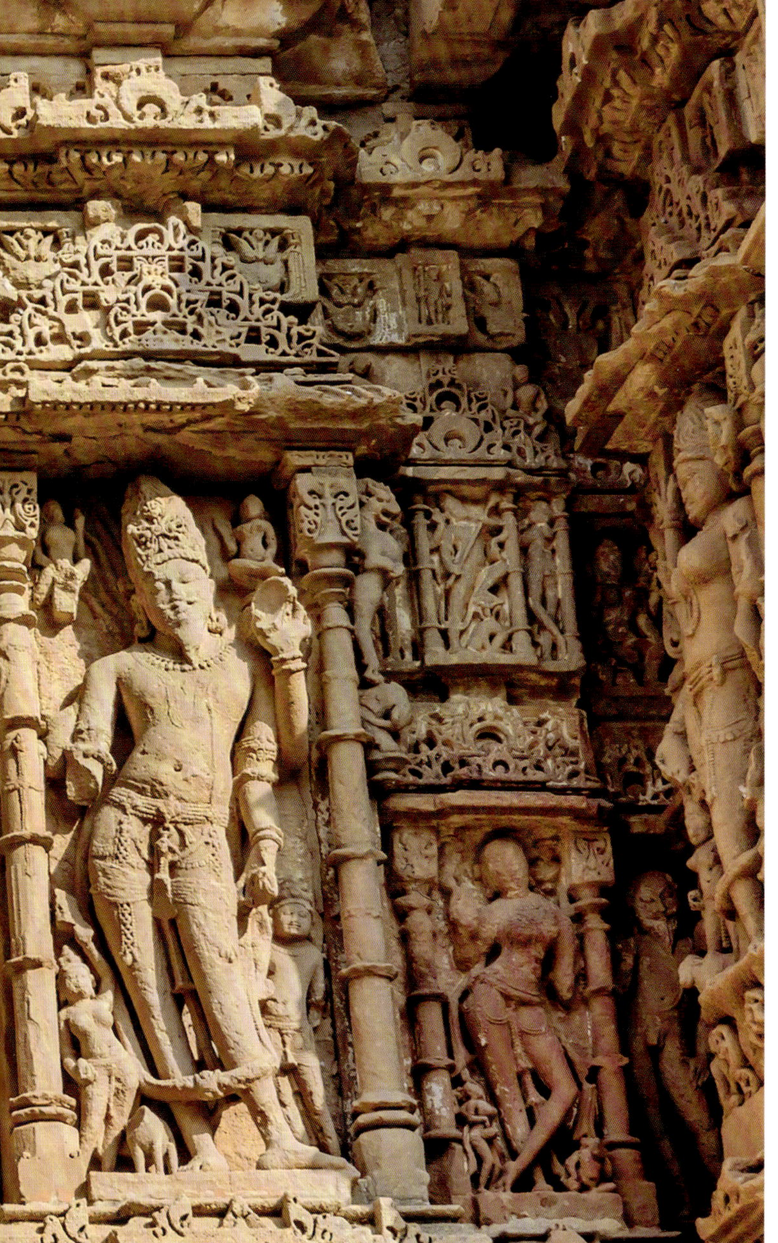

ABOVE:

Lakshmana Temple, Khajuraho, Madhya Pradesh, India

Elephants and warriors march across a 10th century stone panorama on a temple dedicated to Vishnu. Originally, there may have been as many as 83 temples at Khajuraho, but the town was abandoned and reverted to jungle after the Muslim Delhi Sultanate defeated its Hindu rulers in the early 13th century. British explorers rediscovered it in 1883.

LEFT:

Surya Temple, Modhera, Gujarat, India

Riding a celestial chariot pulled by seven horses, the sun god Surya appears in one of 12 niches on this temple, each niche representing a solar month. As in Khajuraho (above), the Surya Temple – built around 1027 CE – is replete with erotic imagery evoking the bond of earth to heaven. Here, Surya's sensuous female attendants can be seen issuing *mudras* (sacred gestures).

Within two centuries of the temple's construction, the region began suffering from earthquakes, and, after the Delhi Sultanate sacked Modhera, Hindus abandoned the town. By the early 14th century, Gujarat had been annexed by the Delhi Sultanate.

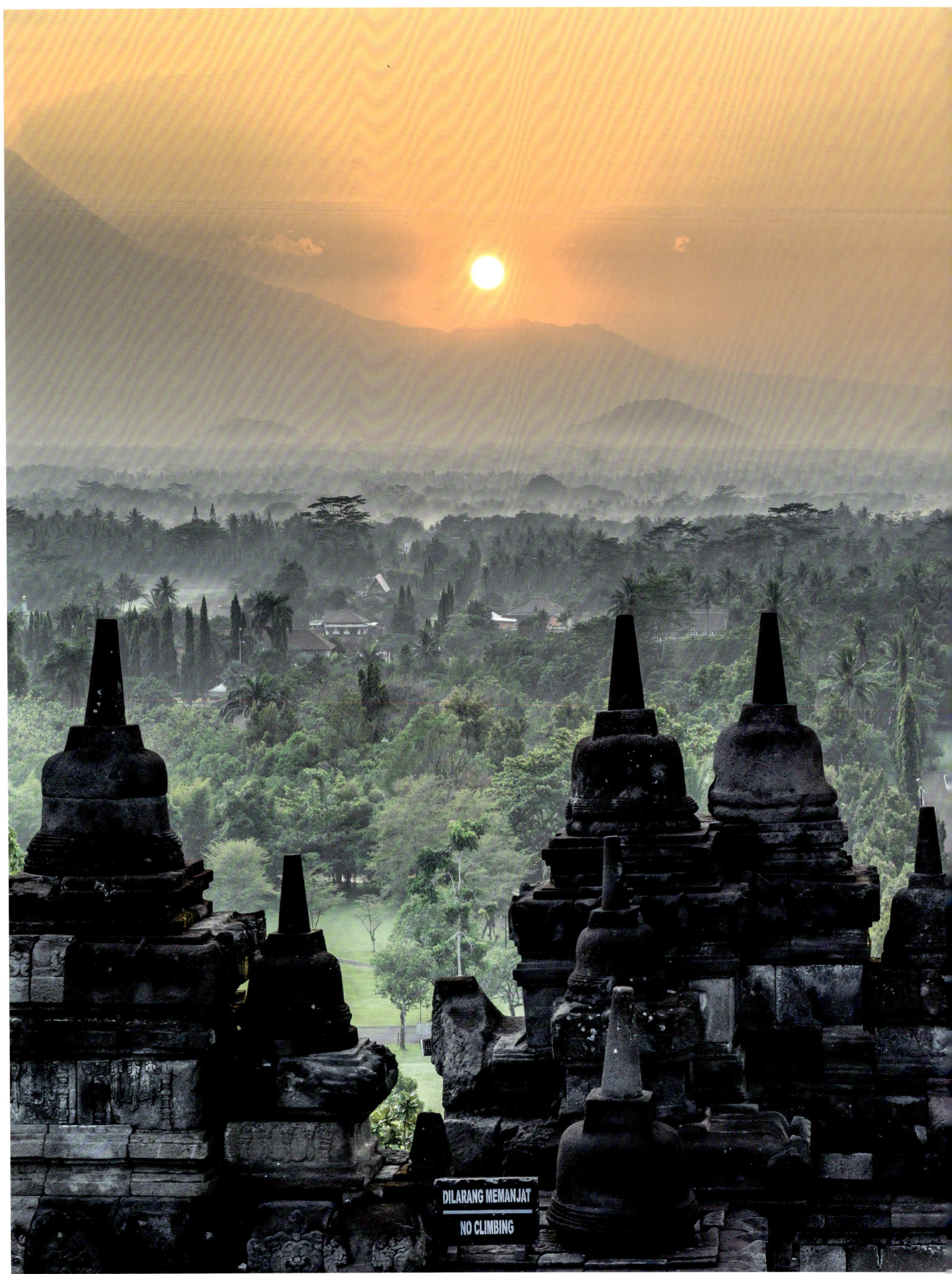
DILARANG MEMANJAT
NO CLIMBING

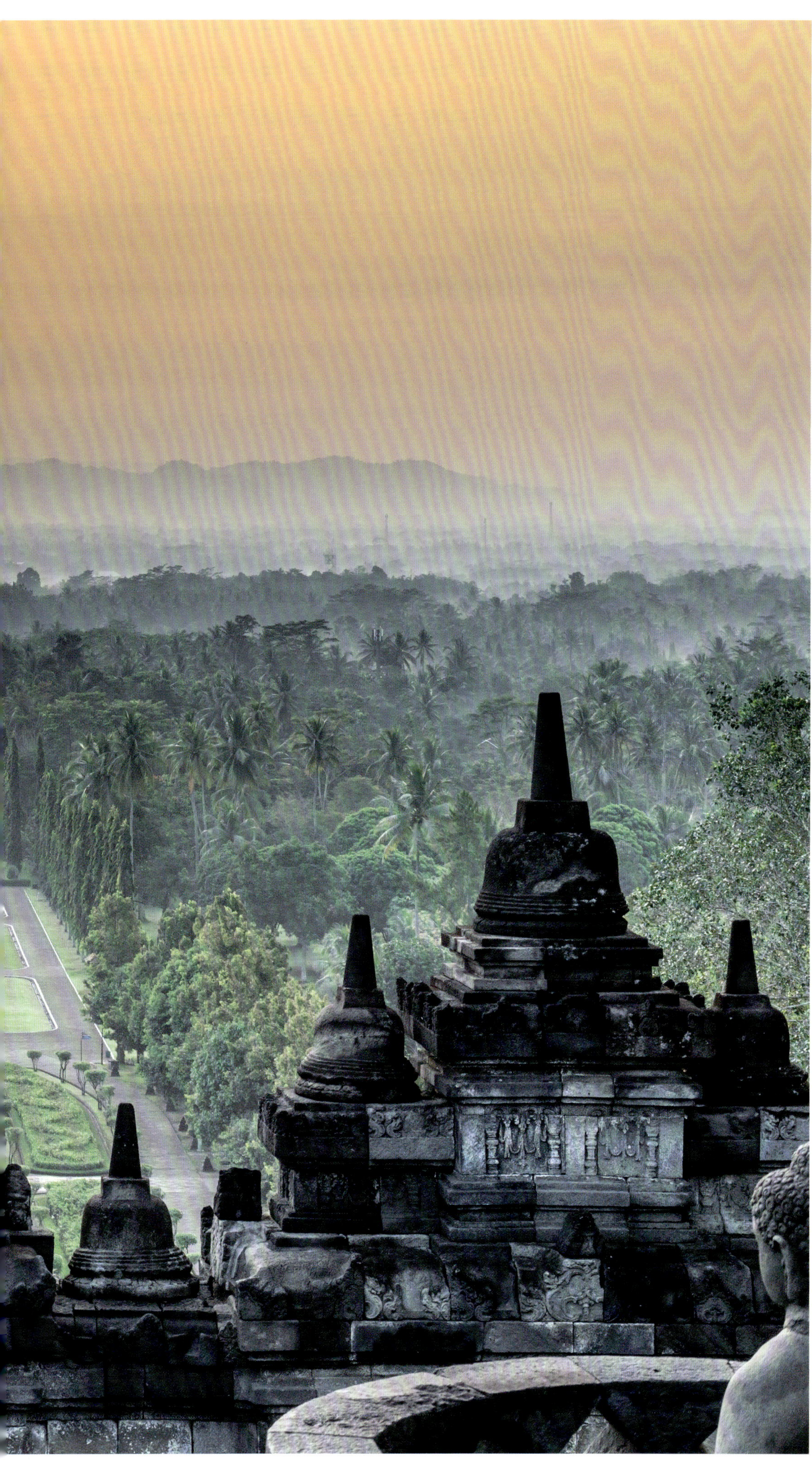

Borobudur, Central Java, Indonesia
Few sights rival that of sunrise over Borobudur, the world's largest Buddhist temple, with Mount Merapi in the distance. Yet there is a dark paradox behind the serene image: Merapi is volcanic, and many scientists now believe that eruptions and earthquakes between 928 and 1006 led monks to abandon Borobudur. British and Dutch explorers only 'rediscovered' the complex in 1814, after which it was renovated.

The Mataram Kingdom erected Borobudur in around 824 CE. That means it enjoyed barely 200 years of use before the forest reclaimed it. Structurally Borobudur works as a giant explanatory book: its 10 concentric rings stand for the ascending steps needed to achieve the perfection of the Buddha.

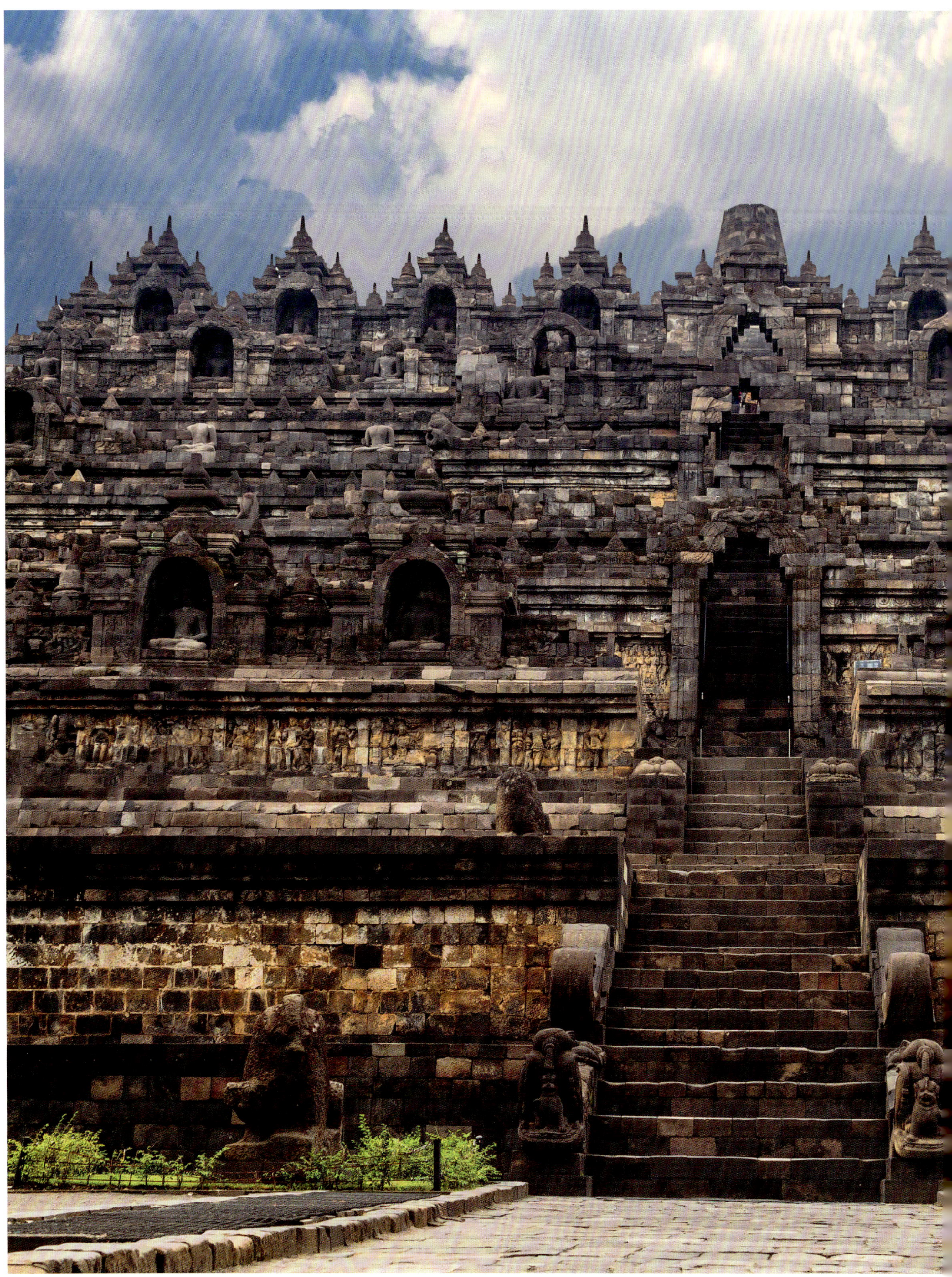

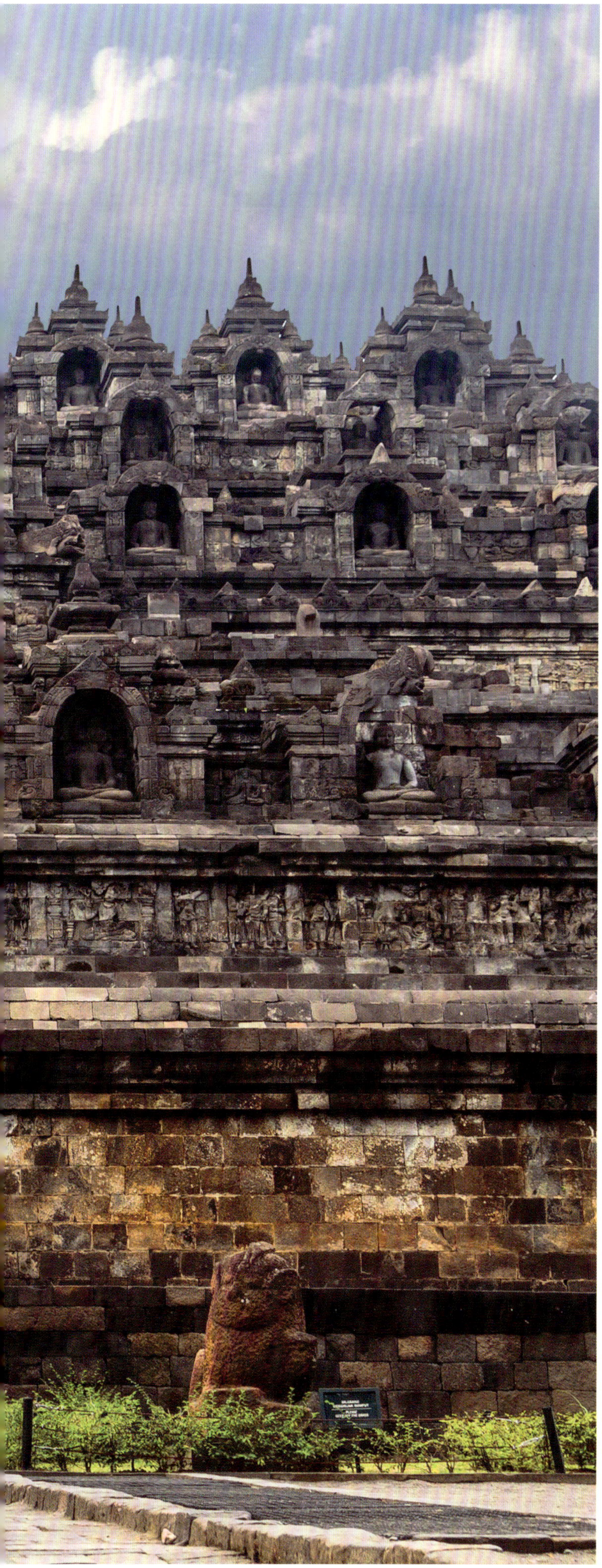

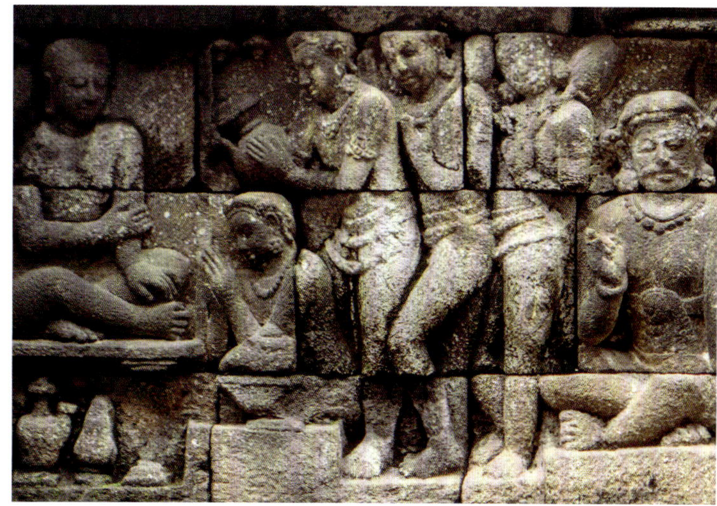

BOTH PHOTOGRAPHS:

Borobudur,
Central Java, Indonesia

(Left) Around 1000 years ago this gateway led Buddhist pilgrims into the first of 10 levels of Borobudur's pyramidal temple. Not all the temple's iconography, however, depicted spiritual scenes: the bas-relief (above) shows everyday life in the 9th century.

Present-day Indonesia has the world's largest Muslim population; officially just 1.2 per cent of citizens are Buddhist. So, why is Buddhism's greatest monument sited here? The answer is that Buddhism and Hinduism once formed the majority faiths in Java. Islam only came to dominate Java in the late 1500s – well after Borobudur's fall.

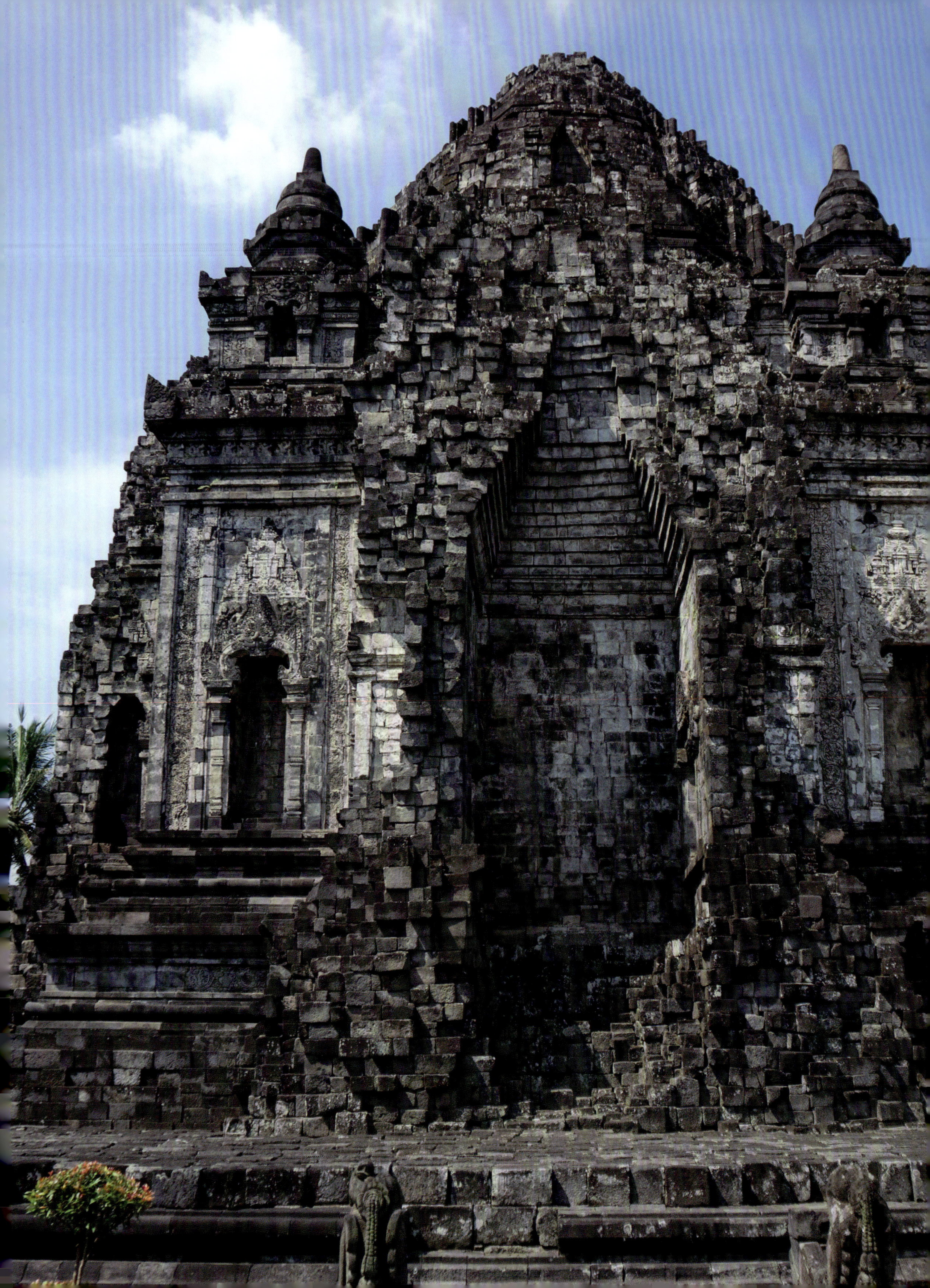

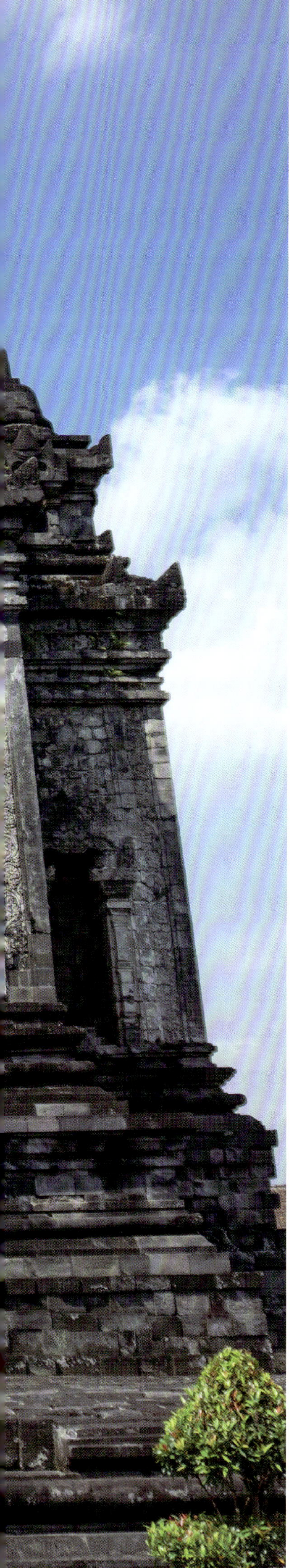

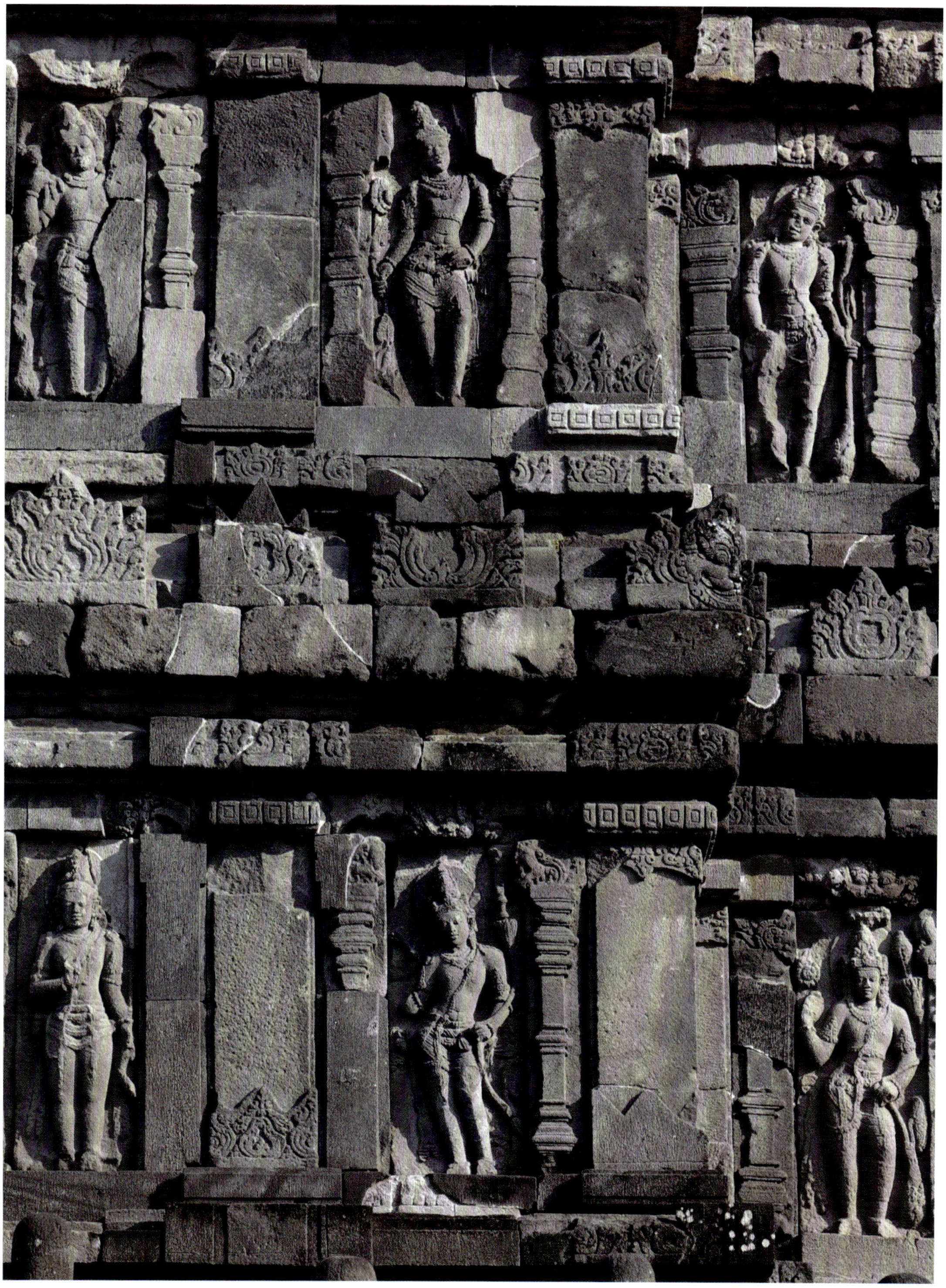

LEFT:

Kalasan Temple, Prambanan, Java, Indonesia

Kalasan Temple illustrates the religious harmony of Indonesia 1200 years ago. Dedicated to the Buddhist deity Tara, it was built for the Shailendra dynasty in the late 8th century CE and forms part of the Prambanan complex, where most of the temples are devoted to Hindu gods.

Prambanan declined after Mataram kings moved their court eastward in the 930s. The temple was rediscovered around 1895.

ABOVE:

Nandi Temple, Prambanan, Java, Indonesia

Divine yet very human in their stances, Hindu gods adorn panels at Nandi Temple, one of 242 shrines surrounding the great Shiva Temple at Prambanan. The Sanjaya dynasty initiated most building here in around 850 CE, reputedly as a Hindu answer to the massive Buddhist complex at Borobudur 51km (32 miles) away.

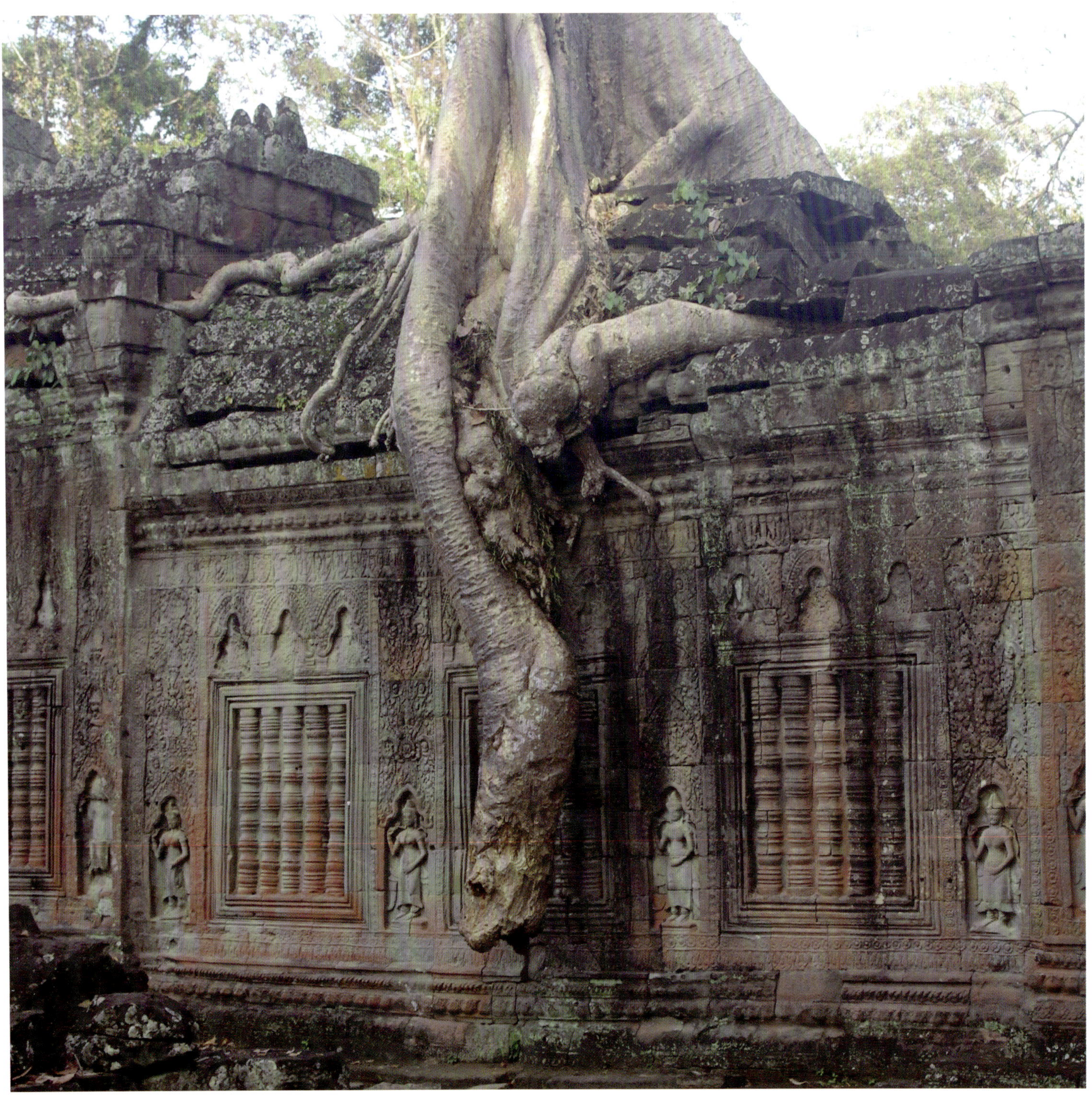

ABOVE:
Preah Khan, Angkor, Siem Reap, Cambodia
Trees have nearly overtaken the labyrinthine temple-monastery of Preah Khan, built in the Khmer capital of Angkor by King Jayavarman VII to commemorate his victory over the Cham Kingdom of southern Vietnam at this spot in 1191 CE.

OPPOSITE:
Ta Prohm, Angkor, Siem Reap, Cambodia
At Jayavarman VII's Ta Prohm Temple the gates contain a massive head of a Buddha – or possibly of the king himself. Ta Prohm crumbled after the Khmer Empire collapsed in the 15th century. The ruins of the city of Angkor were not rediscovered until 1838.

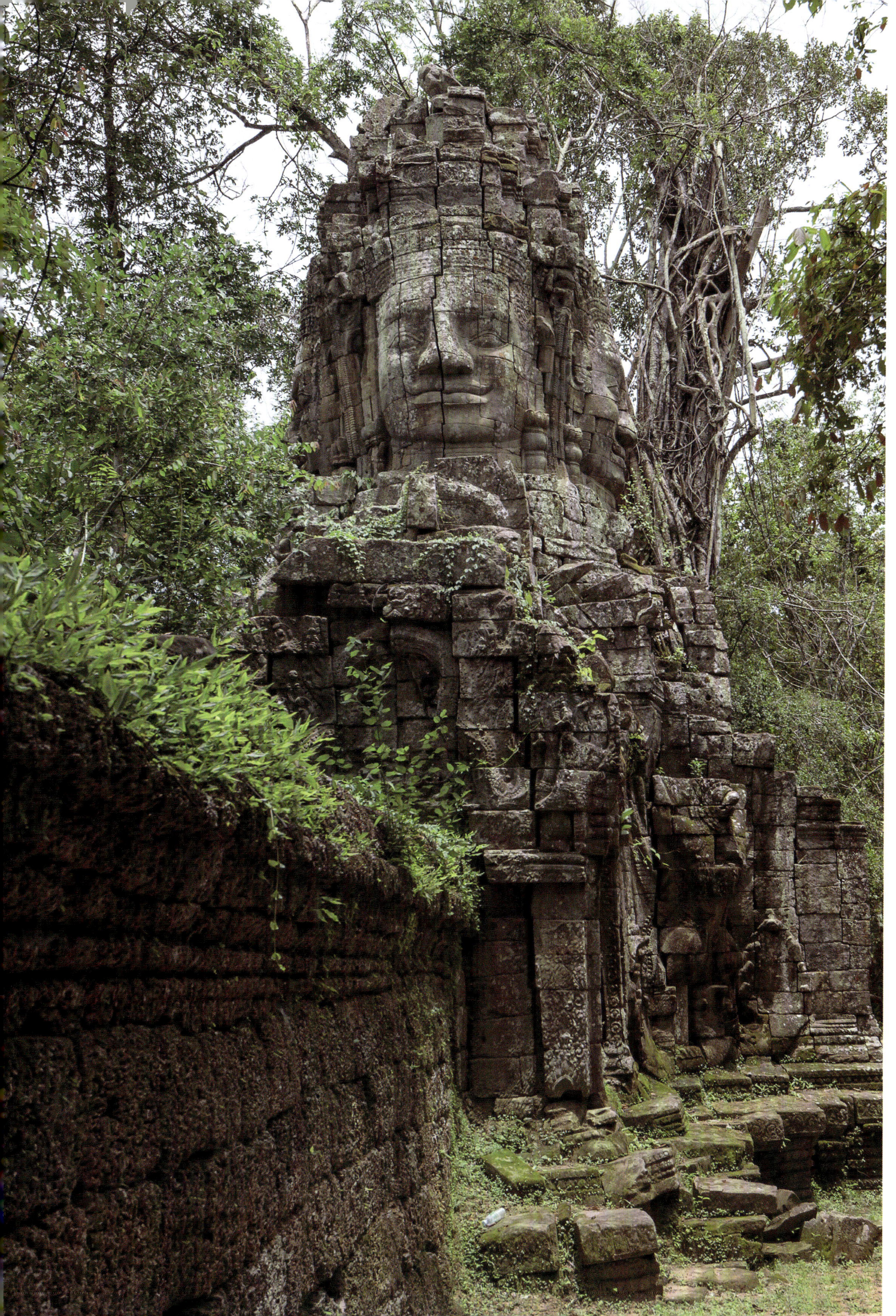

Phimeanakas, Angkor, Siem Reap, Cambodia
Encircled by a moat – Angkor had a highly sophisticated water system – and shaped as a three-tier pyramid, Phimeanakas was begun as a Khmer Hindu temple in the latter part of King Rajendravarman's reign (941–968 CE). Today it is located within the walled enclosure of the Royal Palace of Angkor Thom, which grew up around Phimeanakas at the instigation of the master-builder monarch, Jayavarman VII (ruled 1181–1218).

The later arrival of Theravada Buddhism ultimately spelt doom for the Khmers; the sect rejected any notion of worshipping 'god-kings', which undermined the typically centralized and autocratic Khmer monarchy. The Khmer fell in 1431 to the Thai Ayutthaya Kingdom.

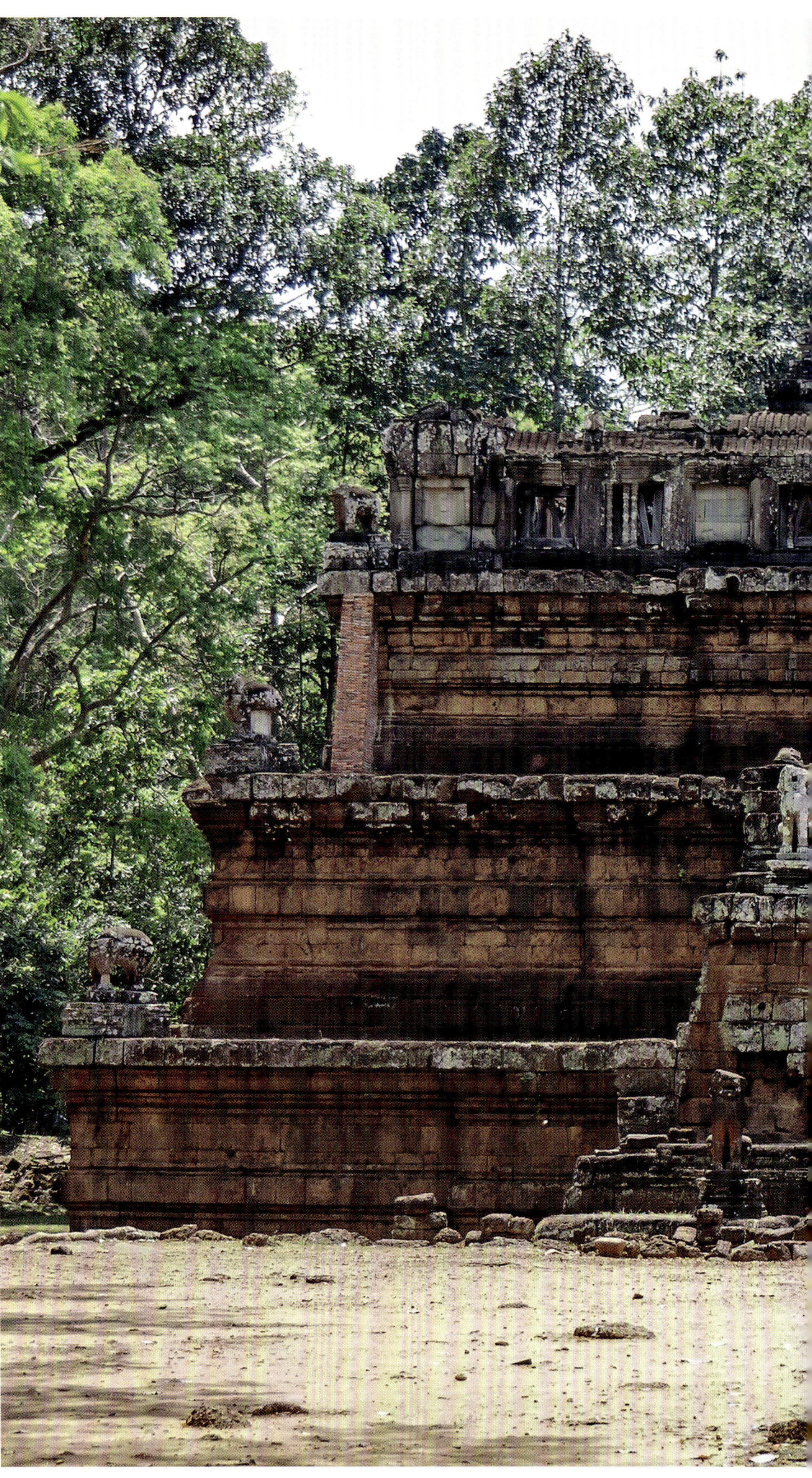

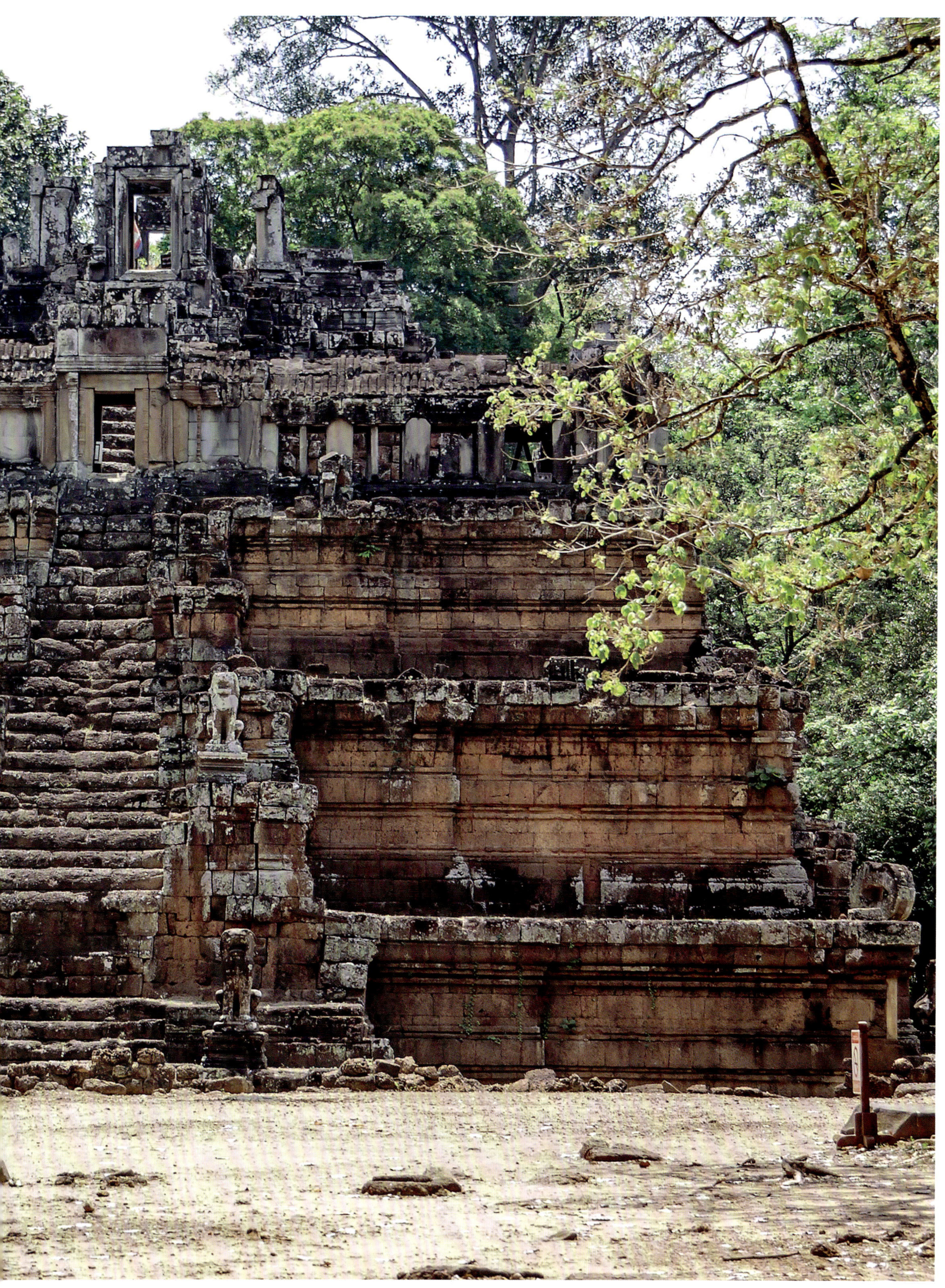

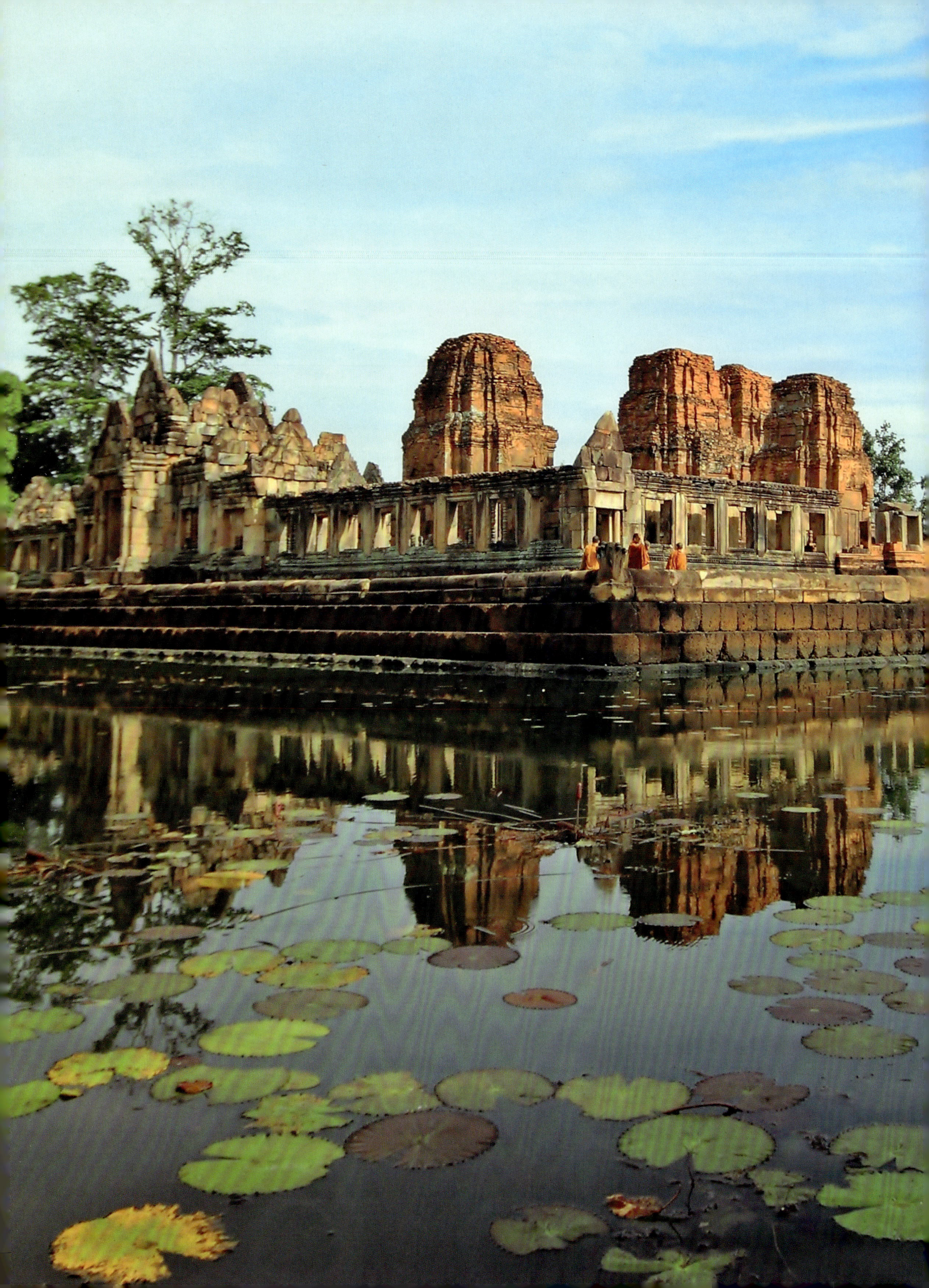

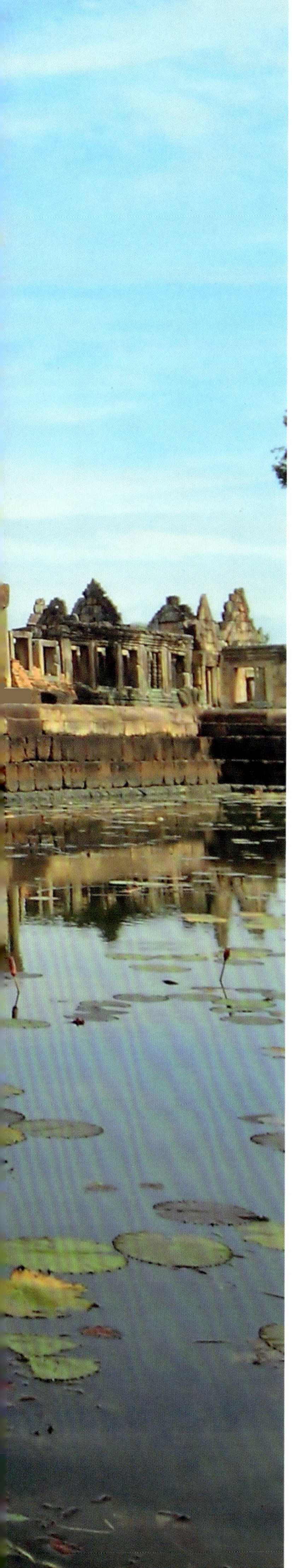

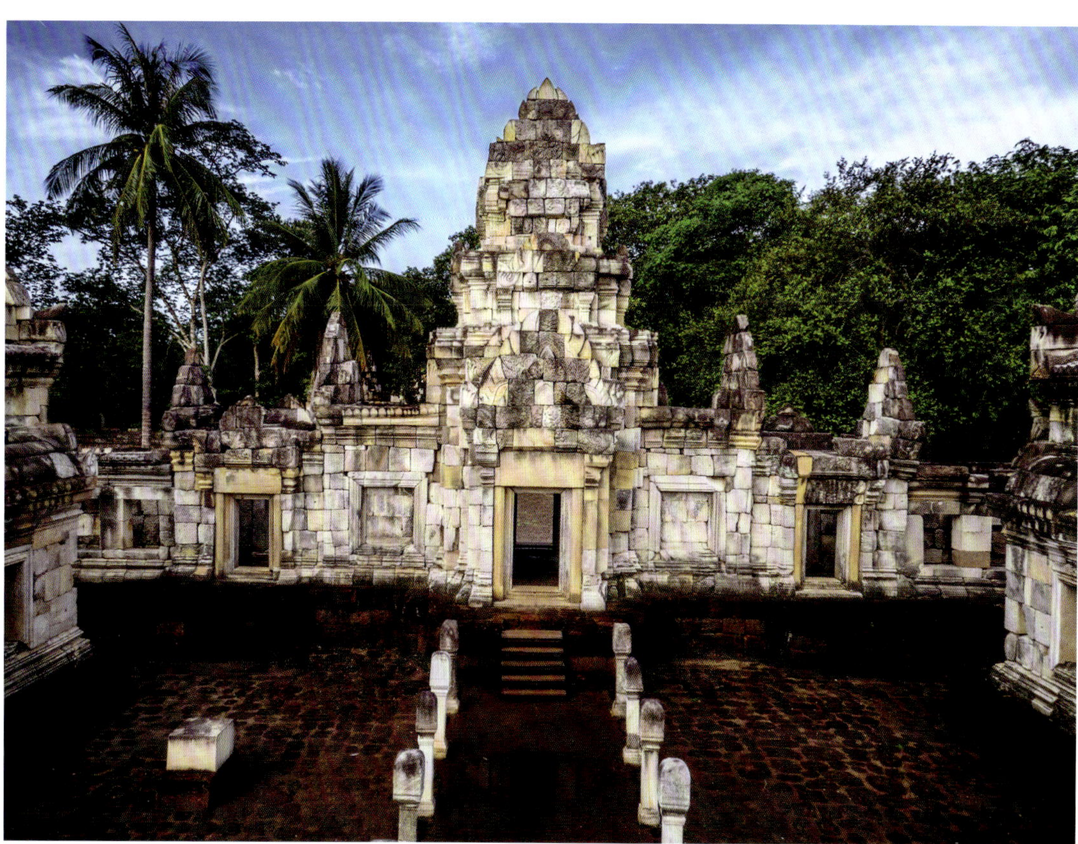

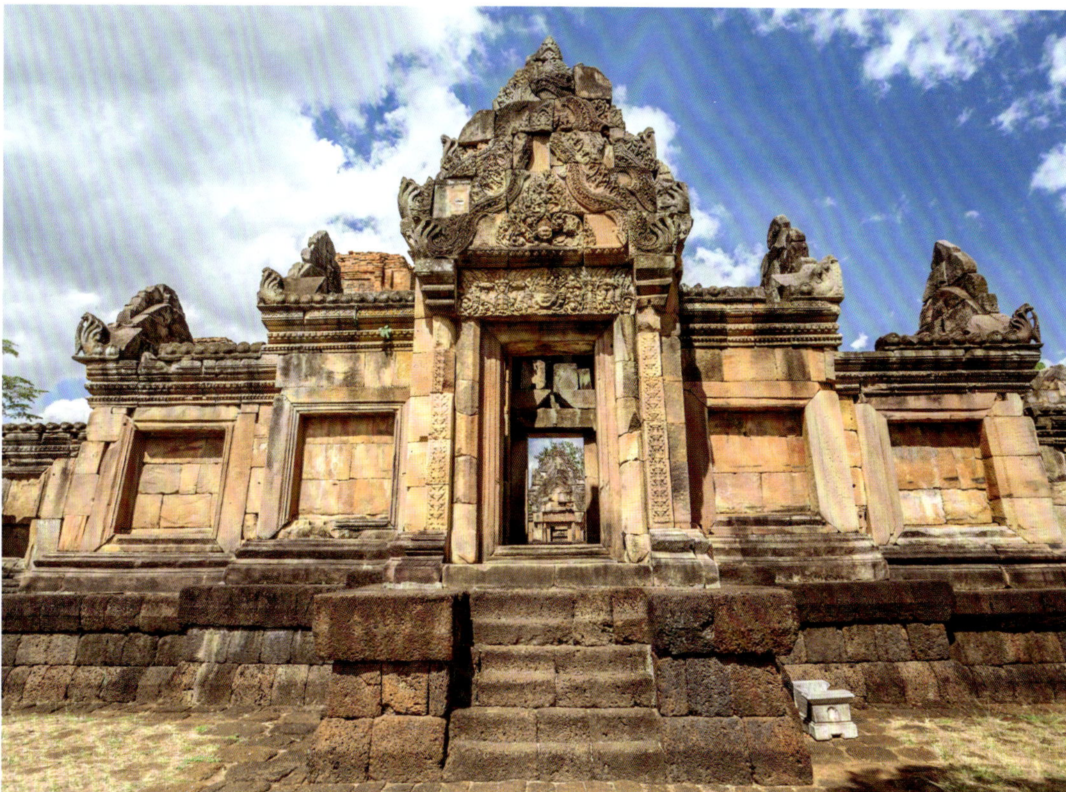

ALL PHOTOGRAPHS:

Prasat Muang Tam, Buri Ram, Thailand

(Left) The ruins of the Khmer Hindu temple of Prasat Muang Tam display a large sandstone porch and an inner sanctuary probably honouring Shiva. Its four brick towers each convey spiritual meaning; the fifth and tallest one, which represented Mount Meru, the centre of the Hindu universe, has collapsed. The temple was built between 900 and 1100 CE.

(Top) An inside-out view of a doorway, now bereft of stucco decoration. Carvings of time-eating demons draw on Hindu mythology.

(Above) An arched doorway is decorated with Hindu legends. The Khmer Empire ruled in Thailand and in much of present-day Cambodia, Laos and Vietnam from the early 9th century to 1431 CE. Their kings favoured Hinduism with aspects of indigenous animism – the belief that objects, places and all creatures have a spirit.

In time, Khmer power waned as Thais migrated into their territory and founded mini-states. The new rulers preferred Buddhism, thus rendering Muang Tam obsolete.

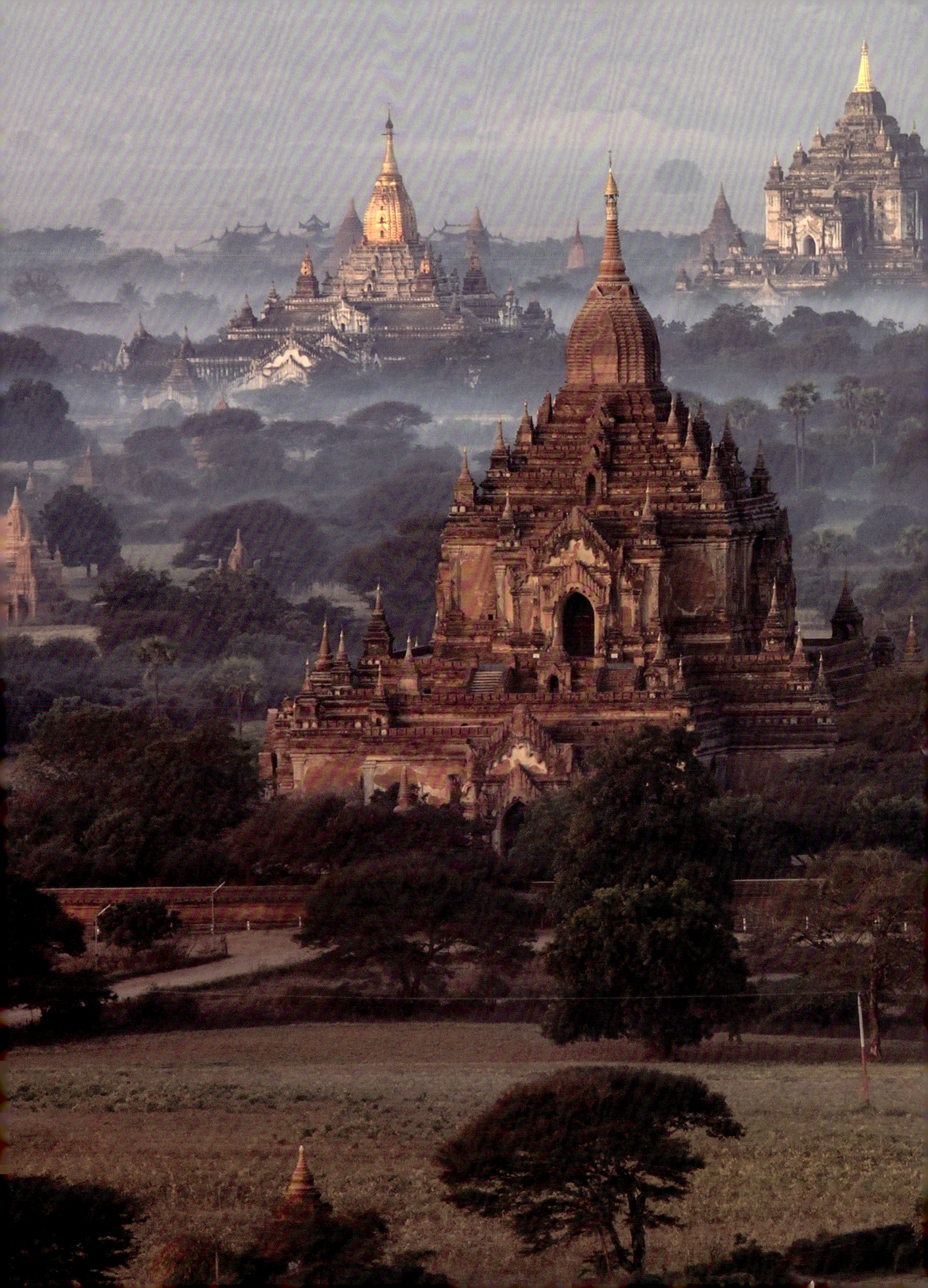

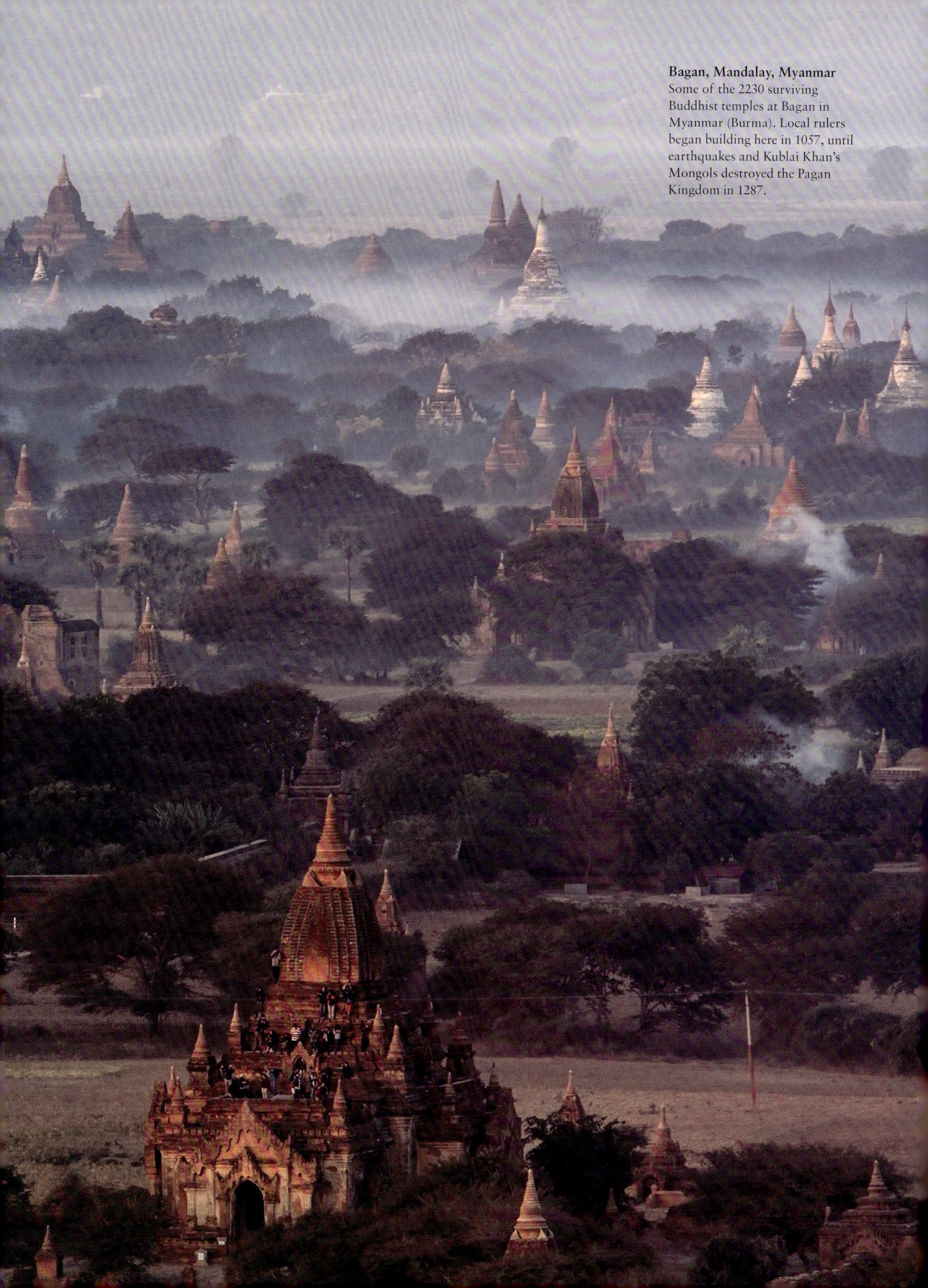

Bagan, Mandalay, Myanmar
Some of the 2230 surviving Buddhist temples at Bagan in Myanmar (Burma). Local rulers began building here in 1057, until earthquakes and Kublai Khan's Mongols destroyed the Pagan Kingdom in 1287.

Bagan, Mandalay, Myanmar
'To build a temple is to earn merit,' runs an old Buddhist adage – a truth ably demonstrated at Bagan. In the top left-hand corner is the all-white Shwesandaw temple, erected by King Anawrahta in 1057. He asserted a uniquely Burmese identity by absorbing the formerly dominant Pyu and Mon people, migrants to Burma and early converts to Buddhism. In the 1230s, the Pagan Empire began to subside, following excessive expenditure, the waiving of taxes on religious institutions and misuse of cultivable land. This led to collapse in 1287 and a power vacuum.

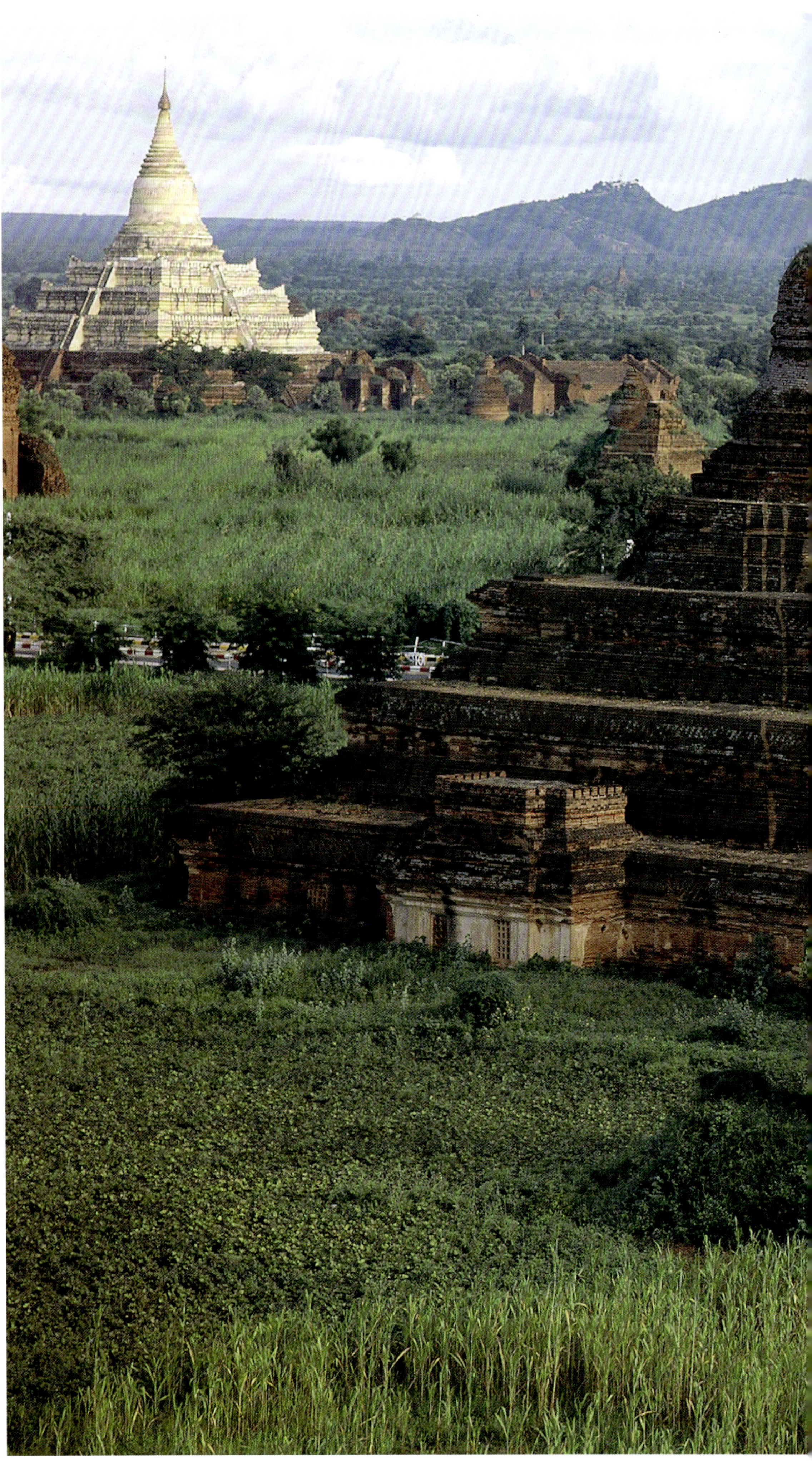

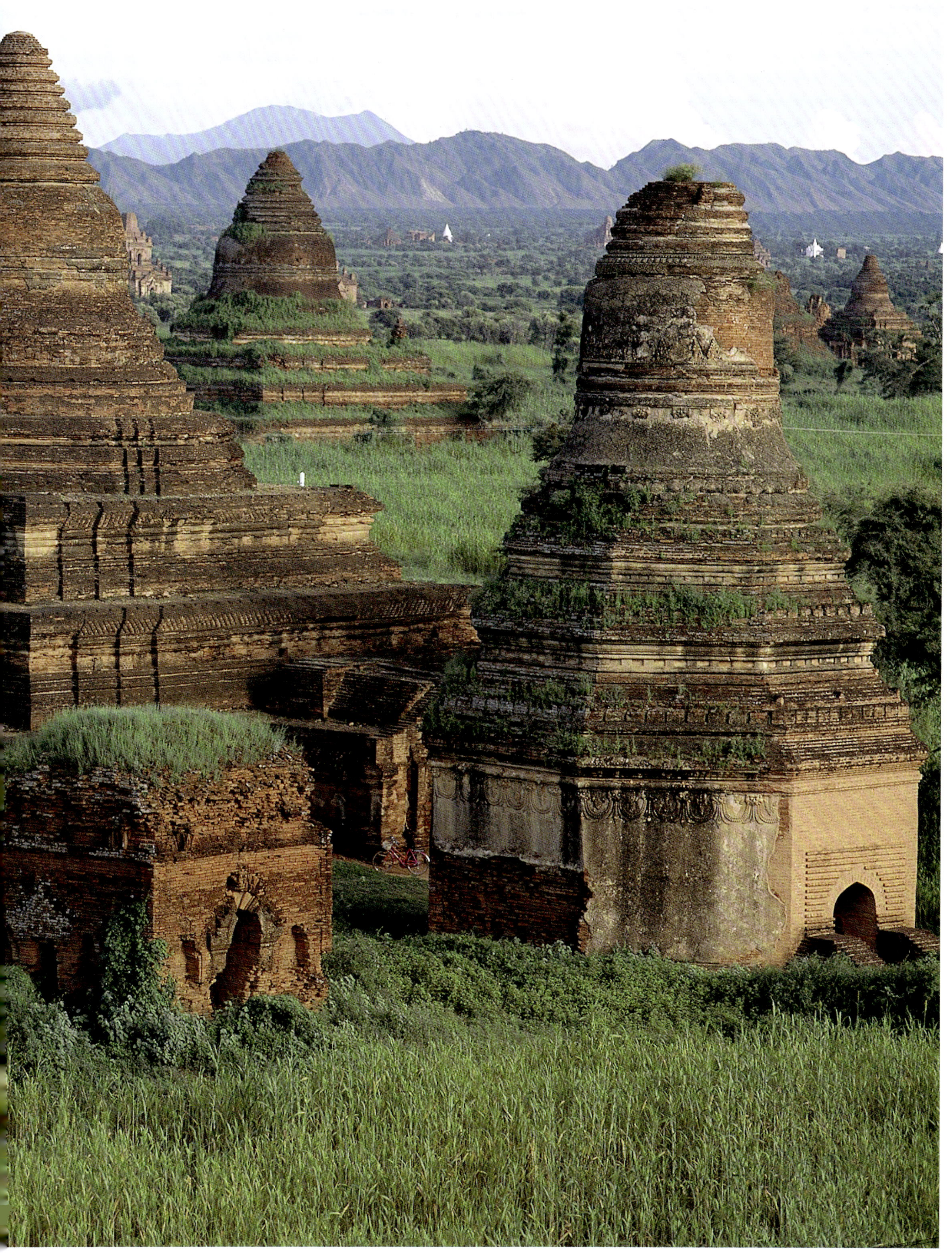

Mogao Caves, Gansu, China

For 1000 years the Mogao Caves served as a magnet for worshippers – and was possibly the world's richest single trove of devotional art. Buddhist monks began carving chambers out of a mile-long cliff face above the Daquan River, near Dunhuang, in 366 CE. Mogao became a welcome stop in the Gobi Desert along the Silk Road. By the 7th century, it was flourishing as East-West commerce boomed. Meanwhile, Buddhism had grown from an obscure foreign sect into China's majority belief system.

In the 11th century, Mogao held 50,000 paintings, manuscripts and icons. By then, however, the Silk Road had switched routes, eventually giving way to sea trading passages. Tibetan and Mongol incursions also contributed to Mogao's decline, although it wasn't finally abandoned until the time of the Ming Dynasty (1368–1644). After that, a few pilgrims visited but otherwise Mogao remained forgotten until a Taoist monk discovered the Library Cave in 1900. There he found documents in Chinese and Sanskrit, and even Old Turkic and Hebrew.

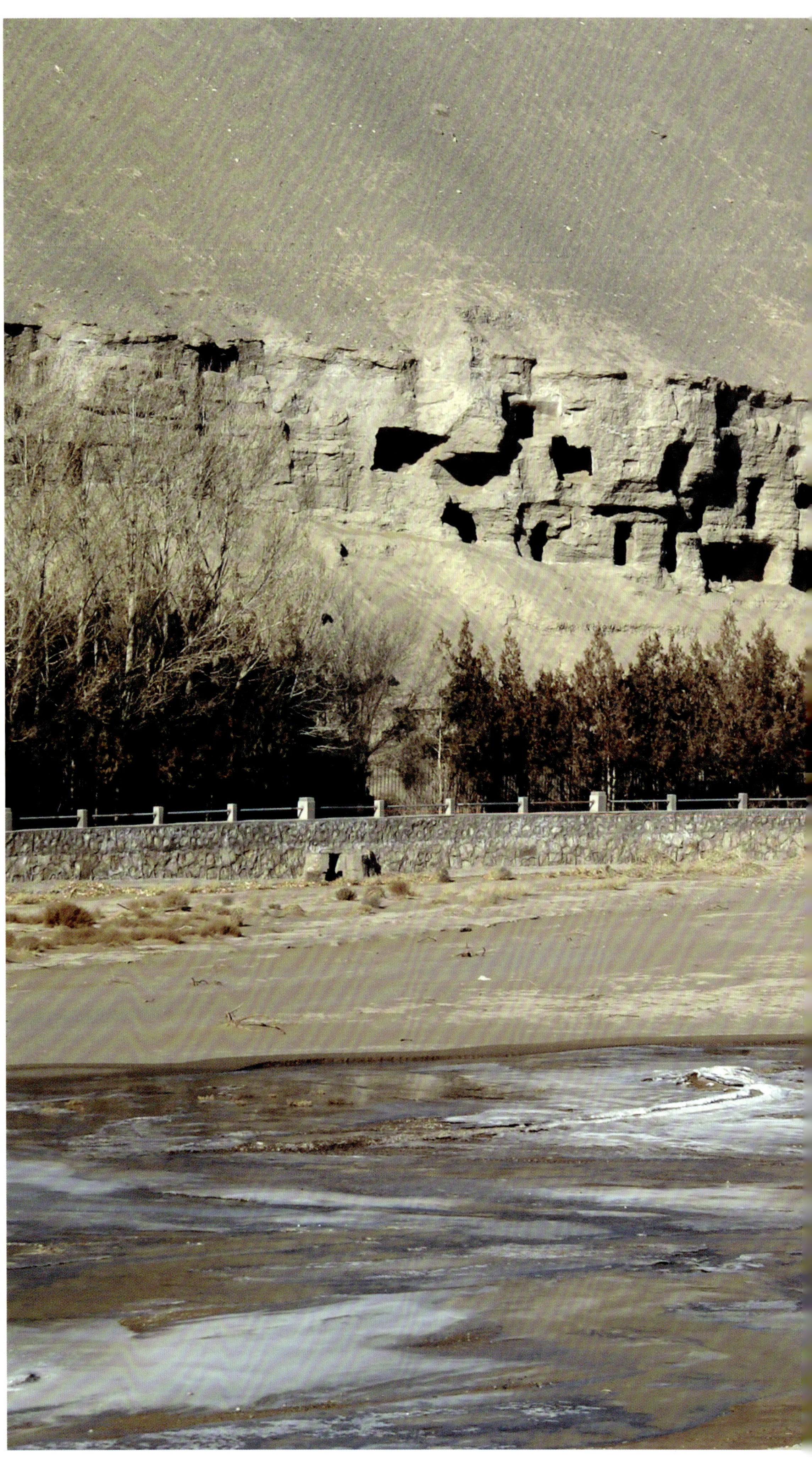

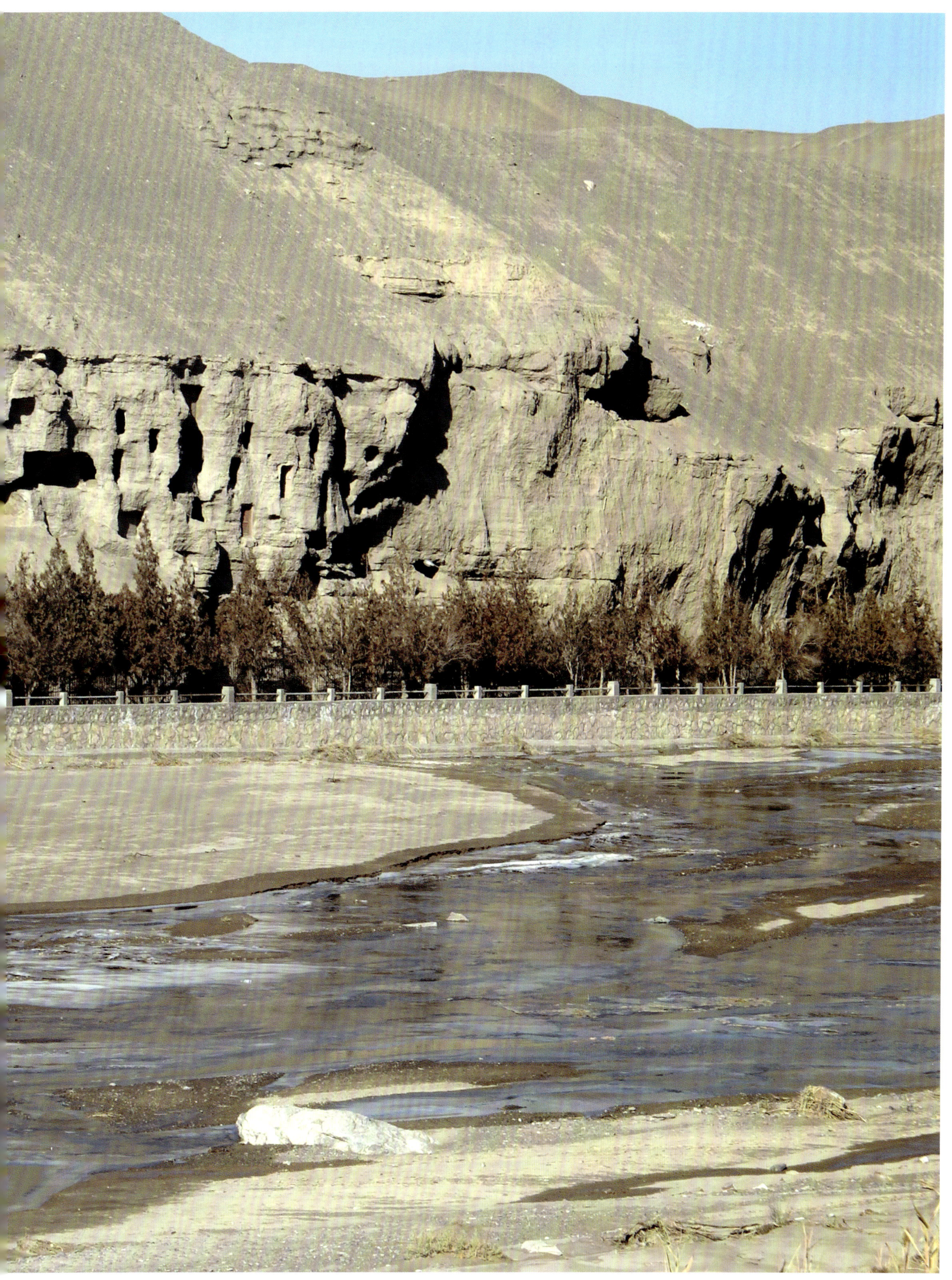

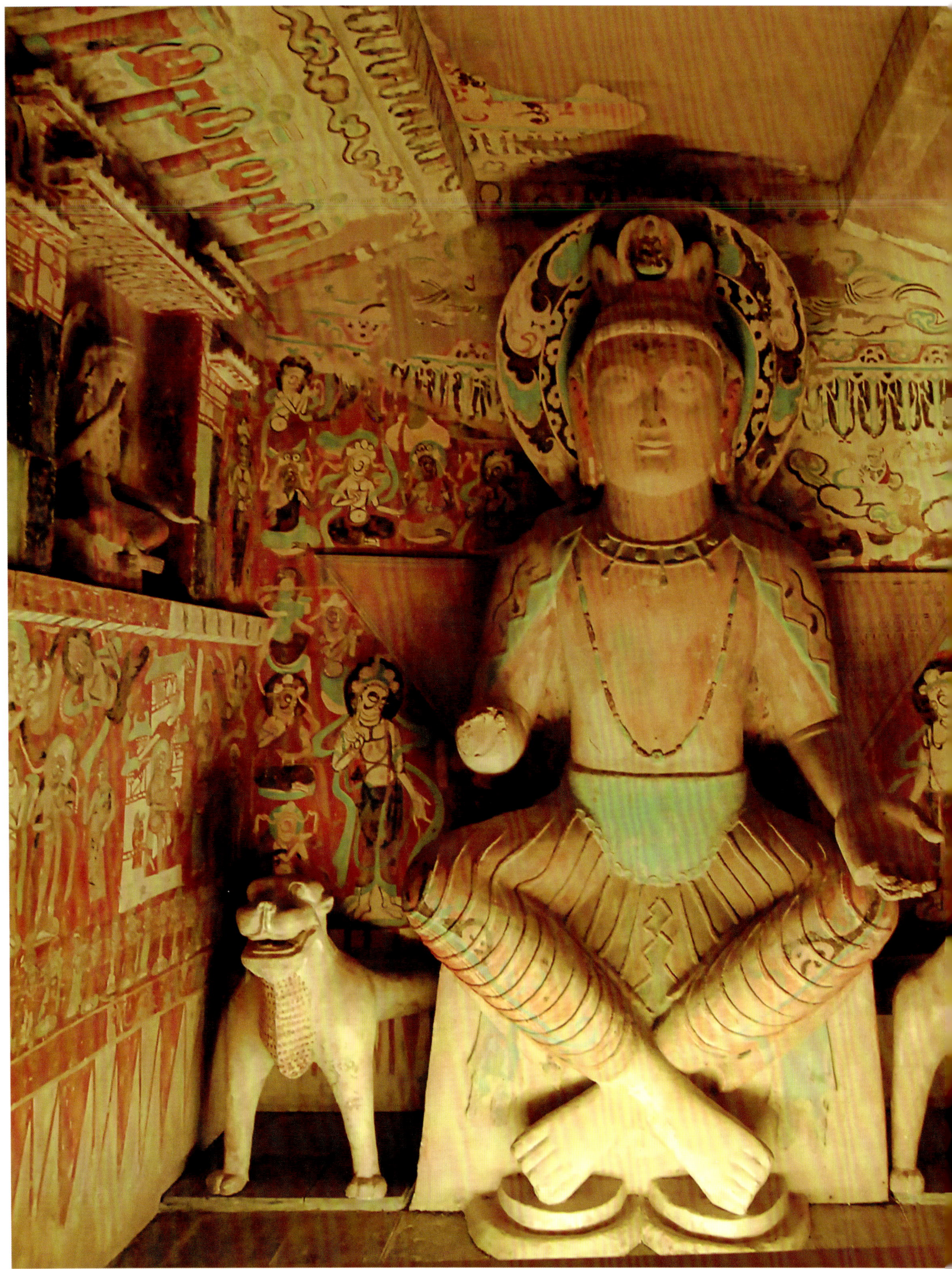

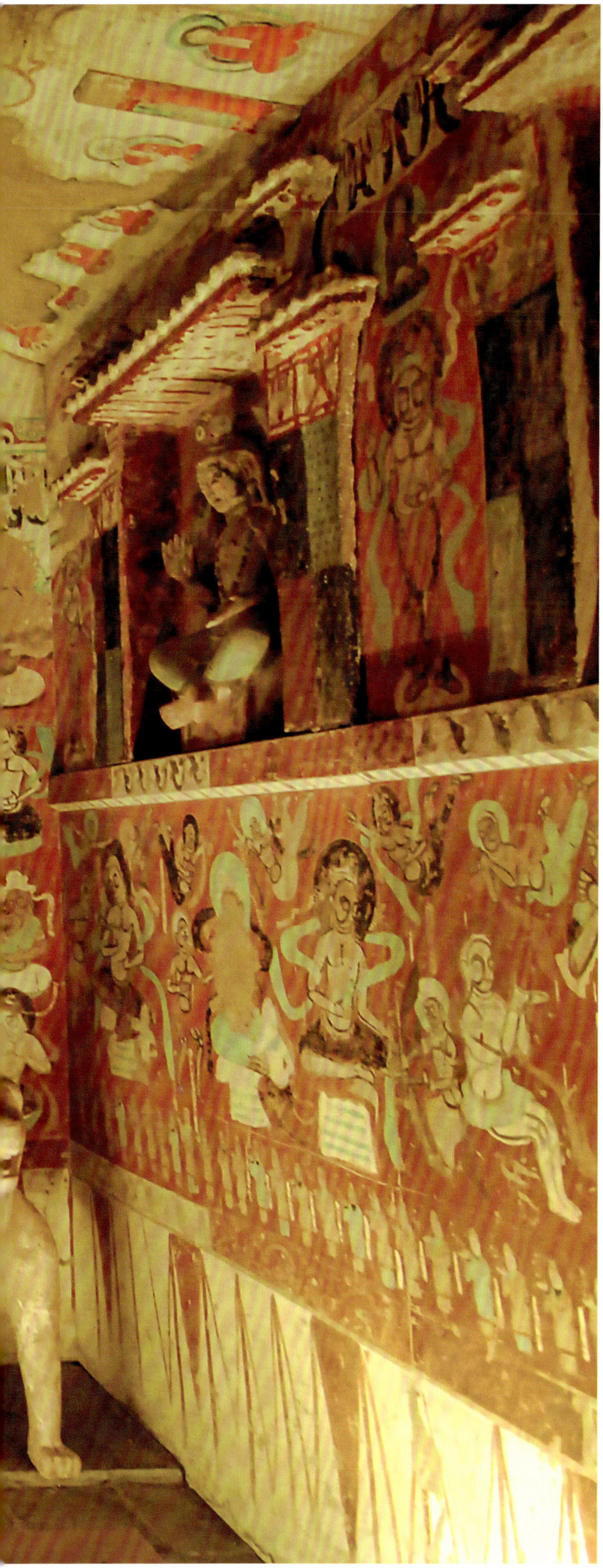

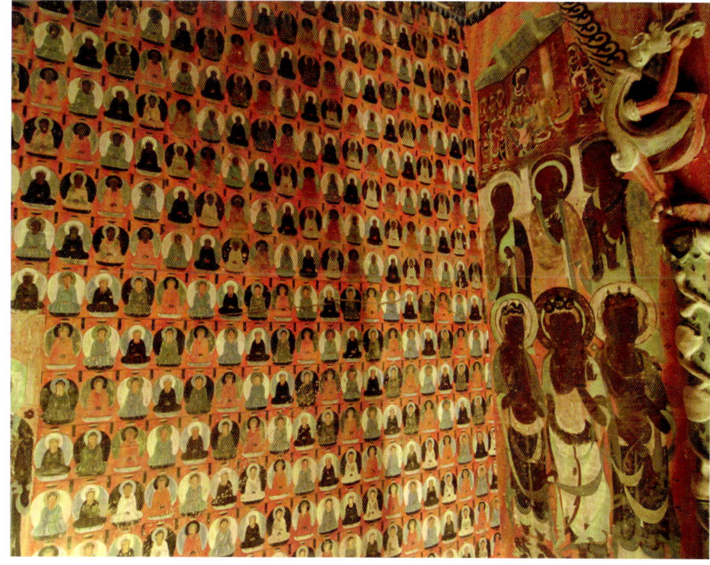

LEFT:
Mogao Caves, Gansu, China
Built of clay, straw and wood, this painted 3.4-metre-high (11ft) statue depicts Maitreya, who was destined to be reborn as the Buddha. He sits in royal pose, cross-legged and flanked by lions. The panel behind shows dancers, musicians and divine creatures. The icon was created in the 5th century CE under the Sui dynasty; Mogao reached its zenith under the T'ang dynasty (618–907 CE).

Mogao's isolation after around 1300 ensured that its art survived anti-Buddhist ire in the 19th century and even the depredations of the 1960s Cultural Revolution.

ABOVE:
Mogao Caves, Gansu, China
Mogao has been called China's art history encyclopaedia in physical form. Through its 492 extant cave-temples we can see how iconography changed over a millennium, as in this mural of a Thousand Buddhas. Dating from the late Yuan Dynasty (1271–1368 CE), it shows how Central Asian, Tibetan and Chinese aesthetics had supplanted the Indian gestures found in art in earlier caves.

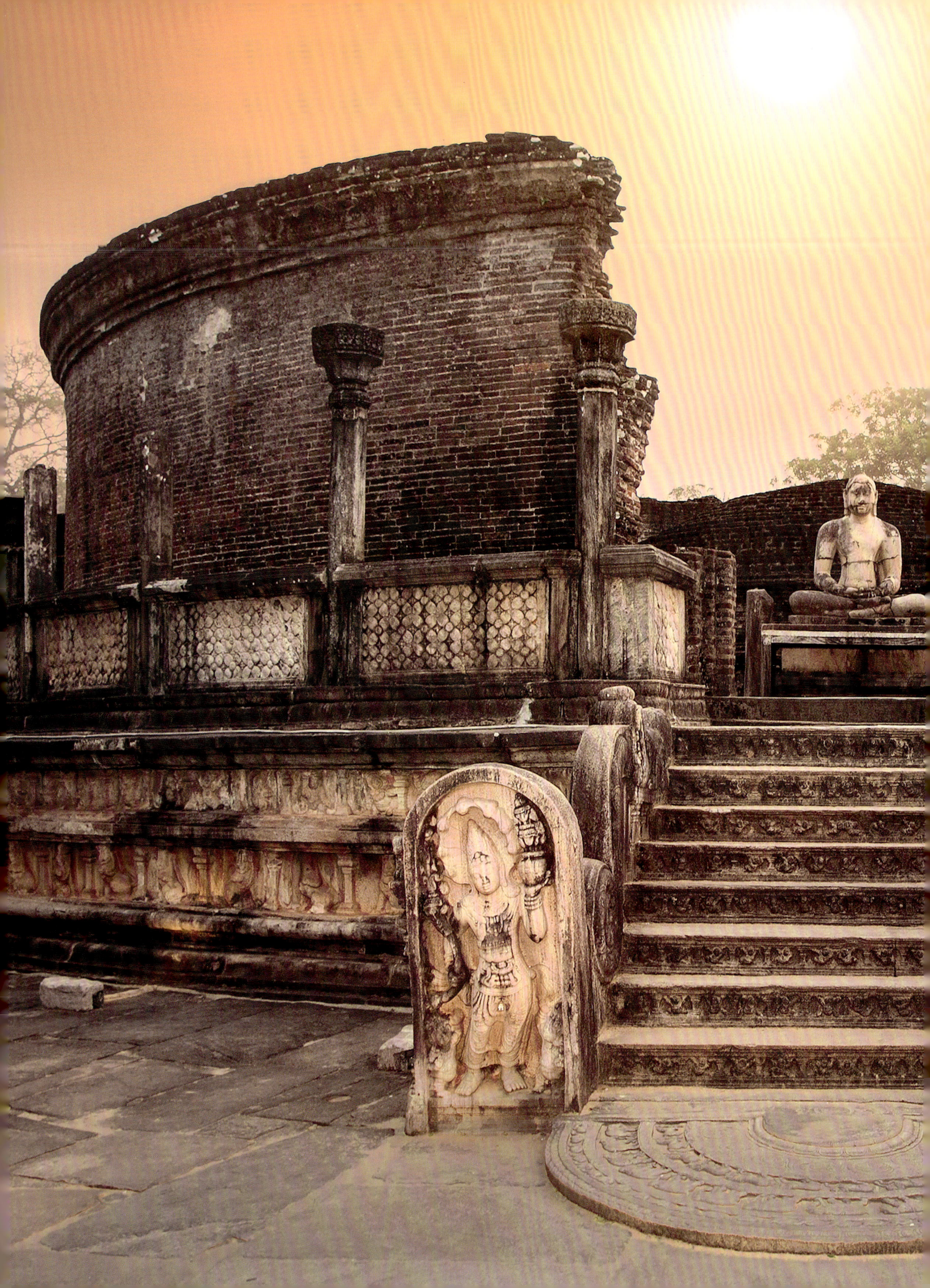

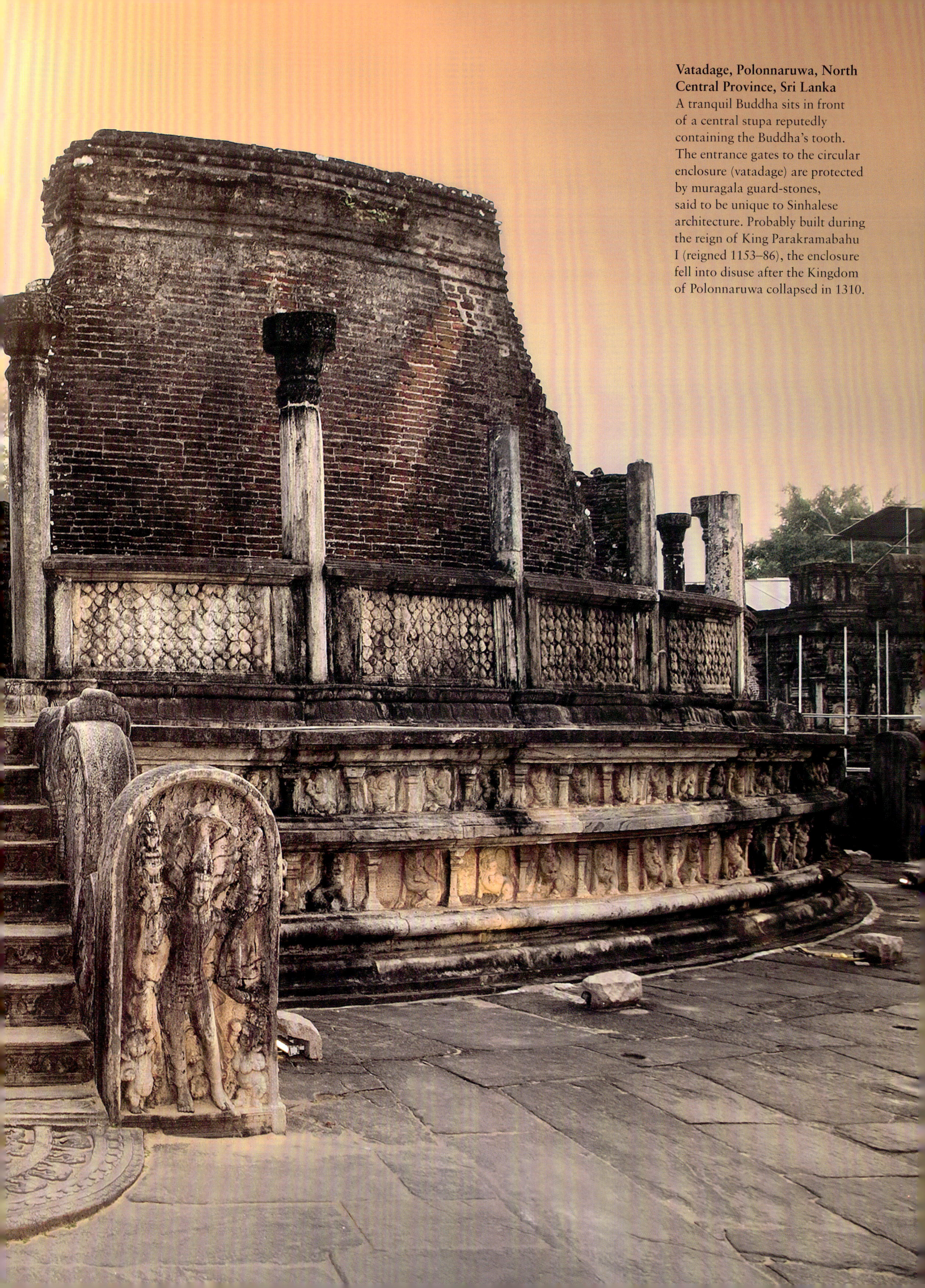

Vatadage, Polonnaruwa, North Central Province, Sri Lanka
A tranquil Buddha sits in front of a central stupa reputedly containing the Buddha's tooth. The entrance gates to the circular enclosure (vatadage) are protected by muragala guard-stones, said to be unique to Sinhalese architecture. Probably built during the reign of King Parakramabahu I (reigned 1153–86), the enclosure fell into disuse after the Kingdom of Polonnaruwa collapsed in 1310.

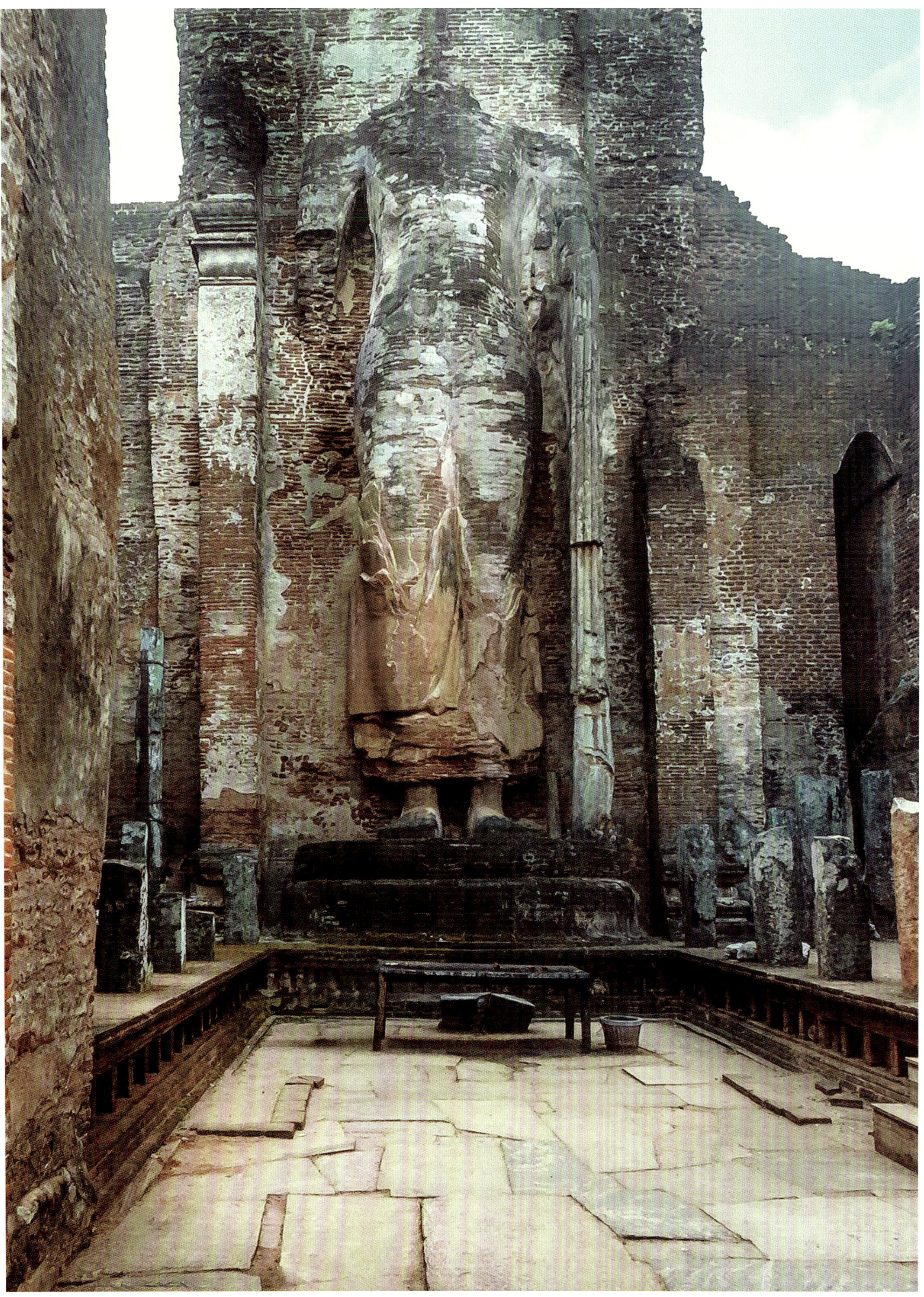

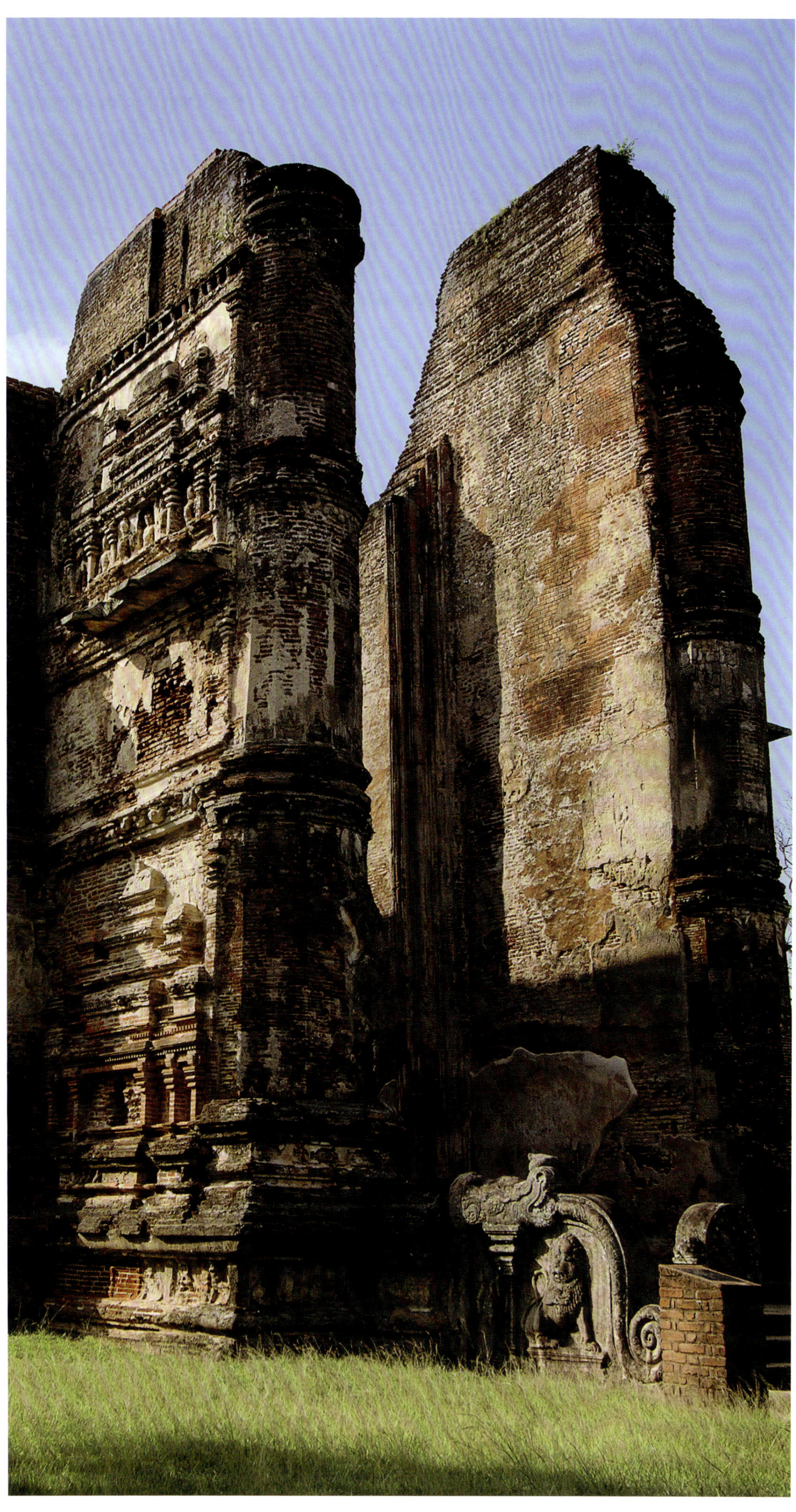

BOTH PHOTOGRAPHS:

Lankatilaka Temple, Polonnaruwa, North Central Province, Sri Lanka

A gigantic standing if now headless Buddha statue commands our attention (opposite). Unusually for a Buddhist temple, Lankatilaka has long, narrow cathedral-like aisles and was originally five storeys tall. Its 17-metre-high (56ft) entrance walls (left) are divided horizontally into five segments, or 'floors', probably representing Vimana, the abode of the gods.

Sri Lanka largely adopted Buddhism when India's Prince Mahinda converted the island's ruler in the 3rd century BCE. Polonnaruwa was founded as the capital of a reunited island after Sinhalese king Vijayabahu I repelled Hindus from South India in 1070, with Lankatilaka built about 100 years later. However, the city began to decline after repeated foreign invasions forced the capital to be relocated in 1303.

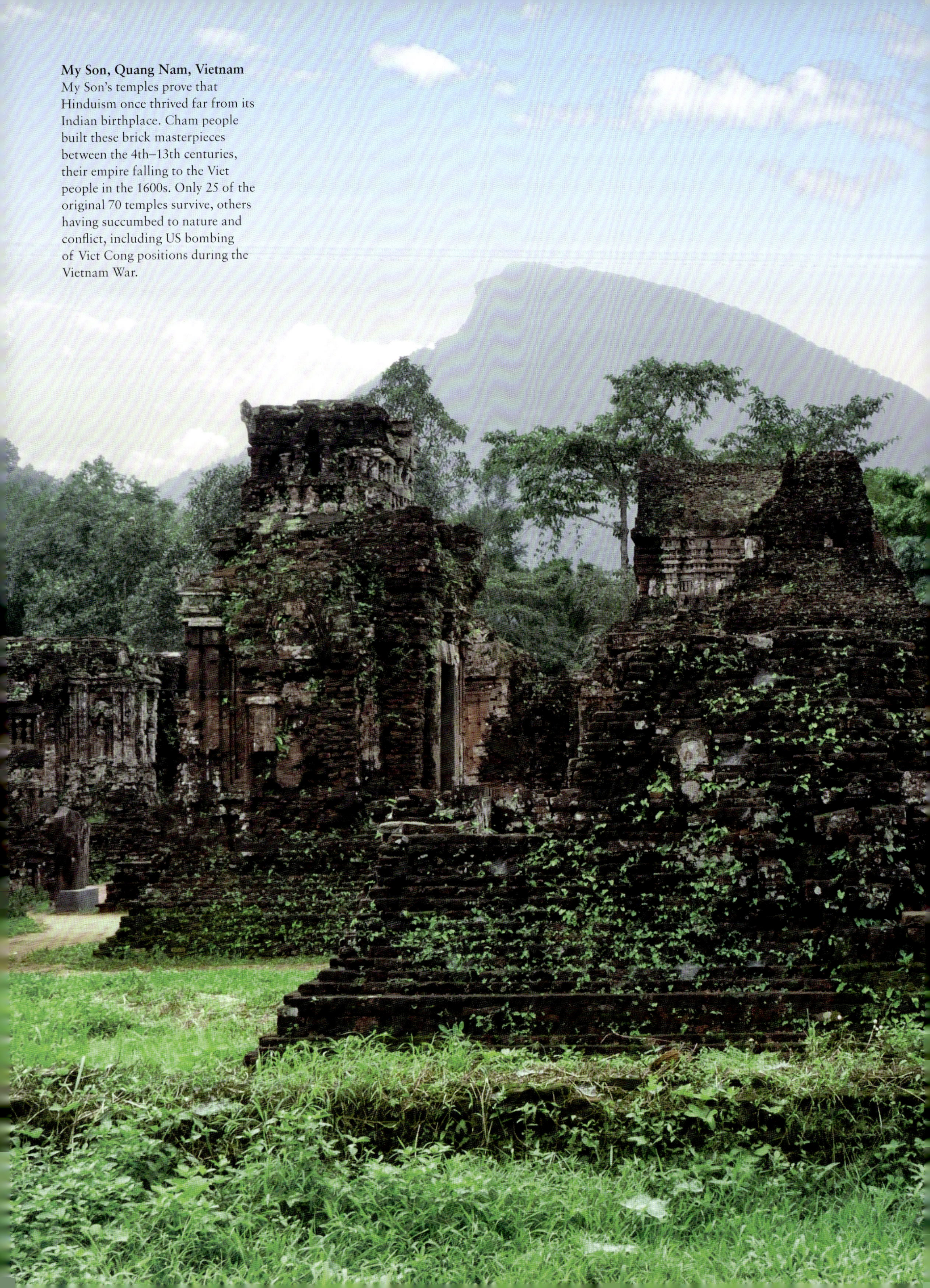

My Son, Quang Nam, Vietnam
My Son's temples prove that Hinduism once thrived far from its Indian birthplace. Cham people built these brick masterpieces between the 4th–13th centuries, their empire falling to the Viet people in the 1600s. Only 25 of the original 70 temples survive, others having succumbed to nature and conflict, including US bombing of Viet Cong positions during the Vietnam War.

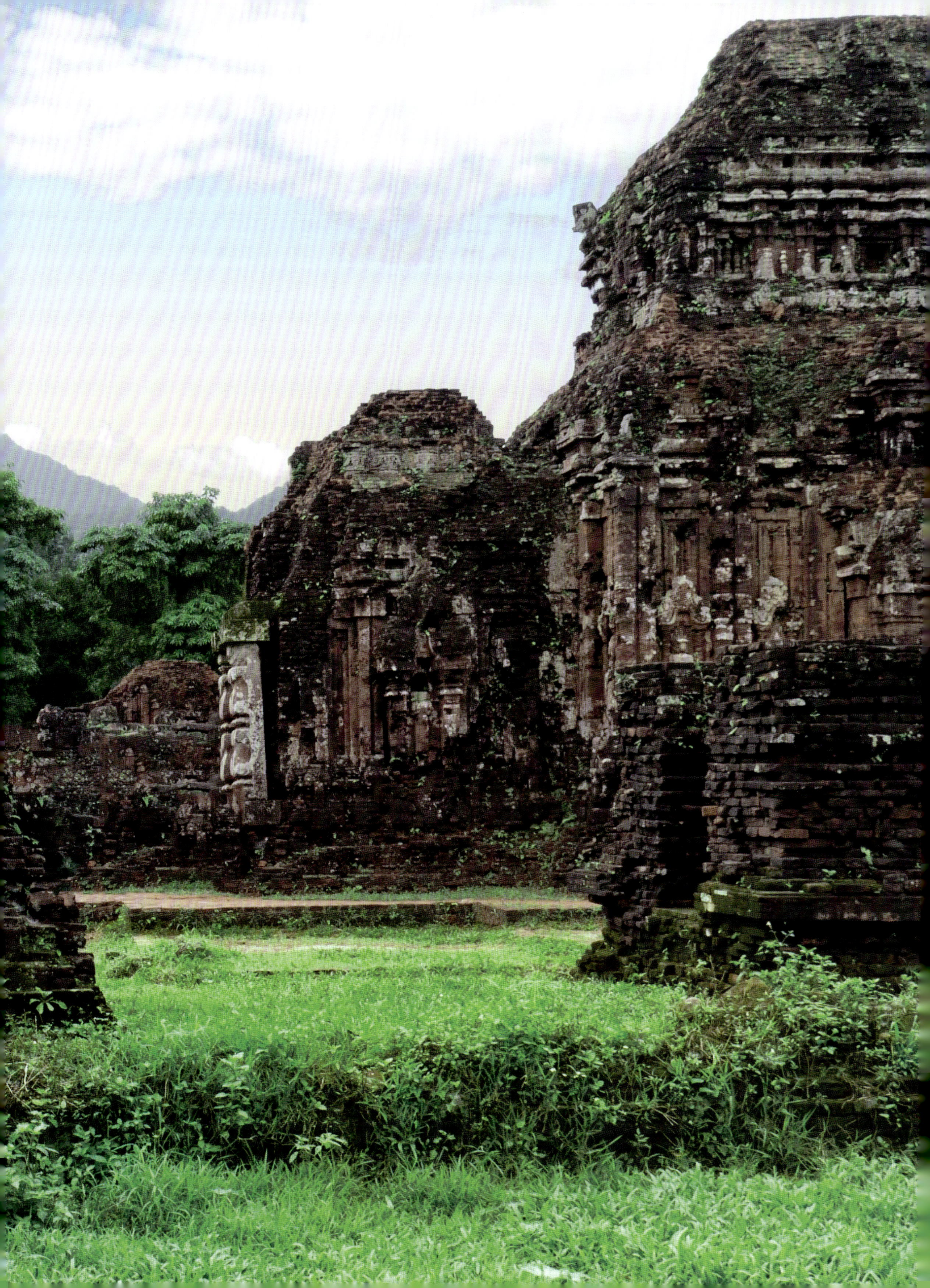

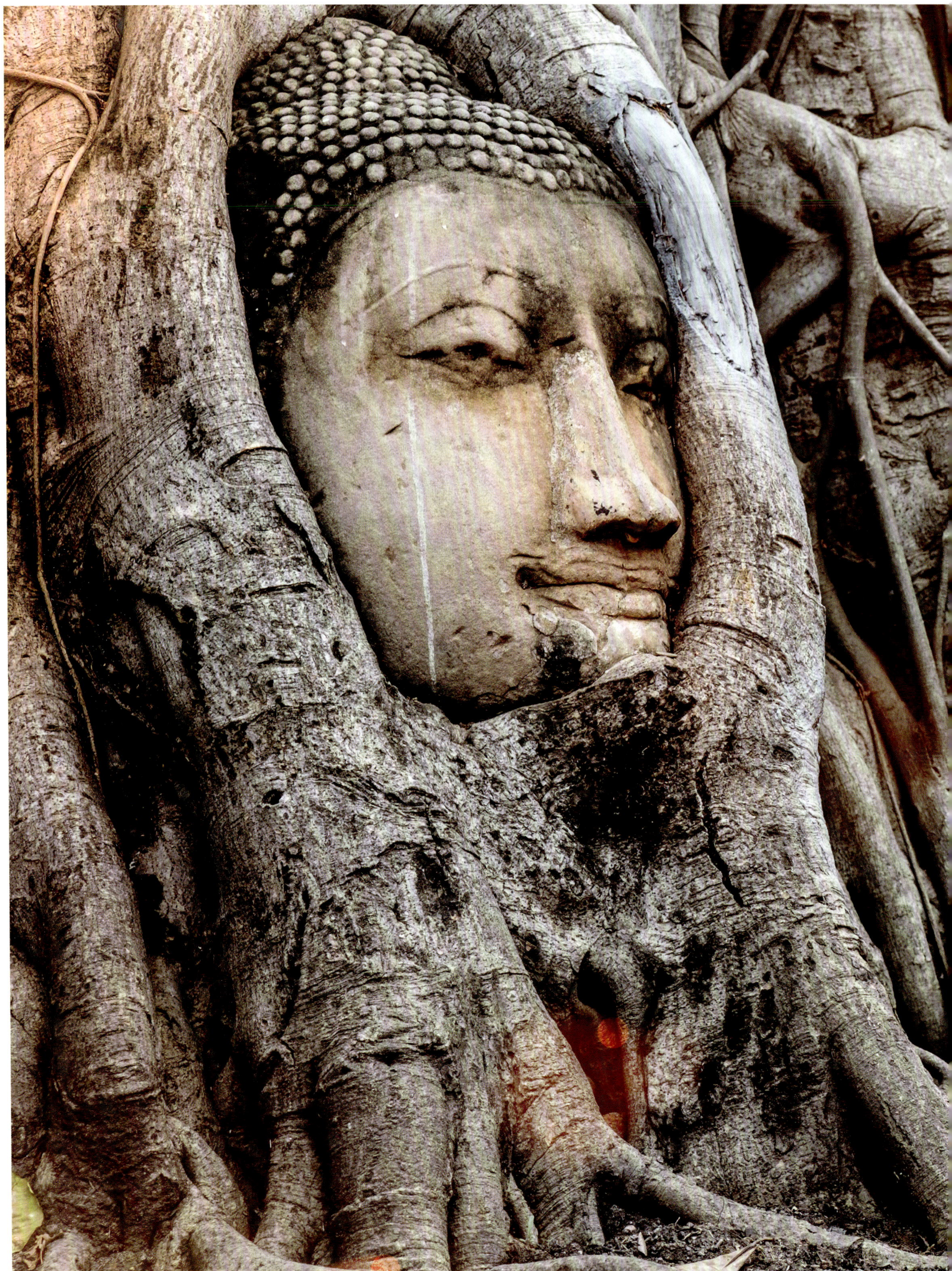

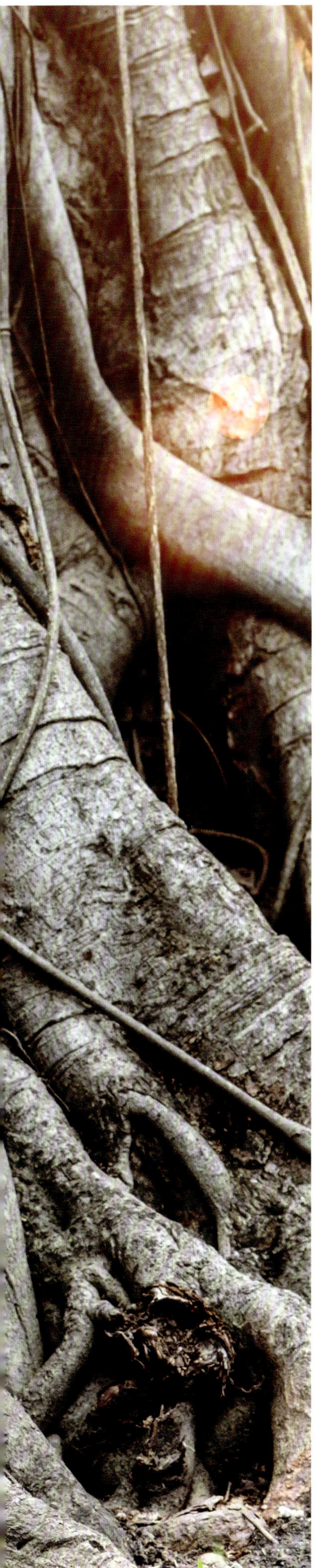

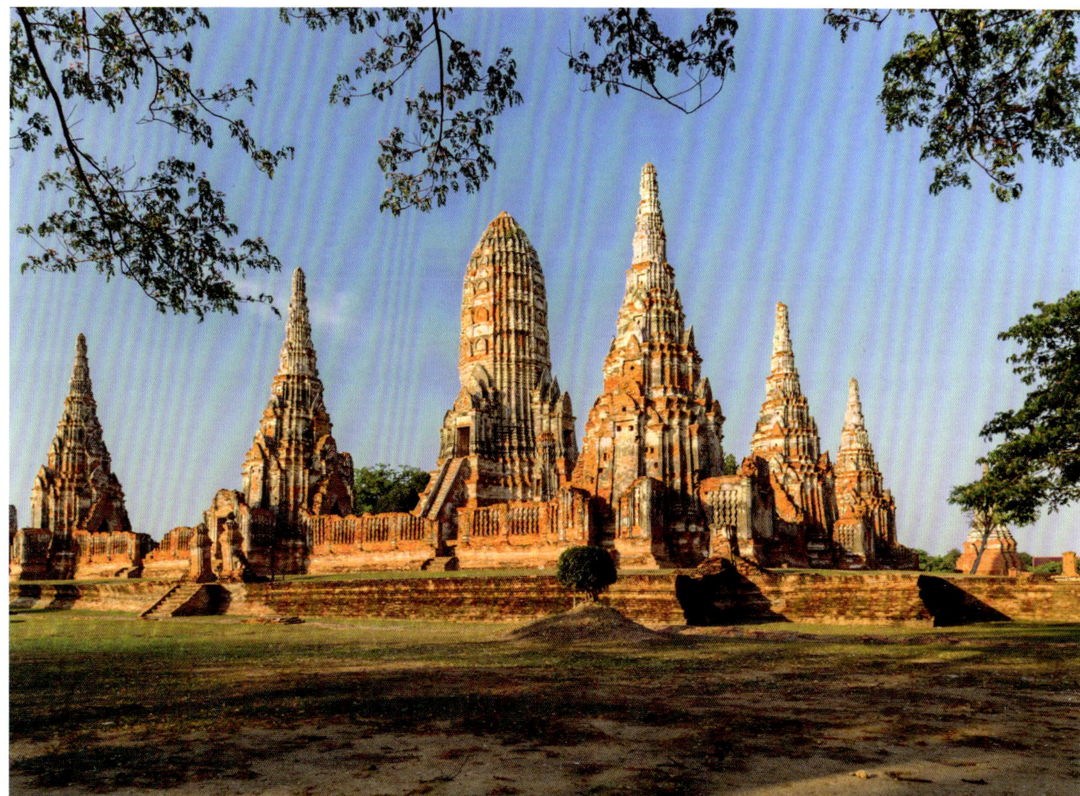

BOTH PHOTOGRAPHS:

Ayutthaya, Phra Nakhon Si Ayutthaya, Thailand

Wat Chaiwatthanaram (above) shows East Asian Buddhist architecture in full bloom. Built in 1630, the temple sits across the Chao Prya River from the older Ayutthaya island compound, the capital of the Siamese Kingdom from the 14th to the 18th centuries. Wat Chaiwatthanaram's 35-metre (115ft) main tower and four lesser spires represent Mount Meru and four symbolic continents. Along the walls once stood 120 Buddhas painted black and gold.

(Left) Next to Wat Mahathat, Bodhi tree roots enwrap a Buddha statue's head like a beard. Begun in 1374, the temple was later expanded with a gold-plated central tower. After taking the city in 1767, the Burmese set fire to the building and the tower fell down in 1904.

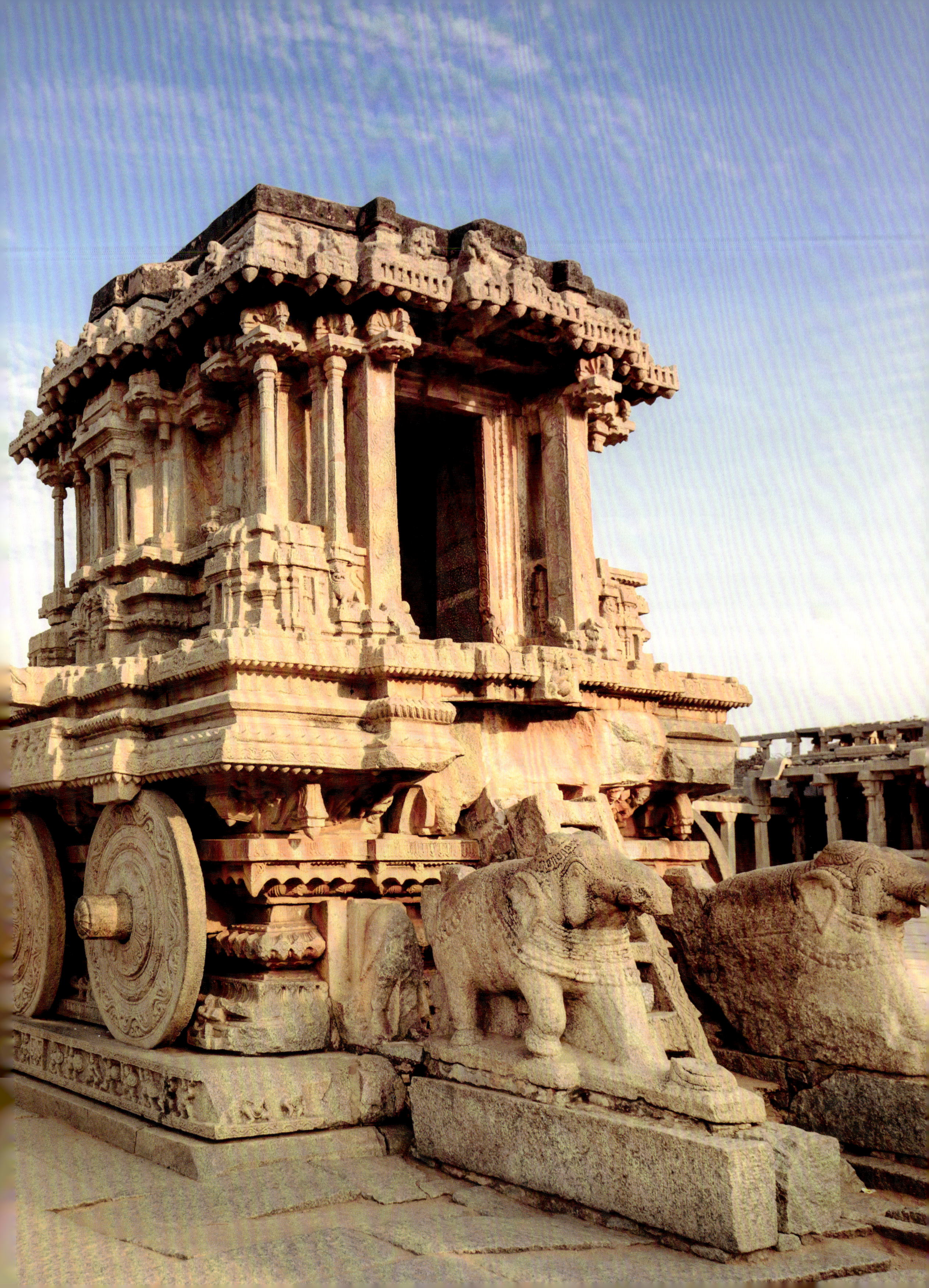

BOTH PHOTOGRAPHS:

Hampi, Karnataka, India

(Opposite) This colossal stone chariot in the courtyard of Vitalla Temple indicates the creativity of south Indian Hindu culture. Built in Dravidian style during King Krishnadevera's reign (1509–29), it was really a disguised shrine for Vishnu's escort Garuda. The temple is decorated with sculptures of warriors, horses, swans and elephants, and has 56 musical pillars that emit distinct notes when lightly tapped.

(Right) Hampi's Lotus Mahal Palace was probably a meeting place for royal women, hence secular in intent. Yet it has clear spiritual resonances. These carved stone arches blend Hindu with Muslim motifs, demonstrating the genius of south Indian craftsmen. Hampi grew up on the ruins of the city of Vijayanagar, the capital of the Vijayanagari Empire, which once reached from the centre of India down to the subcontinent's southern tip.

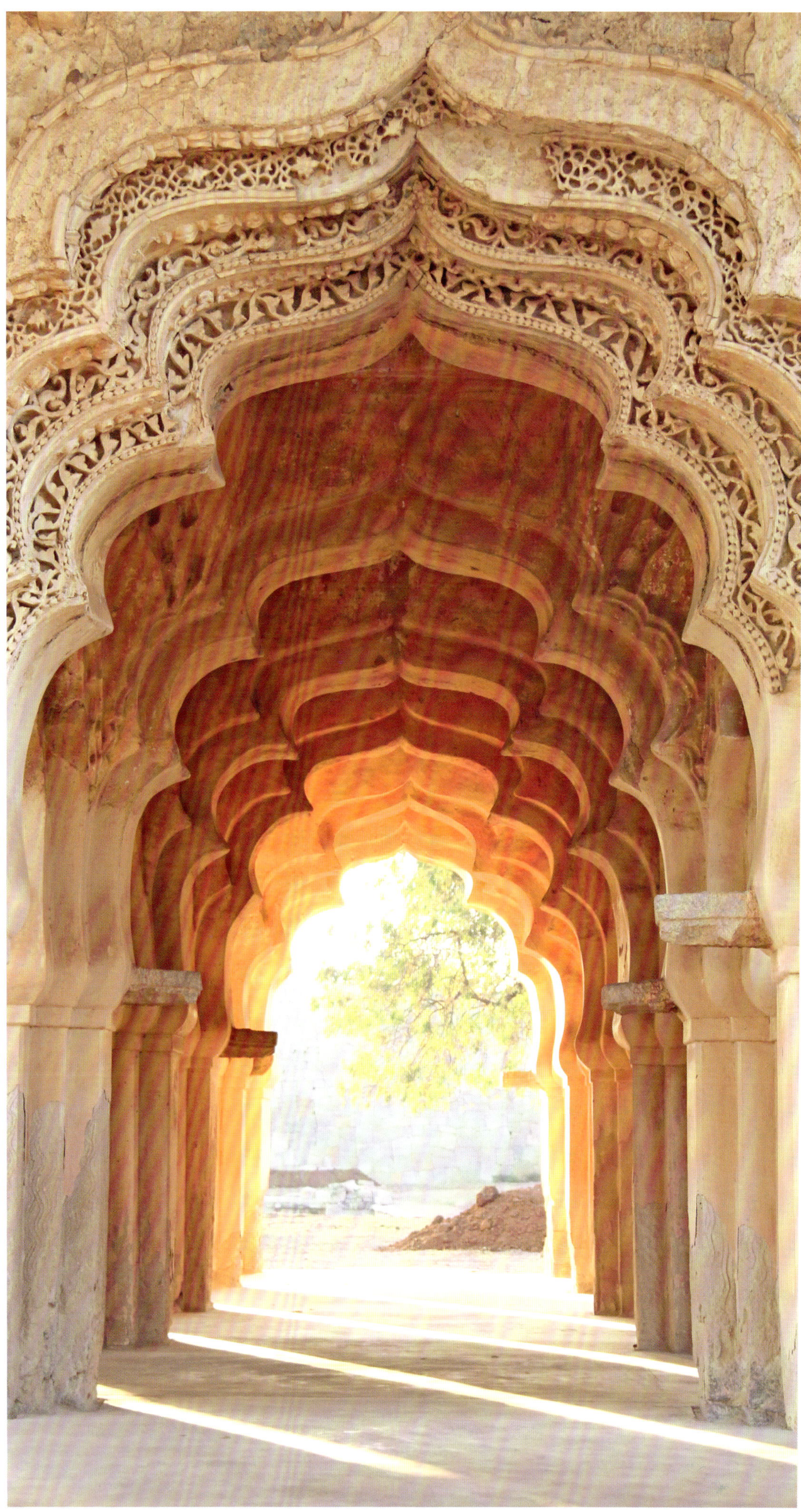

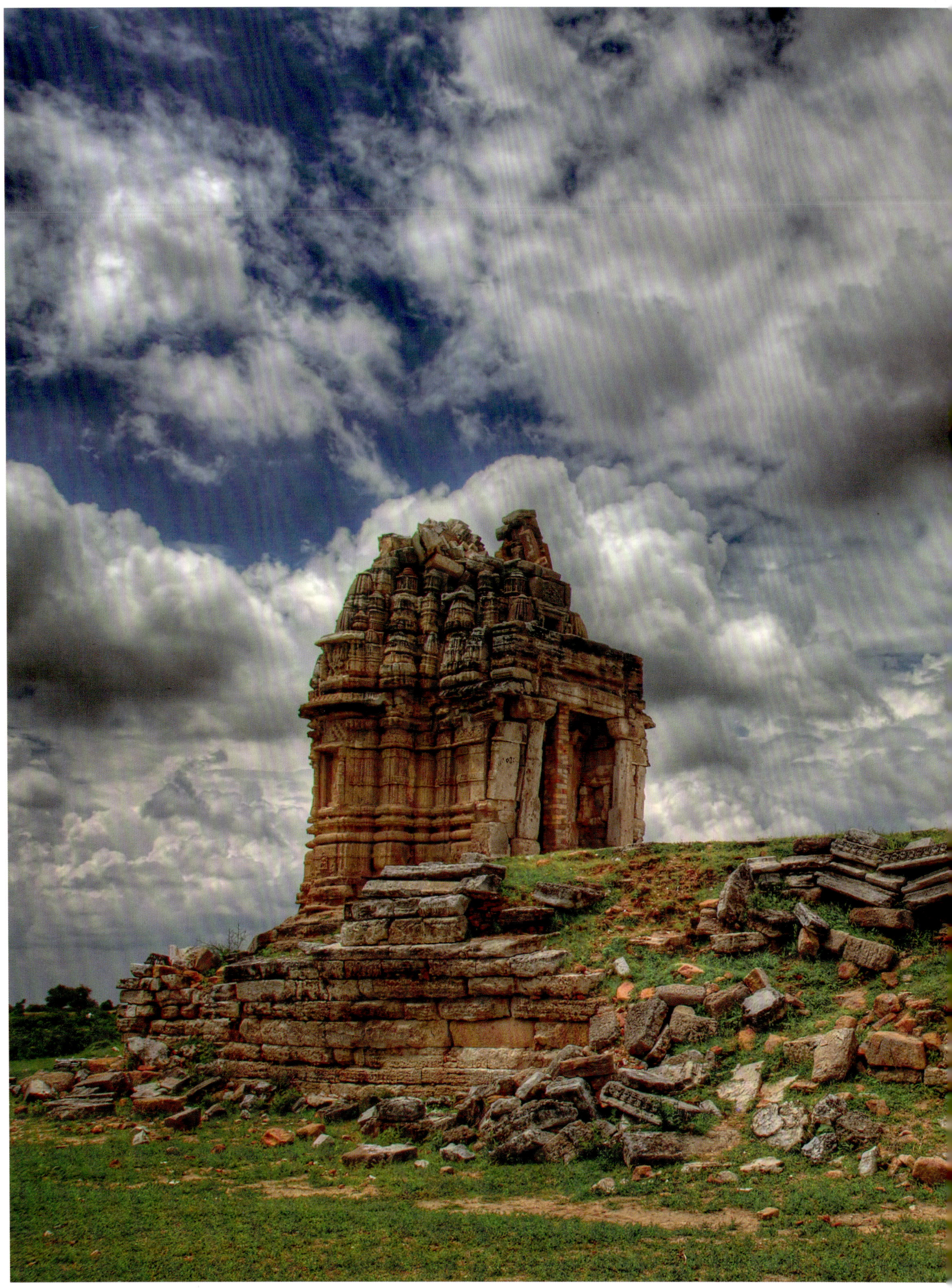

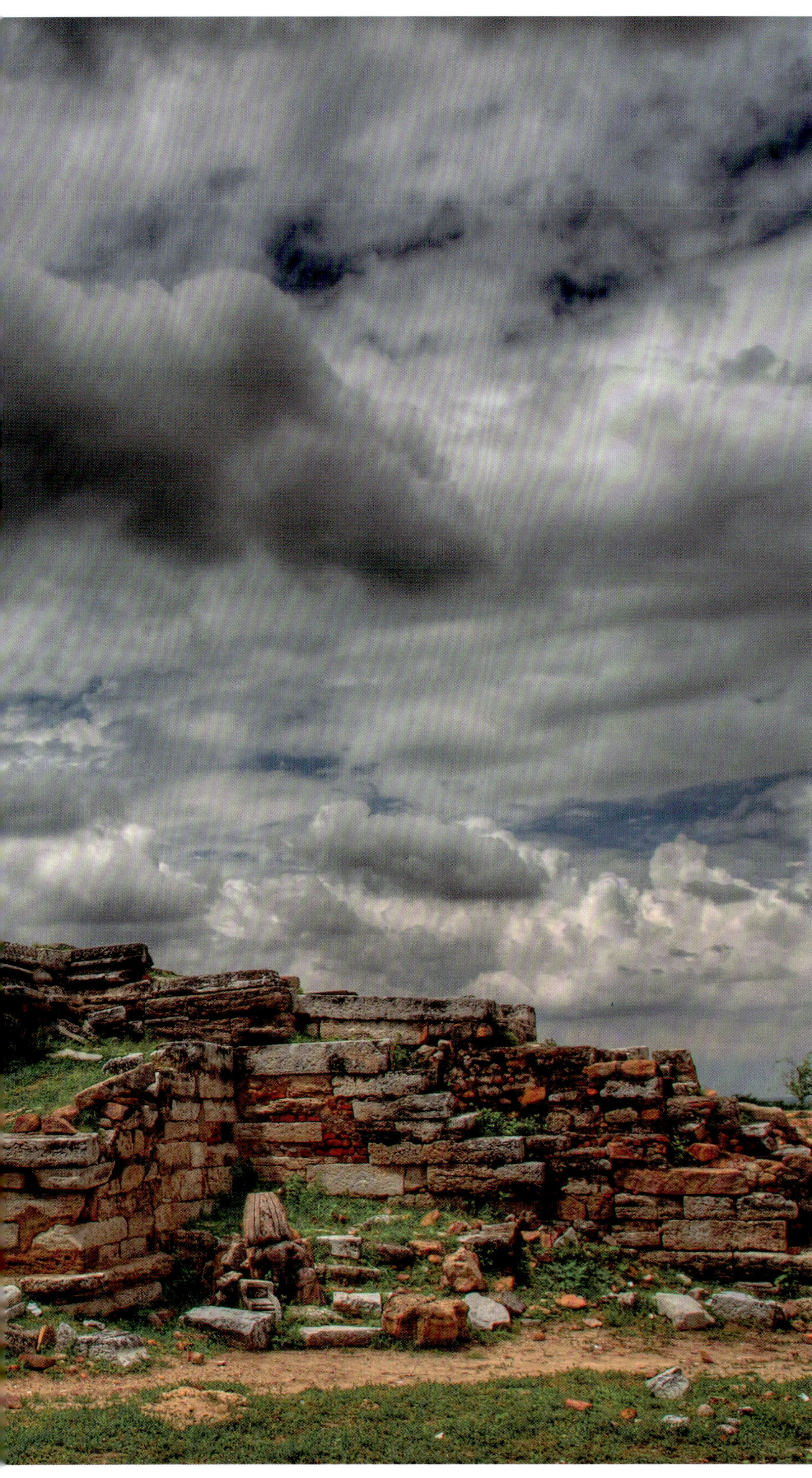

Bodhesar Jain Temple, Sindh, Pakistan
Exposed to the Thar Desert, this 9th century CE Jain temple is the oldest of three built near Bodhesar. Typically these temples have an open hall connected to an intermediate chamber. Raised on a platform, this one was built without mortar, but now its idols have been pilfered and many of its stones taken to build houses.

Shaped by the teachings of Mahariva, a 6th century BCE contemporary of Buddha, Jainism stresses reincarnation and peace to all living beings. Today Jain adherents constitute a tiny proportion of Pakistan's population. Those who didn't flee to India with Partition in 1947 generally left rural areas for the metropolis of Karachi.

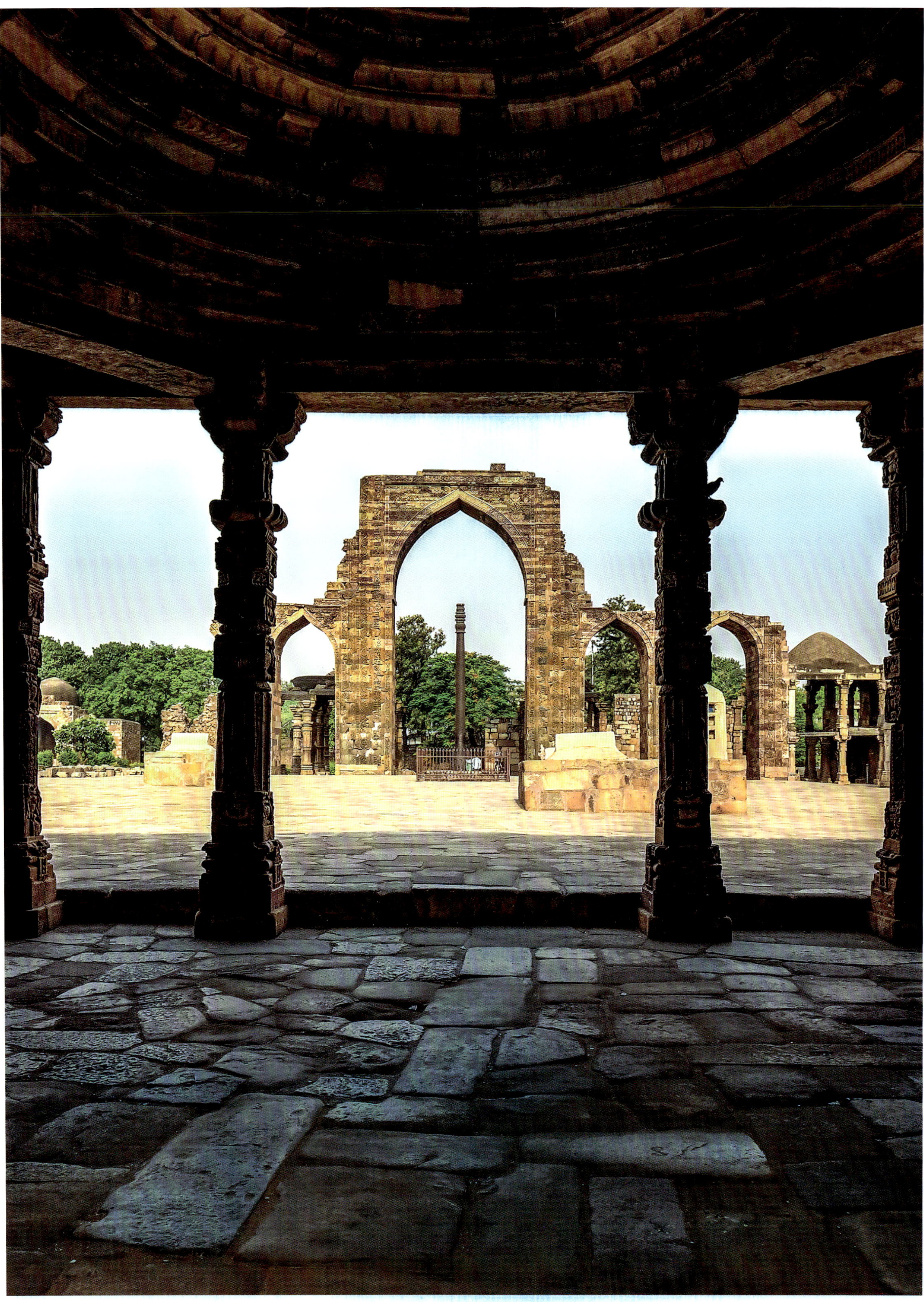

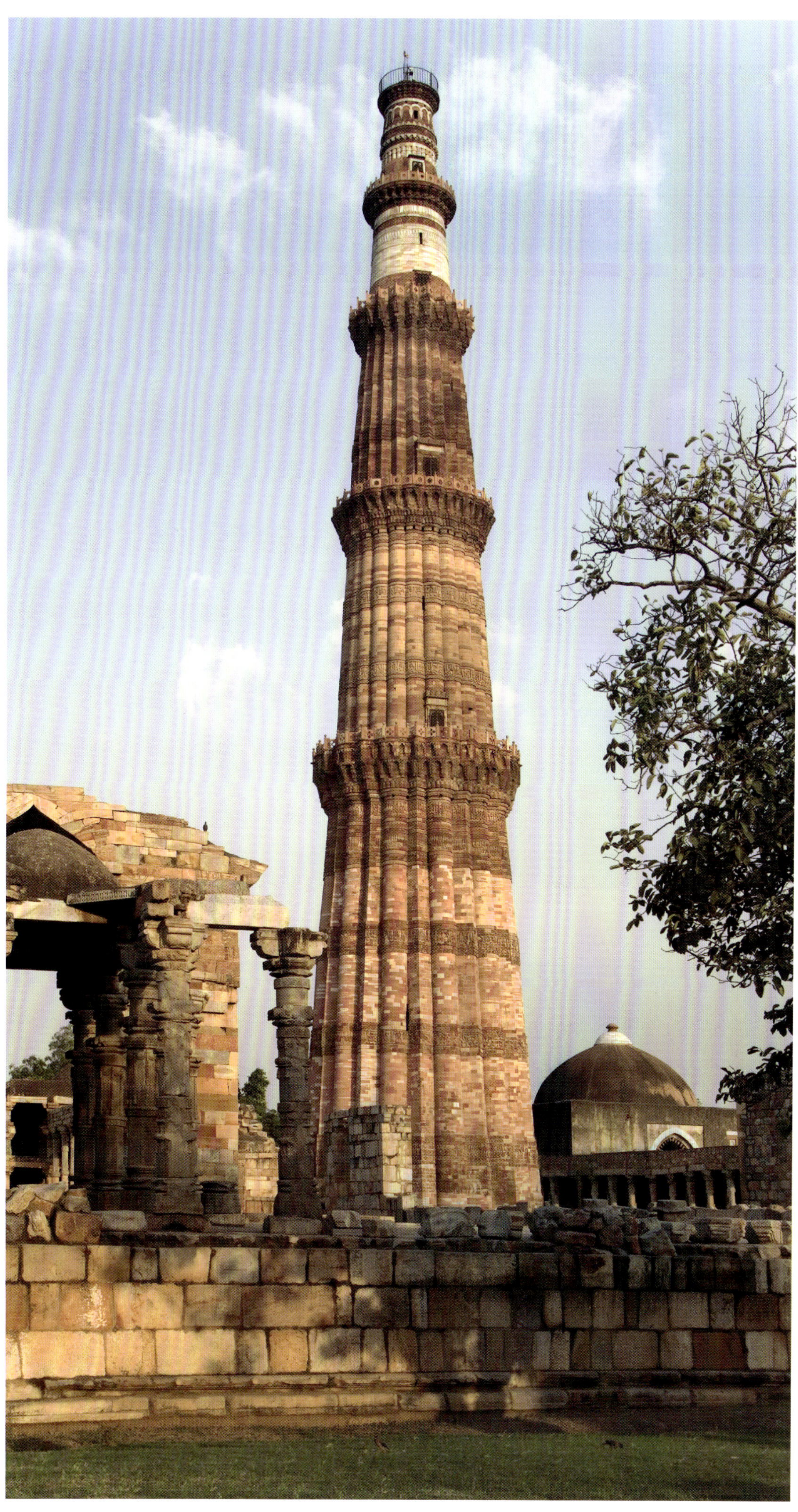

BOTH PHOTOGRAPHS:

Quwwat-ul-Islam Mosque, Delhi, India

Stunning vistas of intricately carved arches, columns and spires typify Quwwat-ul-Islam, Delhi's first mosque (opposite). The architecture evokes the Delhi Sultanate, a Muslim empire that ruled most of India for 320 years from the late 1300s.

(Left) The site is also known as Qutb Minar after the 73-metre-tall (240ft) minaret, which, like the mosque, was begun by Qutb-ud-Din Aibak, a Turkish-born slave turned general, after he captured Delhi in 1192. In his conquest, he reputedly destroyed 27 Hindu temples, using their stones for his building projects.

A century later, Ala-ud-Din Khalji (reigned 1296–1316) doubled the mosque's size and finished the minaret. The site declined after Mughals, Muslims from Central Asia, crushed the Sultanate and made Agra their capital in 1526.

Trai Tim Church, Nam Dinh, Vietnam

Looking like a charming piece of Normandy transplanted to the Vietnamese seaside, Trai Tim Catholic Church was built in 1927 when Vietnam was part of French Indochina. It still just about stands, but lost its last congregants in 1996. Like many churches and villages in Nam Dinh province, it has been the victim of coastal erosion. Yet its frame survives, as does a bell tower that once also served as a lighthouse.

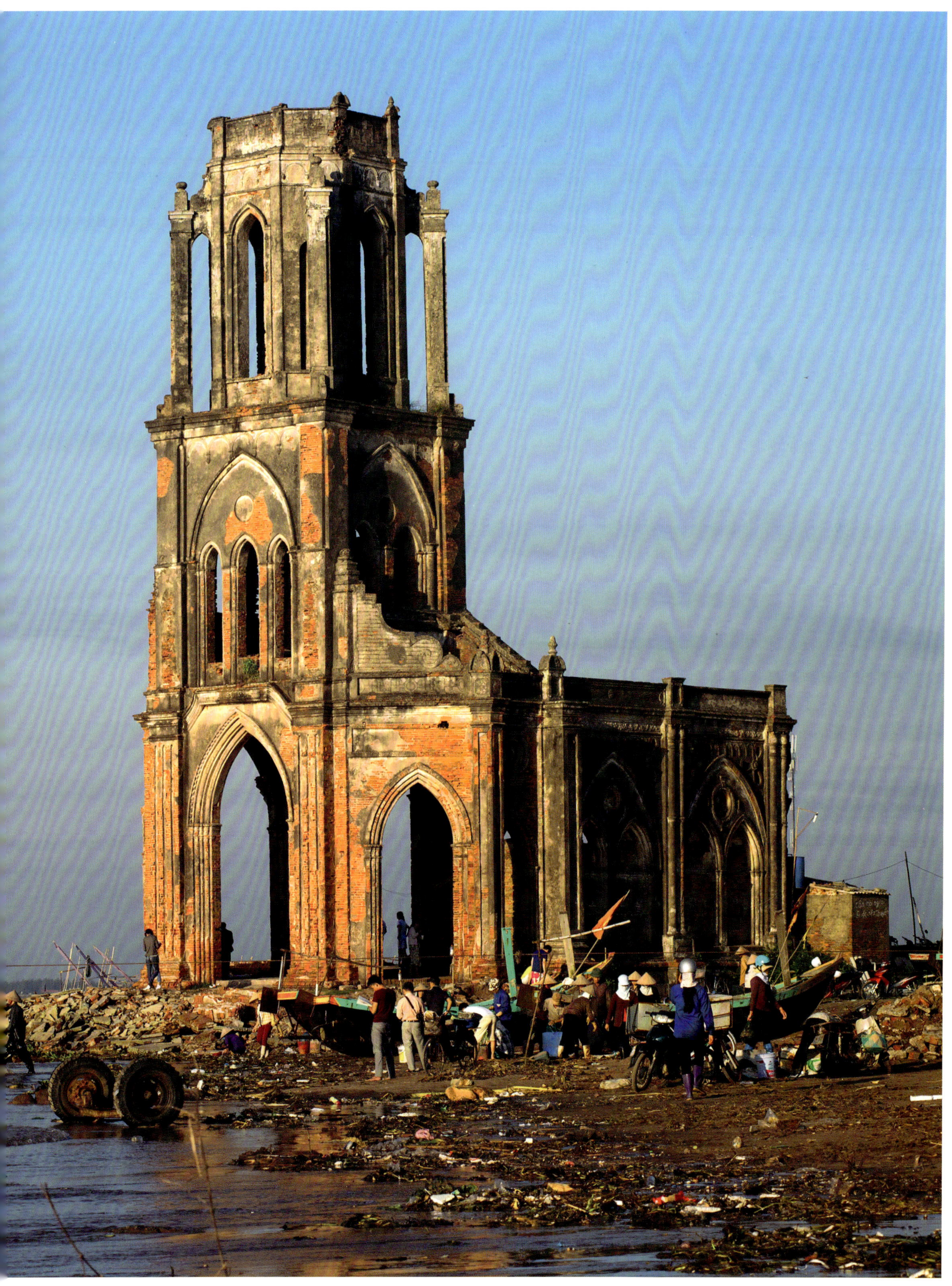

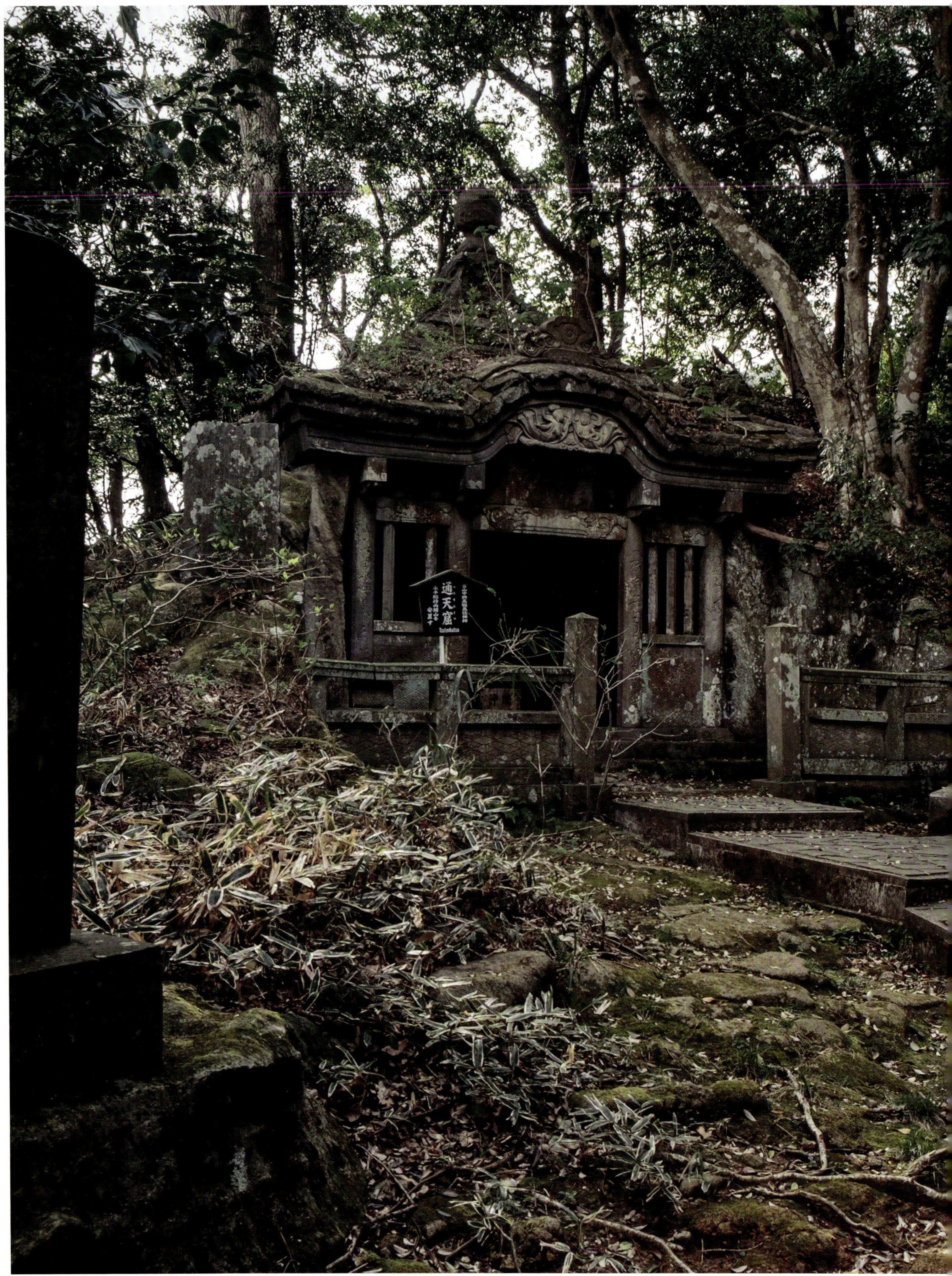
通天窟

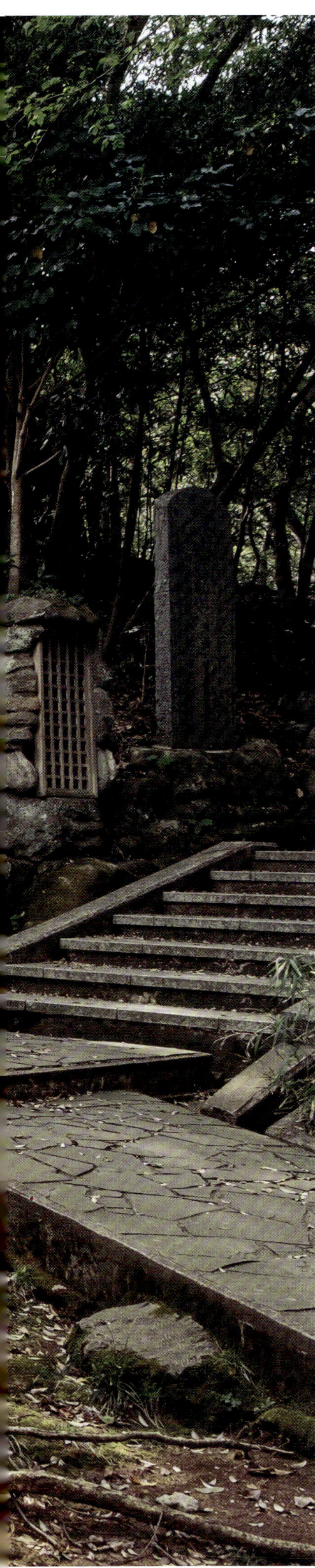

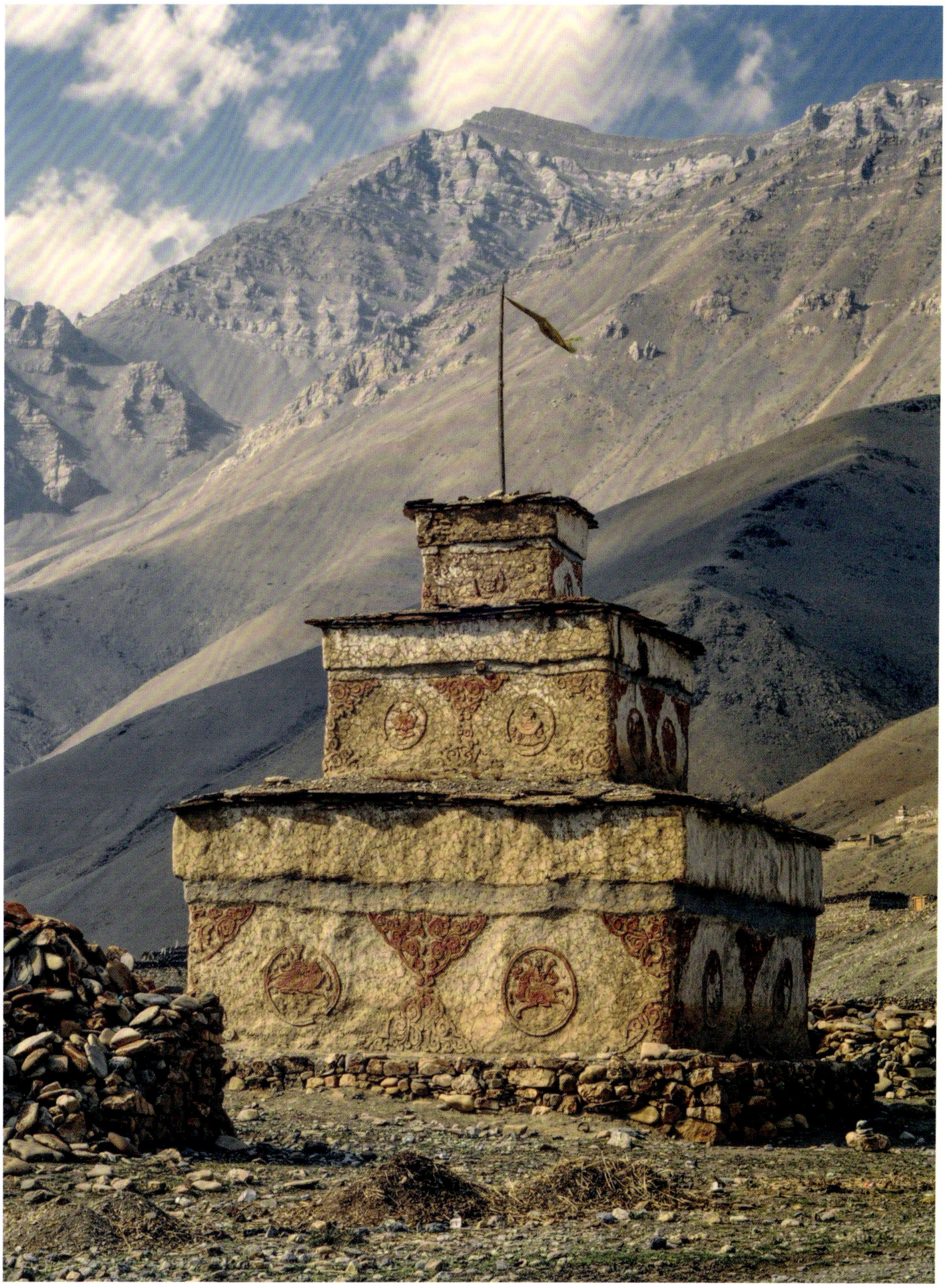

LEFT:
Nihon-ji shrine, Nokogiri, Honshu, Japan
The abandoned shrine of Nihon-ji lies in deep forest on the slopes of Mount Nokogiri. Founded by order of Emperor Shomu in 725 CE, the original Hosso Buddhist temple was burned down in 1331 and, in around 1745, was relocated to its present site. By then it was a Soto Zen sanctuary. Nihon-ji suffered damage during an 1868–74 anti-Buddhist purge and from an earthquake in 1939.

ABOVE:
Buddhist shrine, Nepal
A far cry from the majestic Buddhist structures from India, China and South-East Asia, this squat shrine in the Himalayas reminds us of the faith's simpler ascetic aspects. According to legend, the Buddha was born in Lumbini, Nepal. Despite that, the Nepali Rana dynasty (1846–1951) suppressed all attempts to revive the faith. While just 10 per cent of Nepalis today are Buddhists, many Hindus still observe its customs.

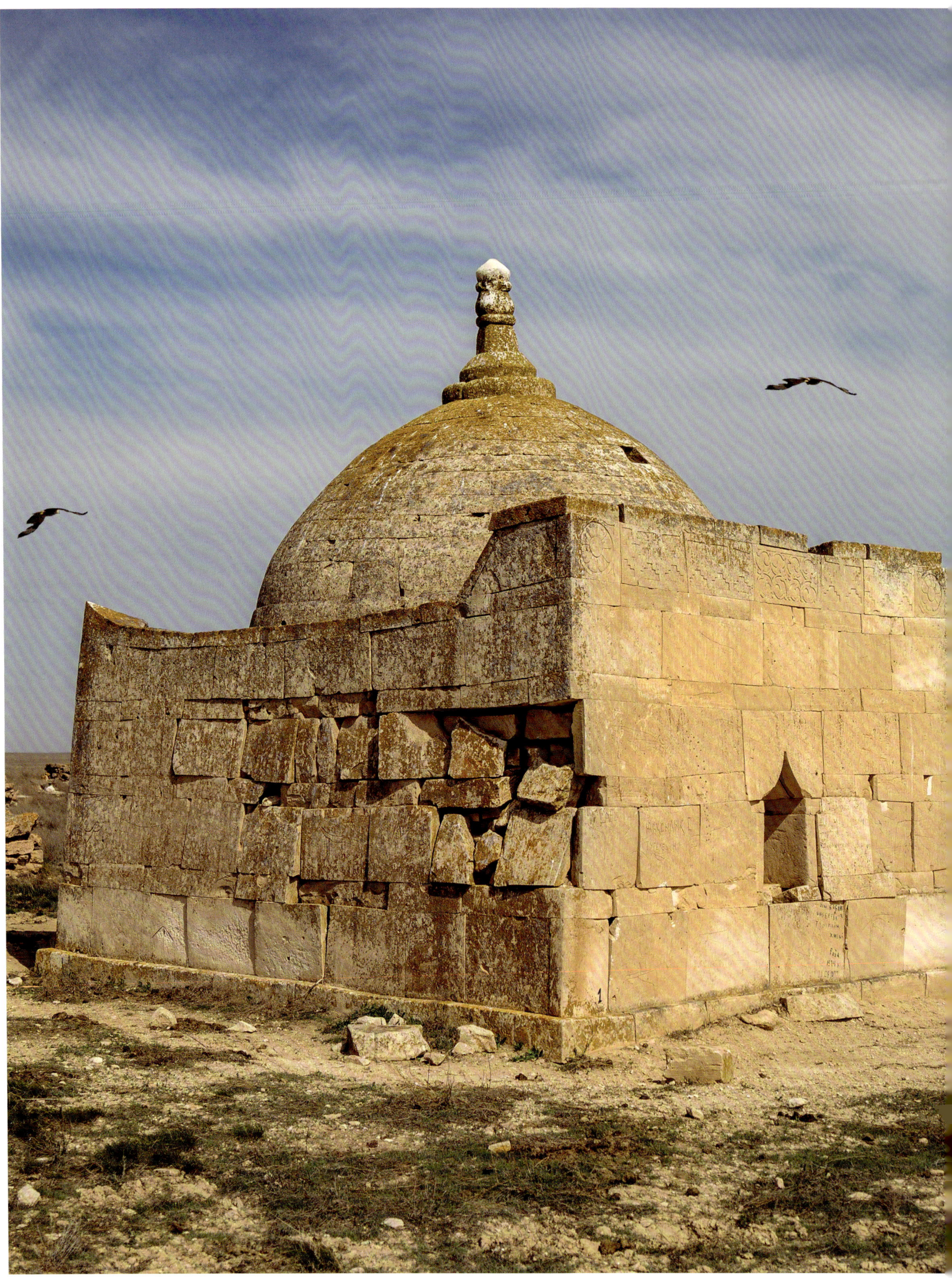

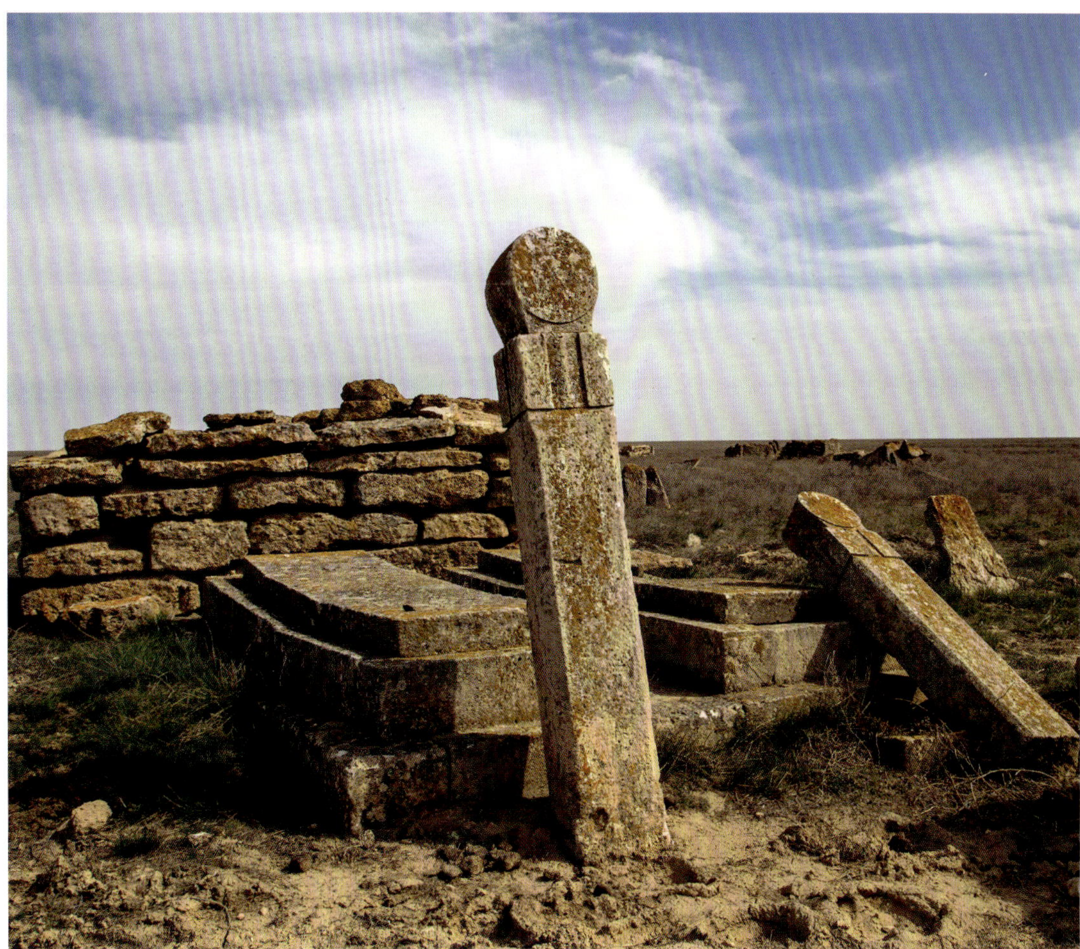

LEFT AND ABOVE:

City of the Dead, Mangistau Region, Kazakhstan

None but the dead and the occasional visitor are found at this once bustling crossroads along a Central Asian branch of the medieval Silk Road. These days the area occupies a largely inaccessible steppe by the Caspian Sea. But what makes it compelling is its city of the dead, where Muslim shrines, such as the one pictured (left), tell of wealthy merchants and Sufi saints. Of the 362 necropolises, some tombs are highly decorated and date back to the 10th century CE.

(Above) Not far away are solitary *shiraktas* – pillars featuring Koranic verses or adorned with images from a deceased person's life.

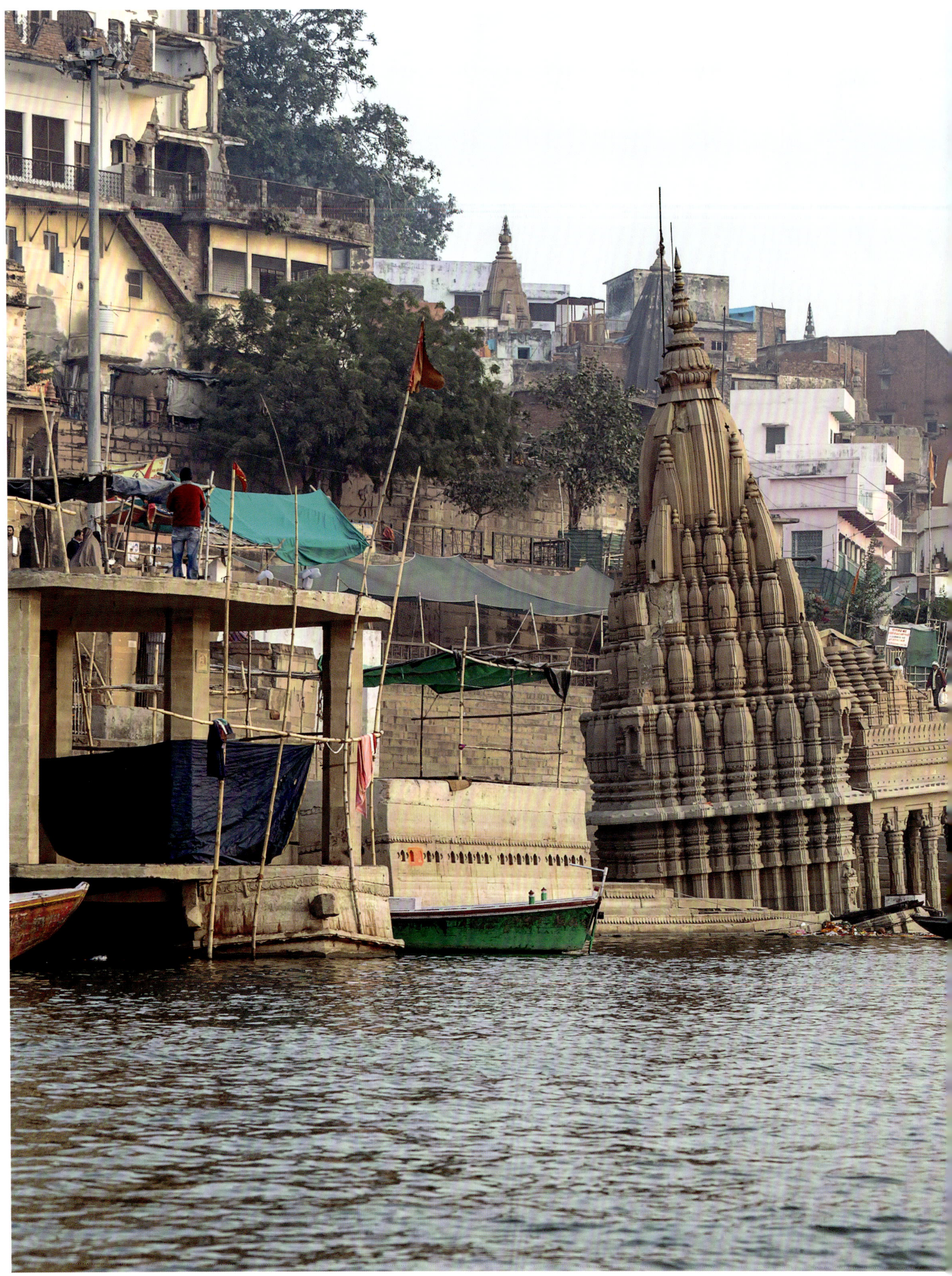

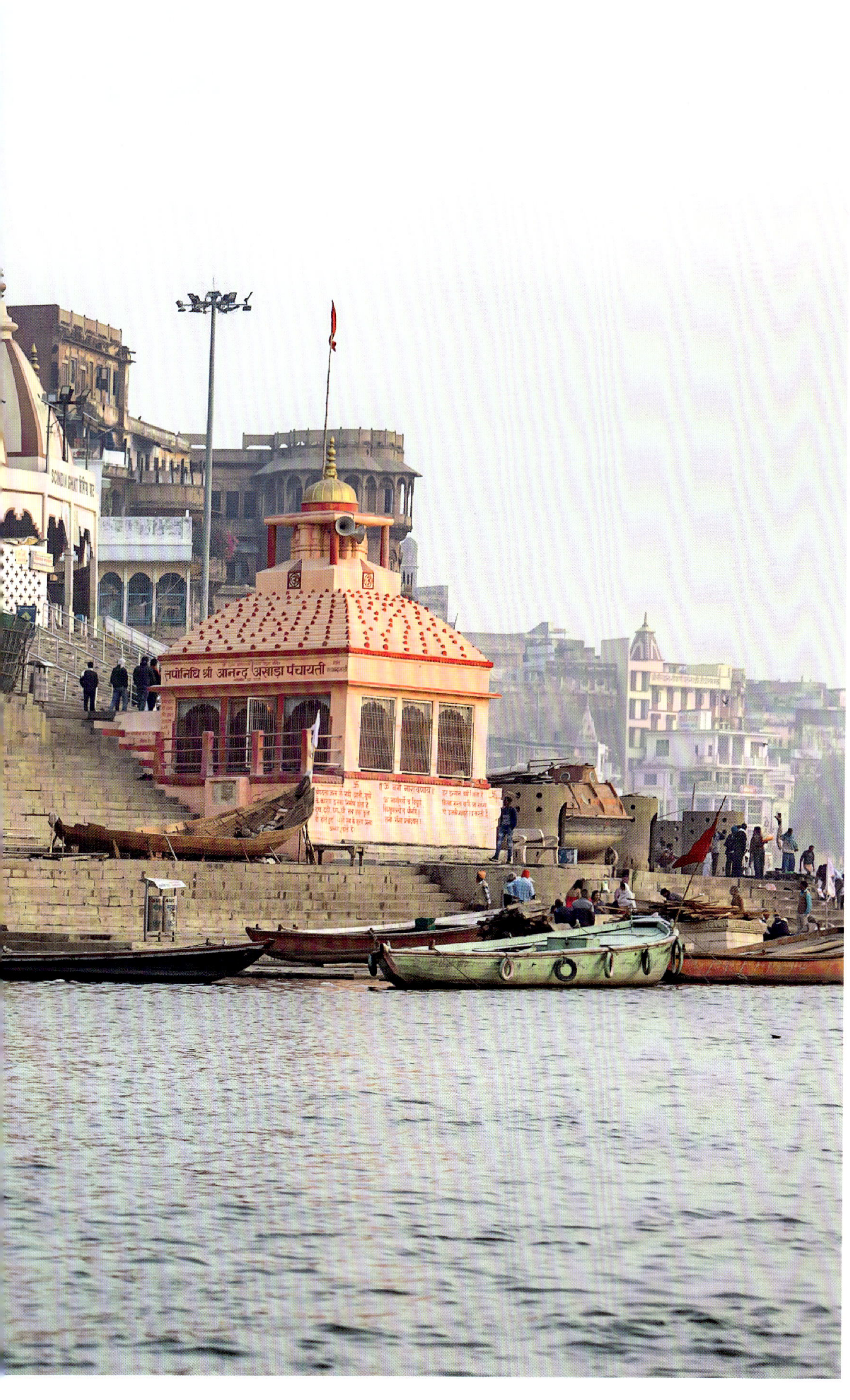

Shiva Temple, Scindia Ghat, Varanasi, Uttar Pradesh, India
Sliding awkwardly into the holy River Ganges, this temple in Varanasi (Benares) reminds us that nature can be as cruel to sacred sites as humans. The shrine most likely collapsed under its own weight, yet still half-rests on a ghat, a stairway leading to the waterline. Some ghats are for bathing, others for cremation. This one, dedicated to Shiva, the legendary founder of Varanasi, was funded by the Scindia dynasty and built by women in 1830.

Each year millions of Hindus visit Varanasi to wash away their sins in the Ganges. Each spot along the river has its own properties. The area around the Scindia Ghat is famed as the birthplace of Agni, Hindu god of fire, and devotees pray here for a son.

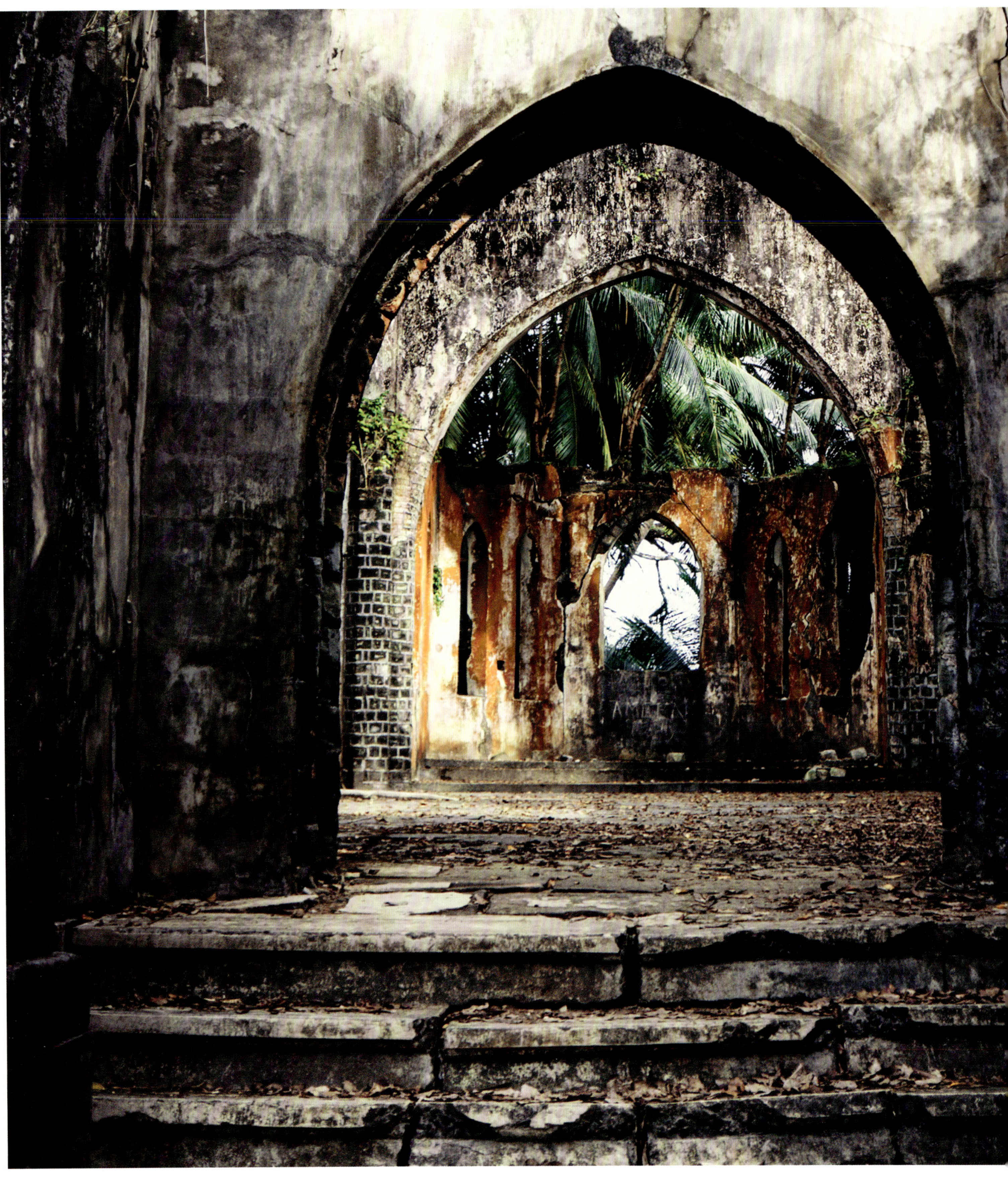

BOTH PHOTOGRAPHS:

Presbyterian Church, Ross Island, Andaman Islands, Indian Ocean

Like a scene out of a tropical horror movie, the church on Ross Island in the Bay of Bengal shows cracked flagstones and faded walls invaded by jungle fronds. In some places mangrove roots have taken over walls, quite possibly holding them in place.

The stone-built chapel was once a proud structure with Burma teak frames and beautifully etched Italian stained glass windows. It served a British penal colony, established after the Indian Rebellion of 1857. In 1941, the island and church suffered two major blows: an earthquake and then capture by Japanese forces, who turned it into a POW camp. The Japanese plan to use the Andamans as a launch pad to invade India, however, never came to fruition.

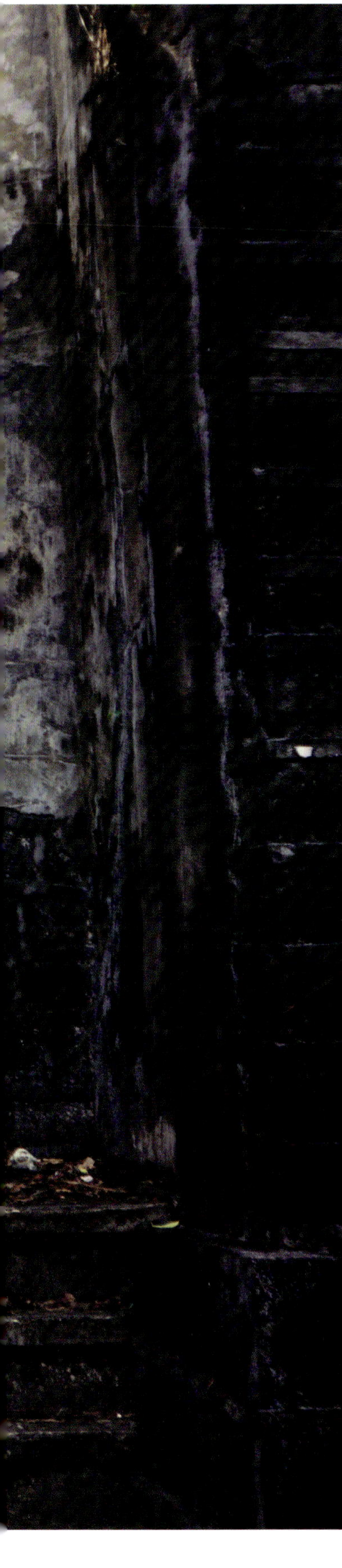

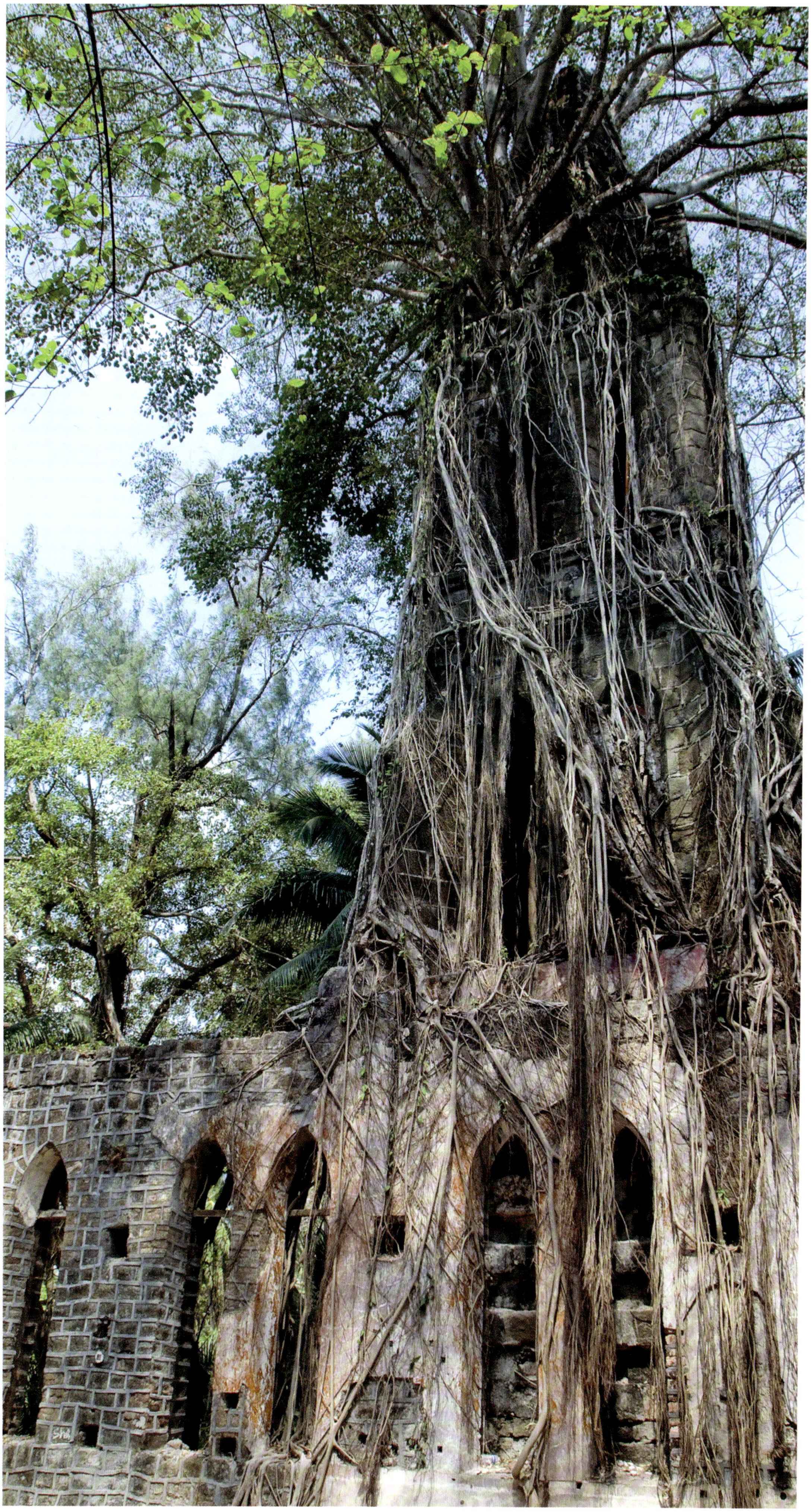

'Chicken Church', Central Java, Indonesia

Daniel Alamsjah says that he was working in Jakarta when a heavenly voice told him to create a sanctuary for all – Muslim, Christian, Buddhist, even atheist. The location for his prayer house would be 550km (342 miles) away in a plot in Java's Magelang Hills. And, despite the nickname 'Chicken Church' (Gereja Ayam), it was meant to resemble a dove, not a fowl.

Construction began in 1992 with the help of 30 villagers, but stopped eight years later when funds ran out and rumours spread that a Christian wanted to convert Muslims. The building barely survived, but tourists flocked in when news about the fantastical project went viral in 2015. Takings from Alamsjah's museum and café are now funding renovations.

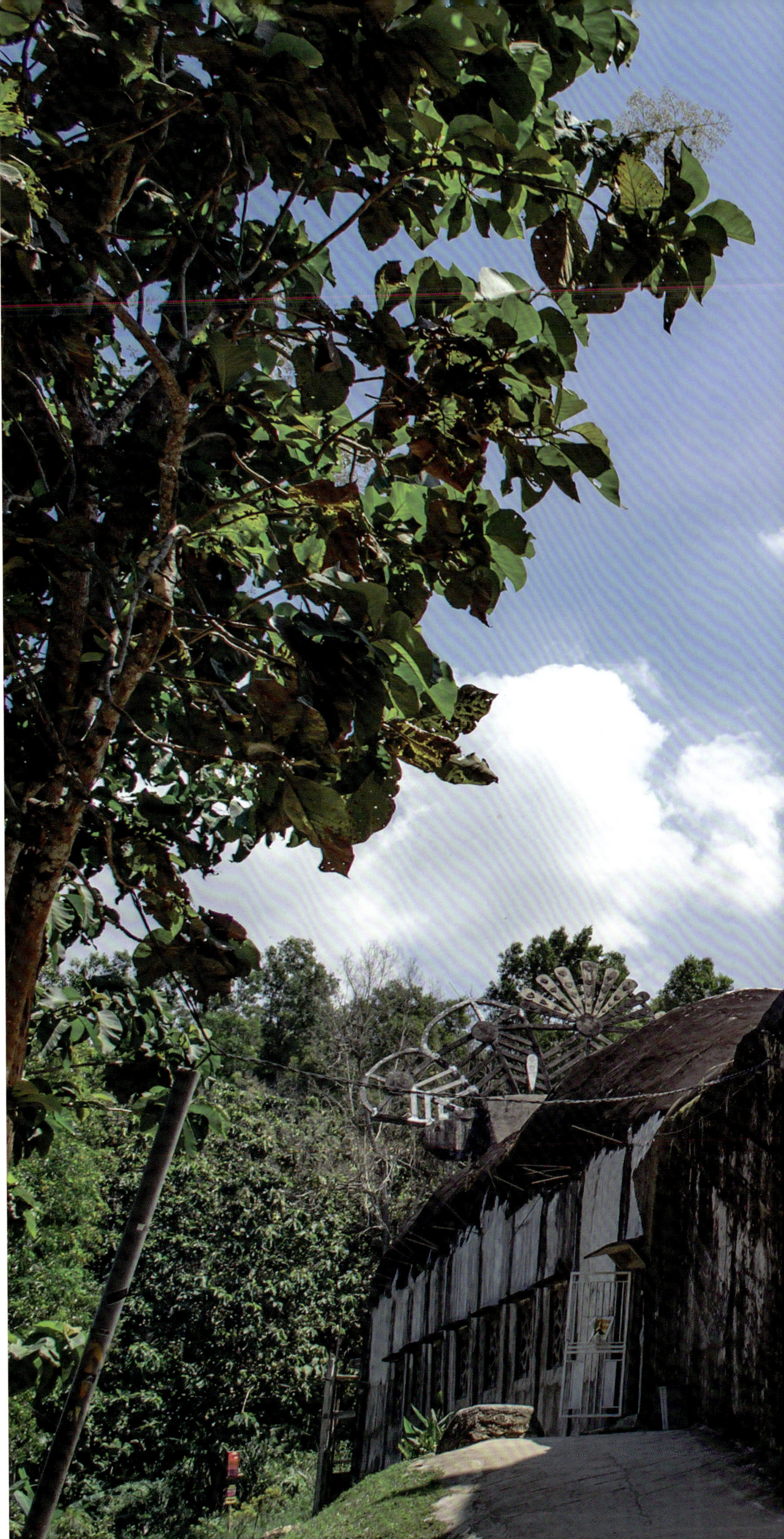

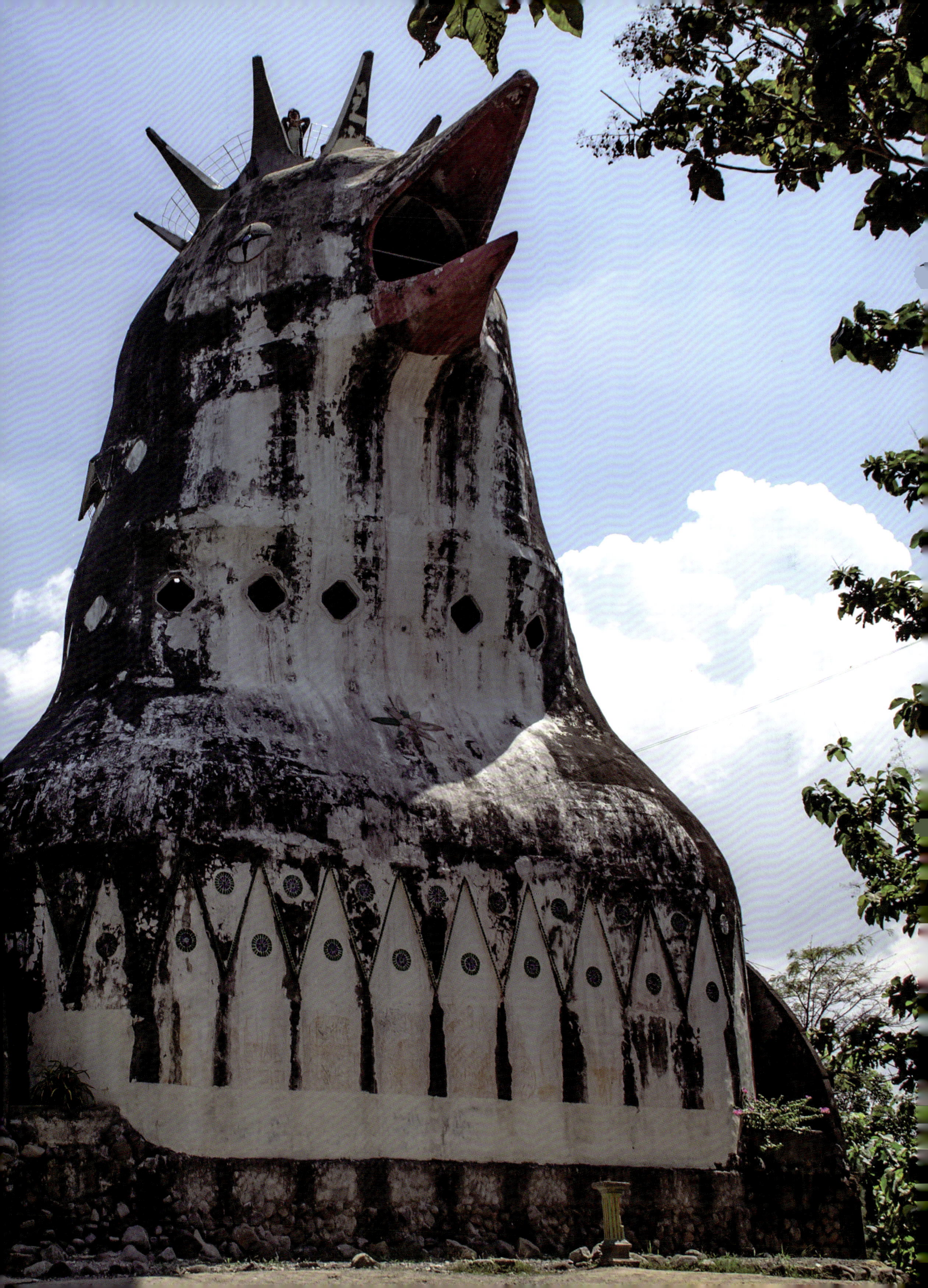

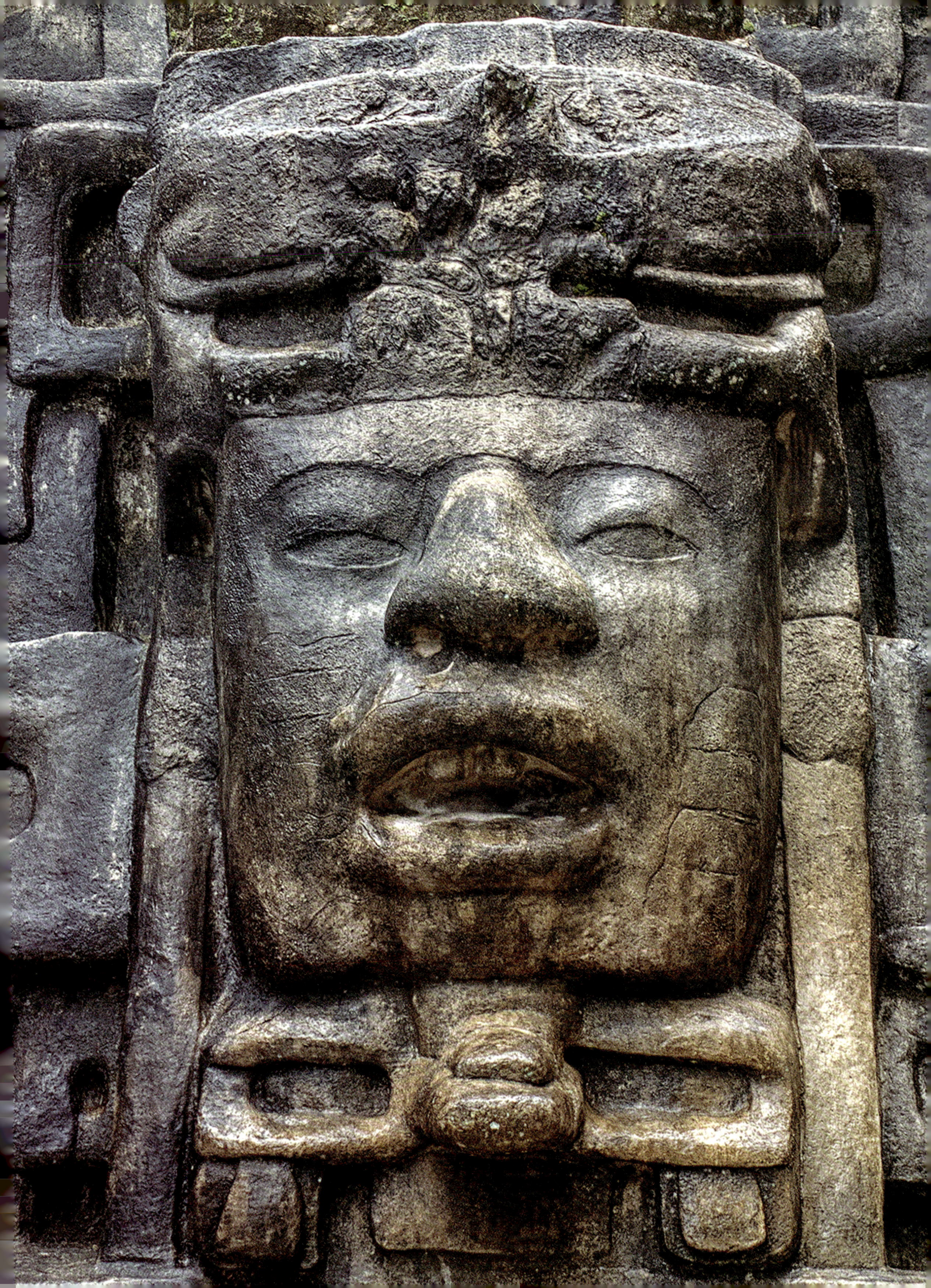

The Americas And The Pacific

Scientists believe that humans first began migrating across the Bering Strait from Siberia to the Americas well over 20,000 years ago. They left behind a trail of artefacts and sacred sites from Alaska in the north to Tierra del Fuego in the south. Only 500 years ago did new immigrants from the West arrive to add their own layers of history. Their appearance had a devastating effect on locals, more often through disease than military conflict. Religious conquest, however, also played its part.

Arguably what survives today of sacred sites is just the tip of the iceberg – earlier structures may have been made of degradable wood, not resilient stone, and hence have long been lost. Some sacred places in these pages, however, are natural formations, such as Guatape in Colombia, or are a cunning adaptation of the environment, such as the Inca Moray circular terraces in Peru.

For the most part, though, the holy sites are manmade, and their construction often defies easy explanation. For without advanced technology, or even beasts of burden, the Maya, for instance, managed to build pyramids to rival those of Egypt.

This tells us two things. Firstly, that only a powerful political authority could corral so many thousands of citizen-labourers to build these structures. Secondly, these holy places were built to last even longer than grand palaces.

OPPOSITE:

Mask Temple, Lamanai, Belize

Peering out across the ages, this gigantic stone-hewn face of an ancient king adorns the Mayan Mask Temple at Lamanai. The edifice covers two tombs and was built between c.200 BCE and c.450 CE, and modified until c.1300 CE. Mayas first settled there in the 16th century BCE, making it probably the longest continuously inhabited site in Central America.

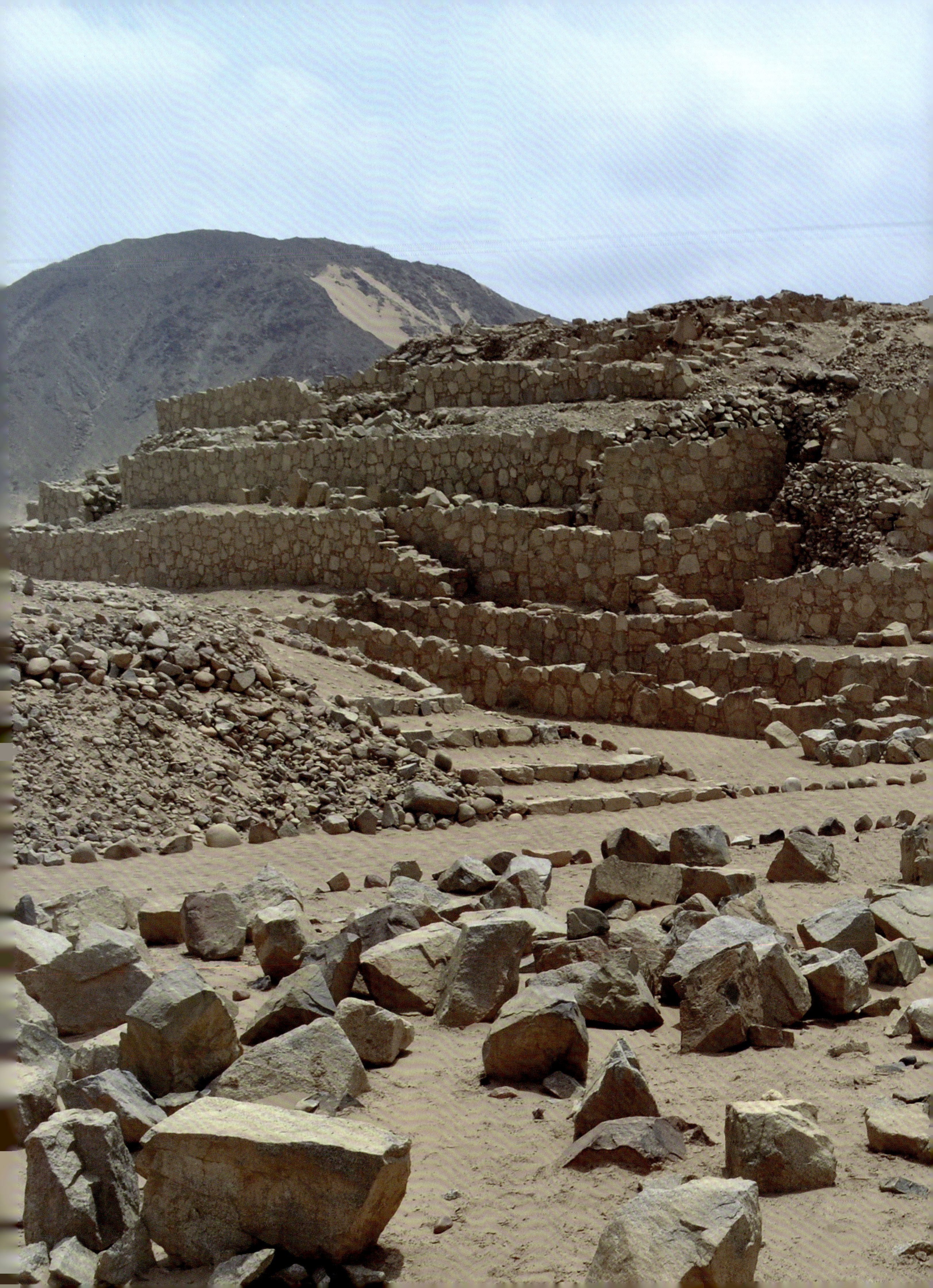

Caral-Supe, Barranca, Peru

An uncut stone stepped pyramid – the oldest known in the world – stands at the centre of the site marking the Americas' most ancient civilization. Caral-Supe covers 626 hectares (1547 acres) and dates back 5000 years. The very act of construction carried religious significance; etchings of a fanged staff-wielding god were found in a nearby valley. Abandoned c.1500 BCE – nearly three millennia before the Incas – it was resettled c.1000 BCE and again during 900–1400 CE; but only around the outskirts, leaving its monumental architecture undisturbed.

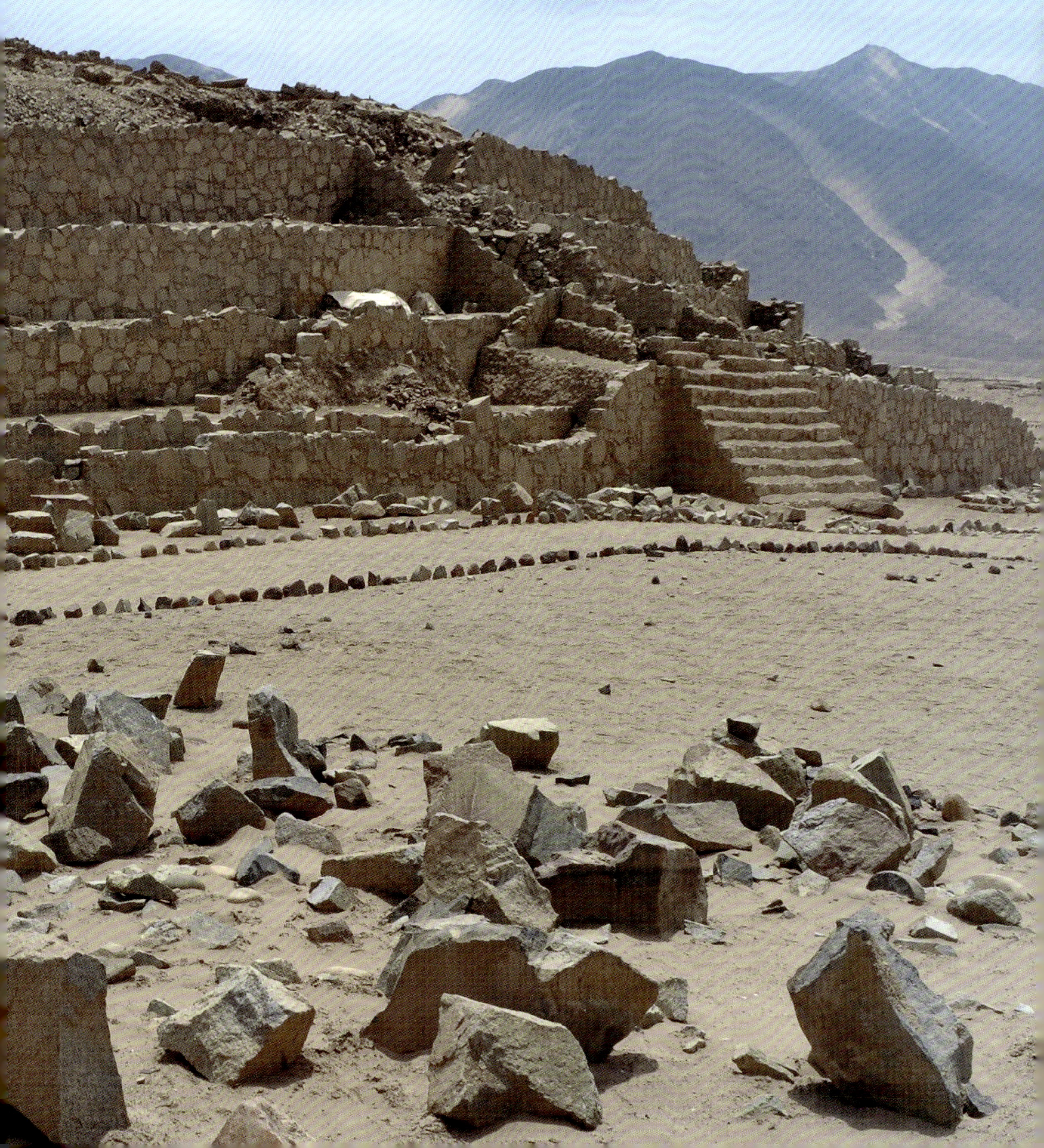

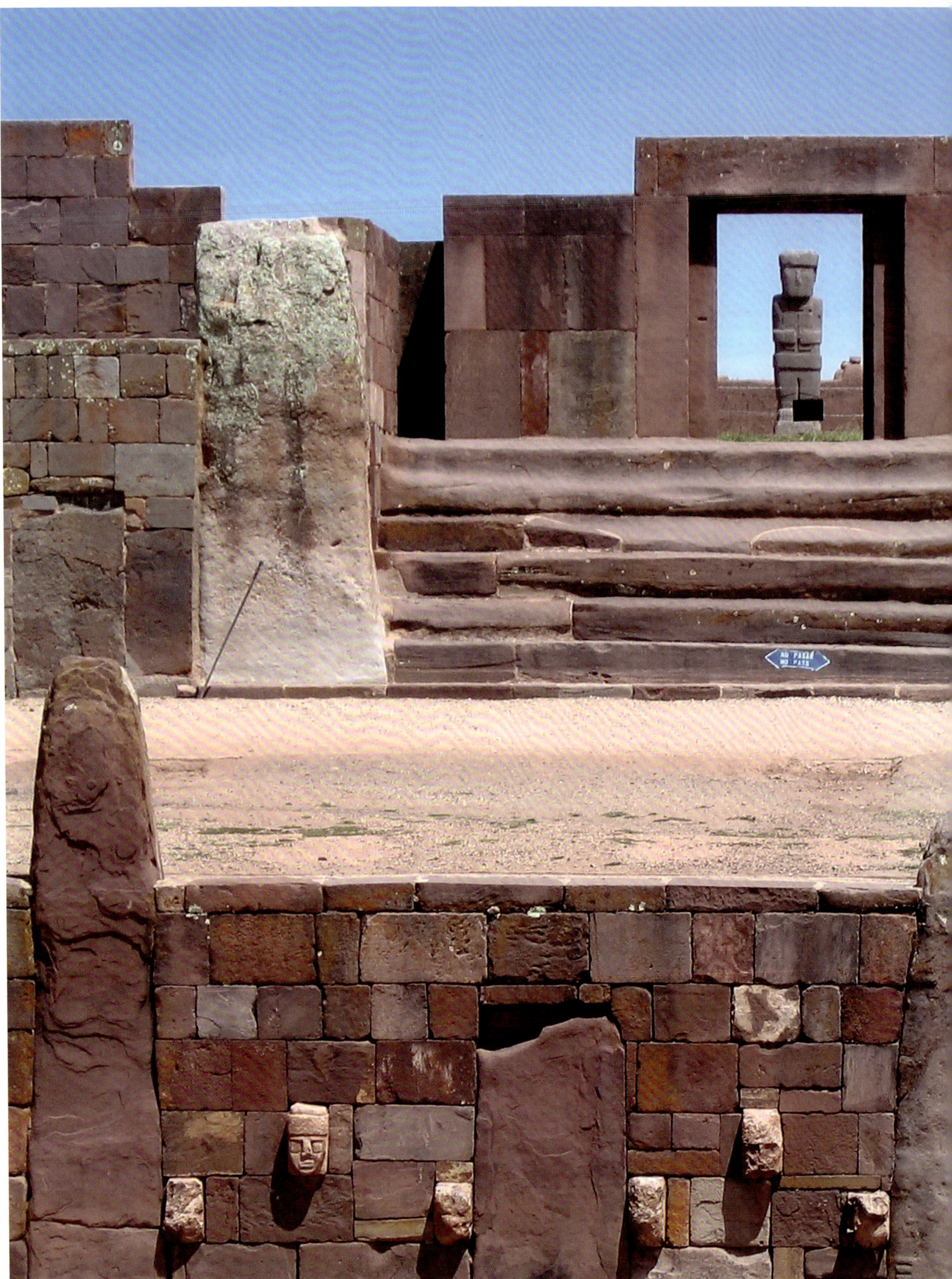

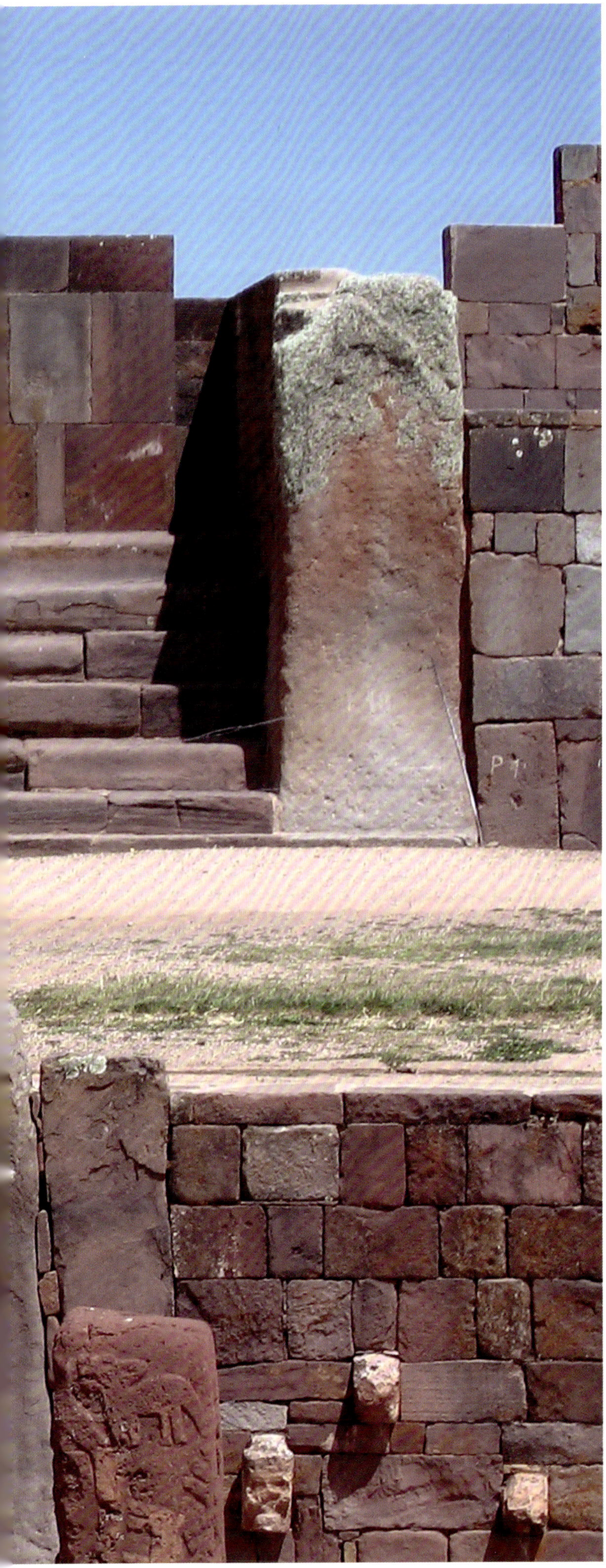

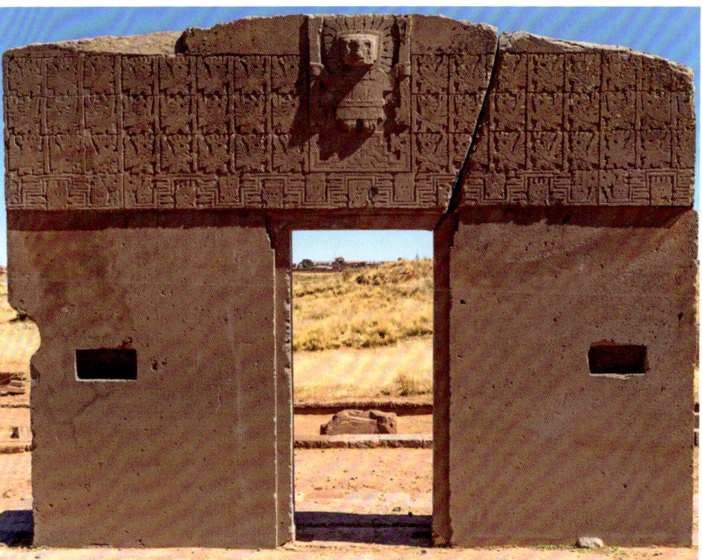

LEFT:

Temple of the Sun, Tiwanaku, Bolivia

Framed by a square gateway, the Ponce Monolith surveys an esplanade at Tiwanaku, on the southern shore of Lake Titicaca. The 3.5-metre-tall (11.5ft) statue may represent a stone giant in pan-Andean mythology, or a fertility symbol. He guards the nearby Kalasasaya 'standing stones' open temple, and once wore coloured textiles stapled with gold pins. At equinoxes the sun shines directly onto the monolith, evidence of the astronomical sophistication of the pre-Inca Tiwanaku Empire, which ruled between c.200–1000 CE.

ABOVE:

Gateway of the Sun, Tiwanaku, Bolivia

Tiwanaku's majestic Gateway of the Sun stands alone on a man-made platform called Pumapunku, or 'door of the puma'. Closer inspection of the gate reveals icons of the Staff God, attendants with bird and human heads and three-dimensional geometric patterns chiselled with extraordinary precision. Along an east-west axis lies the matching, if less ornate, Moon Gate. At its height, 20,000 people might have lived in Tiwanaku, which probably means 'stone in the centre' – or, metaphorically, centre of the world.

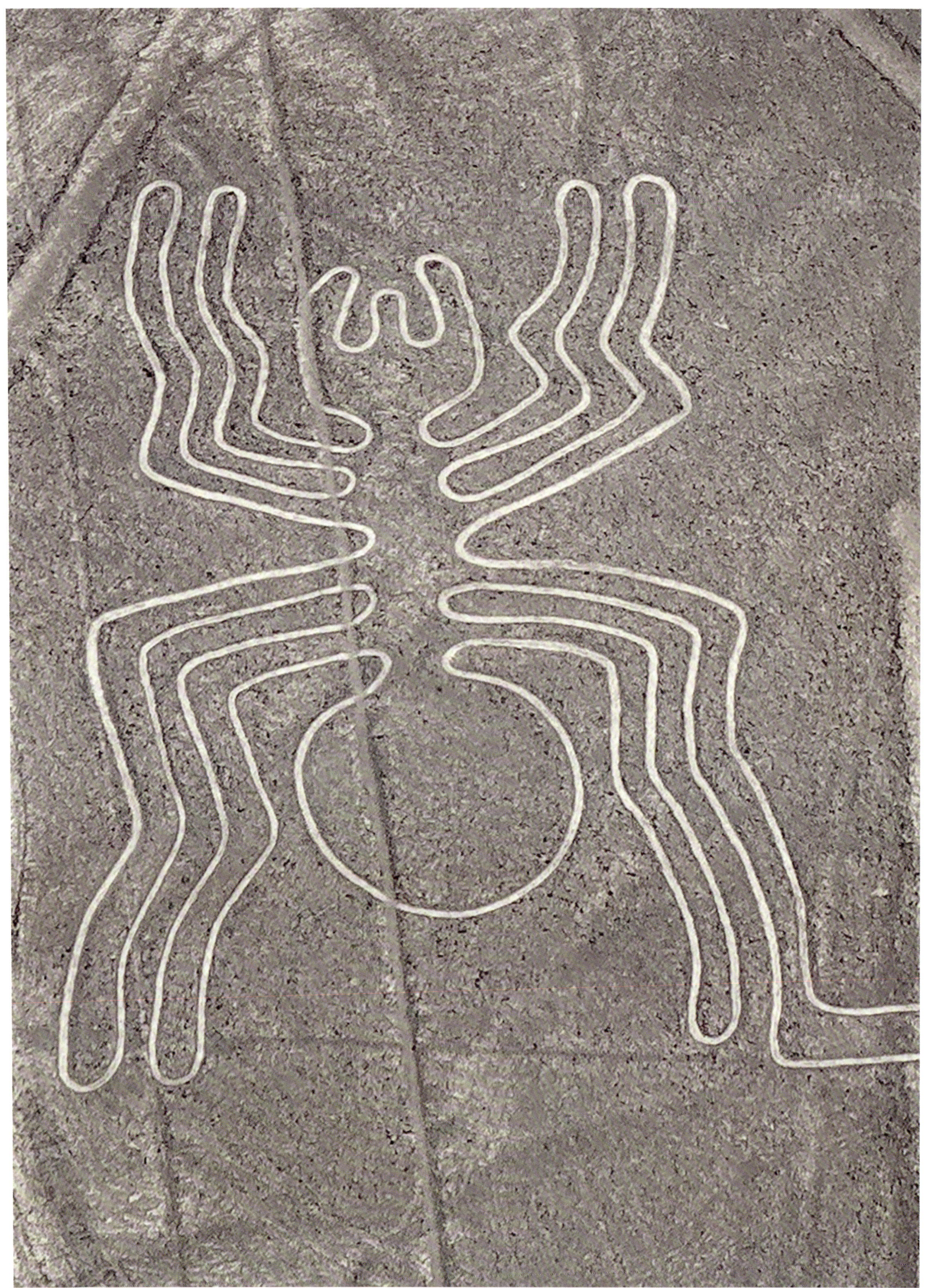

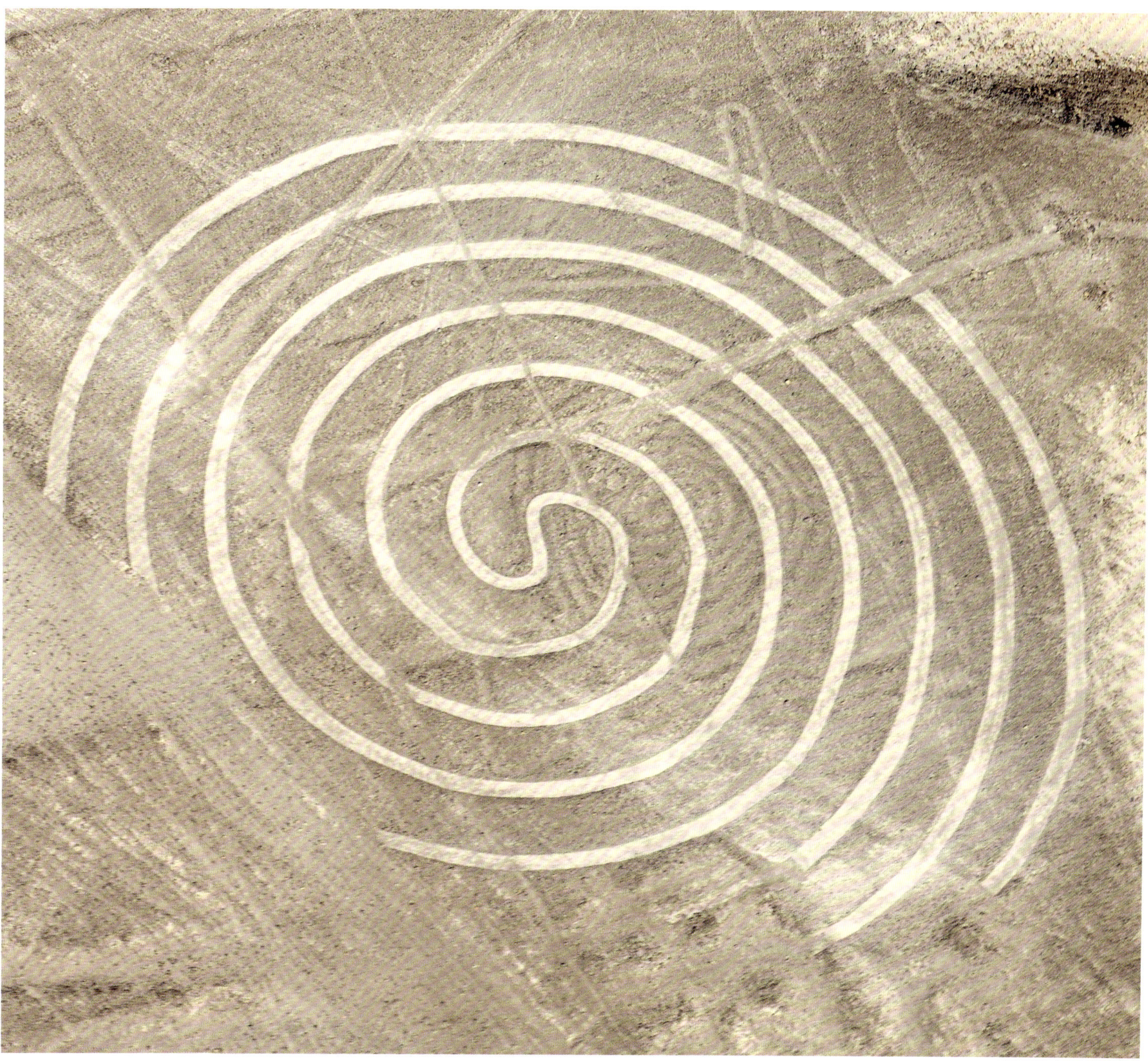

BOTH PHOTOGRAPHS:

Nazca Lines, Peru

(Opposite) Best seen from the air, this gigantic 47-metre-long (154ft) spider – or possibly ant – was created by Nazca people between the 3rd and 8th centuries CE. Other creatures are even bigger: there is a hummingbird of 93 metres (305ft) and condor of 134 metres (440ft).

The Nazca formed such geoglyphs by removing red pebbles to reveal light-coloured lime-rich clay underneath. Perhaps they were meant to encourage sky-gods to water one of Earth's most arid deserts. But while dryness preserves designs, devastating floods probably led to their creators' demise in around 750 CE.

(Above) Most Nazca formations show abstract designs, like this intriguing spiral. Could it have been a mirror to stellar constellations? A maze guiding worshippers praying to one of the Nazca nature-based gods? Or, more prosaically, a representation of man-made subterranean water pumps?

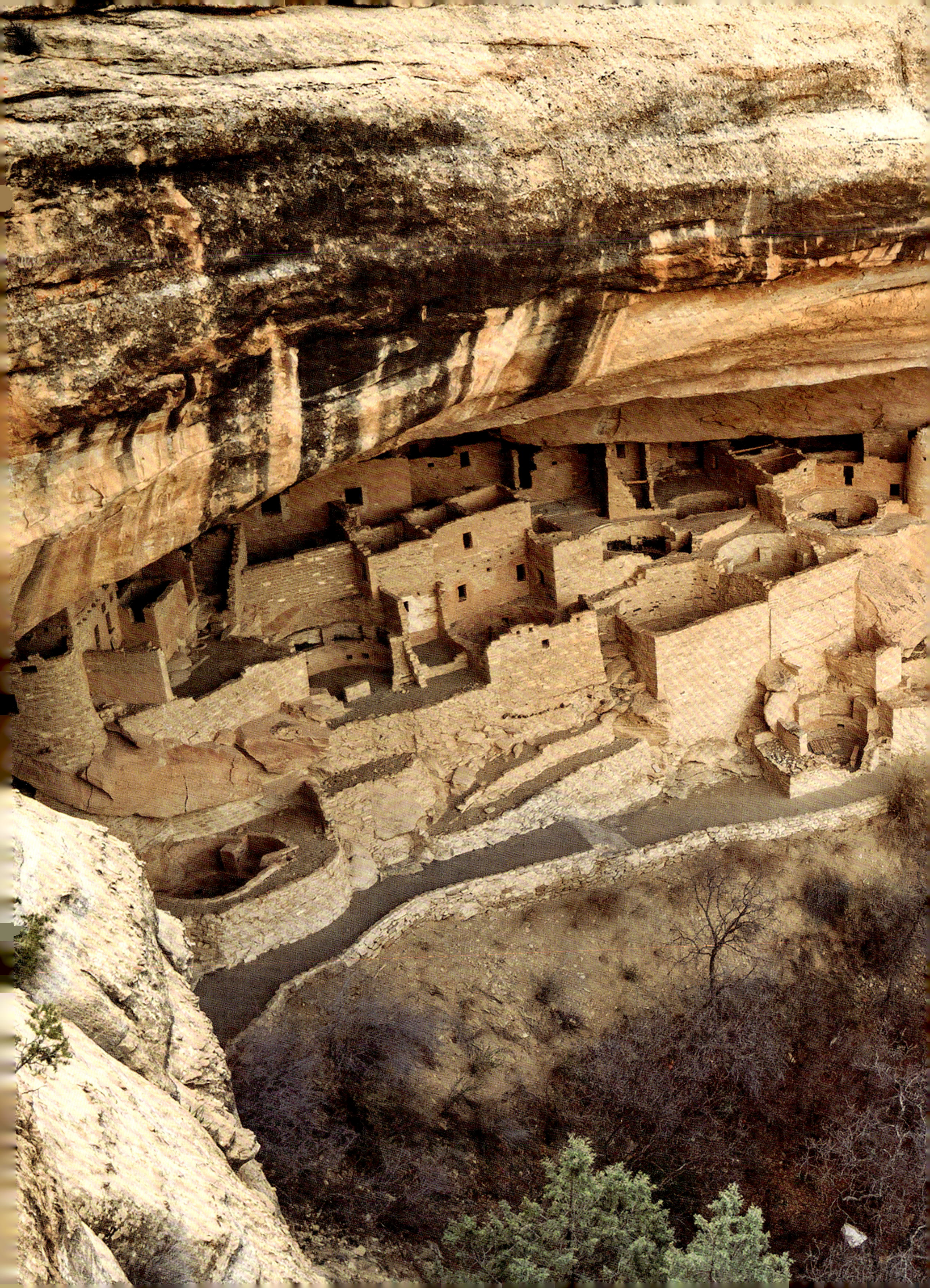

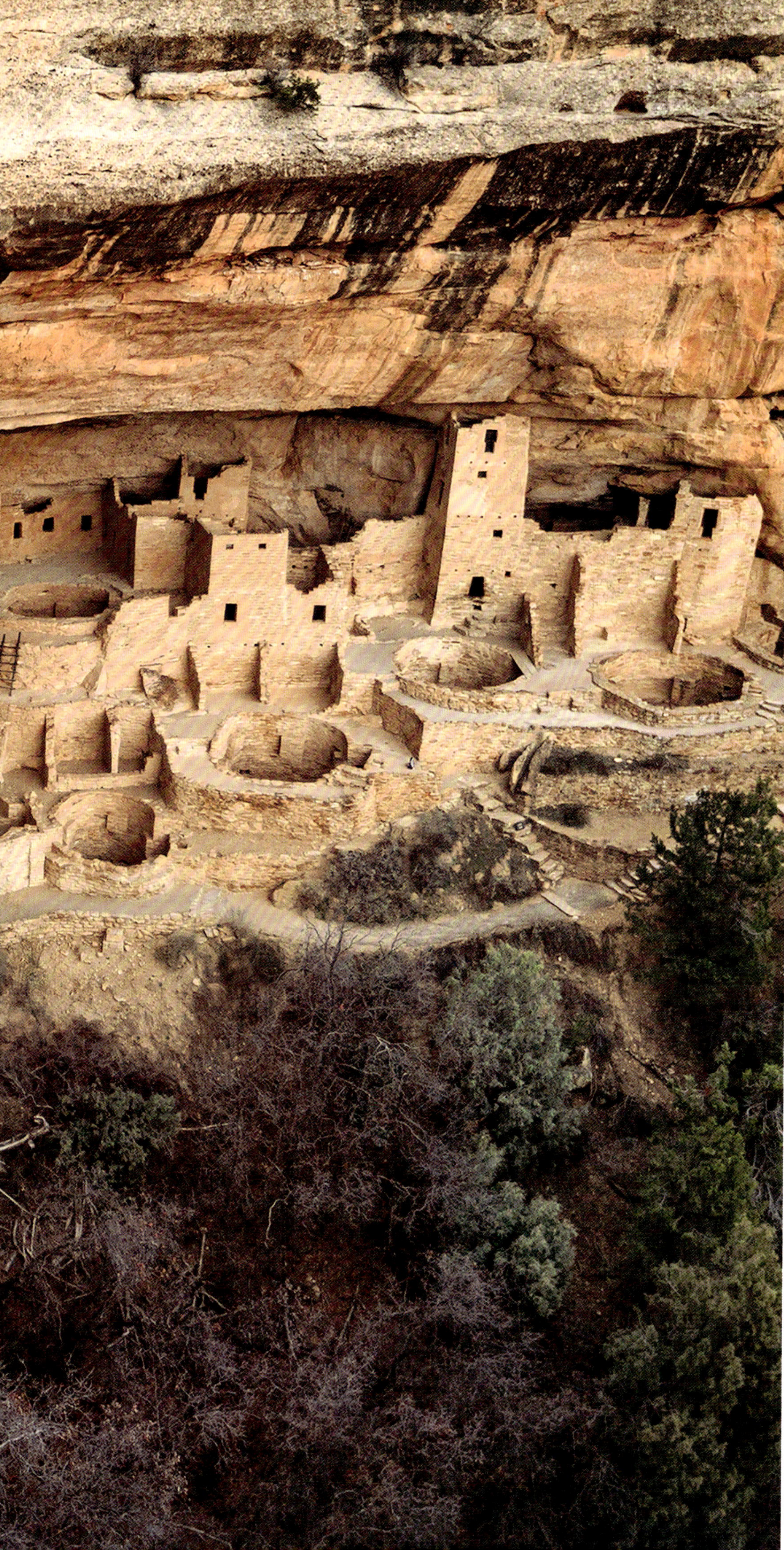

Cliff Palace, Mesa Verde, Colorado, USA
Cliff Palace looks like a quaint residential complex. Yet the multi-storeyed Ancestral Pueblo structure, hewn out of living rock between around 1190–1260 CE, also has spiritual aspects. Those circular sunken rooms are *kivas*, where devotees held ceremonies to honour the Puebloan *kachina* spirits. Many clans lived at this, the largest cliff dwelling in North America, each with its own *kiva*, before a drought around 1300 apparently decimated the community.

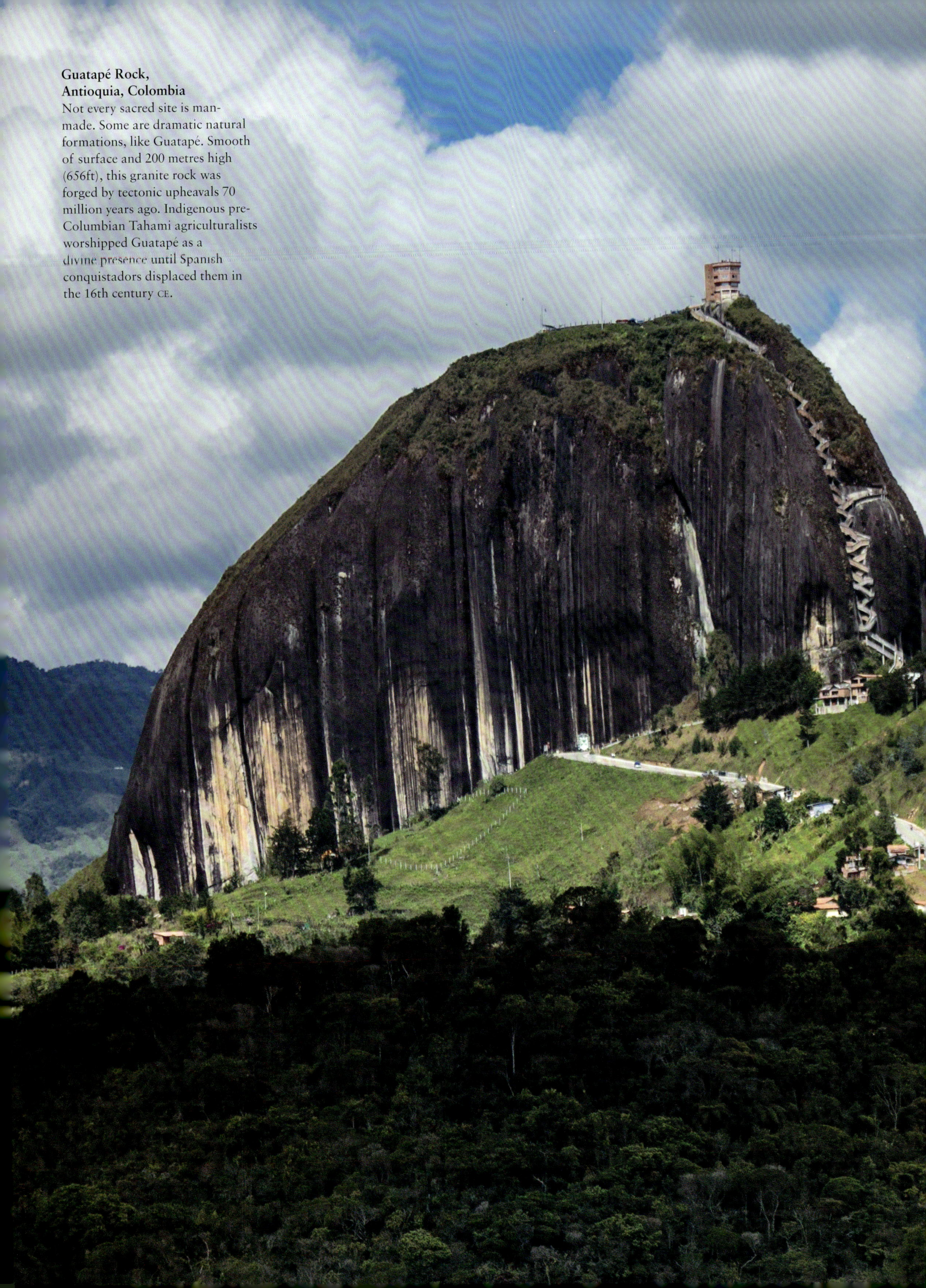

Guatapé Rock, Antioquia, Colombia
Not every sacred site is man-made. Some are dramatic natural formations, like Guatapé. Smooth of surface and 200 metres high (656ft), this granite rock was forged by tectonic upheavals 70 million years ago. Indigenous pre-Columbian Tahami agriculturalists worshipped Guatapé as a divine presence until Spanish conquistadors displaced them in the 16th century CE.

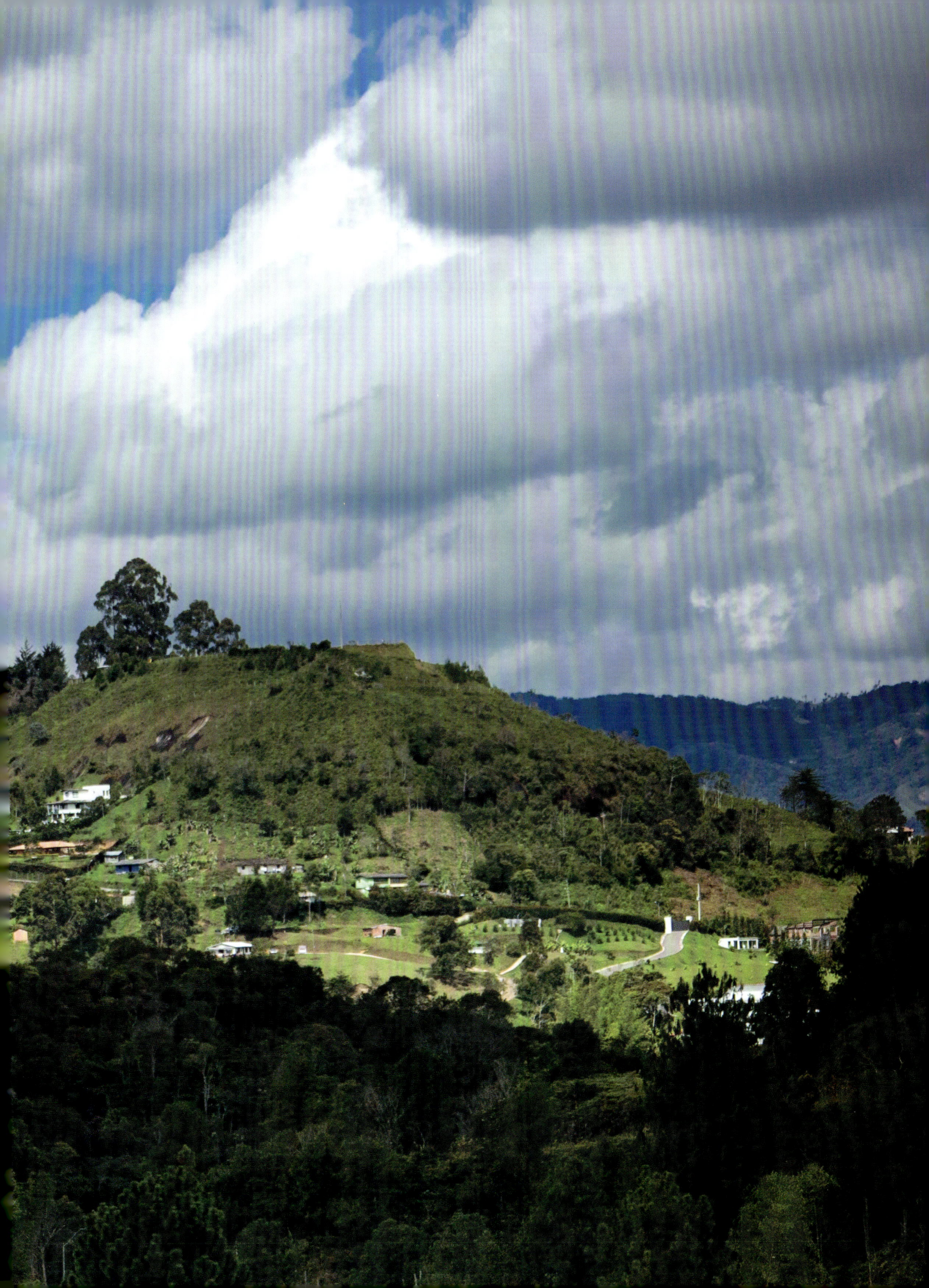

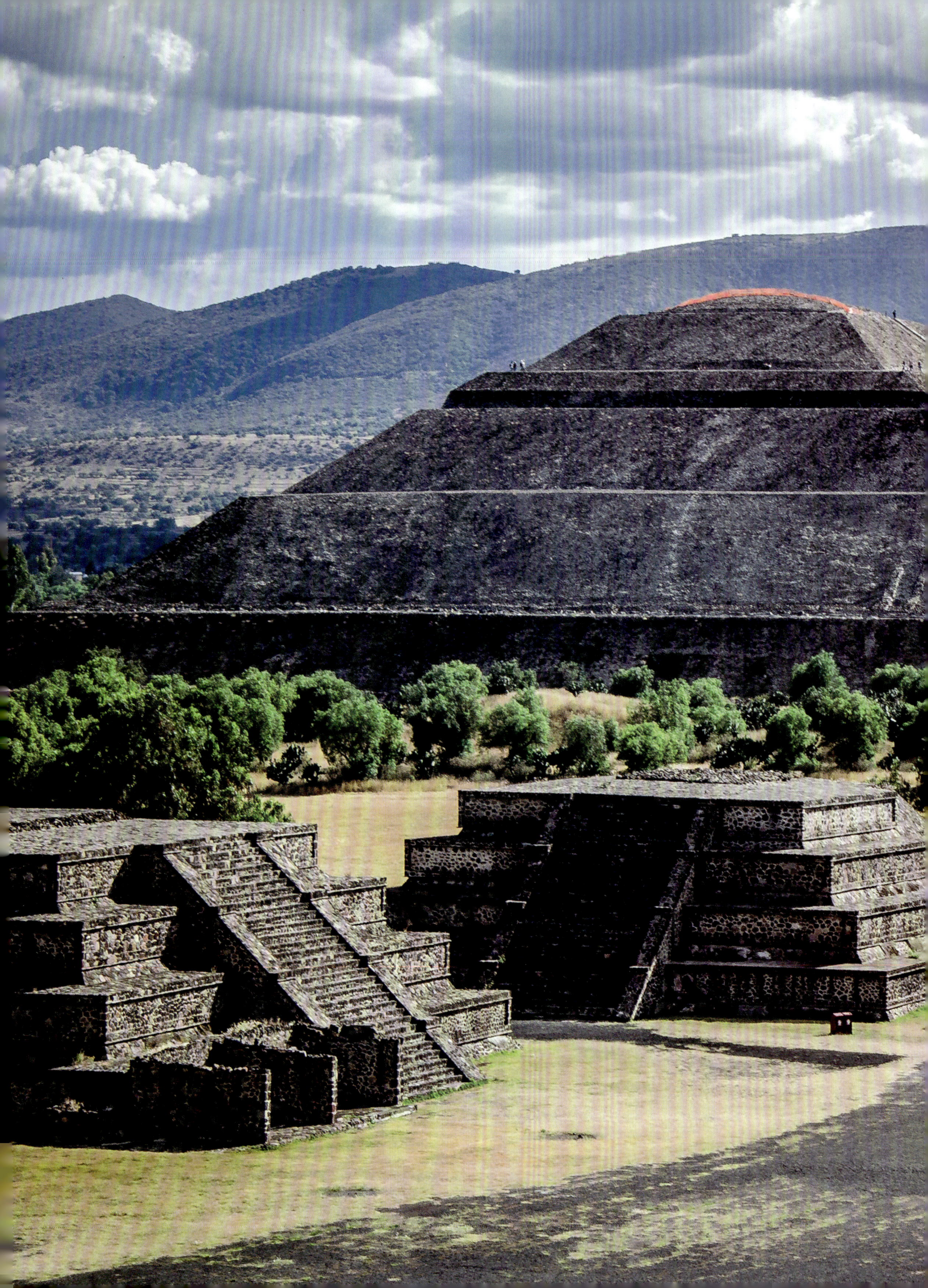

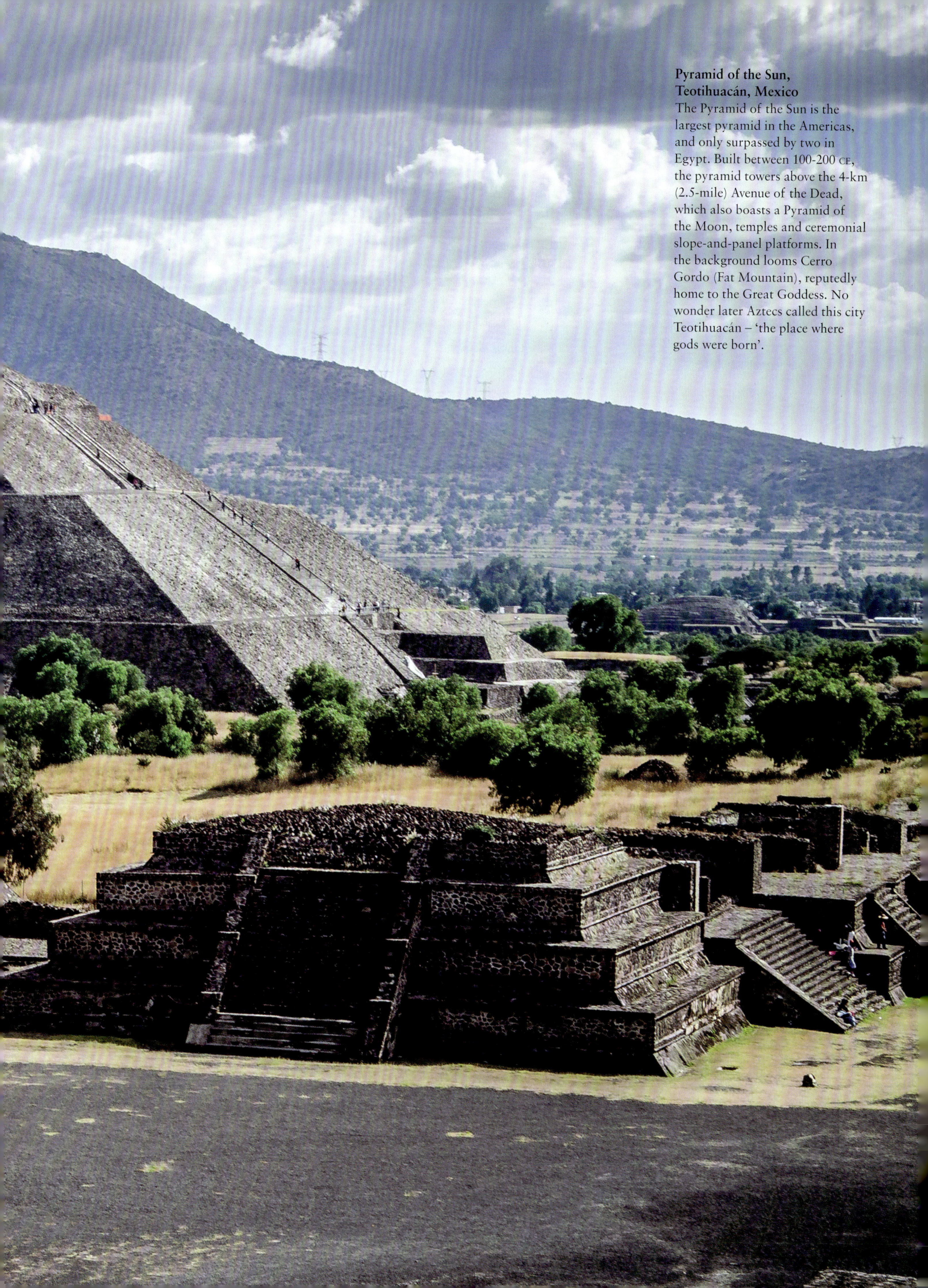

Pyramid of the Sun, Teotihuacán, Mexico
The Pyramid of the Sun is the largest pyramid in the Americas, and only surpassed by two in Egypt. Built between 100-200 CE, the pyramid towers above the 4-km (2.5-mile) Avenue of the Dead, which also boasts a Pyramid of the Moon, temples and ceremonial slope-and-panel platforms. In the background looms Cerro Gordo (Fat Mountain), reputedly home to the Great Goddess. No wonder later Aztecs called this city Teotihuacán – 'the place where gods were born'.

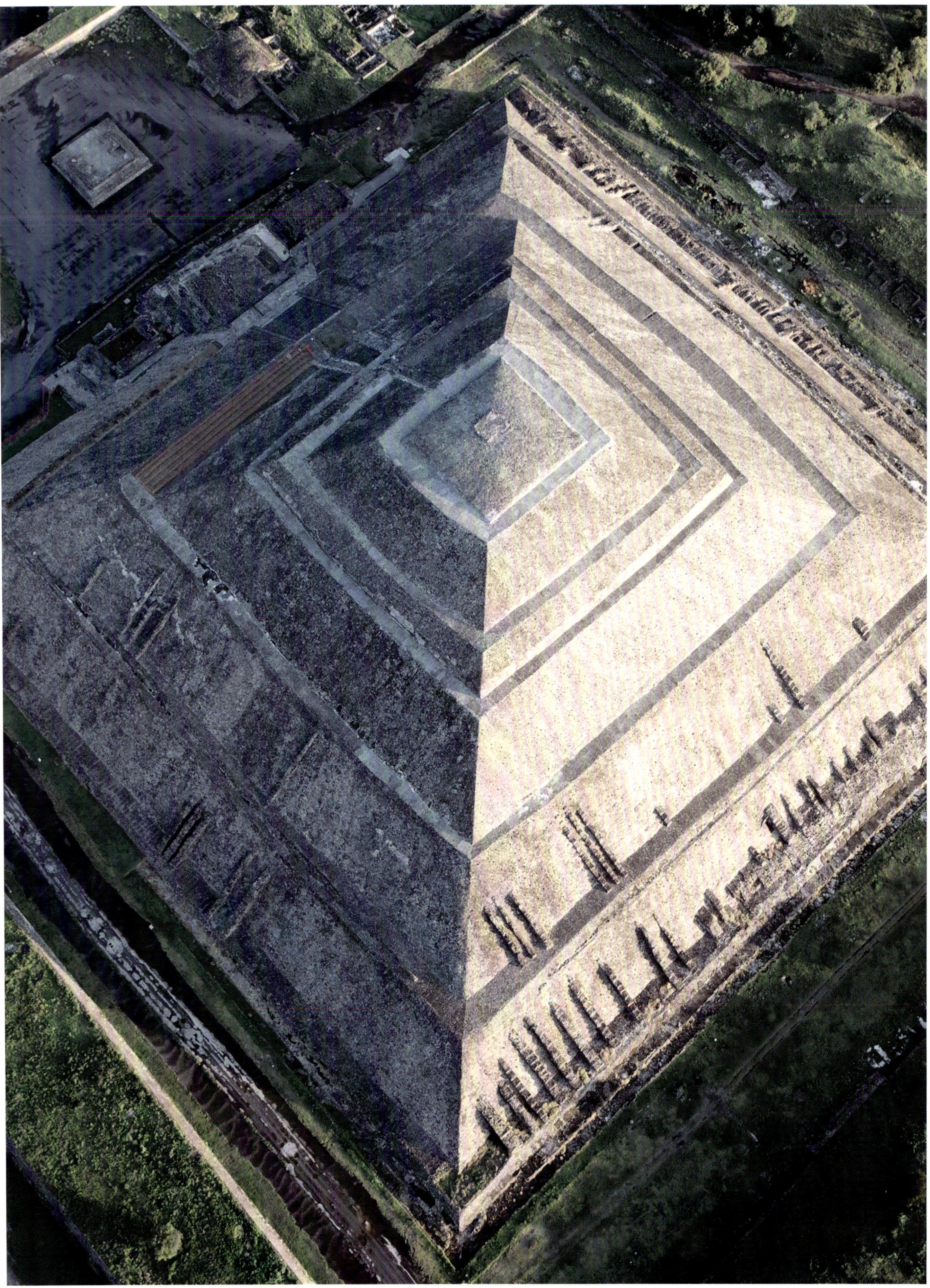

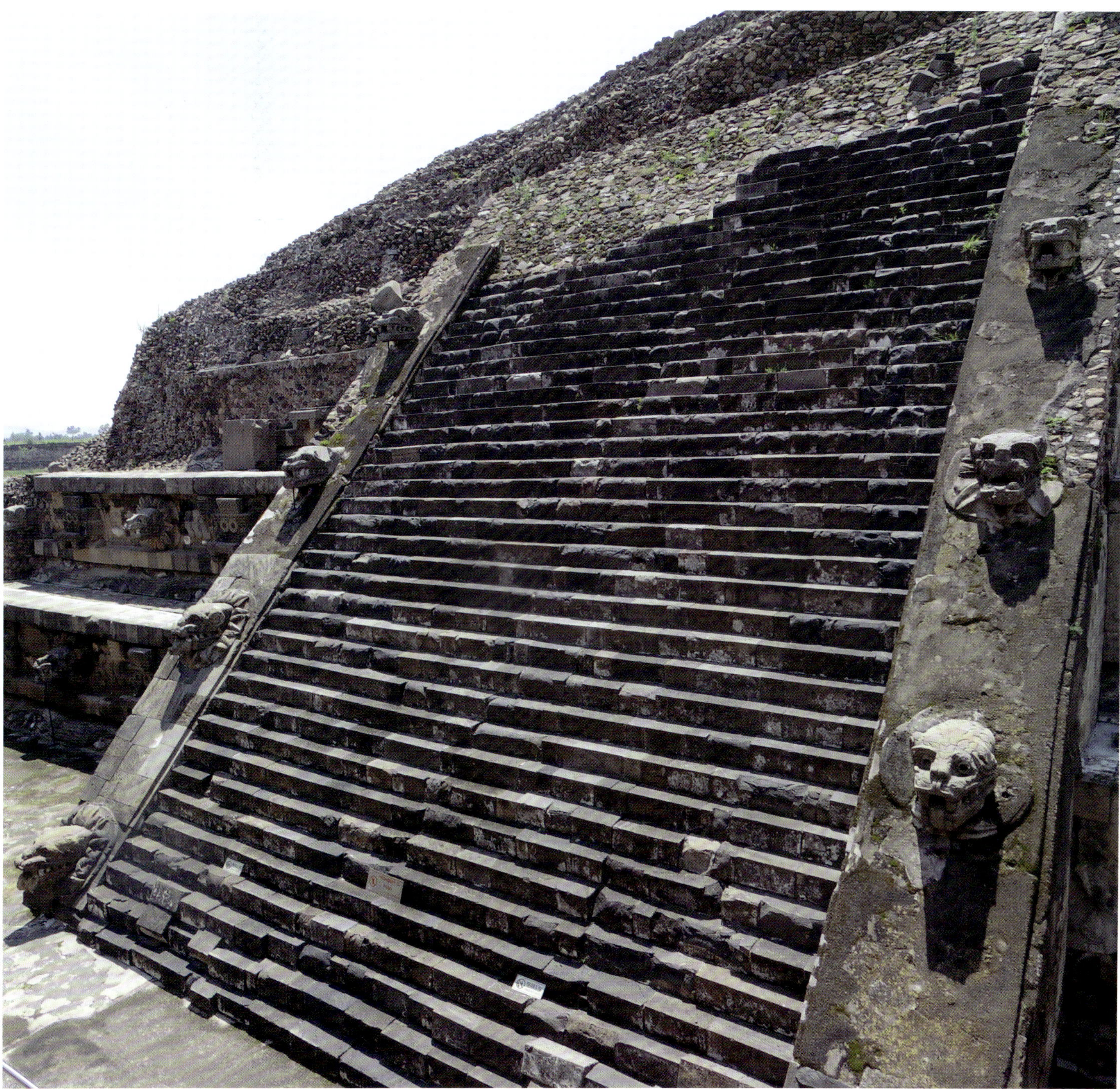

OPPOSITE:

Pyramid of the Sun, Teotihuacán, Mexico

Exquisitely designed shapes emerge from an aerial view of the multilayer Pyramid of the Sun. Teotihuacán's advanced grid plan suggests a powerful centralized government capable of corralling hordes of workers. Yet the site lacks evidence of military structures. The later Aztecs believed that the gods created the sun from this pyramid. Its true function, however, and even the identity of its original worshippers, remains a mystery.

ABOVE:

Temple of the Feathered Serpent, Teotihuacán, Mexico

Leering animal heads adorn a staircase on Teotihuacán's once red-painted Temple of the Feathered Serpent, Quetzalcoatl, the god of life and harvest. Underground chambers reveal greenstone statuettes, a carved figure of the storm god Tlaloc, and bones signifying the possible sacrifice of 200 humans. The multi-ethnic nature of Teotihuacán explains its diverse religious motifs. By 400 CE, 125,000 lived in the city, making it the largest in the Western Hemisphere. Sacked in around 650 CE, Teotihuacán was rediscovered by the Aztecs around 1300 CE.

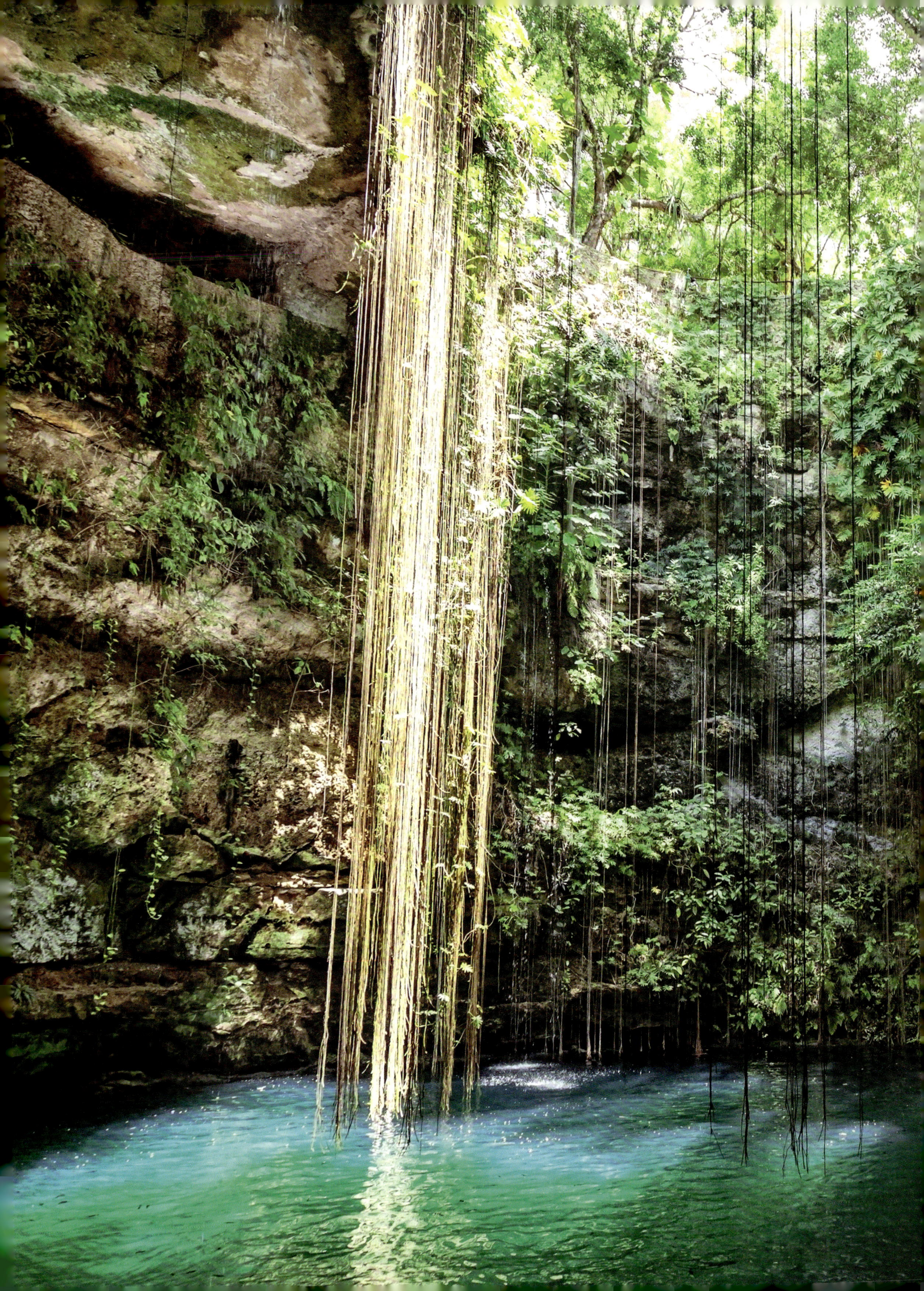

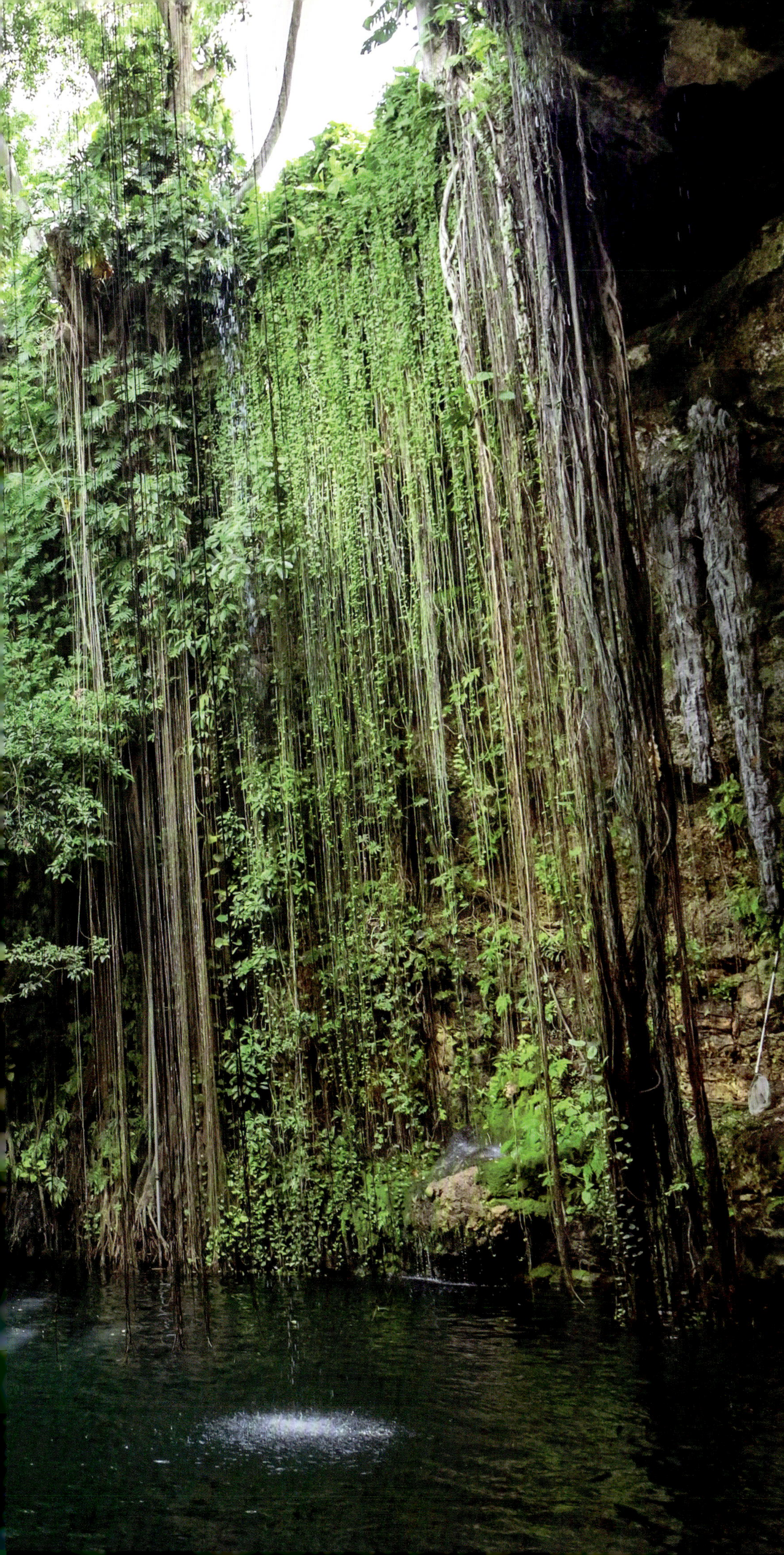

Sacred Cenote, Ik-Kil, Mexico
The Maya quite reasonably venerated Ik-Kil's *cenote* – a groundwater-rich natural sunken well – in the Yucatán Peninsula. Yet its placidity is deceptive. Skeletons discovered in the depths, along with jade and gold objects, speak of human sacrifices to the rain god Chaac.

Nearby lies the city of Chichen Itzá, founded by the Maya in the 6th century CE and conquered by Toltecs in the 10th century CE. Chichen Itzá contains more fearsome cultural clues: a Temple of the Jaguars, fanged rattlesnake sculptures, ceremonial pyramids and a court for *tlachtli*, a sacred ball game where losing teams literally lost their heads.

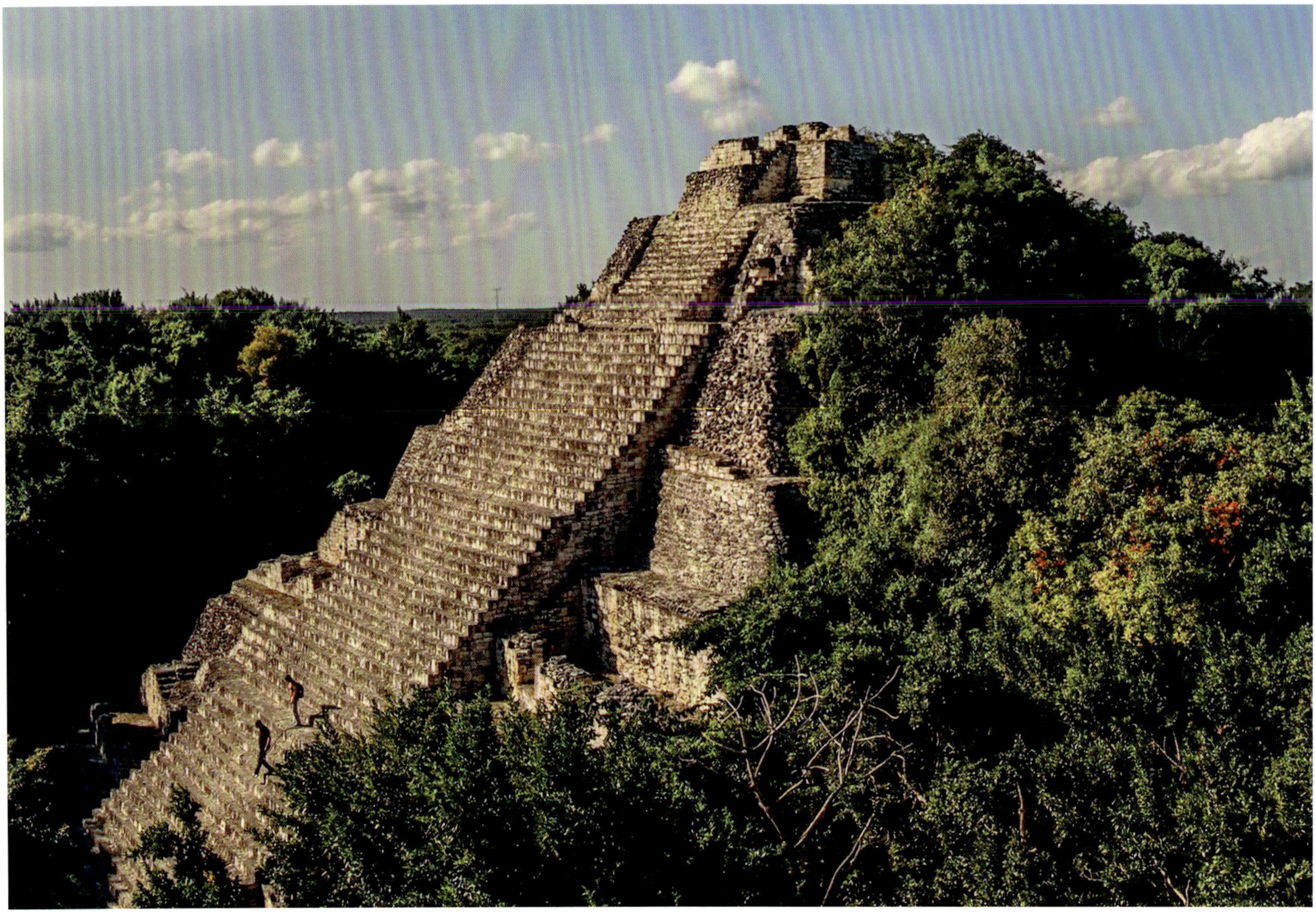

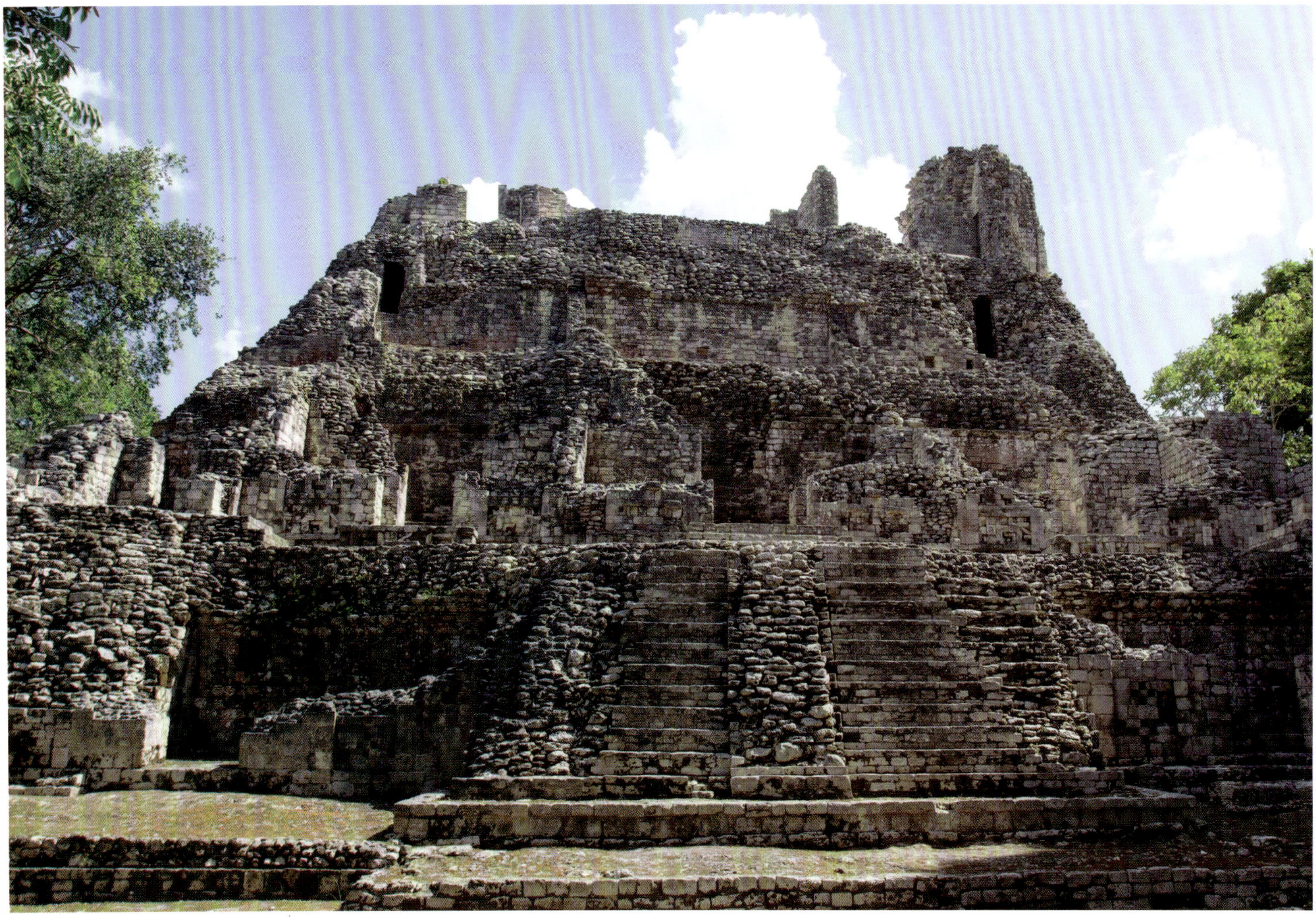

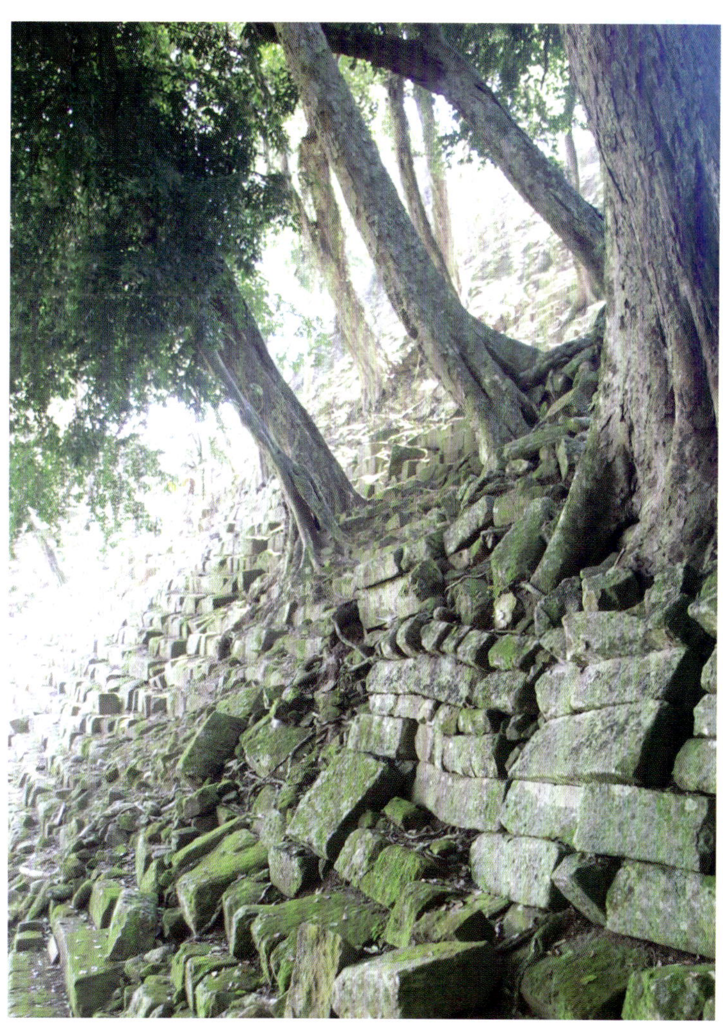

OPPOSITE, ABOVE:

Becán, Yucatan, Mexico

Becán's pyramid soars above the tropical forest in Mexico's Yucatán Peninsula. Topped by a temple, it features a steep outside staircase hewn from limestone. The site's name means 'ravine formed by water', referring to its defensive moat, unique in the Maya world. First occupied c.550 BCE, Becán developed as a ceremonial centre during 300 BCE–100 CE, and thrived as the strategic crossroads of several trade routes.

OPPOSITE, BELOW:

Becán, Yucatan, Mexico

This temple at Becán probably honoured the earth monster Itzamna, whose giant stucco masks dot the site. Maya elites dwelt in vast chambers near the town centre, while false stairways and hidden tunnels suggest that Becán was a military centre – and target. Becán dramatically revived c.500 CE after a long decline, before being abandoned by 1200 CE.

LEFT, TOP:

Copán, Honduras

Forgotten until its rediscovery in the 1840s, Copán was capital of an astonishingly creative Maya kingdom from the 5th–9th centuries CE. It marks the southern outpost of Classic Period Maya civilization, situated today near Honduras's border with Guatemala. Rivals surrounded Copán on all sides, yet ultimately disease, overpopulation, crop failure and dynastic strife spelled its demise. Here trees bind shards of stones that once built a mighty city-state.

BELOW:

Copán, Honduras

A growling skull and demons stare out from a temple entrance. The glyphs convey a date – 29 November 711 CE – coinciding with a unique juxtaposition of Venus, Sun, Moon and the Milky Way. What that event portended in the Maya calendar remains unknown. The sculptures probably aided worship of the temple's guardian creator gods, who the Maya believed held up the skies.

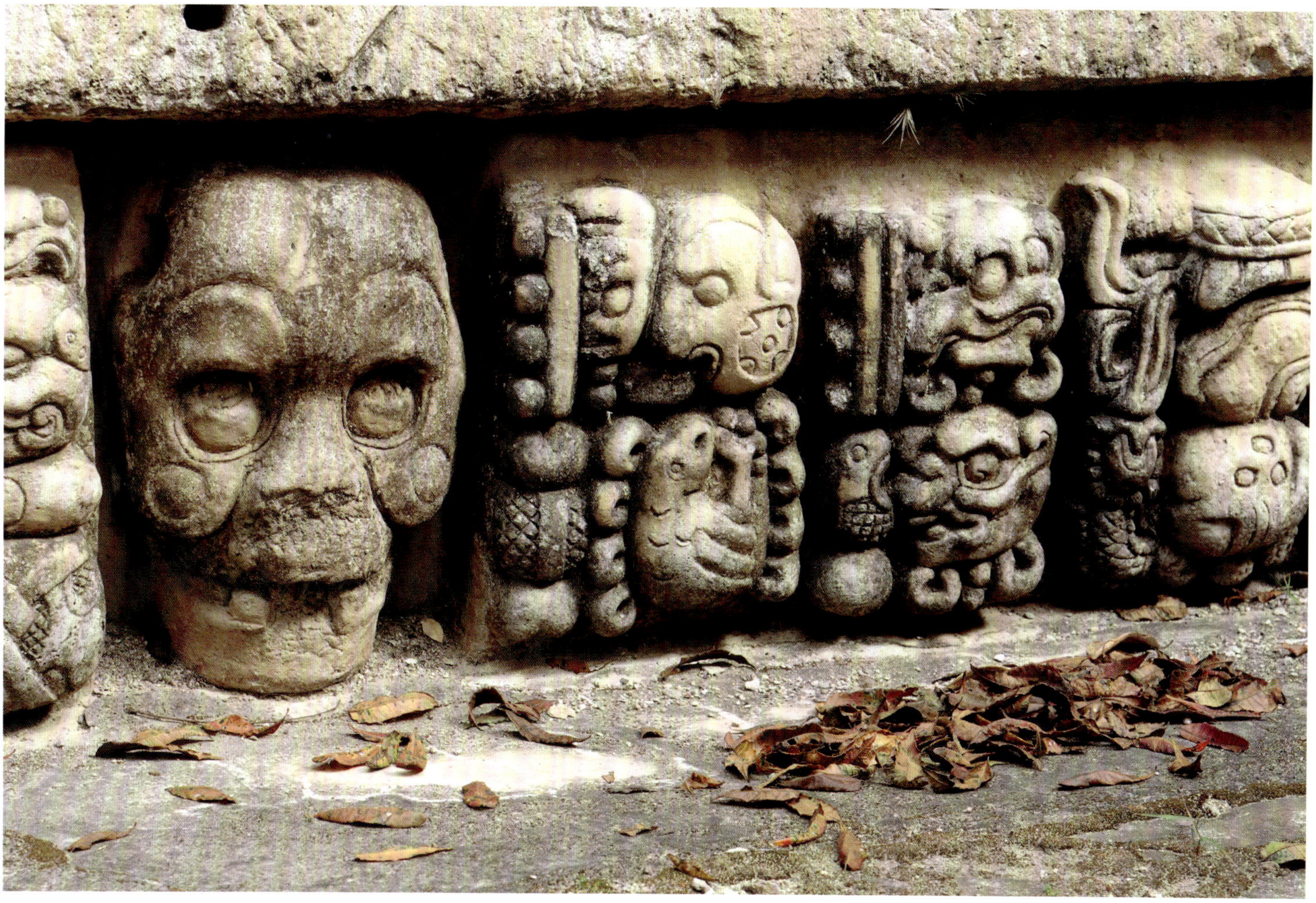

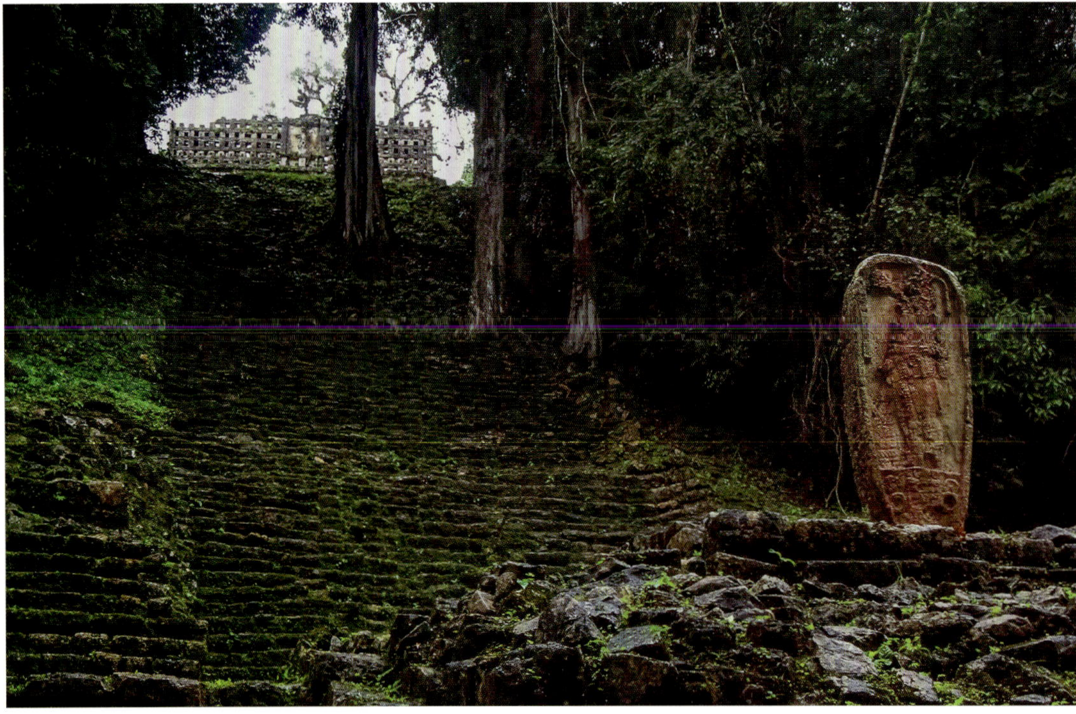

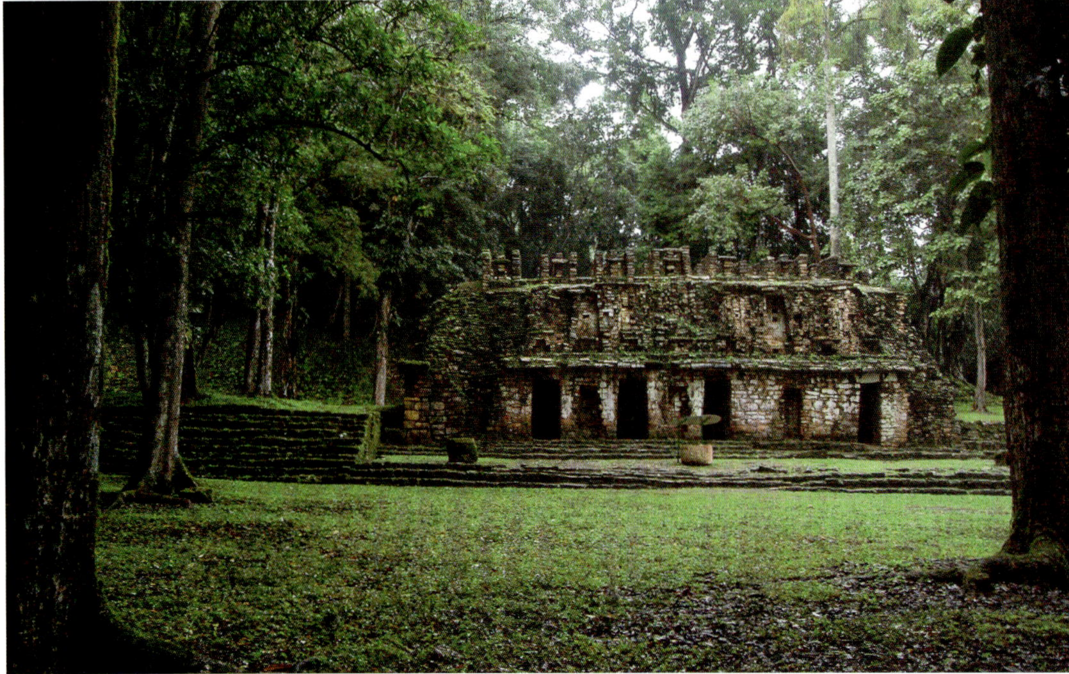

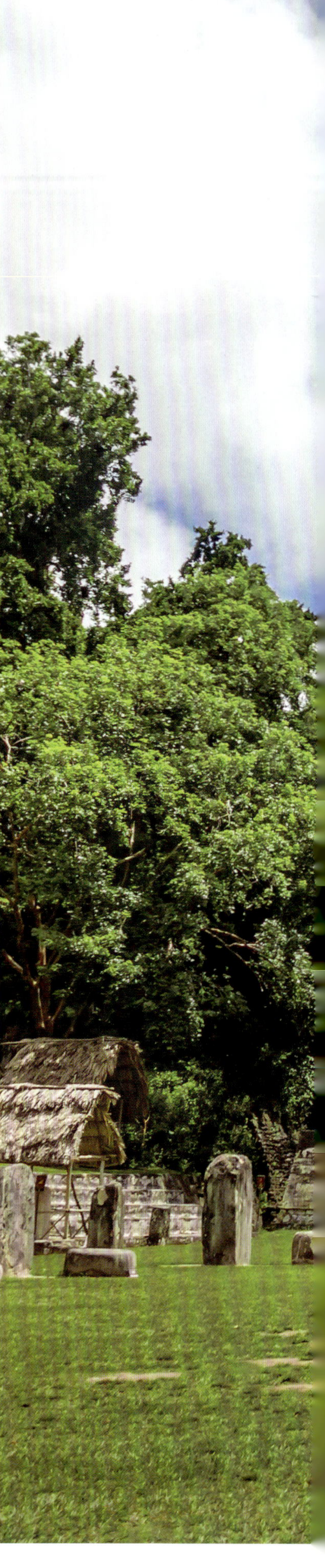

TOP:

Temple, Yaxchilan, Mexico

Today Yaxchilan peeps out of thick jungle foliage and largely lies in ruins. Yet in the 7th century CE this Maya city attracted pilgrims from far and wide. Situated besides the Usumacinta River, Yaxchilan contained a lattice wall-topped pyramidal temple (top), ball-court, three acropolises, *yotoot* (palace building) and dazzling carved depictions of historic victories and events.

BOTTOM:

Temple, Yaxchilan, Mexico

Yaxchilan reached its zenith under King Itzamnaaj B'alam II, who ruled during 681–741 CE. In one stone lintel carving the king looks on as his wife, Lady K'ab'al Xook, pulls a spiked rope through her tongue. In another, the storm god Tlaloc emerges from the mouth of a double-headed Vision Serpent. Nature and mythology blend together, whether in a stele built from an otherworldly stalactite, or in the cries of jungle howler monkeys, as heard today.

RIGHT:

Tikal, Guatemala

Lofty edifices inspired awe among Maya peasants and this temple at Tikal was the tallest. Such feats of engineering still baffle us today. For despite their astronomical, mathematical and artistic prowess, the Maya lacked draft animals or knowledge of the wheel. A funereal shrine for King Jasaw Chan K'awiil (reigned 682–734 CE) crowns the temple. His tomb lies deep within. The building's nine stepped levels probably mirror the nine strata of the Maya underworld.

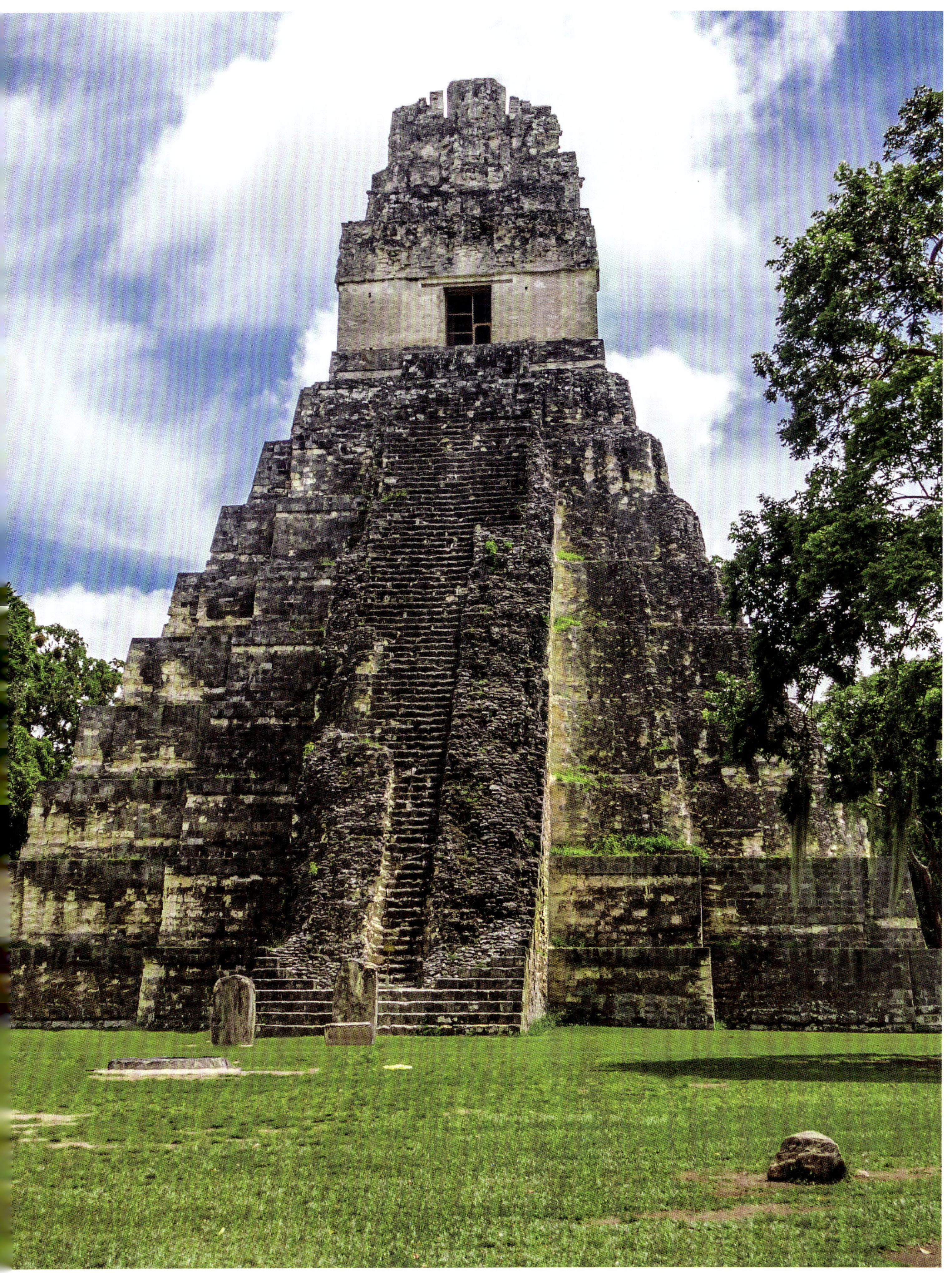

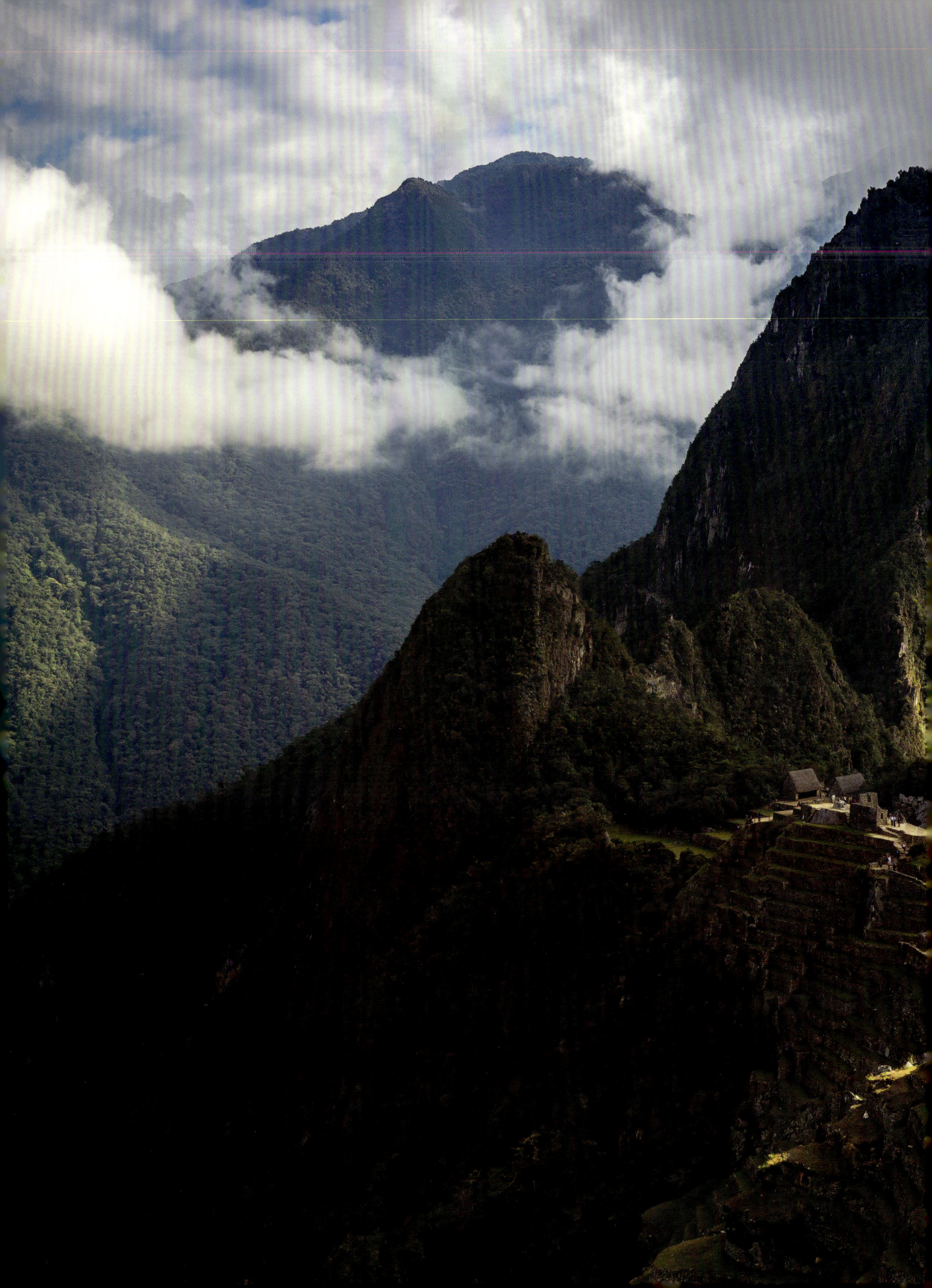

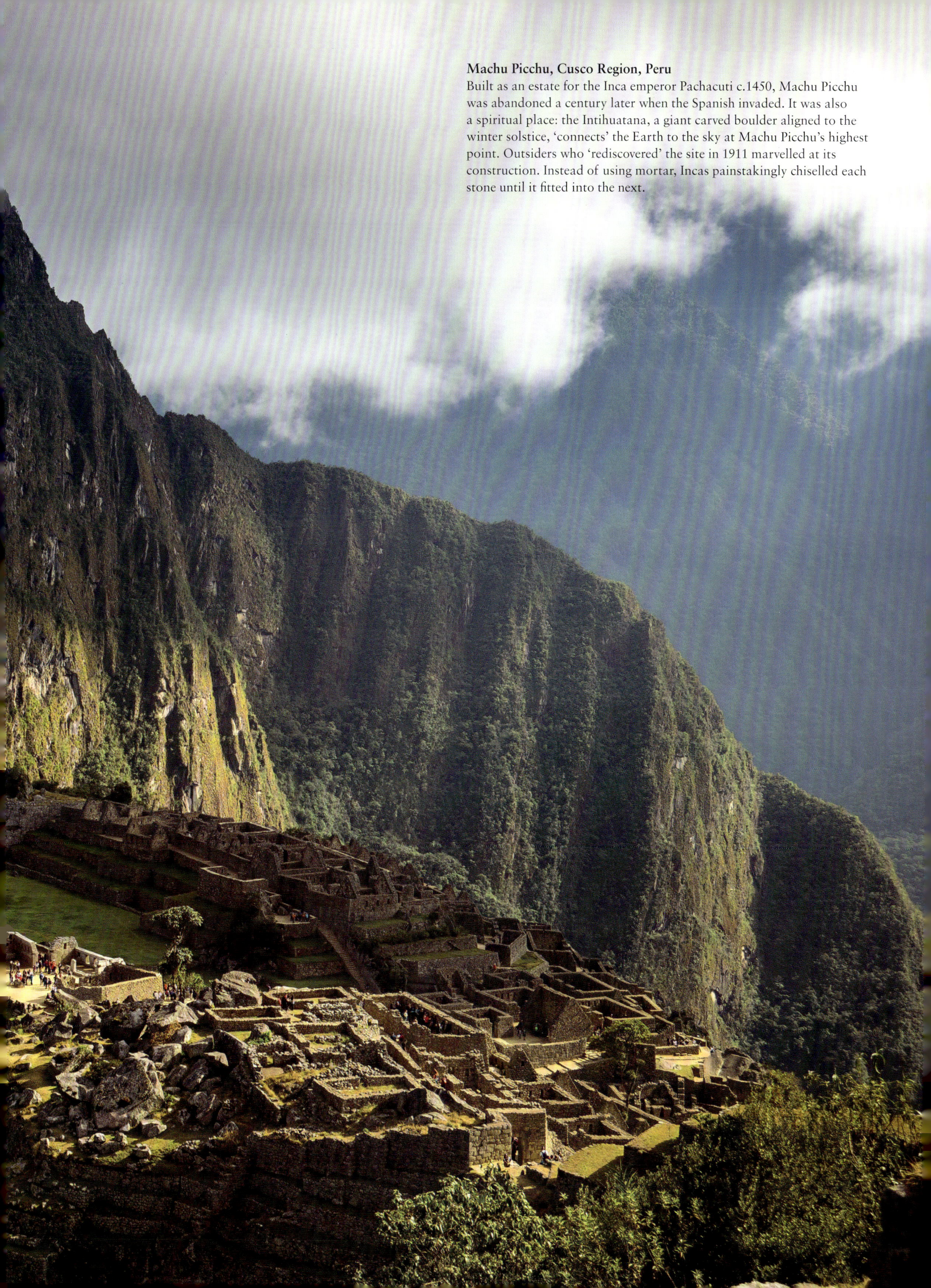

Machu Picchu, Cusco Region, Peru
Built as an estate for the Inca emperor Pachacuti c.1450, Machu Picchu was abandoned a century later when the Spanish invaded. It was also a spiritual place: the Intihuatana, a giant carved boulder aligned to the winter solstice, 'connects' the Earth to the sky at Machu Picchu's highest point. Outsiders who 'rediscovered' the site in 1911 marvelled at its construction. Instead of using mortar, Incas painstakingly chiselled each stone until it fitted into the next.

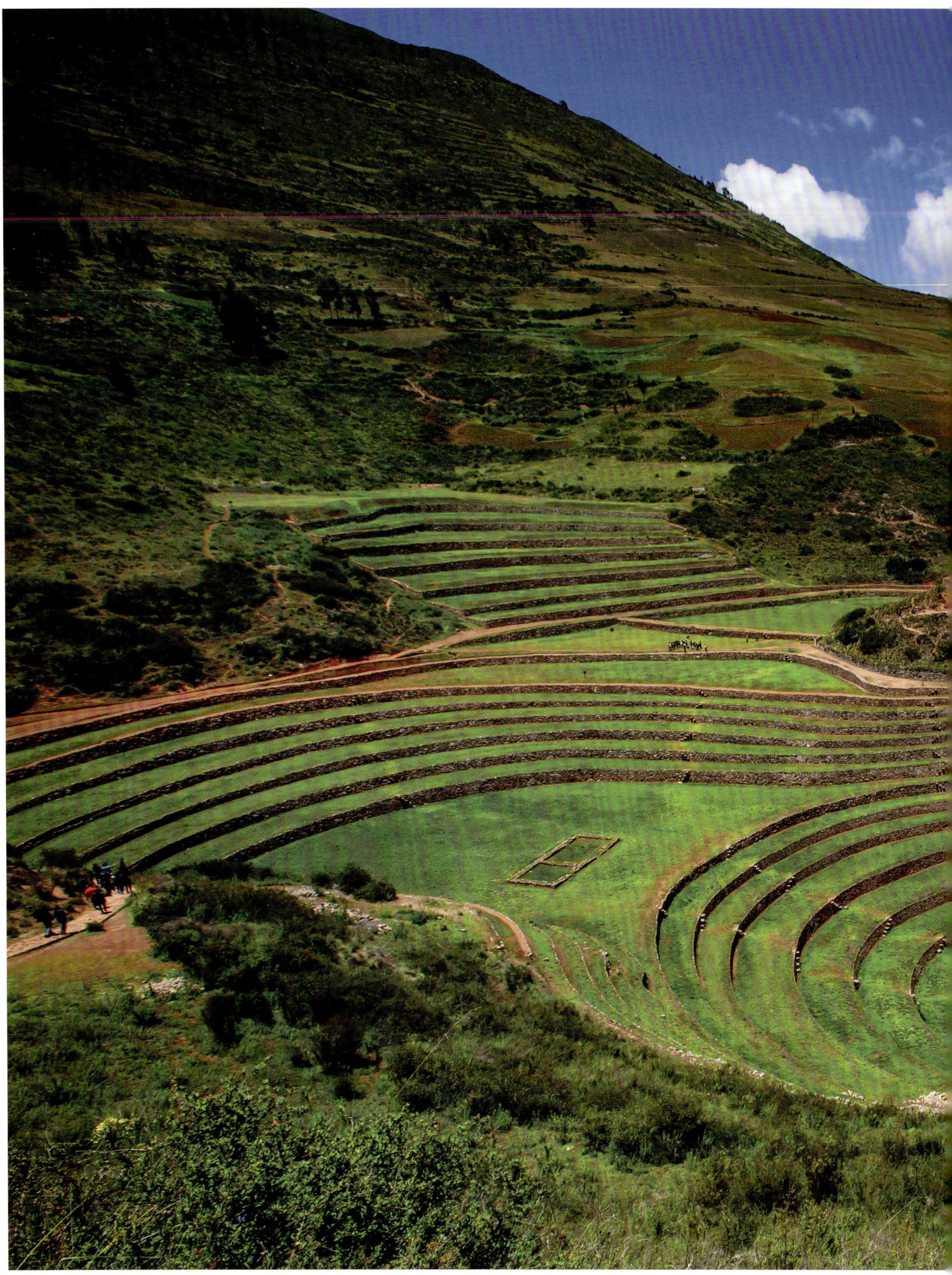

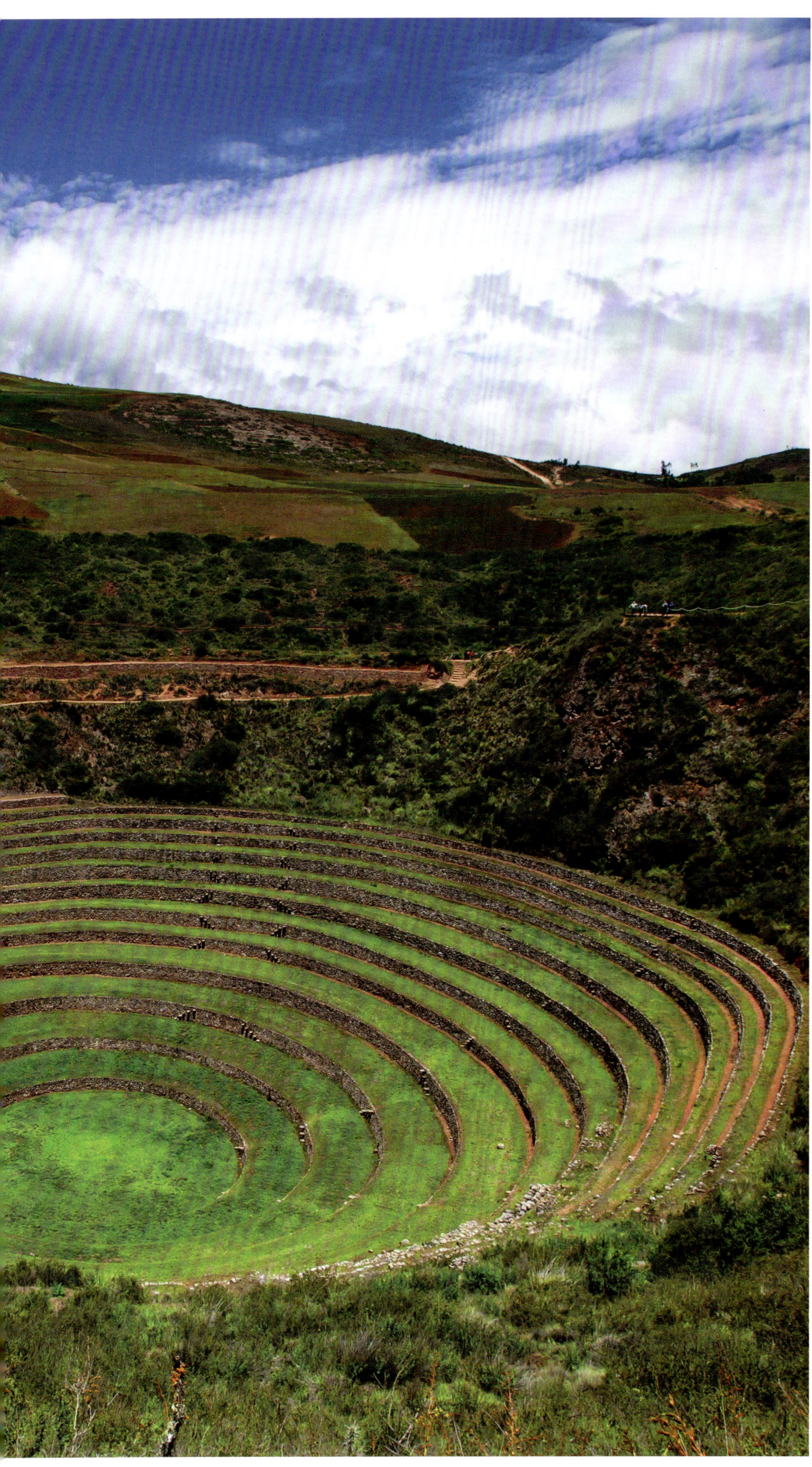

Moray Circles, Cusco Region, Peru
Incas designed these concentric circular terraces at Moray quite brilliantly. Still today, each level generates its own microclimate and air temperatures drop markedly over just a few feet. The site might have been an experimental nursery that developed superior forms of vital crops: maize, quinoa, squash, potatoes and coca. Moray abuts Peru's Sacred Valley, so perhaps it had spiritual functions, too – as an open air temple to Pachamama, the Earth Mother; or an attempt to regularize the Earth itself according to mythological geometry.

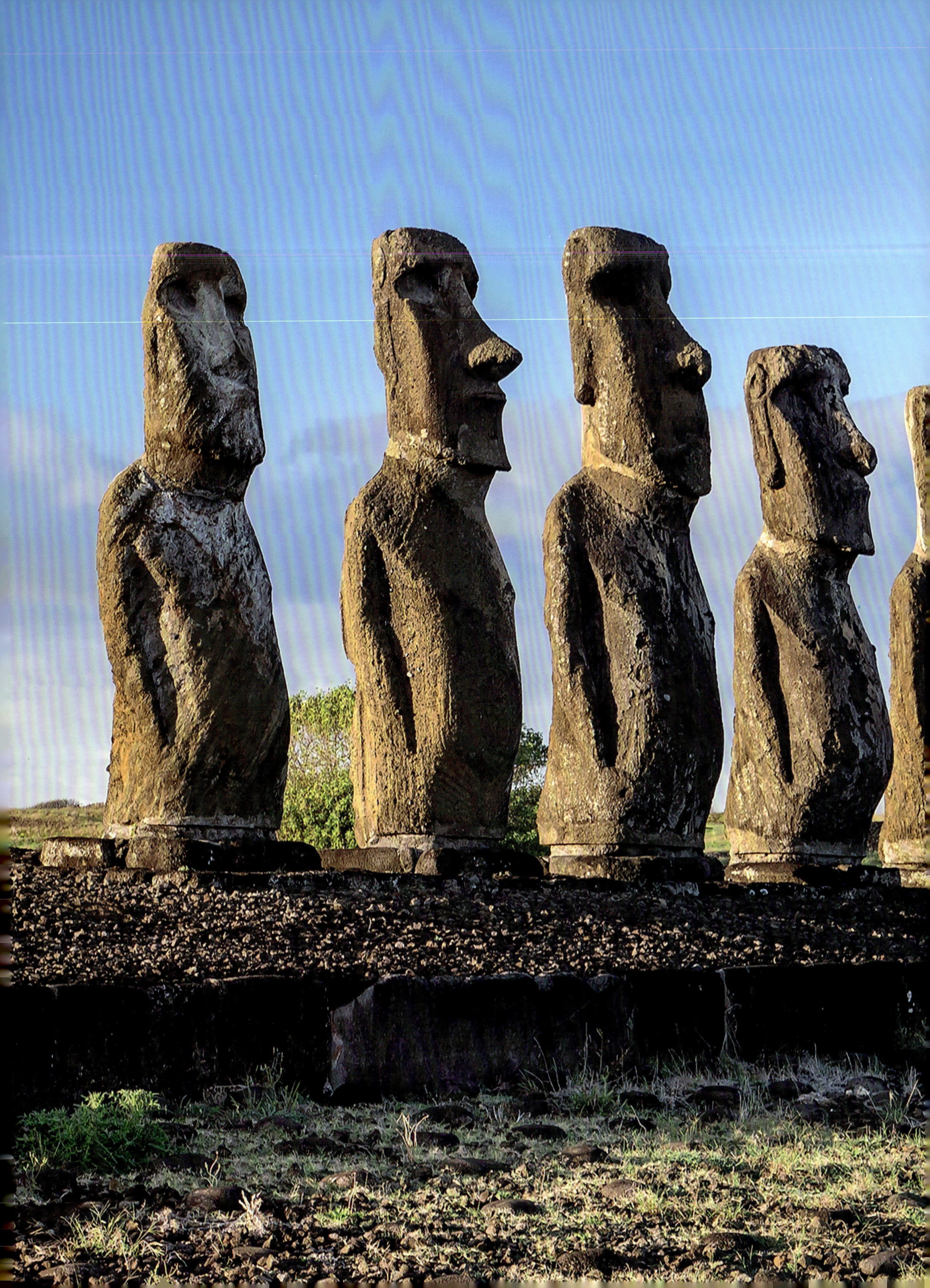

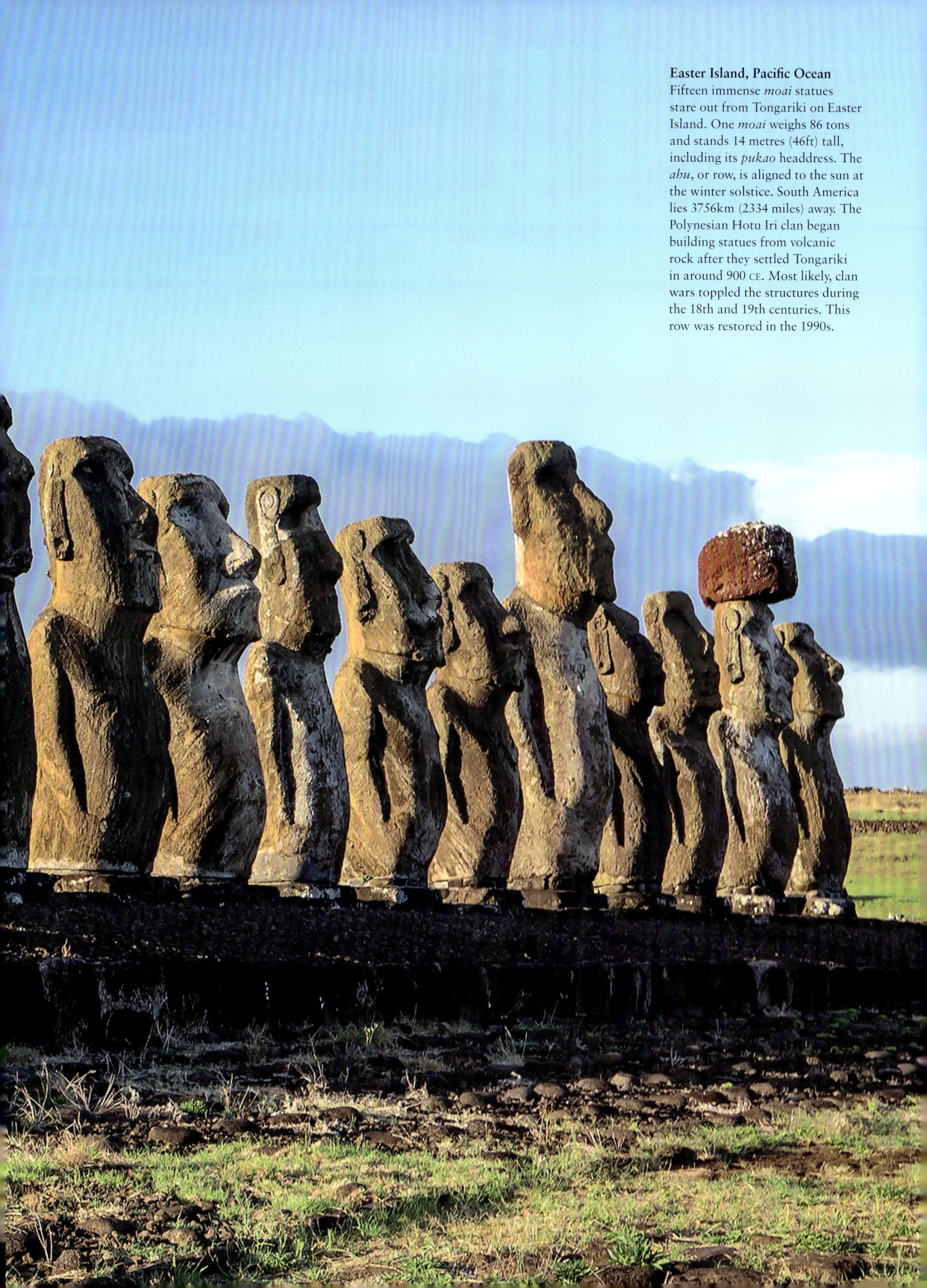

Easter Island, Pacific Ocean
Fifteen immense *moai* statues stare out from Tongariki on Easter Island. One *moai* weighs 86 tons and stands 14 metres (46ft) tall, including its *pukao* headdress. The *ahu*, or row, is aligned to the sun at the winter solstice. South America lies 3756km (2334 miles) away. The Polynesian Hotu Iri clan began building statues from volcanic rock after they settled Tongariki in around 900 CE. Most likely, clan wars toppled the structures during the 18th and 19th centuries. This row was restored in the 1990s.

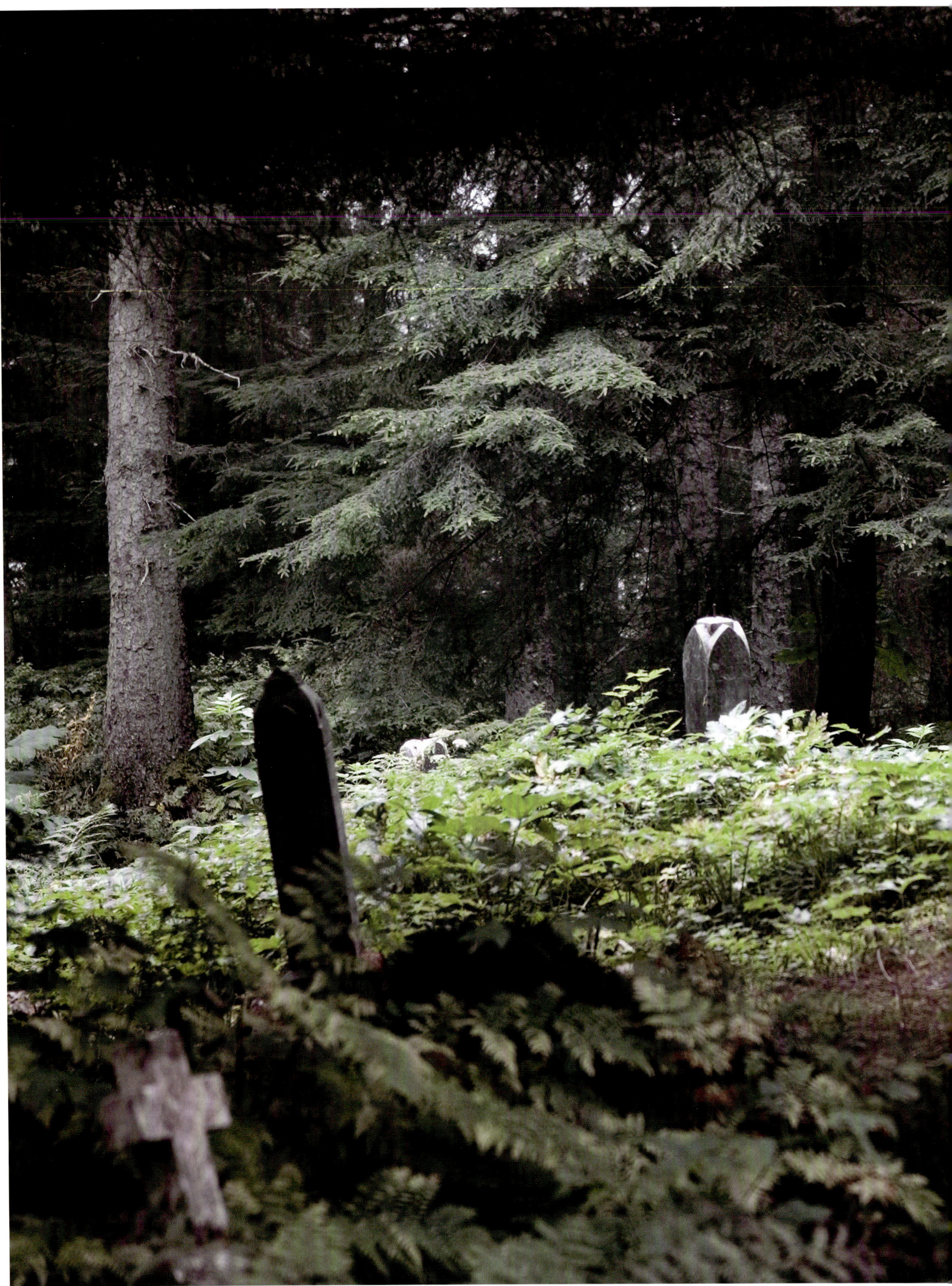

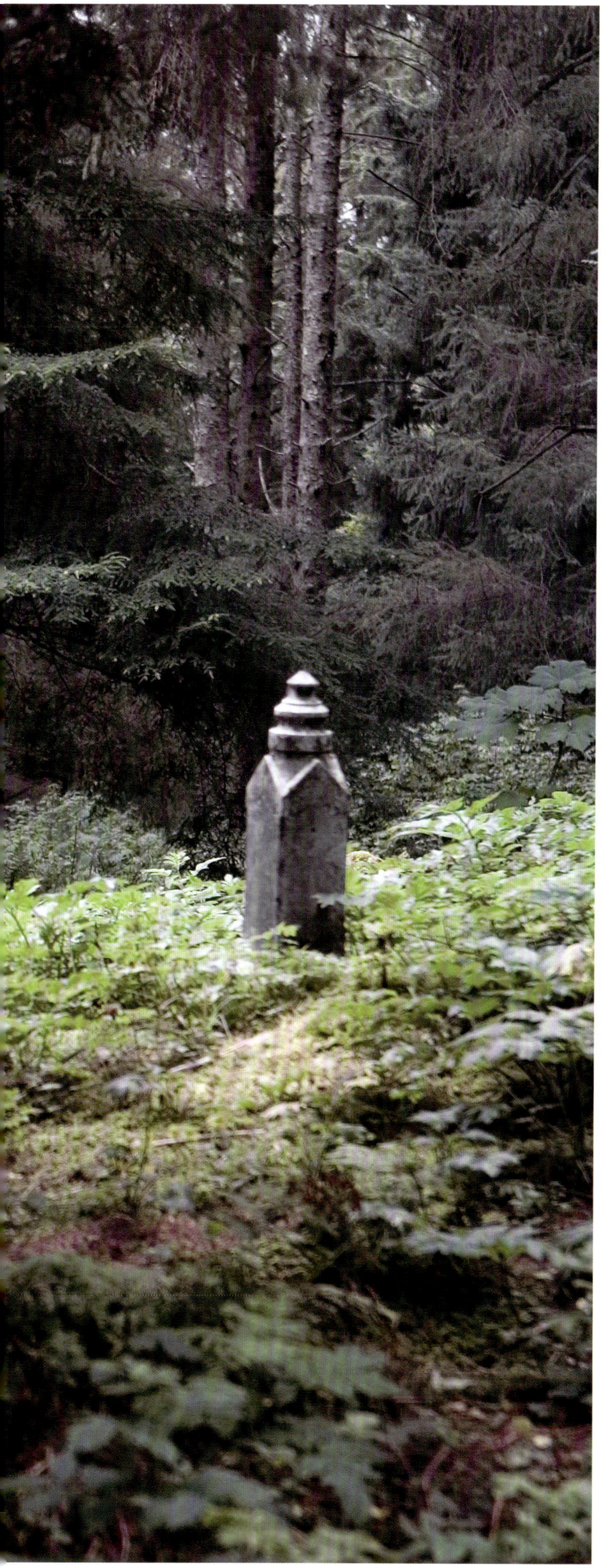

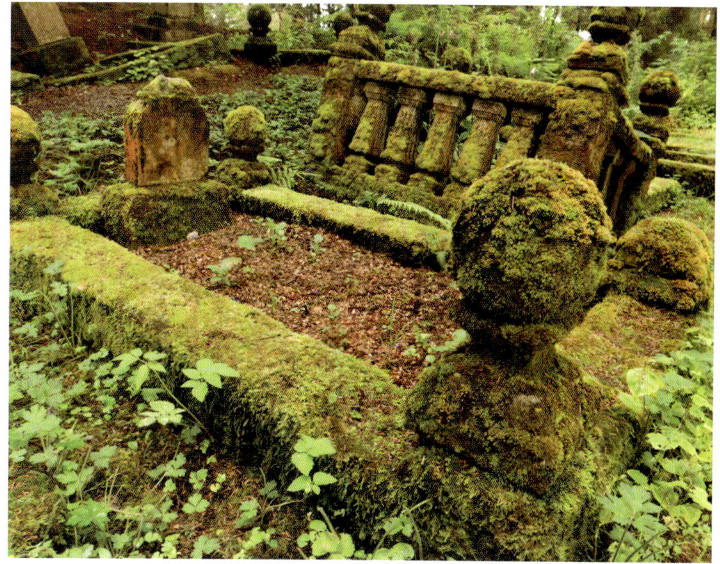

BOTH PHOTOGRAPHS:
Russian Cemetery, Sitka, Alaska, USA
Mostly Orthodox Christian Russian fur traders settled in Alaska in 1784. One such settlement was Sitka, named after an indigenous Tlingit clan, but renamed New Archangel by Tsarist forces in 1804. In 1848, the Russians built the Cathedral of St Michael at Sitka, the first Orthodox cathedral in the New World. But overhunting depleted the number of sea otters and, with Russian interest in the region waning, in 1867 the Russian Empire sold Alaska to the USA for $7.2 million.

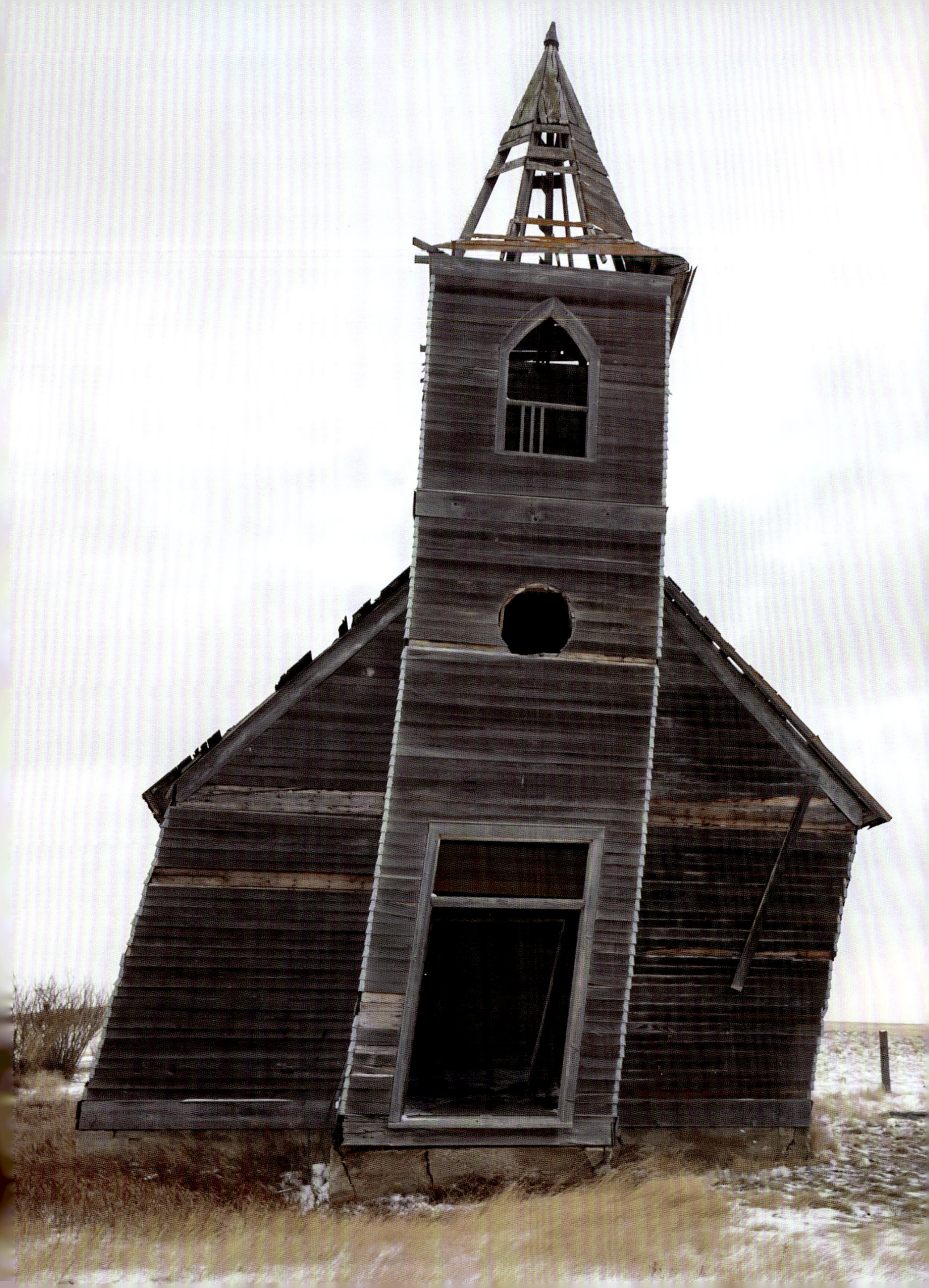

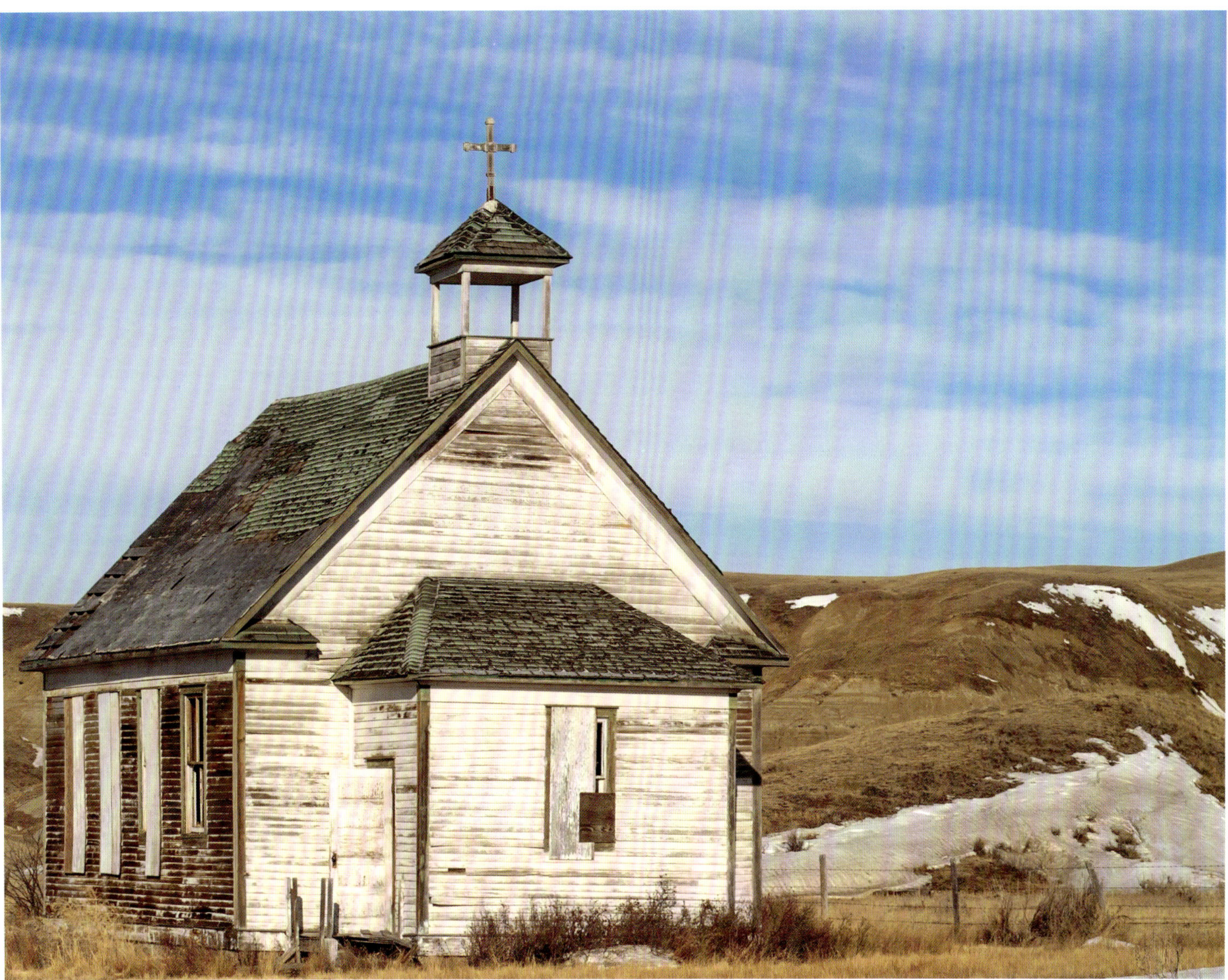

OPPOSITE:

Rocky Valley Lutheran Church, Dooley, Montana, USA

The only substantial building left in Dooley, Rocky Valley Church was built in 1915 and deserted 30 years later. Dooley's economy collapsed after repeated crop failures, a rash of fires, armyworm infestations and cold winters that froze railway lines. Ultimately Dooley became a ghost town – a sad yet not uncommon counter-narrative to the American dream.

ABOVE:

Catholic Church, Dorothy, Alberta, Canada

In the 1920s prospects looked good for Dorothy. Founded by hardworking pioneers in 1895, the hamlet of about 100 residents had its own postmaster, grocery store, railway station, ferry service, three grain elevators and a school. The Catholic Church opened in 1945, but shut in 1967 as the shift from coal to oil cost miners their jobs, and saw railway routes suspended. Today only nine people live in the valley town.

Calvin Presbyterian Church, Godmanchester, Quebec, Canada
The haunting remains of Calvin Presbyterian Church speak volumes about how economic change can devastate communities. Alexander McBain founded the largely Scottish town in 1823 as lumbering boomed in Canada. The church opened in 1851, a Protestant island within mostly French Catholic Quebec. But a nearby canal had already begun flooding Godmanchester, and the town's narrow wharves could not accommodate newer steamships. Residents quickly fled and the church closed for good in 1941.

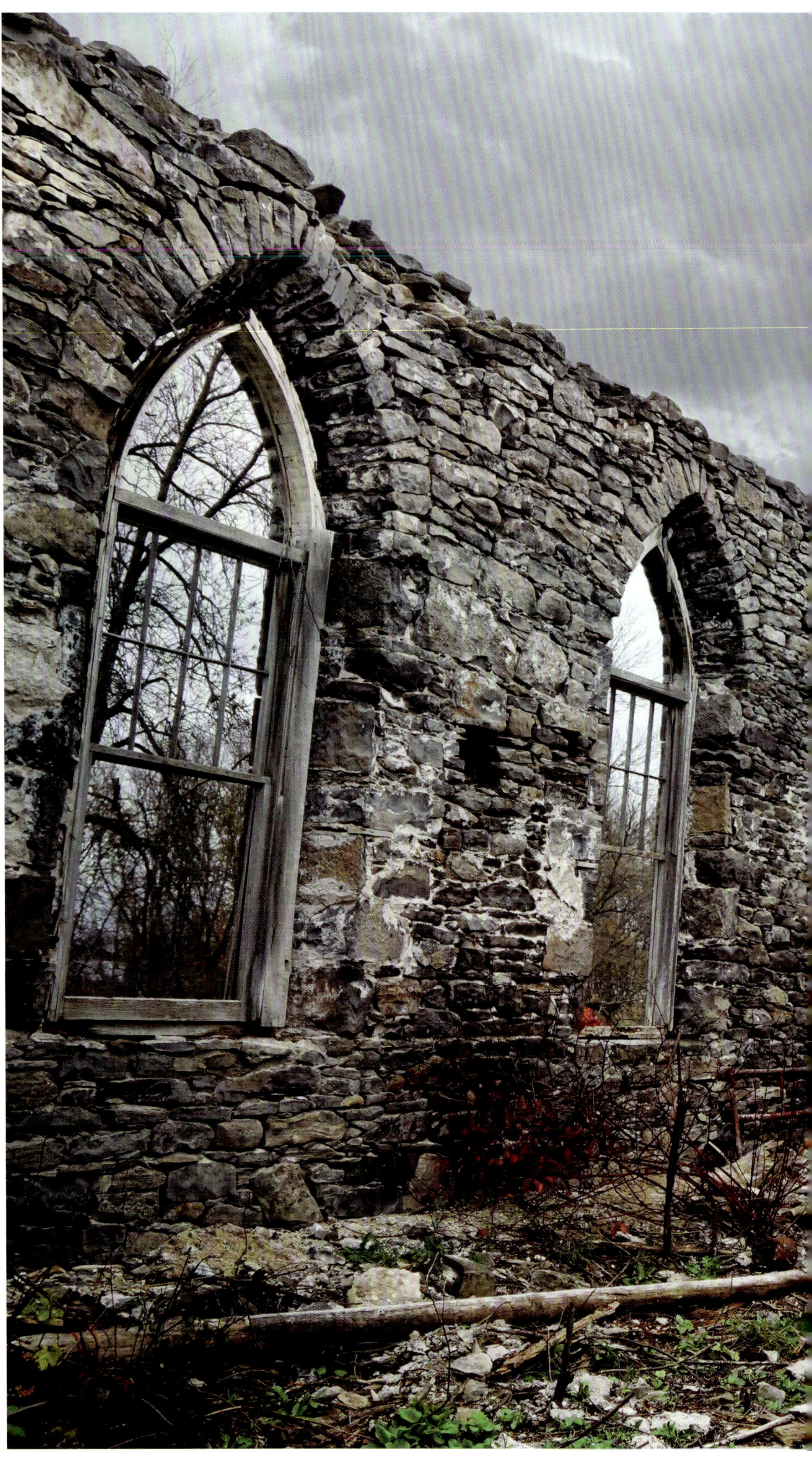

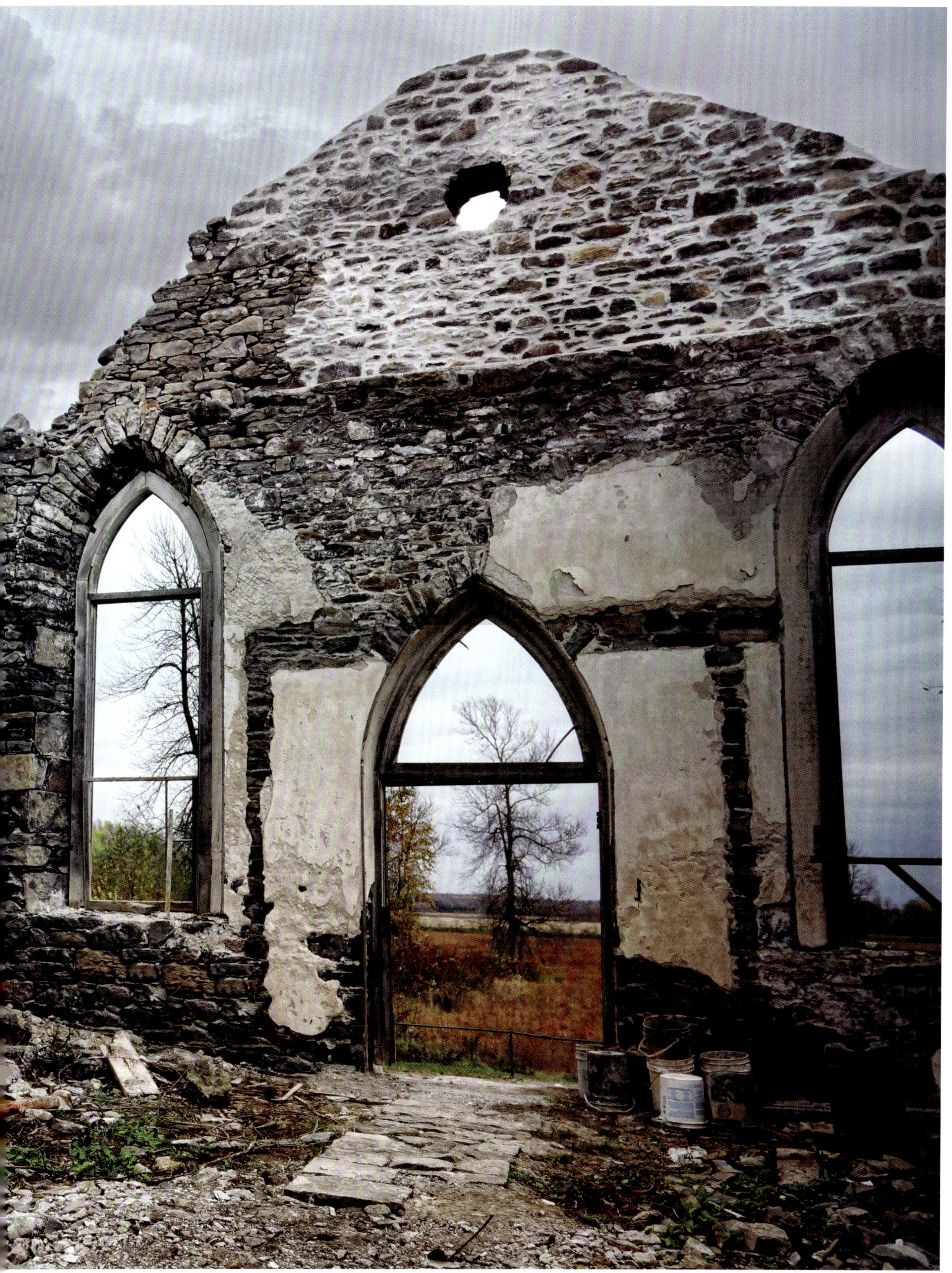

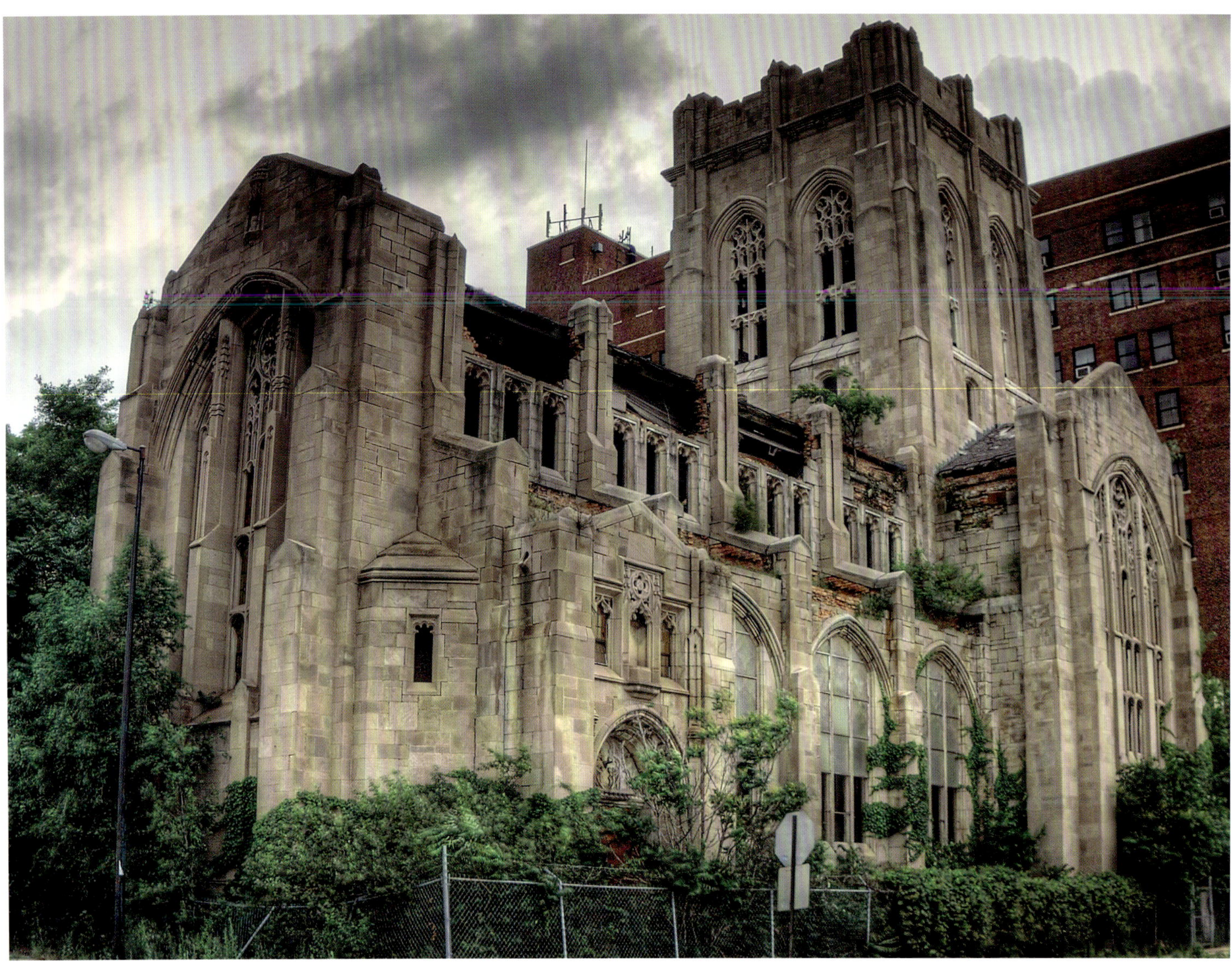

BOTH PHOTOGRAPHS:
City Methodist Church, Gary, Indiana, USA
The City Methodist Church was a hub of 1950s urban life in Gary. Its congregation exceeded 3000 and its surrounding nine-storey complex had a theatre, gymnasium and university annexe. The church's vaulted ceiling and massive internal columns express the confidence of its founder, Methodist minister and social activist William Grant Seaman. In the 1920s, he persuaded US Steel to bequeath inner city land for a church to improve the morals of residents who lived near brothels and speakeasies. To an extent he succeeded – until the church closed in 1974.

So what caused its demise? In a nutshell, de-industrialization: Gary, 64km (40 miles) from Chicago, was renowned for its steel mills and associated businesses. Then economic malaise destroyed jobs and churches like City lost their congregants, who fled to the suburbs.

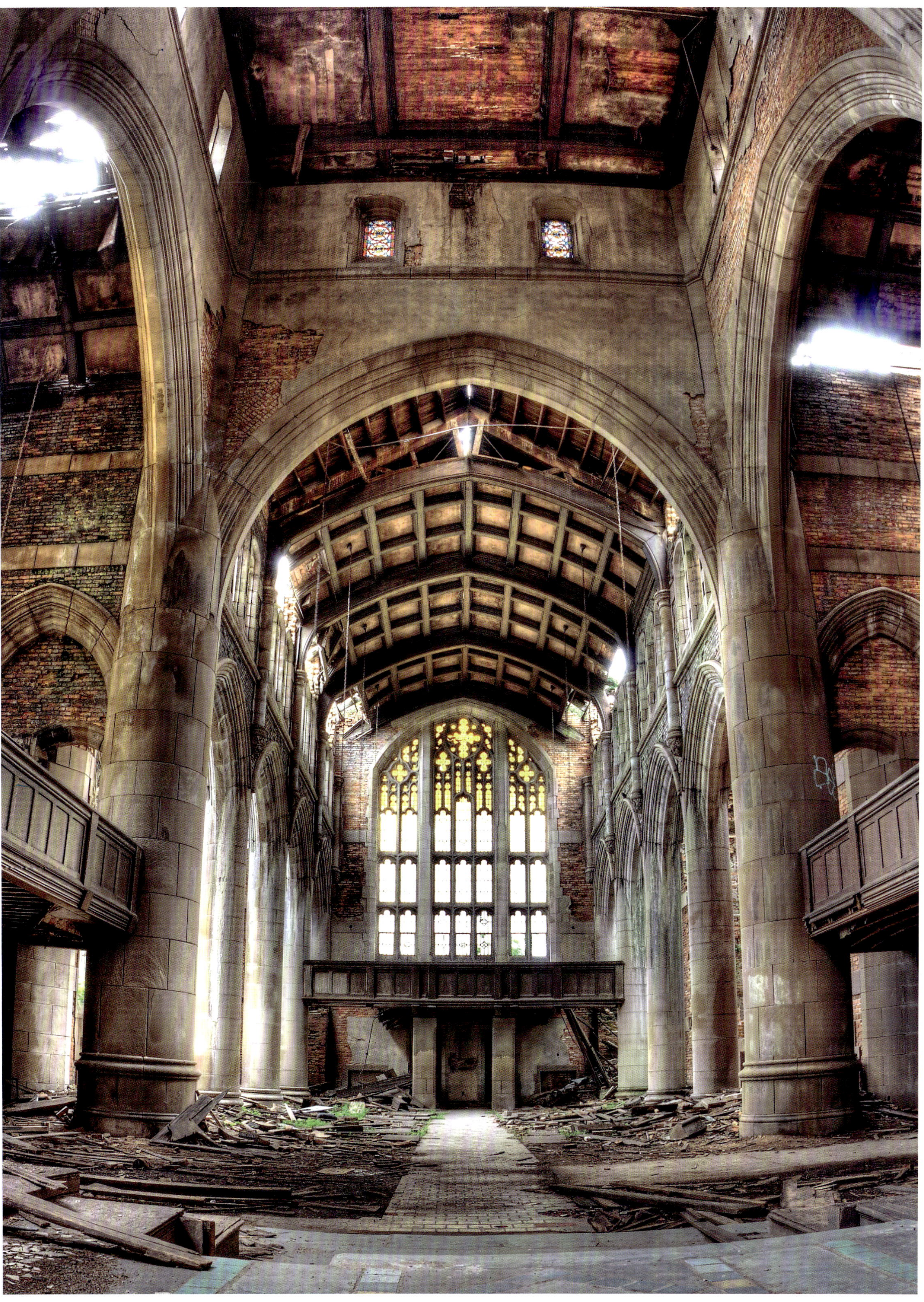

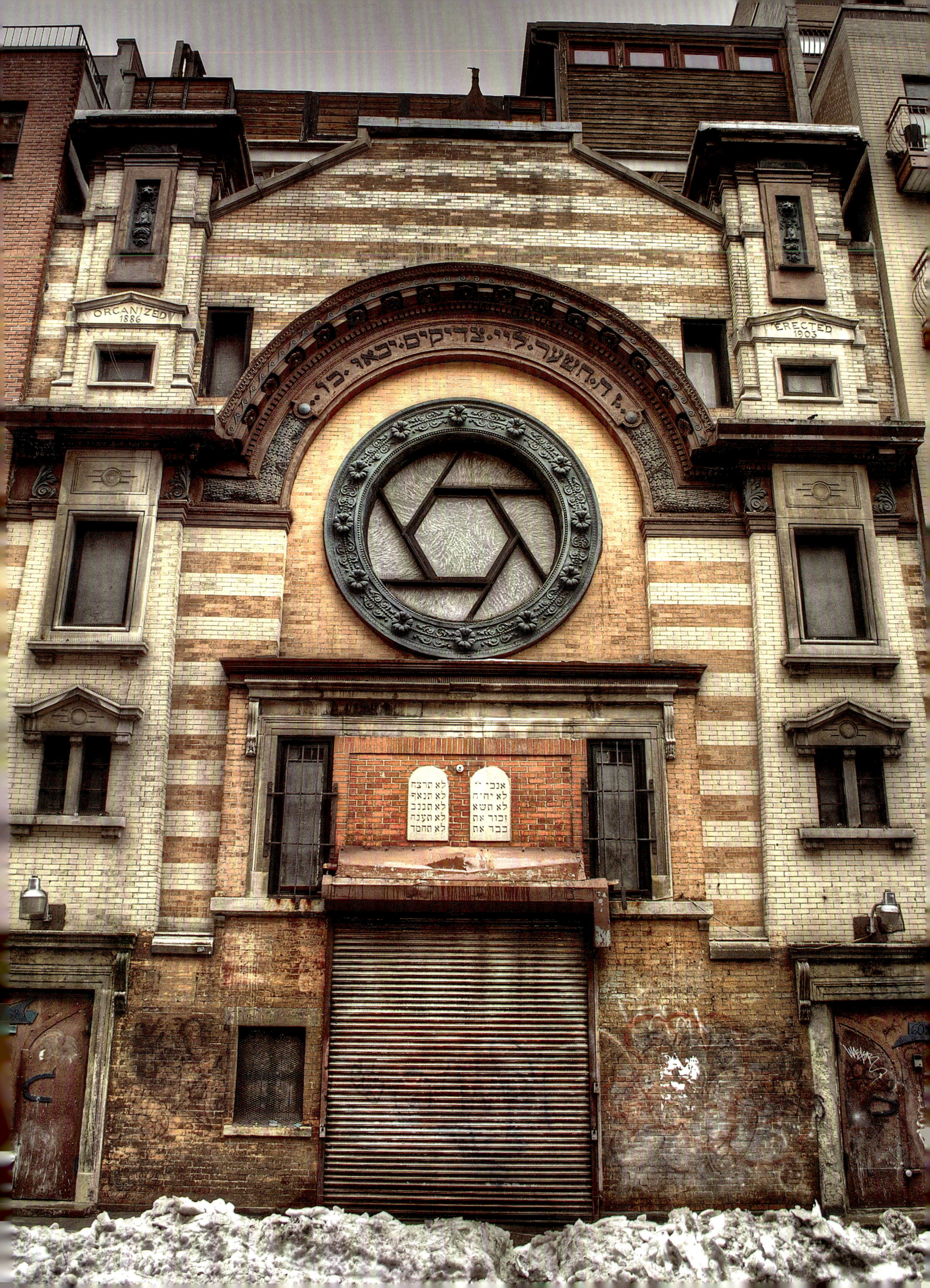
ORGANIZED 1886
ERECTED 1903
זה השער ליי צדיקים יבאו בו

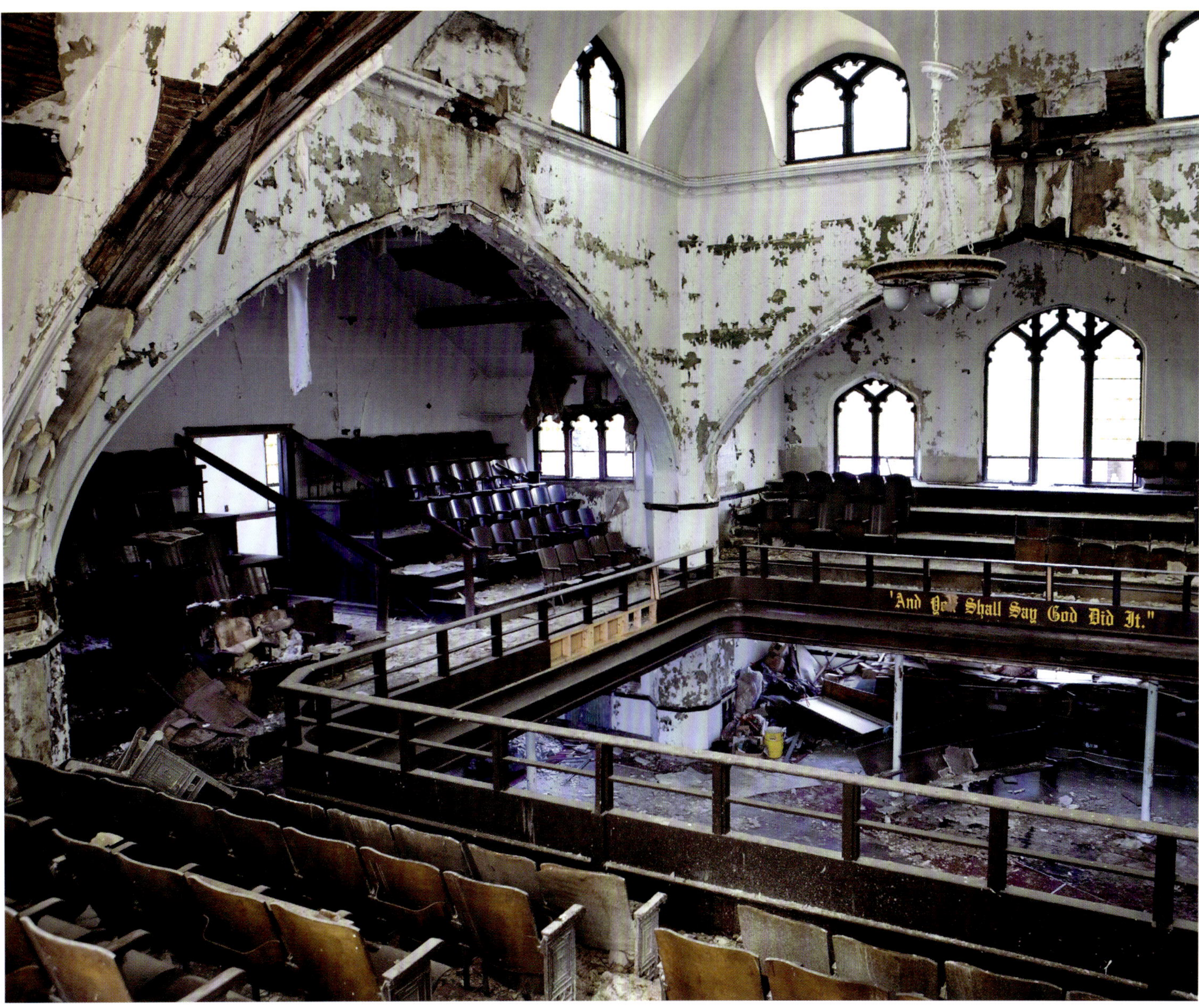

OPPOSITE:

Adath Jeshurun of Jassy Synagogue, New York City, USA

More Jews live in New York than any other city; at last count more than 1.5 million, or three times those in Jerusalem itself. Yet demographic shifts have led several synagogues to shut, even in the Big Apple. One is Adath Jeshurun of Jassy Synagogue in the Lower East Side. Its front exterior displays the Ten Commandments on two tablets, along with a curious circle-framed emblem that once was a Star of David, until certain mullions were peeled off.

Built in eclectic Moorish Revival style in 1904, it originally served Jews from Romania, before passing hands to a Polish community in 1912. Most congregants left in the 1950s and Adath closed its doors two decades later. In recent years the building has been repurposed for artists' studios.

ABOVE:

East Methodist Church, Detroit, Illinois, USA

Crumbling seats and mildewed walls reveal little evidence of the East Methodist Church's former elegance. It is found in Detroit, once famous for its massive car industry and soul music label Motown. But industrial collapse denuded the city of 60 per cent of inhabitants over as many years; one-third of houses lie in ruins, rioting dispelled investors and nature has reclaimed large areas. In 2009, the city filed the largest municipal bankruptcy in US history.

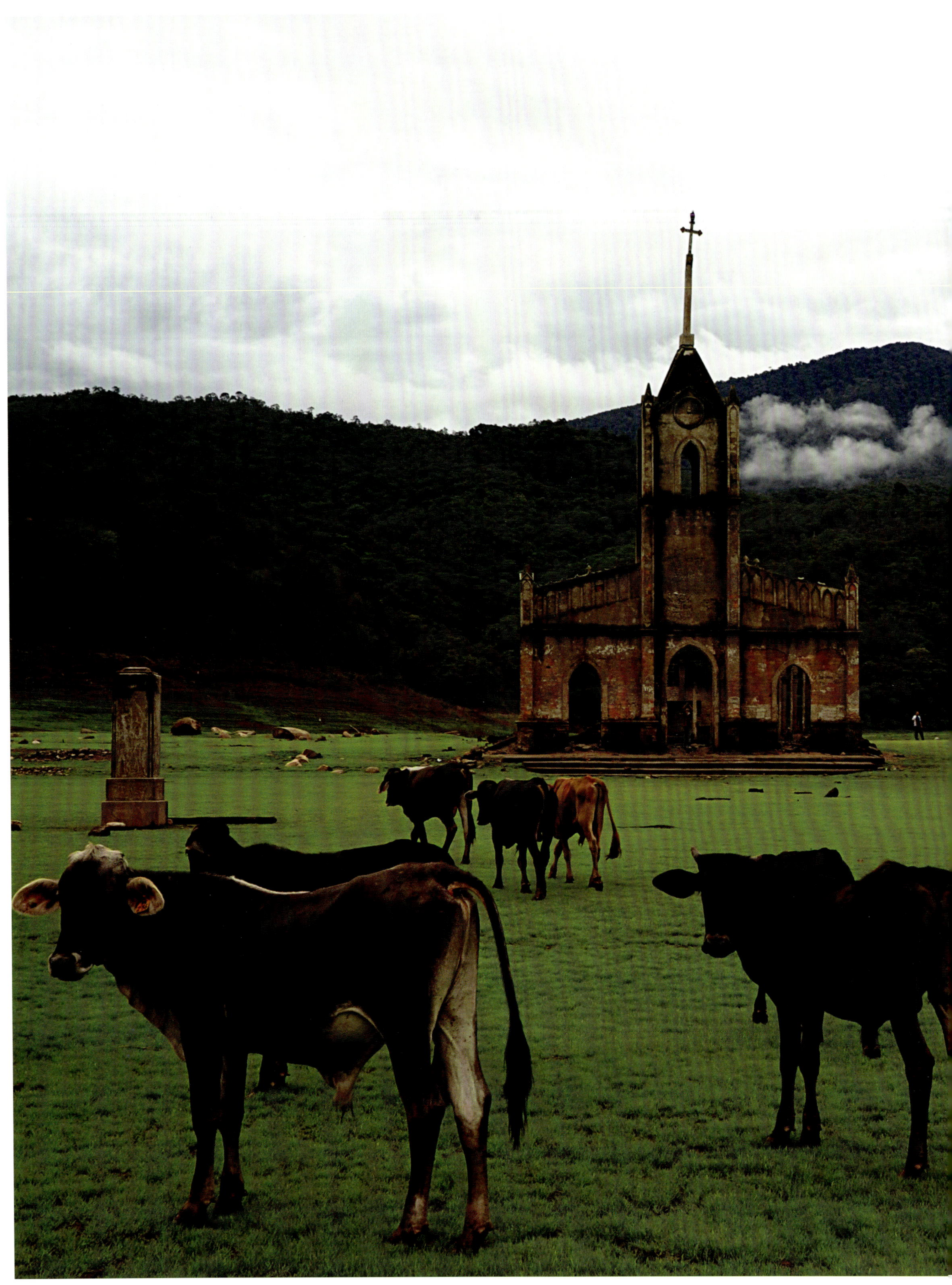

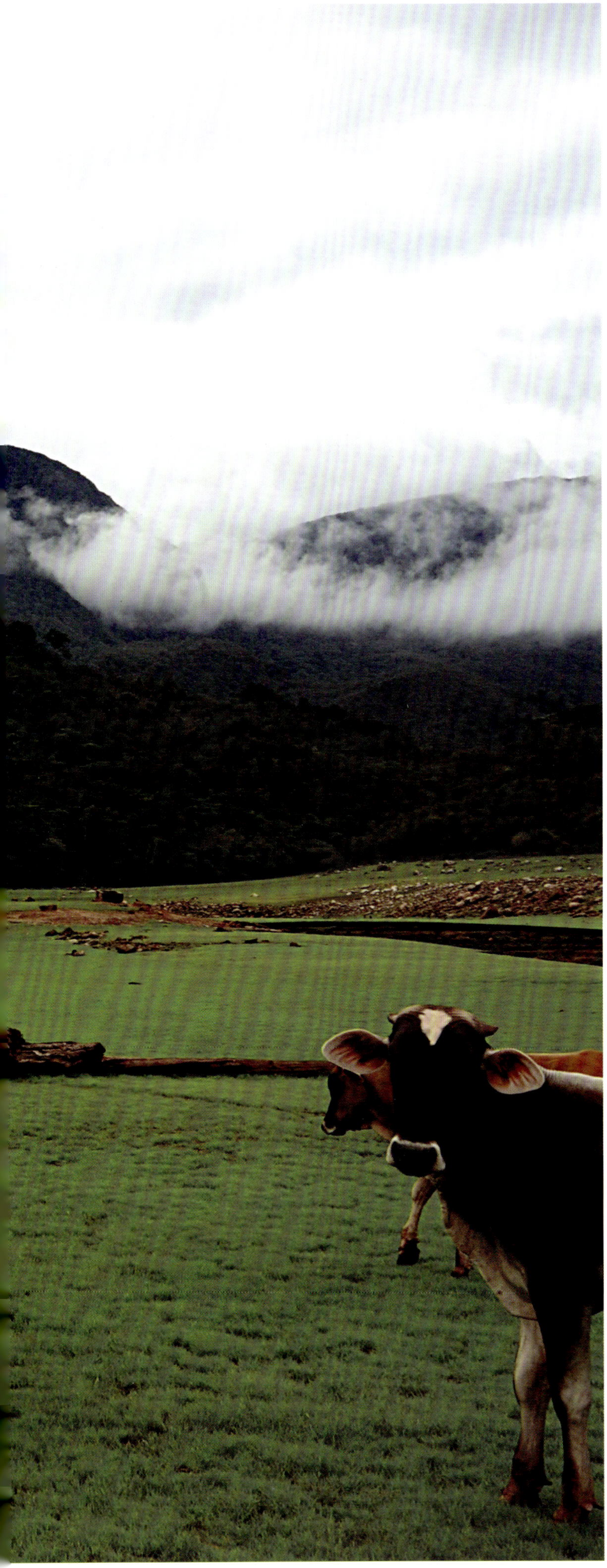

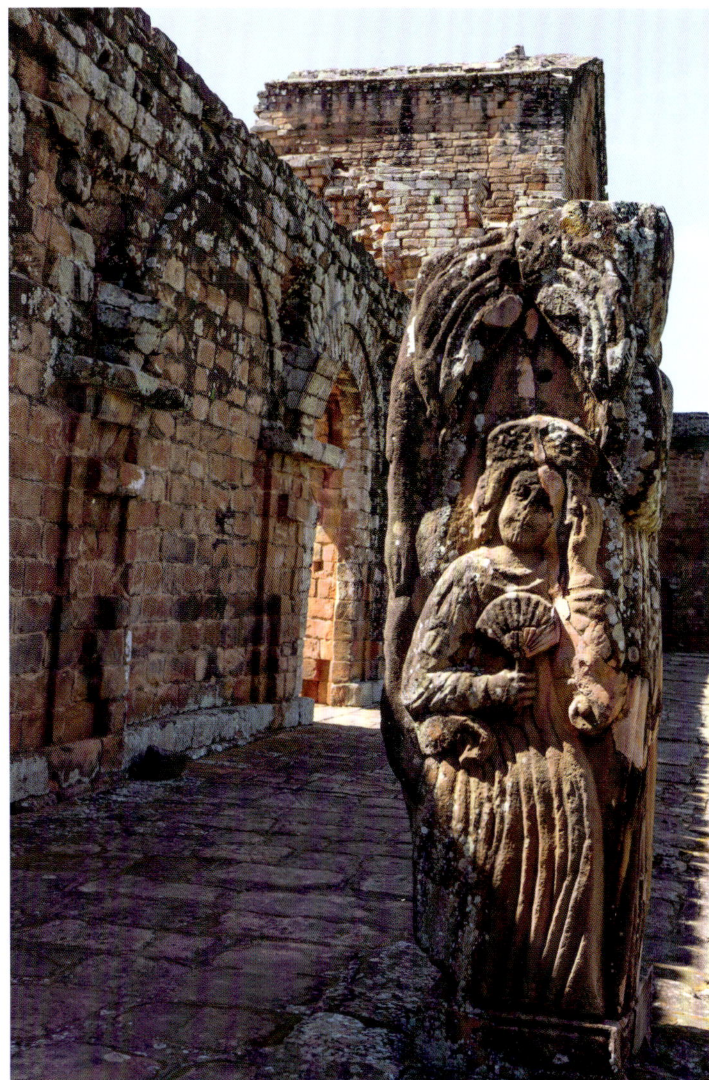

LEFT:

Potosi Church, Táchira State, Venezuela

Nature triumphed over politicians in Potosi, but not by enough to get congregants back to their church pews. In 1985, President Carlos Andres Perez ordered Potosi's 1200 residents to leave and make way for a huge hydroelectric dam. The town disappeared underwater. All that peeped above the waterline was the colonial era church's steeple. Then in 2010 Potosi spookily re-emerged after drought reduced Uribante Reservoir's water levels. What we see, however, is a facade; the church interior is totally gutted.

ABOVE:

Jesuit Mission, La Santisima Trinidad de Paraná, Paraguay

The grandly named La Santisima Trinidad de Paraná, or Most Holy Trinity of Paraná, well deserves its status as one of Paraguay's two UNESCO World Heritage Sites. Founded in 1712, it was a self-sufficient Jesuit mission largely run by converted Amerindians. Ultimately Paraguay's expulsion of Jesuits in 1767 and a deluge of looting and killing thereafter led to Trinidad's downfall.

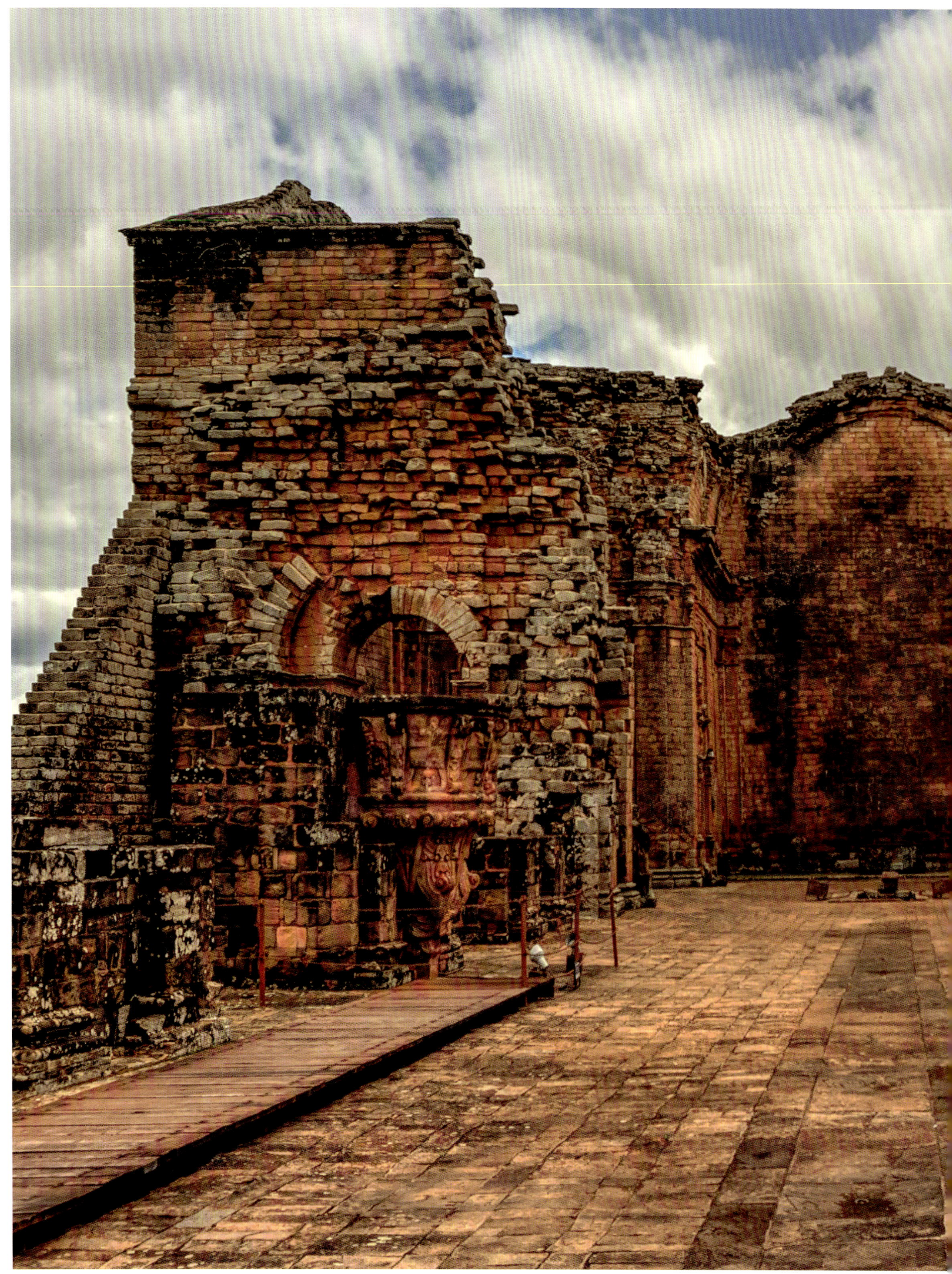

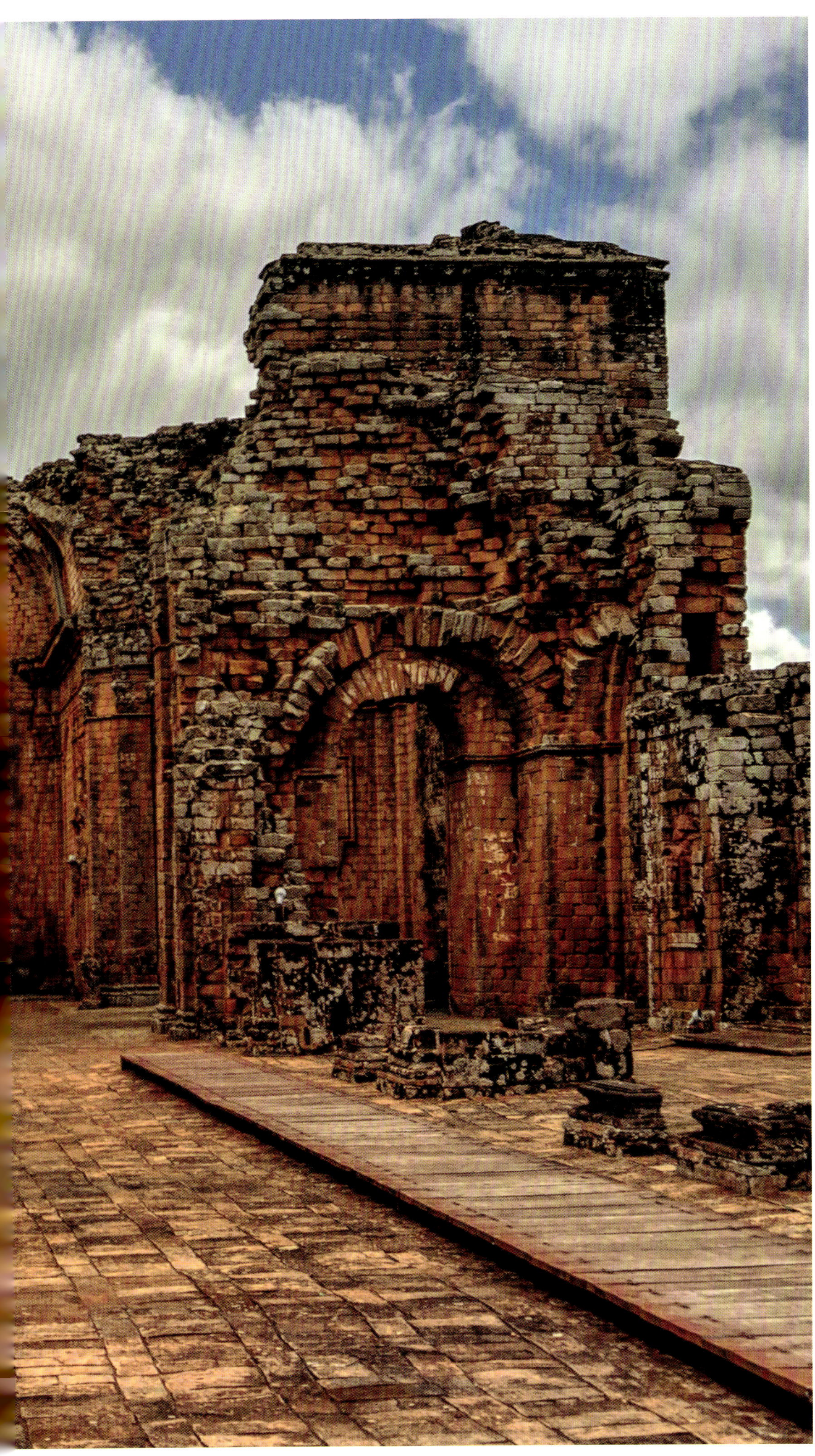

Jesuit Mission Jesus de Tavarangue, Itapua, Paraguay
This handsome, unfinished mission church for the Christianized Guarani people resembles a corner of Italy transplanted to South America. Building began in 1760 to a design replicating the Baroque-style Church of Ignatius of Loyola at Campus Martius in Rome. Construction was still underway when Spanish authorities drove the Jesuits out of Paraguay seven years later. Madrid felt that Jesuits were too close to the Pope and too scornful of secular authority.

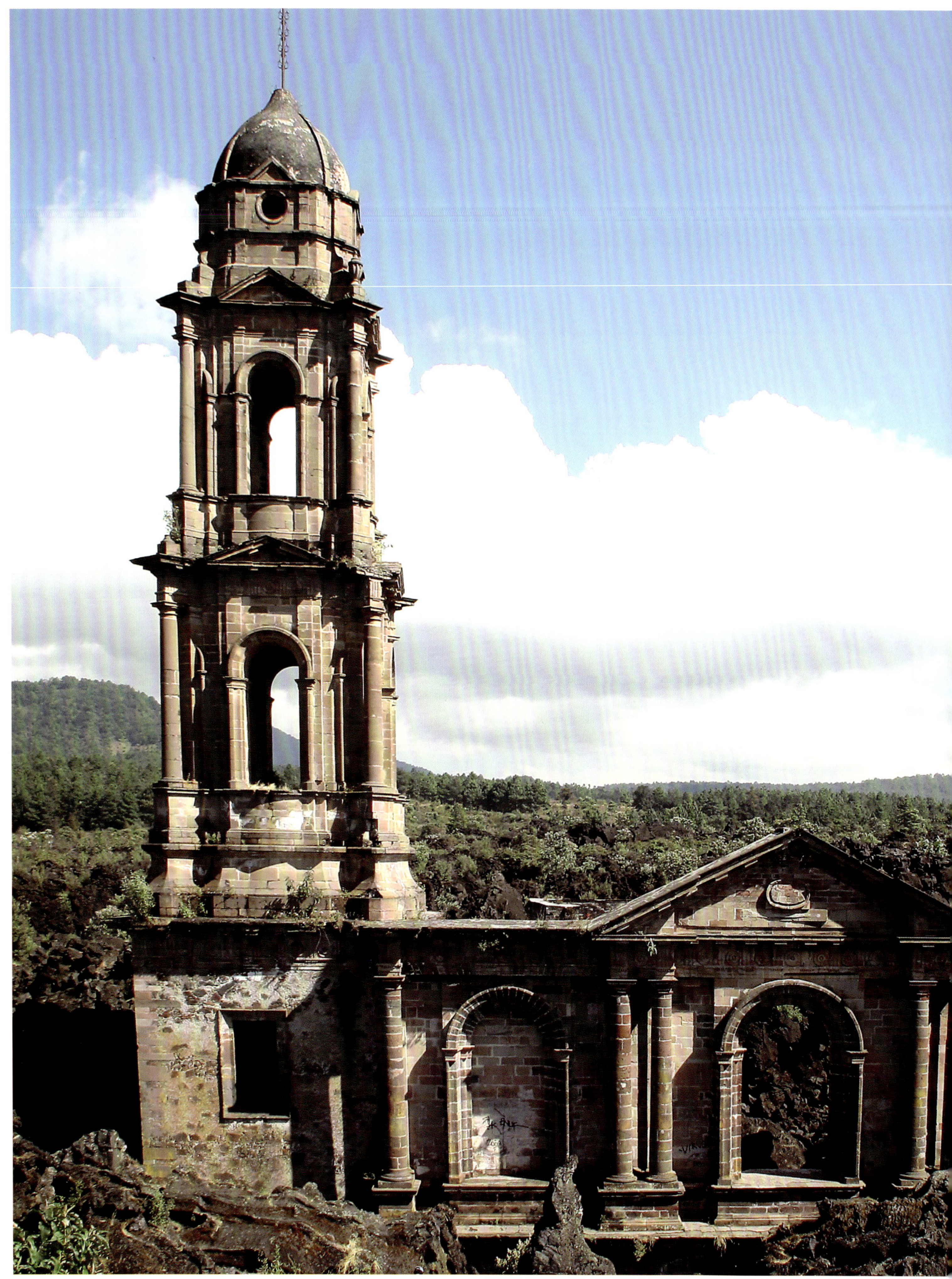

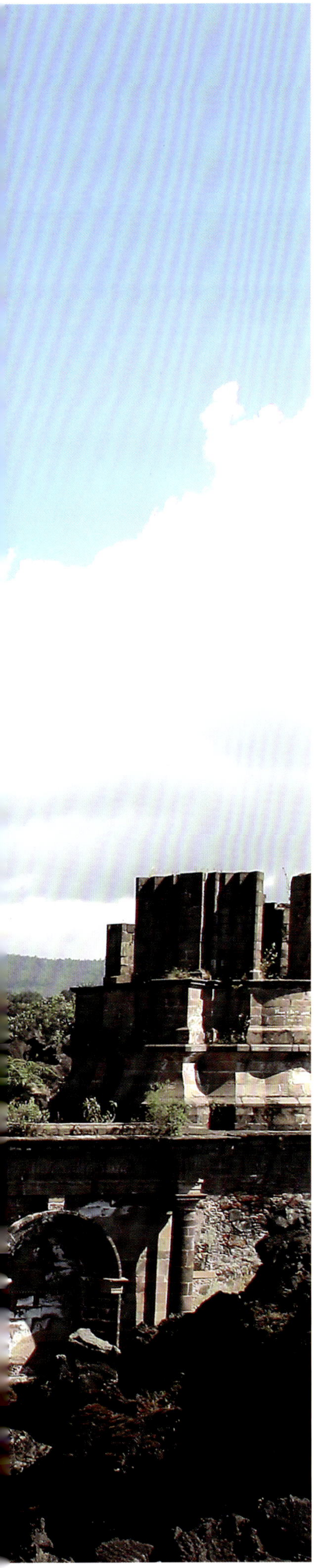

BOTH PHOTOGRAPHS:
San Juan Parangaricutiro, Michoacán Province, Mexico
A deluge of ash and lava destroyed the town of San Juan Parangaricutiro in 1943, yet this church tower still proudly emerges above the black debris. Matter accumulated over the next eight years and created the world's youngest volcano, Mount Paricutin, which eventually topped 2800 metres (9186ft).

The Basilican-style church probably survived the eruptions because of the expertly engineered solid slabs that Augustinian monks used when they began building it in the mid-1600s. Pilgrims used to flock to the old church to marvel at the reputedly miracle-working crucifix of El Señor de Los Milagros (Lord of Miracles). Since 1943 a new town has sprouted beside the old. Its church houses the wooden image of a saint that fleeing parishioners rescued from their former sanctuary.

Curiously, the town's name means St John of the Bedspreads.

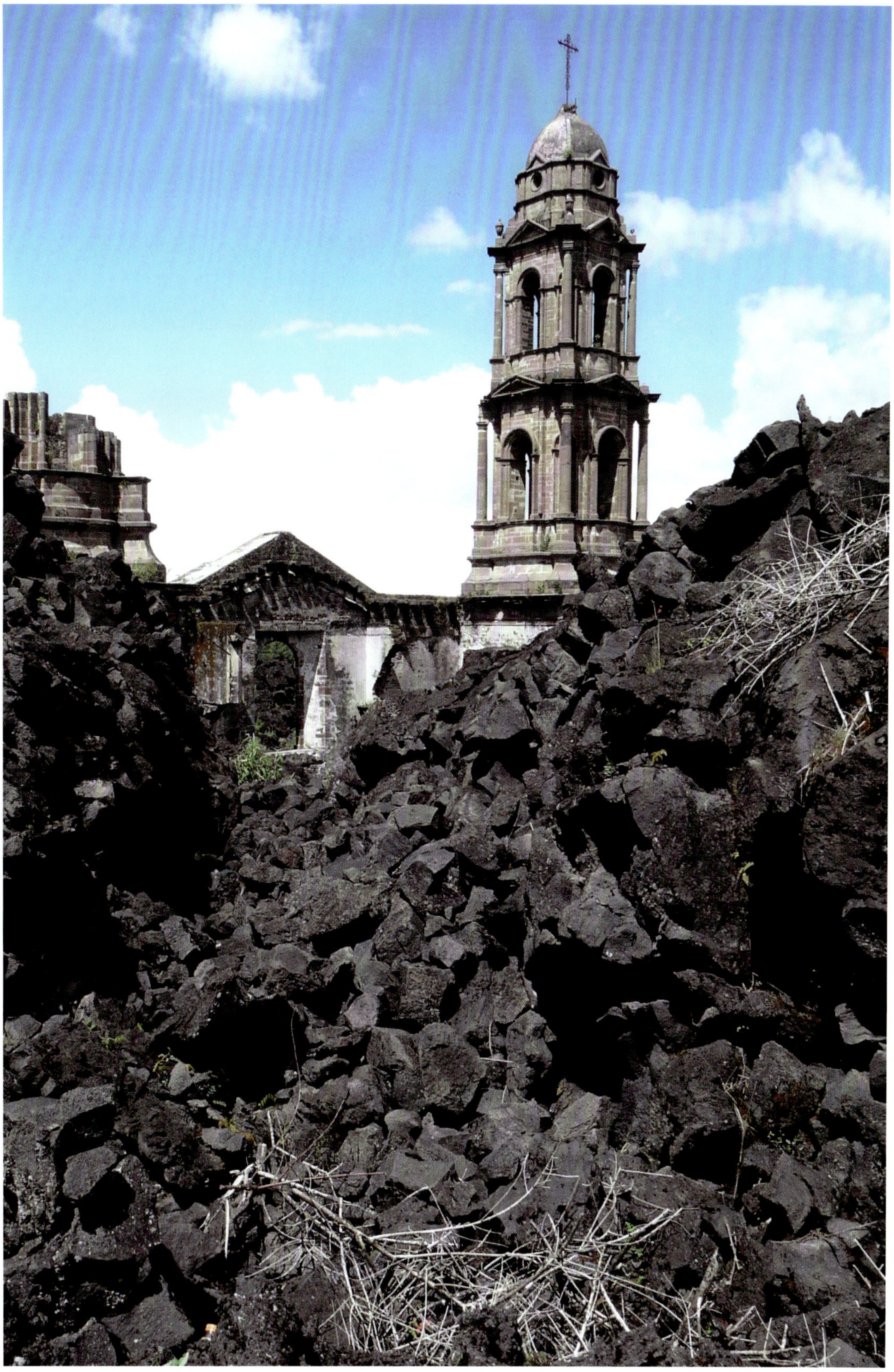

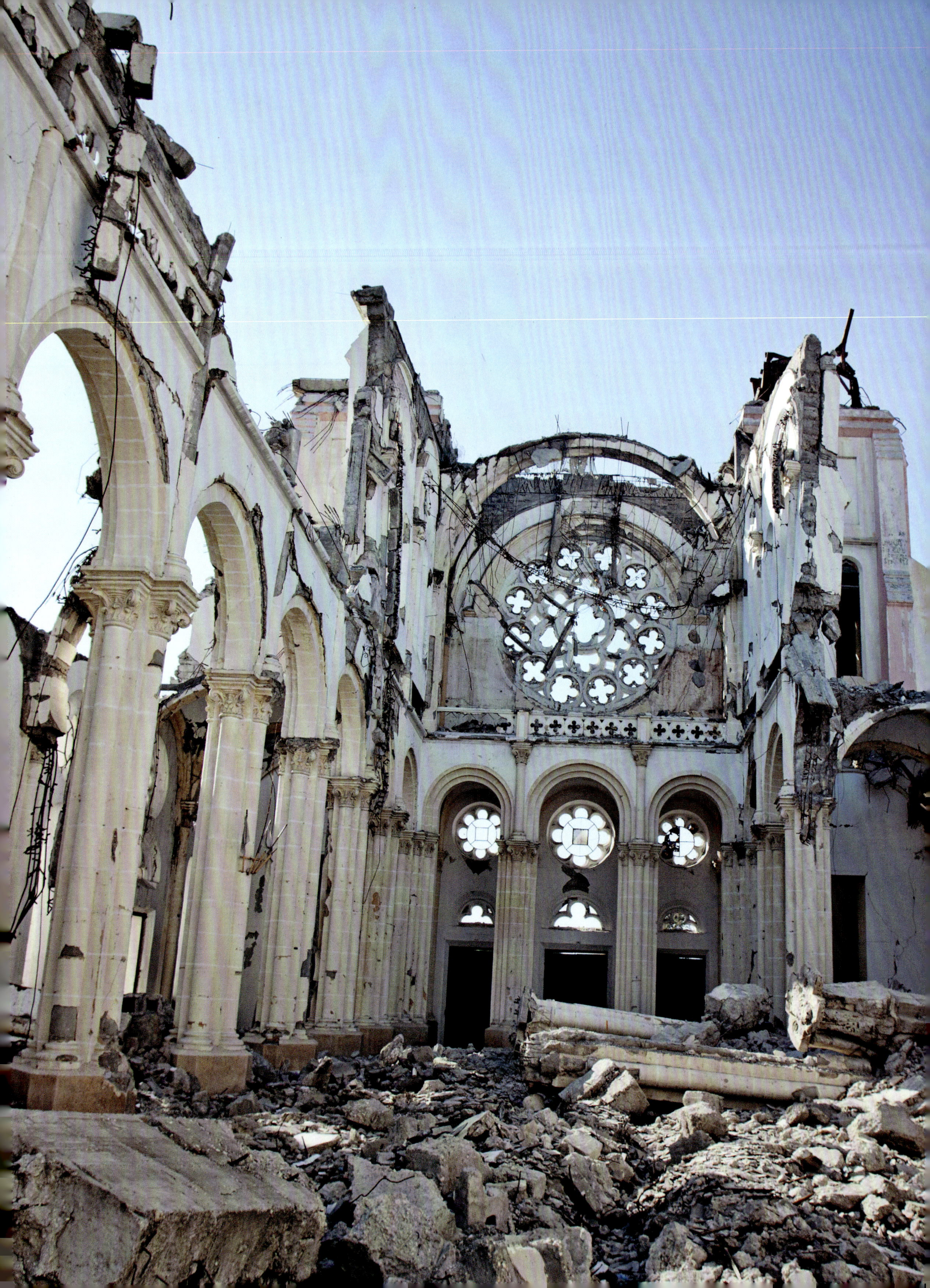

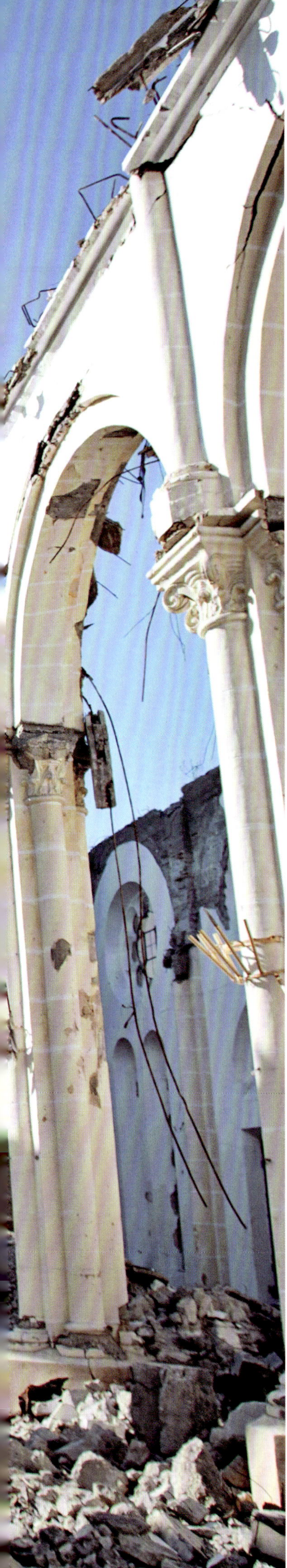

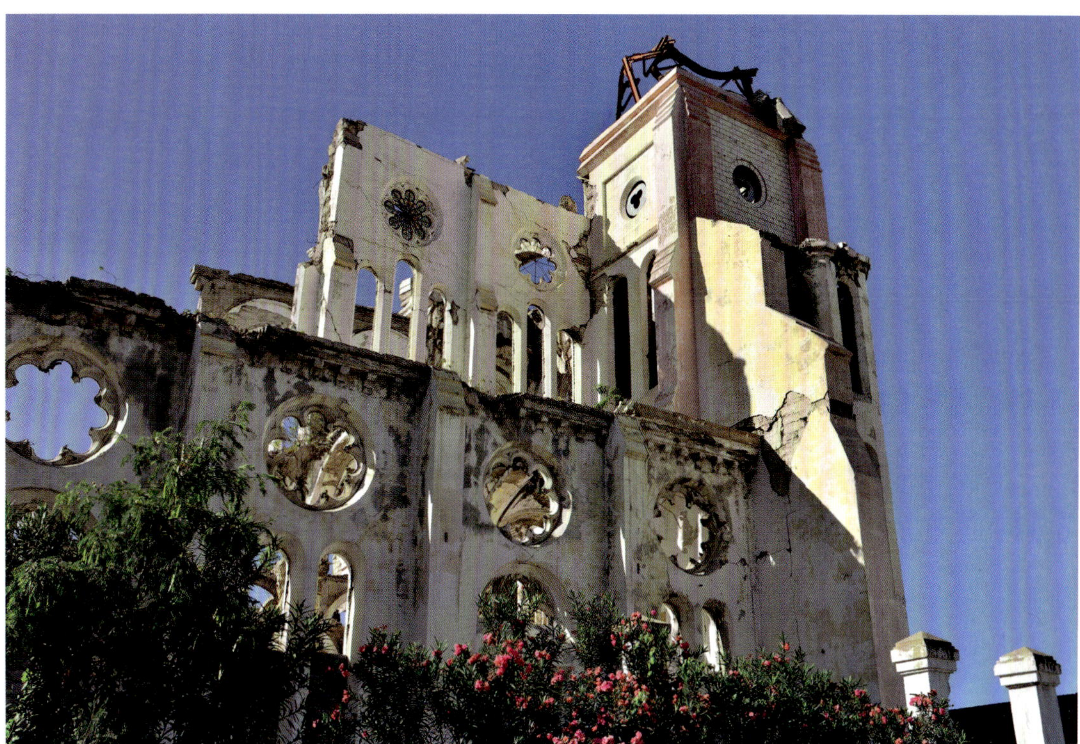

BOTH PHOTOGRAPHS:

Cathedral of Our Lady of the Assumption, Port au Prince, Haiti

Lovingly built over 30 years from 1884–1914, the Cathedral of Our Lady of the Assumption took only a few seconds to crash to the ground on 12 January 2010. Well, certainly the roof and entrance columns did – somehow the main structure survived the great Haitian earthquake, albeit badly damaged.

Still visible are the outlines of elegant grand round stained glass windows, redolent of the Gothic Revival style of fin de siècle Europe. Standing high over the city, one of the cathedral's Coptic spires had even served as a lighthouse.

Some 300,000 Haitians died in the 2010 disaster, including Archbishop Joseph Serge Miot, who was buried under rubble at the cathedral. In 2012 a Puerto Rican architect won a competition to redesign the cathedral. Unfortunately political tussles seem to be delaying delivery.

Church, Port Arthur, Tasmania, Australia

This discarded Gothic style church may look like a Disney castle, but it has a much darker history. The chapel served inmates of Port Arthur, Australia's largest and most notorious prison colony. Many were re-offenders from Australia's original wave of 'transported' convicts. Some were juveniles as young as nine. They worked away under strict surveillance in prison dockyards and other industries – and built this, their own non-denominational church.

Port Arthur became a penal colony in 1833. Hard labour and regular compulsory church services were considered as twin pathways to 'rehabilitation' on this isolated peninsula. In 1877, however, the enterprise was shut down, and in 1895 and 1897 fires gutted many buildings.

In a gruesome epilogue to Port Arthur's already turbulent history, the popular tourist site witnessed the worst mass shooting in Australian history, when 35 visitors were killed in April 1996.

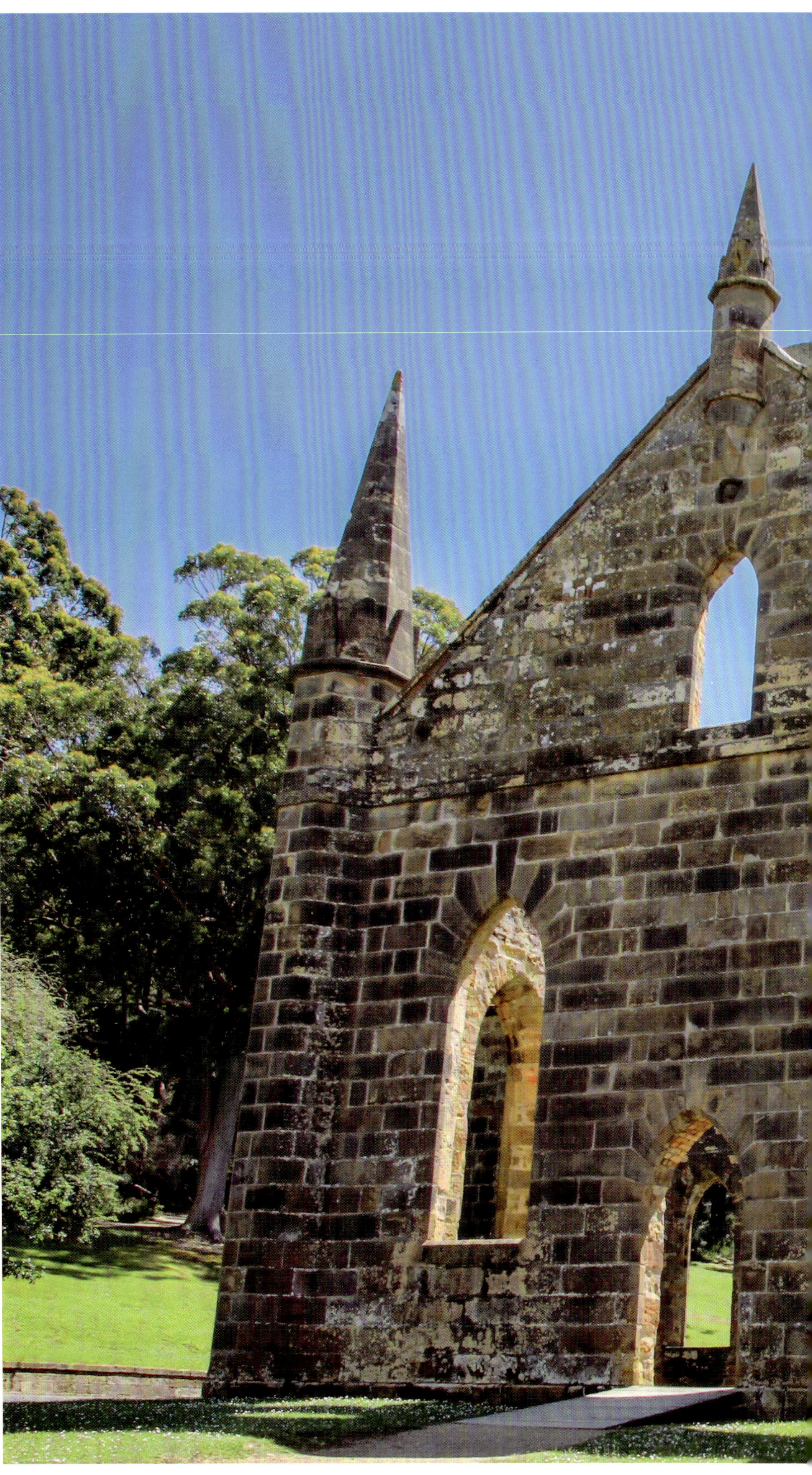

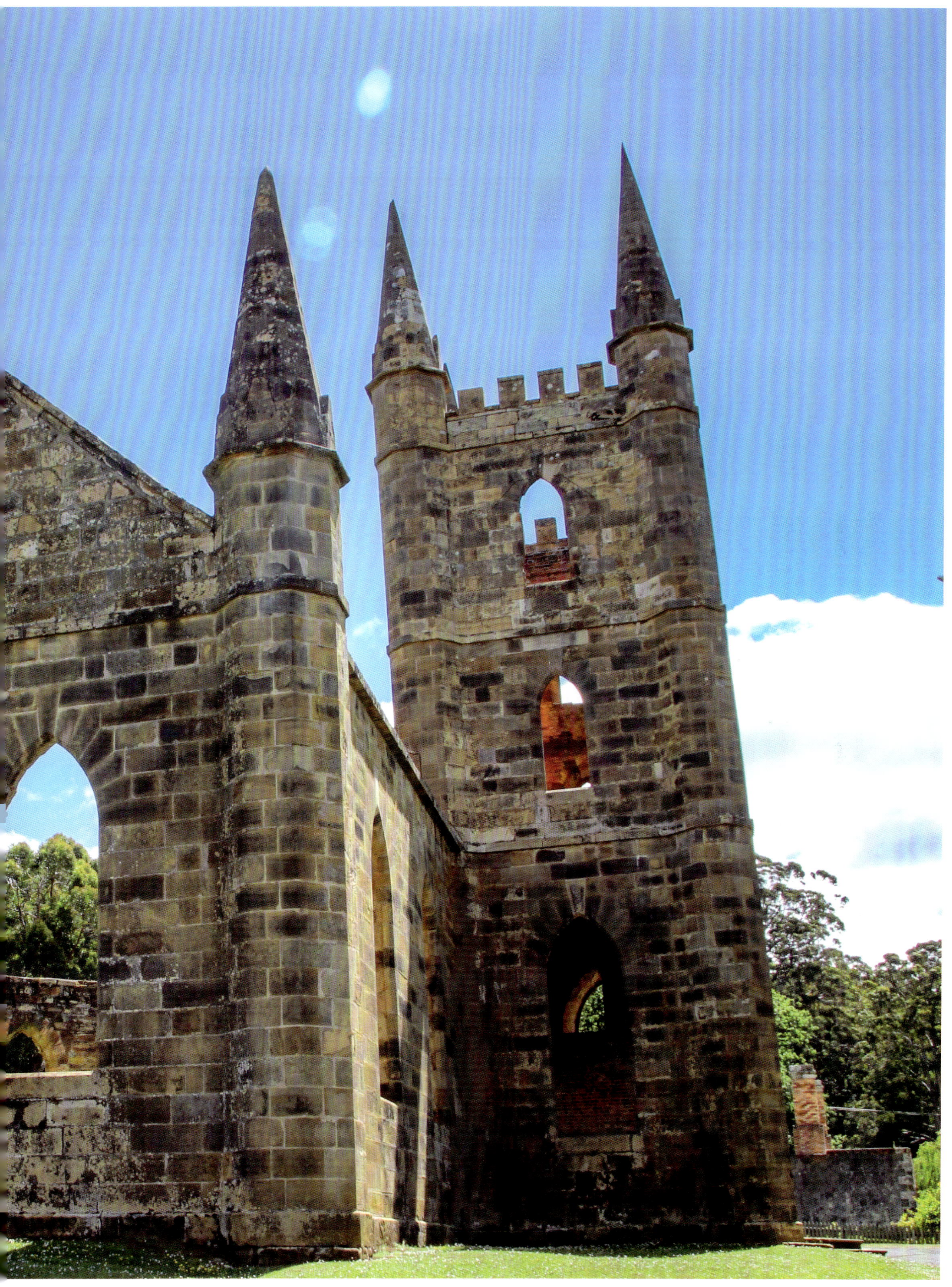

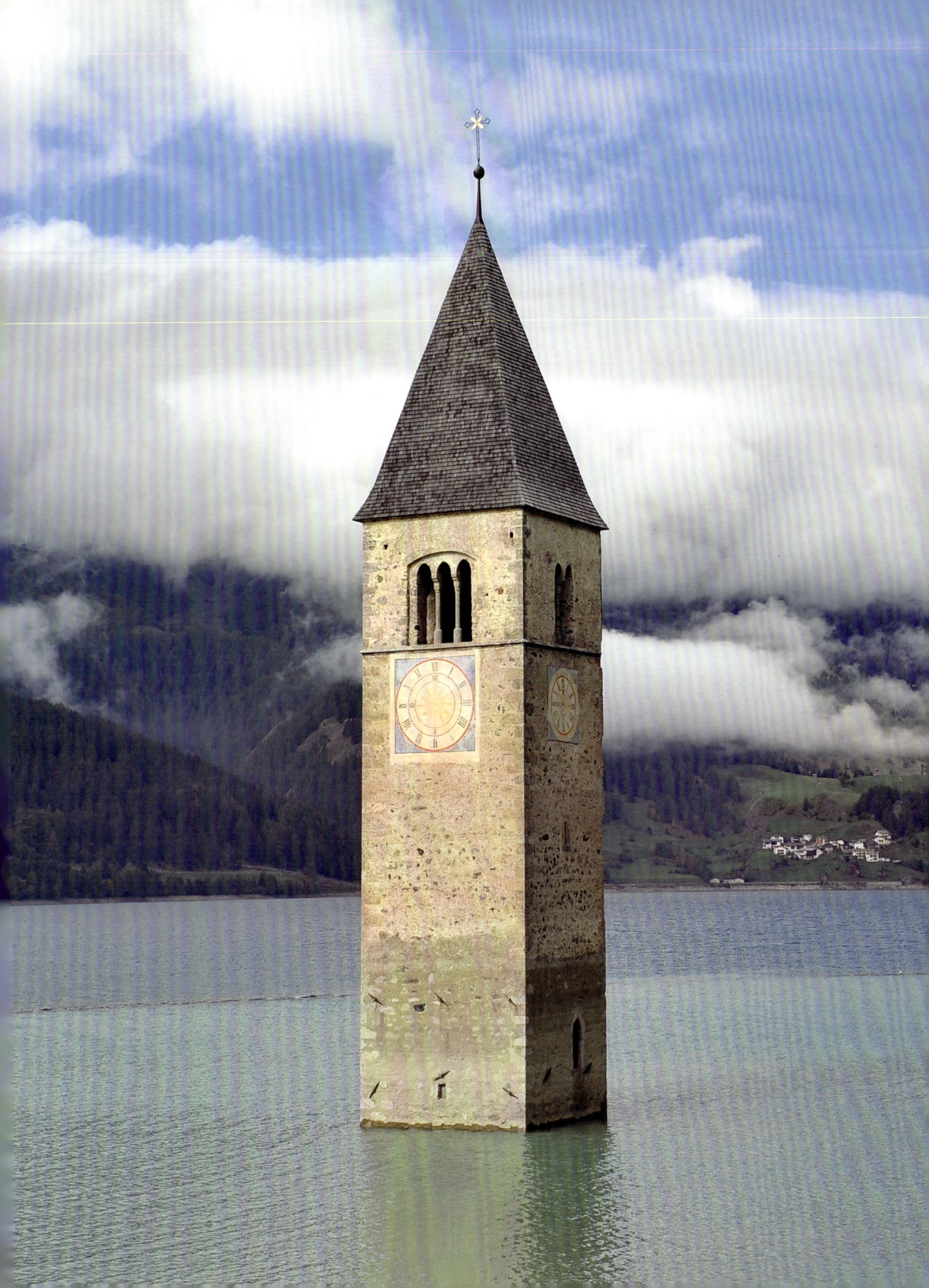

Europe

Christianity and Europe are often considered synonymous. Europe's first cultures, however, were 'pagan': Stonehenge in England or Hagar Qim in Malta, sites whose function still leave us puzzled; or outstanding Greek remains such as the Parthenon and Delphi. The religious turning point came in 380 CE when the Roman Empire adopted Christianity.

So why have so many churches been deserted? Battles *within* Christendom provide one answer. King Henry VIII of England's break with papal authority and closure of all Catholic institutions blighted hundreds of English monasteries, priories and convents. Militant Protestants ransacked Scotland's Elgin Cathedral. Antireligious French Revolutionaries devastated Belgium's longstanding Villers Monastery. More recently, aerial bombing during World War II nearly destroyed St Luke's Church in Liverpool and Berlin's Kaiser Wilhelm Church.

Economics is another factor: the desire for hydroelectric power created lakes that submerged cathedrals and churches. Moreover, Nazi genocide against Jews left just ruined synagogues behind; while an atheist Soviet Union deliberately neglected many churches. Nature, too, has played its role: an earthquake in 1887 capsized the baroque chapel at Bussana Vecchia in Italy. At least renewed interest in such sites recalls the rich heritage they represent.

OPPOSITE:
Church, Reschensee, South Tyrol, Italy
Like something out of a fairytale, a Romanesque church spire dating back to 1355 pokes above the surface of Reschensee. Yet in 1950, the image resembled a nightmare for 150 families who were forced to flee the deliberate flooding of their village to create a reservoir.

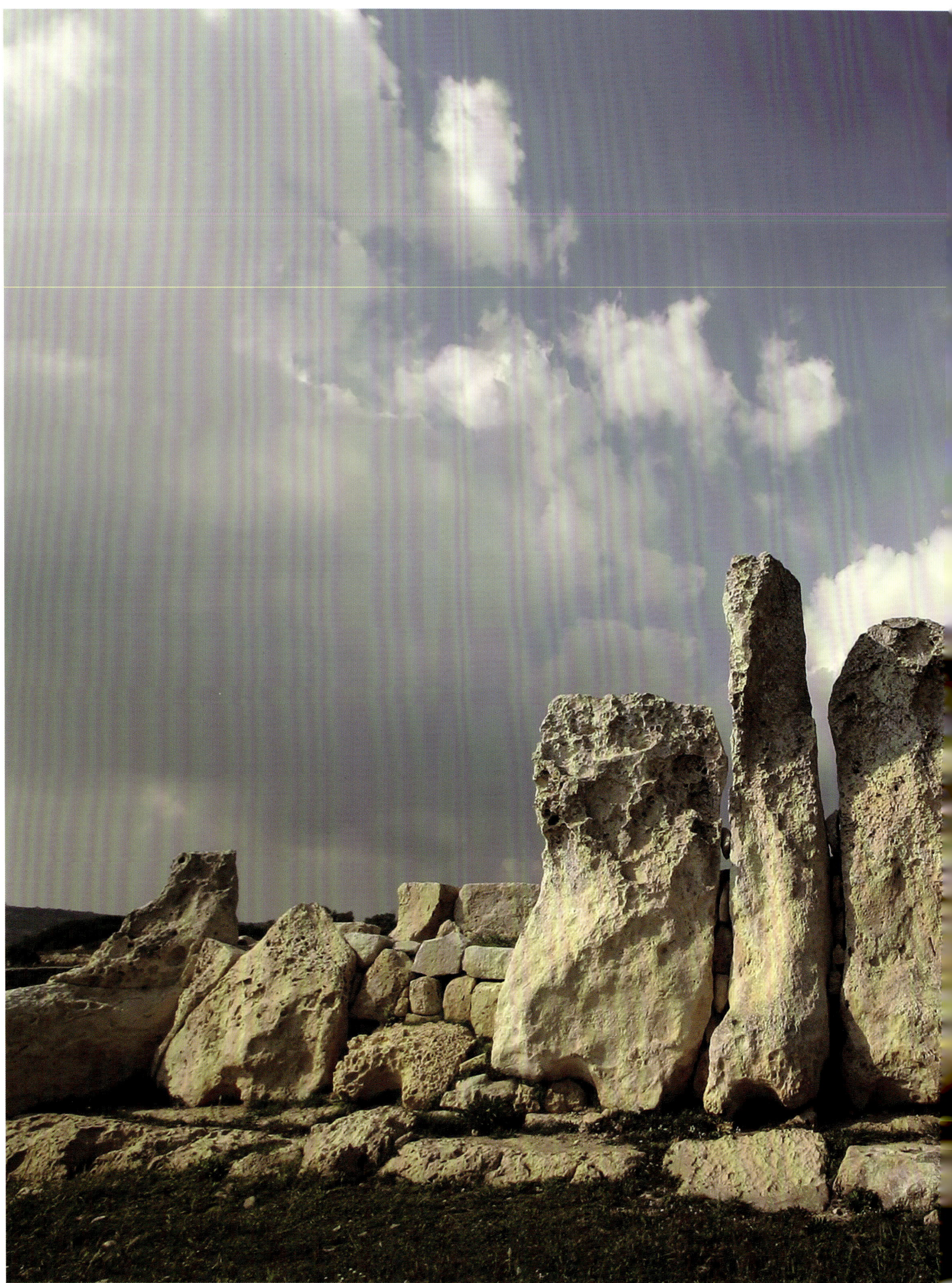

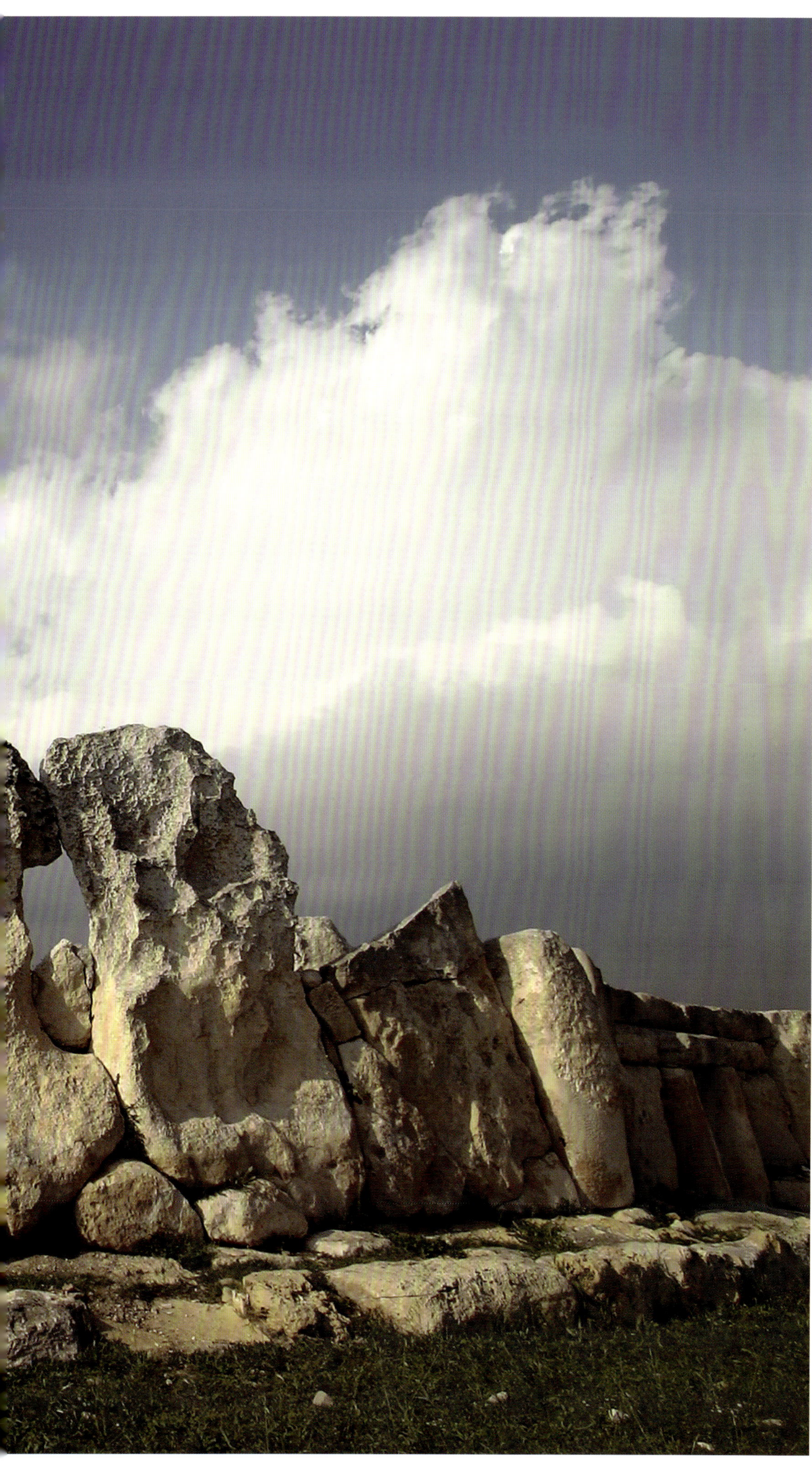

LEFT:

Hagar Qim, Malta

Holy to humans for thousands of years before the Torah, Bible and Koran were written, Hagar Qim has been carbon dated to c.3100 BCE. Its limestone facade hints that it was once almost twice its present height. Its largest block weighs 70 tons and stands 7 metres (23ft) long.

Sacred objects found on site include mother-goddess statuettes, solar wheel-inscribed pottery and a 5.2-metre-high (17ft) menhir – possibly a phallic shrine. Moreover the gates and rooms were designed to catch the winter solstice and equinox sun, indicating that the complex functioned as an astronomical calendar.

NEXT PAGE:

Stonehenge, Wiltshire, England

Every year people flock to Stonehenge to celebrate the winter and summer solstices. But what did the site really mean to the Neolithic and Bronze Age people who built and worshipped there? The answer is still cloaked in mystery.

We do know that Stonehenge was built in six stages between 3000–1520 BCE. Uniquely, the circular monument consists of artificially shaped sarsen stones, along with smaller bluestones that prehistoric Britons somehow carried from south Wales up to 240km (150 miles) away. Scholars have theorized that Stonehenge functioned variously as an eclipse-predicting 'computer', a monument to the ancestral dead, a seasonal gathering place located at the intersection of other prehistoric sites, or a site of sacred healing.

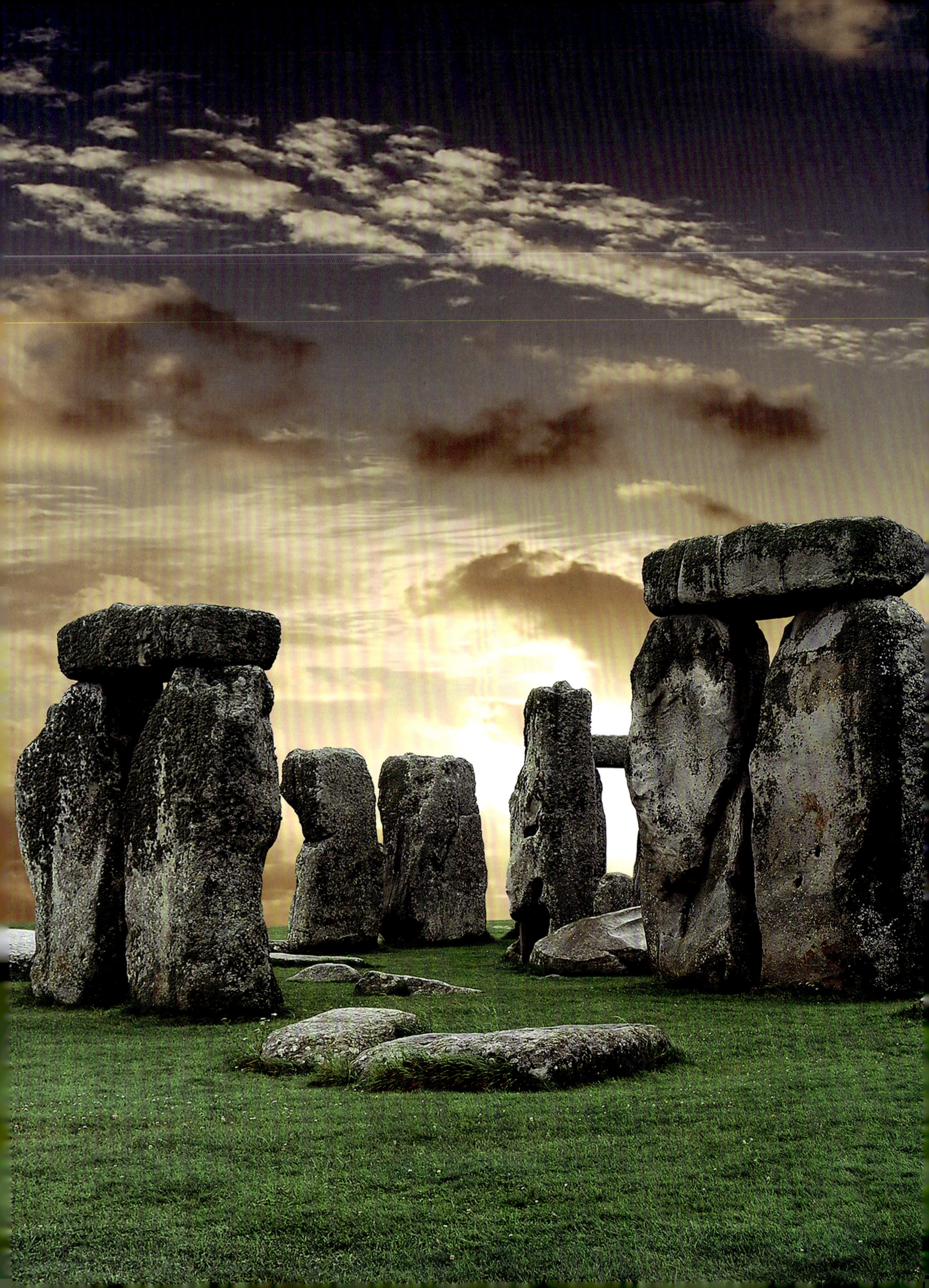

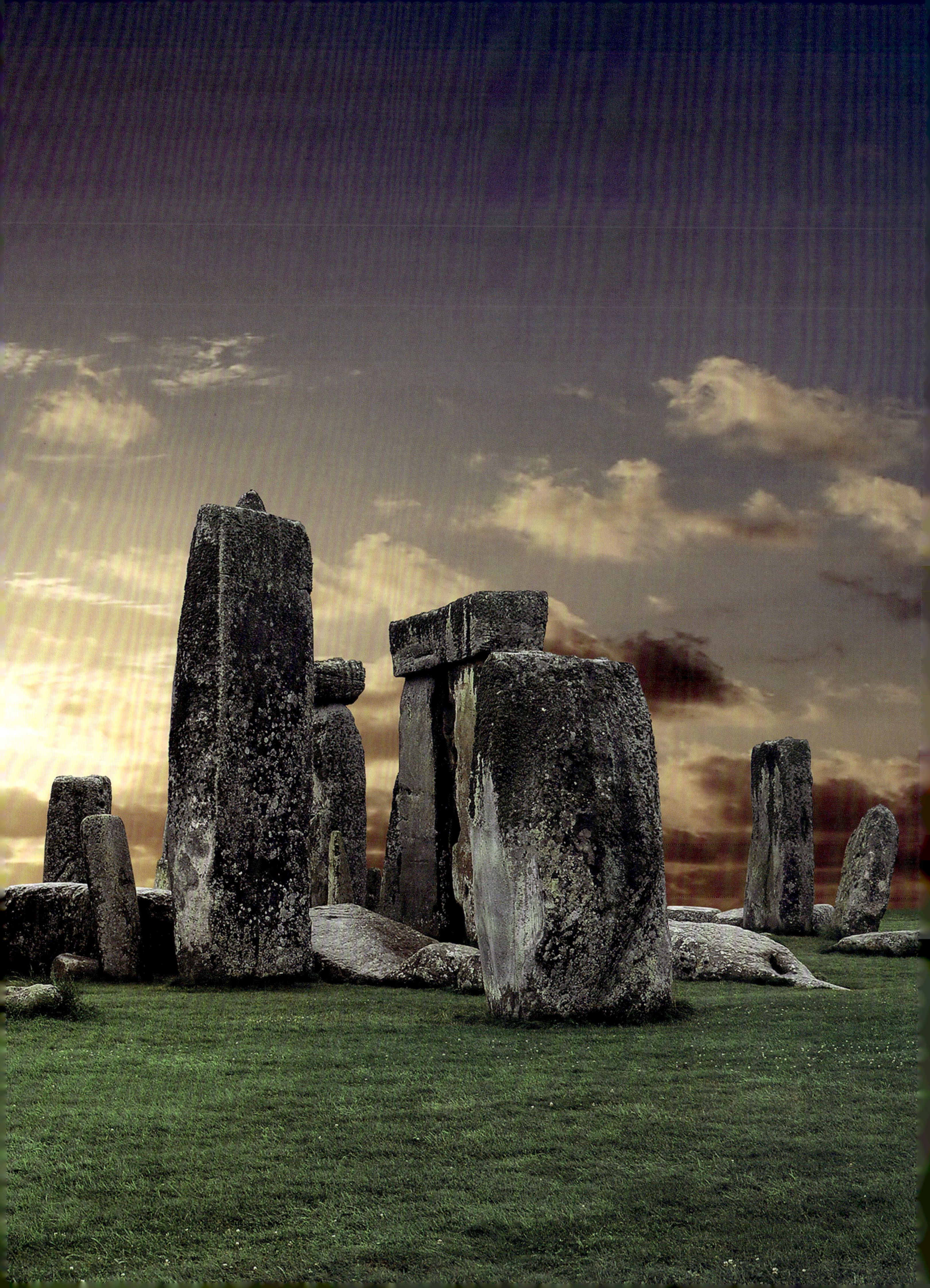

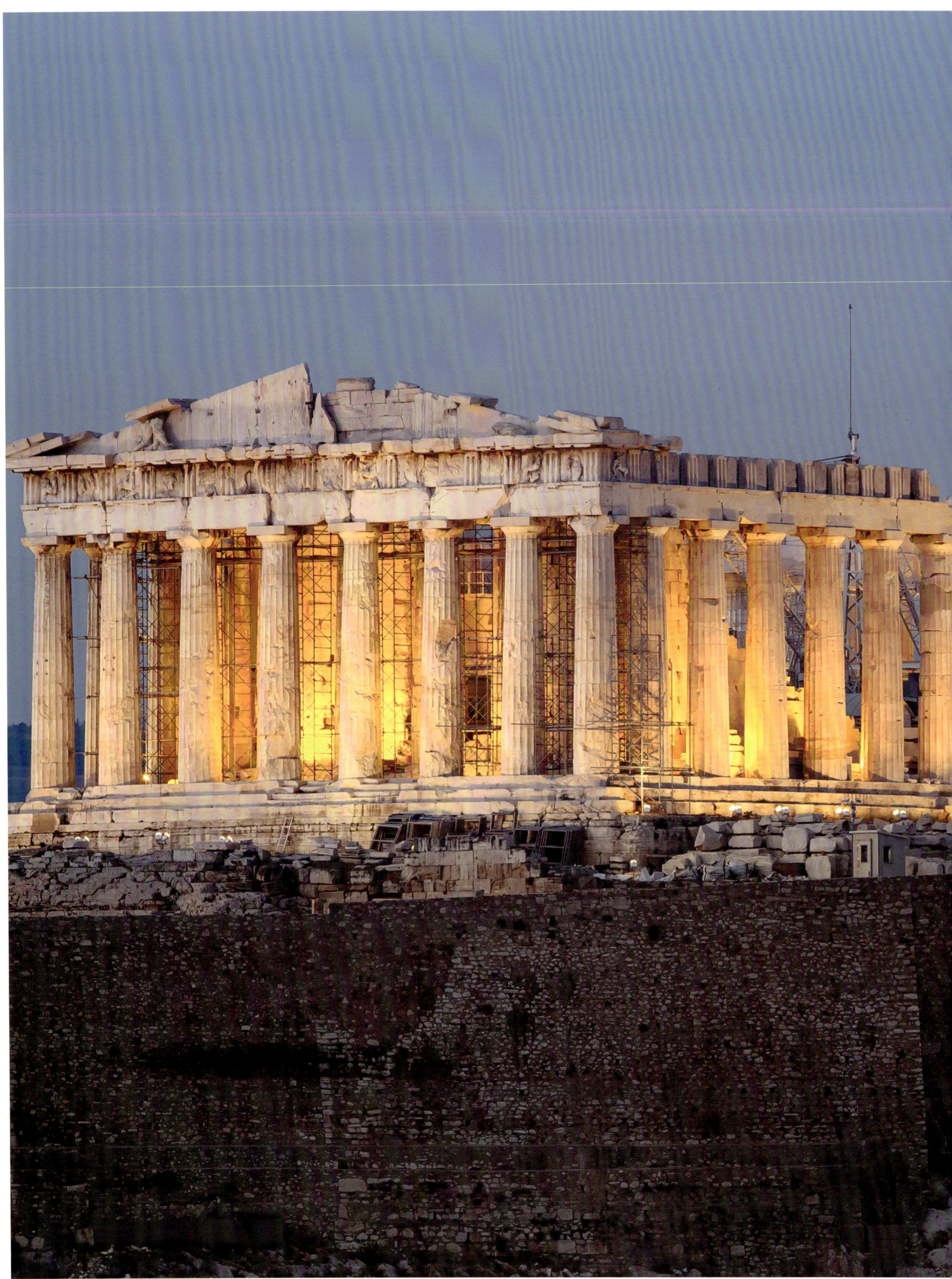

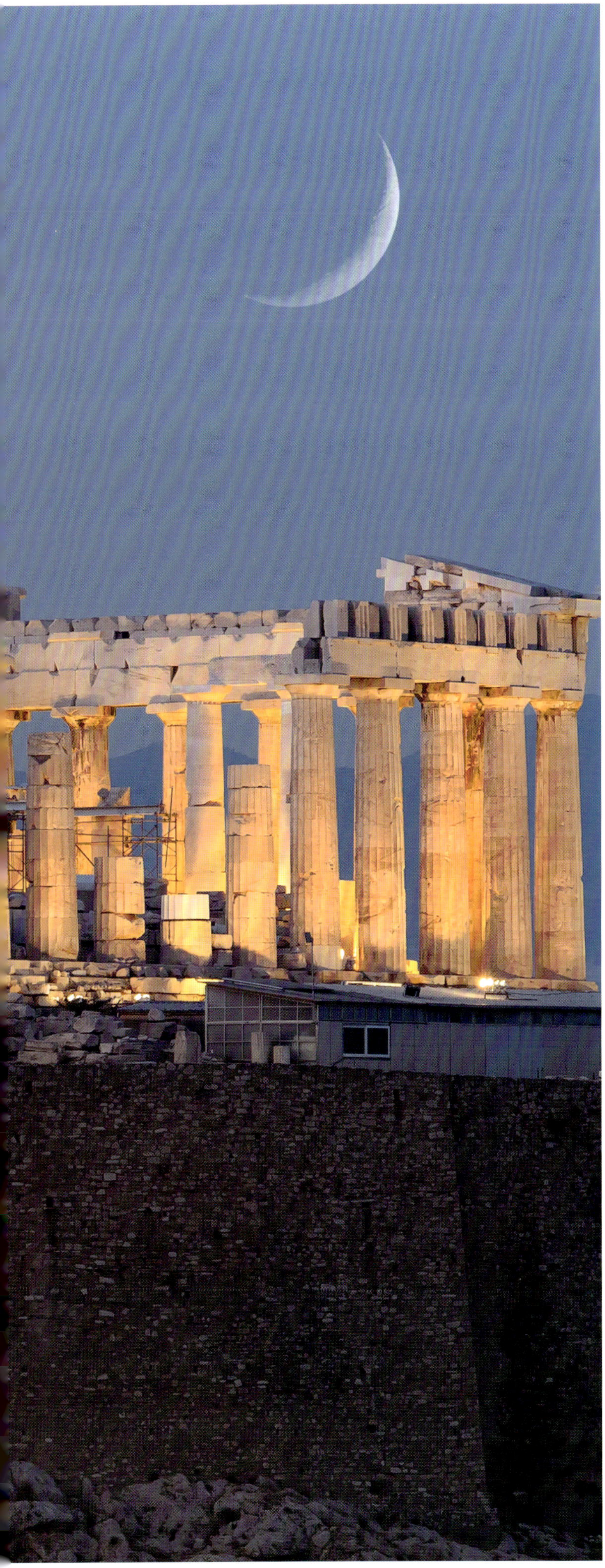

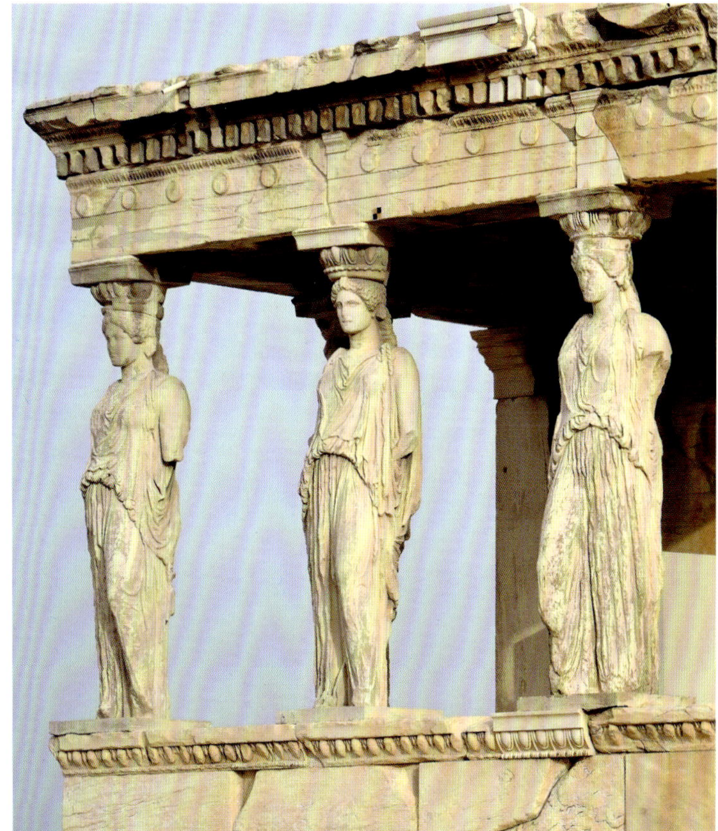

LEFT:

Parthenon, Acropolis, Athens, Greece

Expelling the Persians from Athens after a 29-year-long war, general Pericles ordered new shrines to be built on the Acropolis, the most striking of which was the Parthenon, completed c.432 BCE. For 1000 years this was Athens's religious apex, a place of 'pagan' sacrifice, until it became a church in the 5th century CE.

In 1458, Muslim Turks converted the building into a mosque. Then in 1678 a Venetian shell hit gunpowder stored in the Parthenon, and many of its friezes and sculptures went up in smoke. Lord Elgin 'rescued' surviving artefacts and gave them to London's British Museum in 1816. The Greeks have wanted them back ever since.

ABOVE:

Erechtheion, Acropolis, Athens, Greece

Built between 421 and 406 BCE, the Erechtheion was a temple associated with various Greek relics and beliefs. The eastern part was dedicated to the goddess Athena Polias, Protector of the City, while the western part was dedicated to Poseidon-Erechtheus, an early mythical king of the city. In the later Middle Ages, the temple became a palace and, for a time after the Ottoman Conquest in the 15th century, a residence for the Turkish commander's harem.

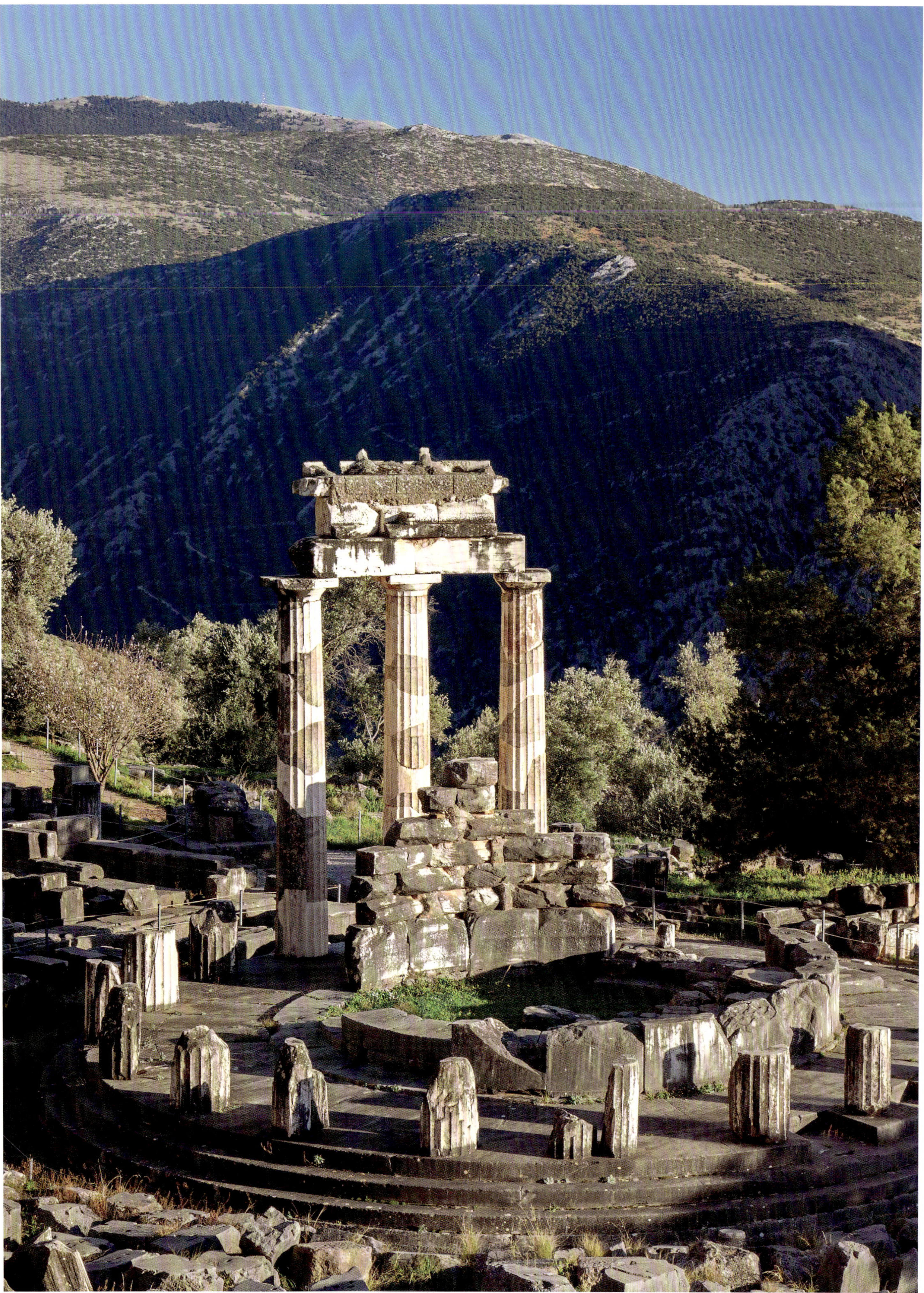

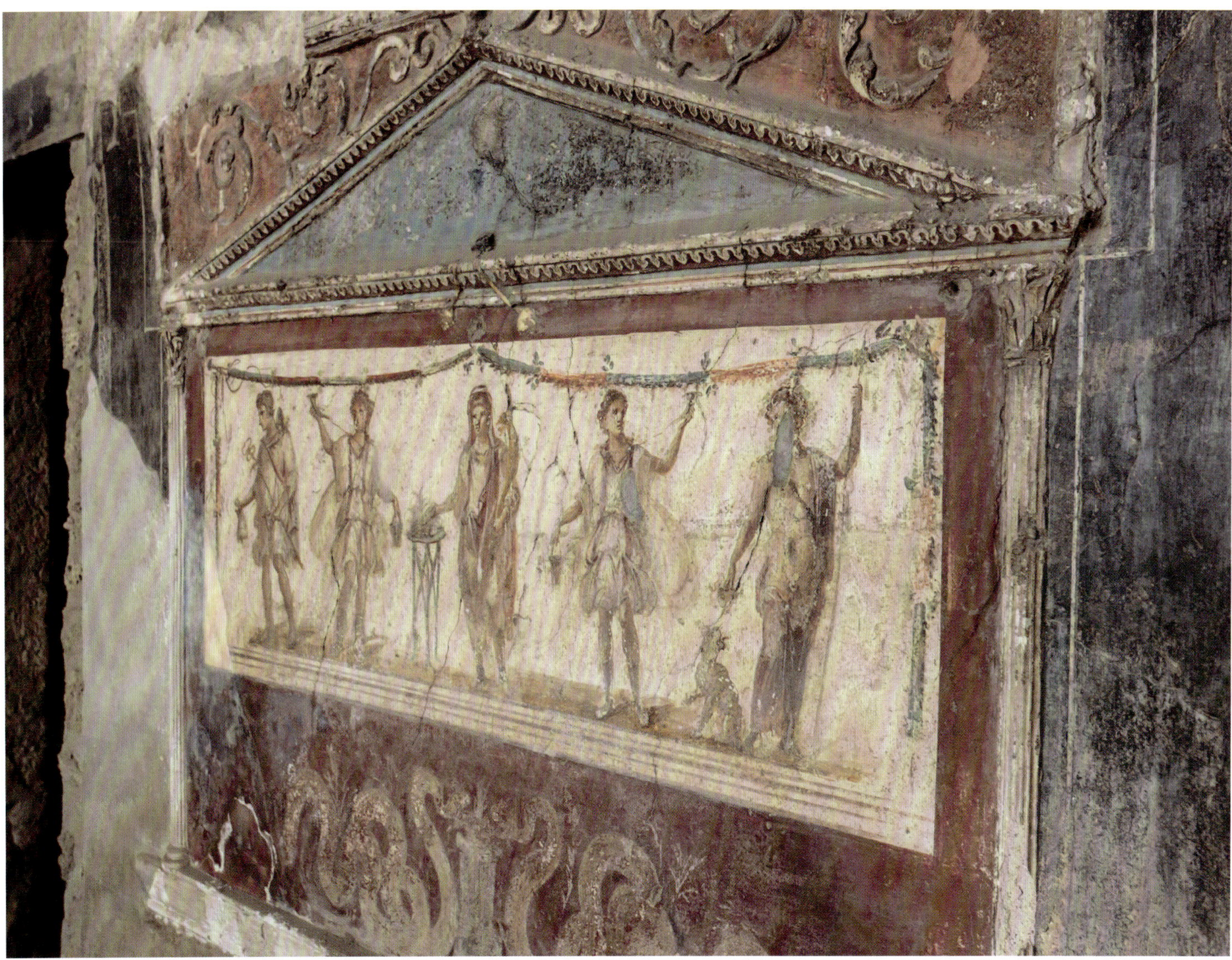

OPPOSITE:

Sanctuary of Athena, Delphi, Phocis, Greece

Predicting the future obsesses humankind – and no more so than at Delphi on the slopes of Mount Parnassus. At Delphi's Temple of Apollo, a high priestess – the Oracle – would divine petitioners' fates in daylong rituals. Some 800 metres (2625ft) away stands this once-domed circular *tholos* at the Sanctuary of the goddess Athena, built around 380 BCE. Eventually Delphi ceased functioning when the Christian Roman Emperor Theodosius banned pagan practices in 390 CE.

ABOVE:

Domestic Altar, Pompeii, Campania, Italy

A perfectly preserved fresco from a domestic altar in Pompeii blends public and private faith. Vetutius Placidus placed it in his dining room, from which he sold food to hungry passersby. The scene shows Mercury, Roman god of commerce, and Dionysus, god of wine, beside a sacrificial pedestal.

Everyone in Pompeii died when Mount Vesuvius erupted in 79 CE and covered the town in six metres (20ft) of volcanic ash. Yet, preserved by that ash, Vetutius's faith in household deities lives on.

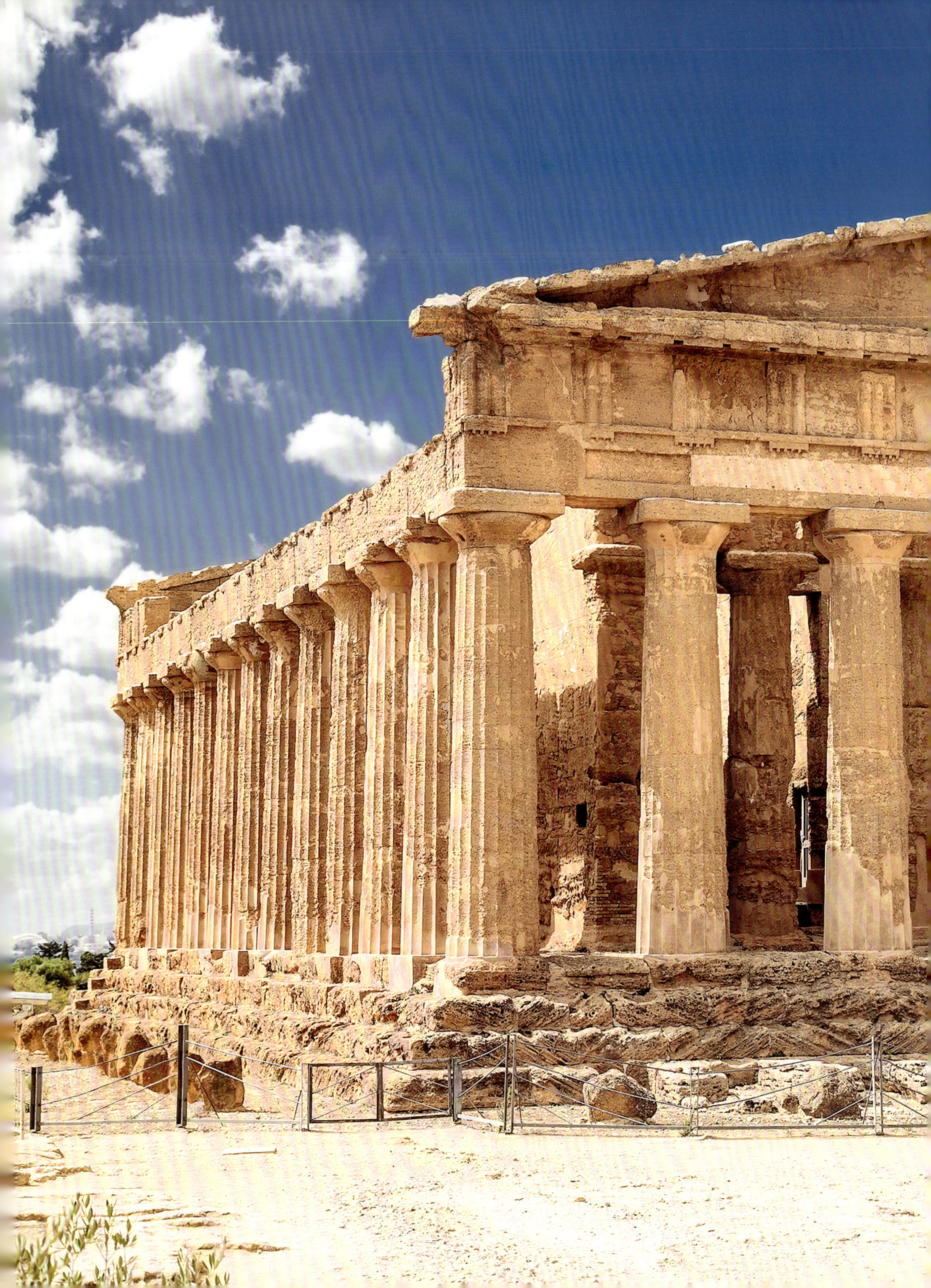

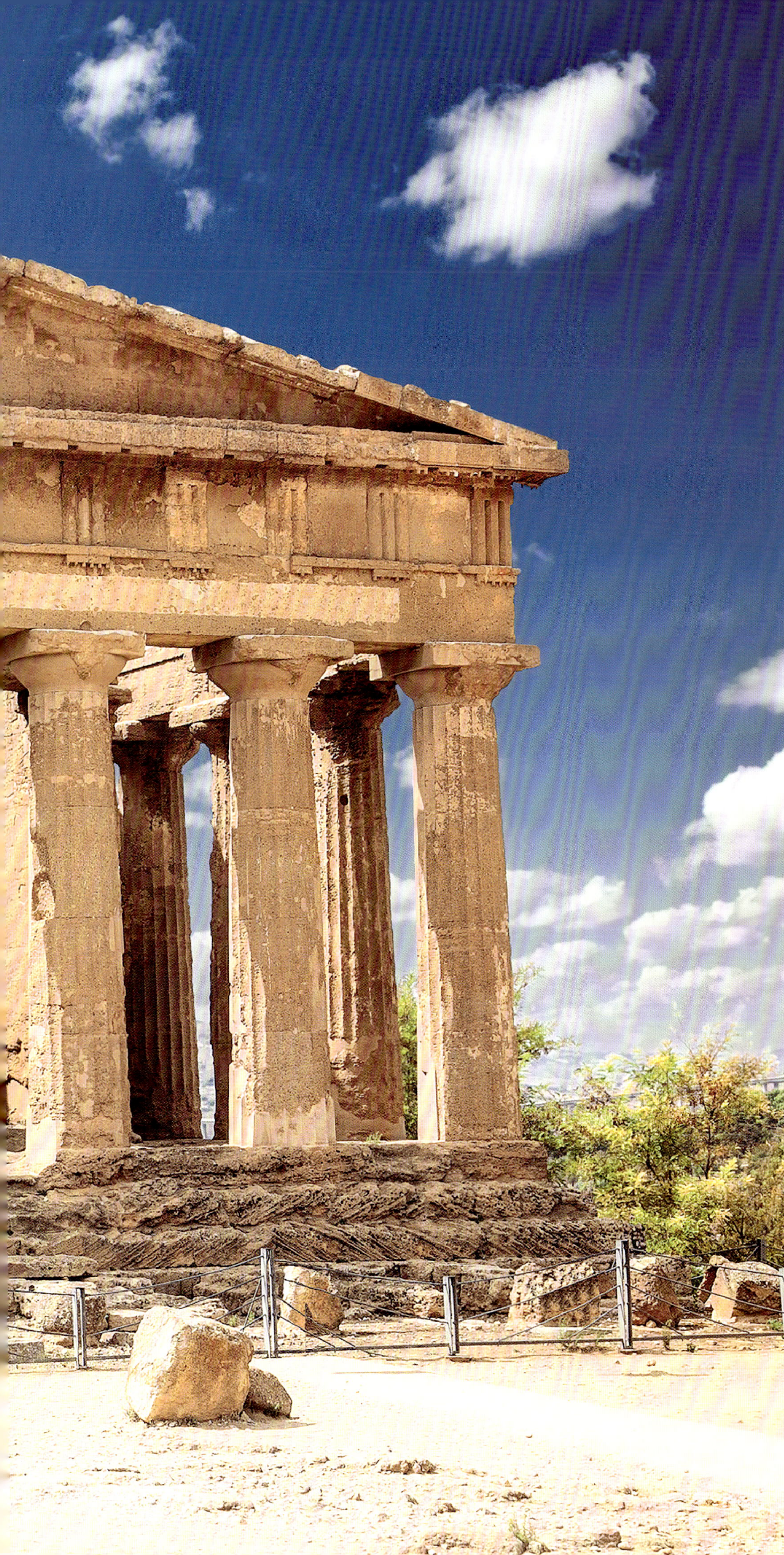

Temple of Concordia, Agrigento, Sicily, Italy
The enchanting Valley of Temples in Agrigento houses some of the most outstanding Ancient Greek monuments in the world, Sicily having been colonized by the Greeks in the 8th century BCE. The largest and best preserved of these monuments is the Doric style 34-columned Temple of Concordia, a secular edifice that became a holy site in the 5th century BCE. Other nearby sanctuaries commemorate soldiers who fell in wars against the Carthaginians, or honour Ancient Greek deities.

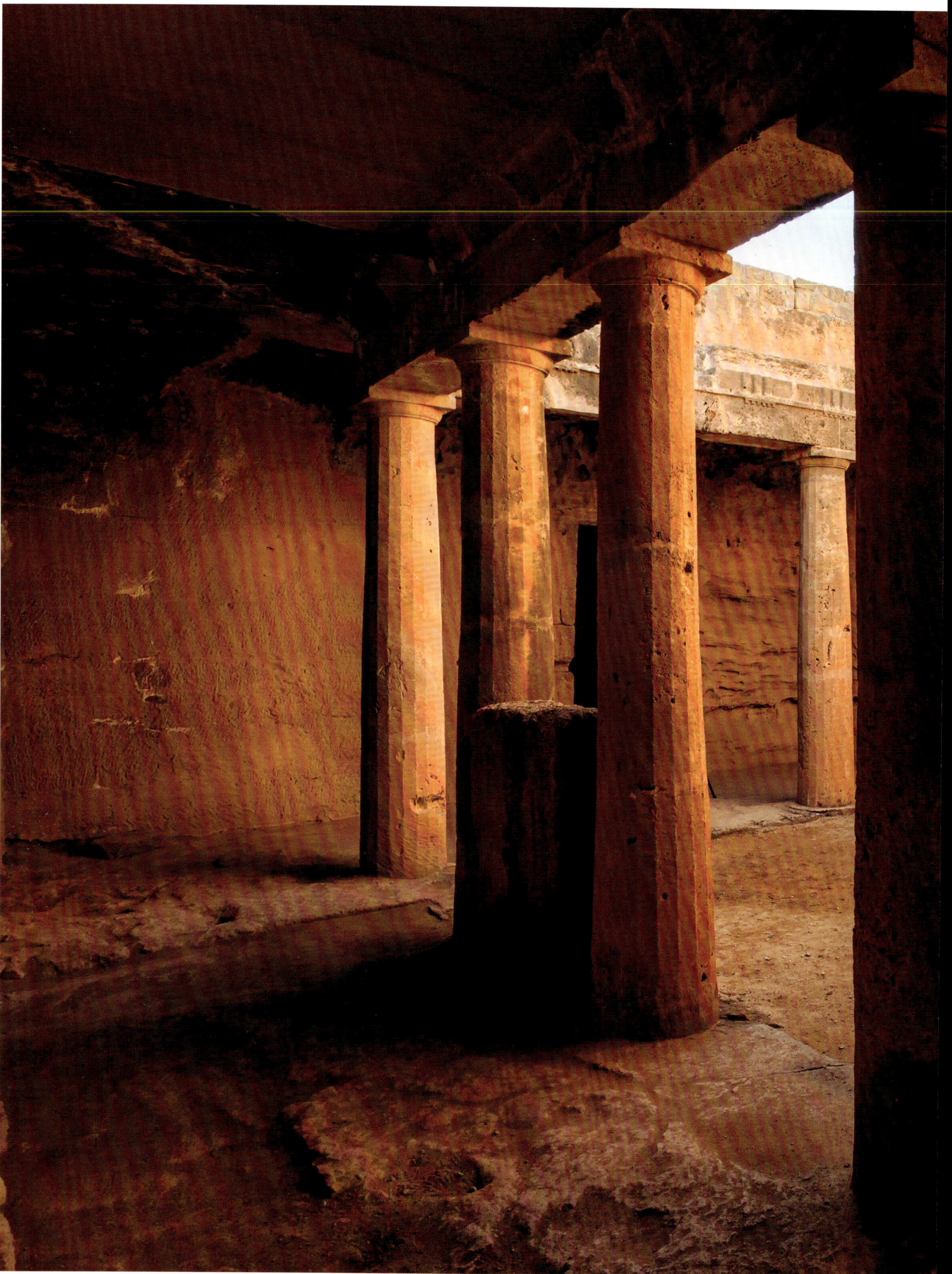

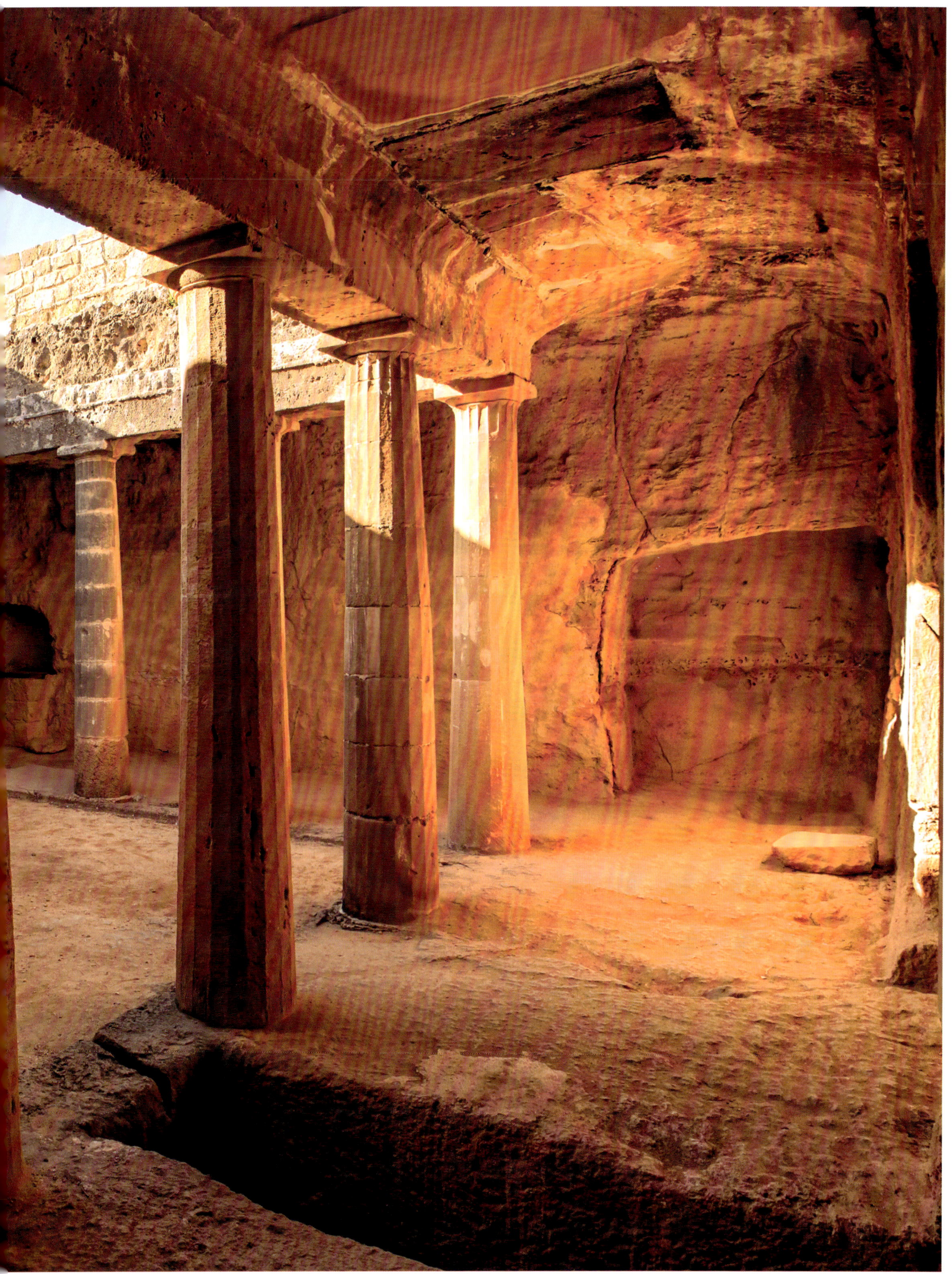

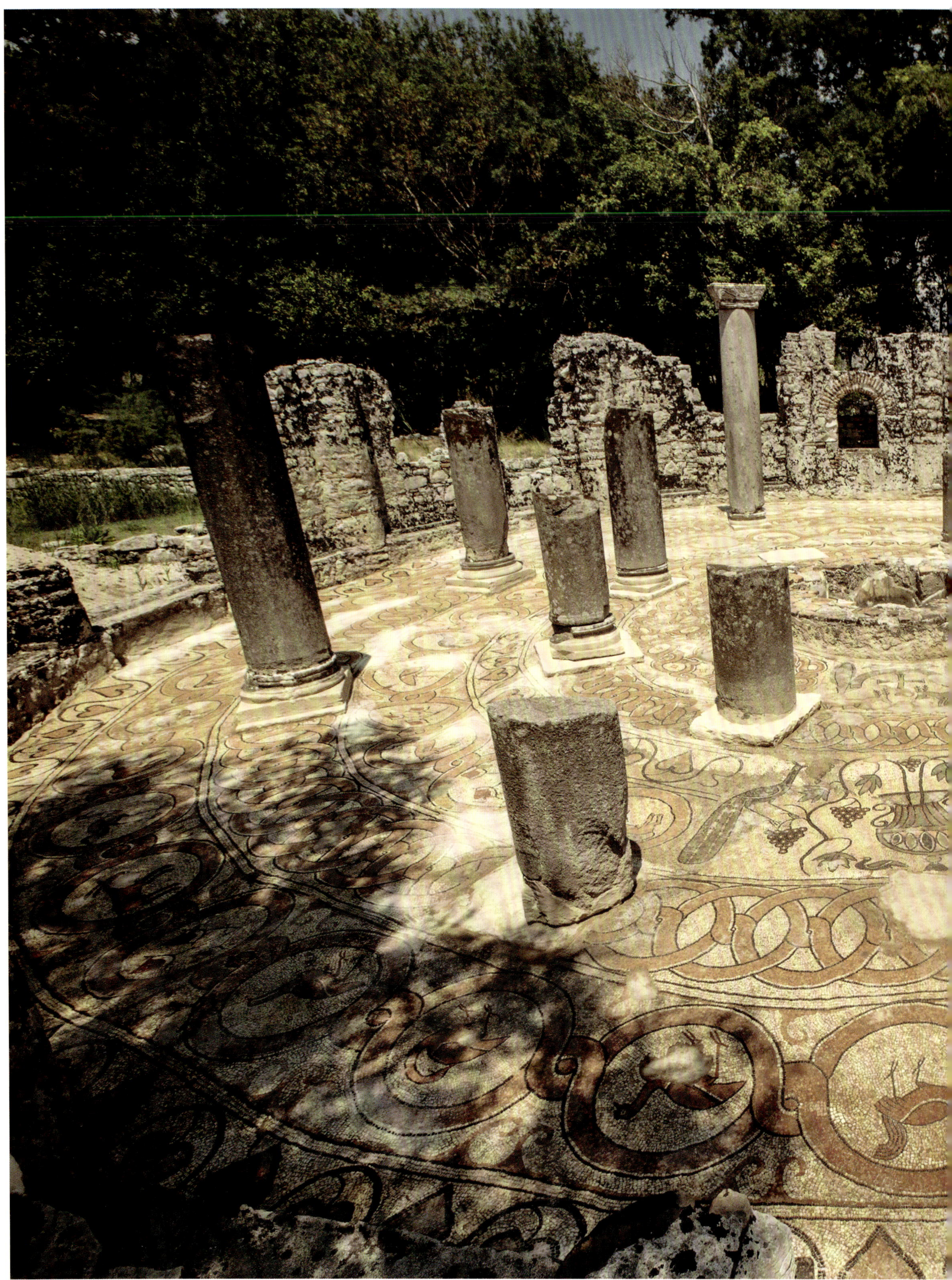

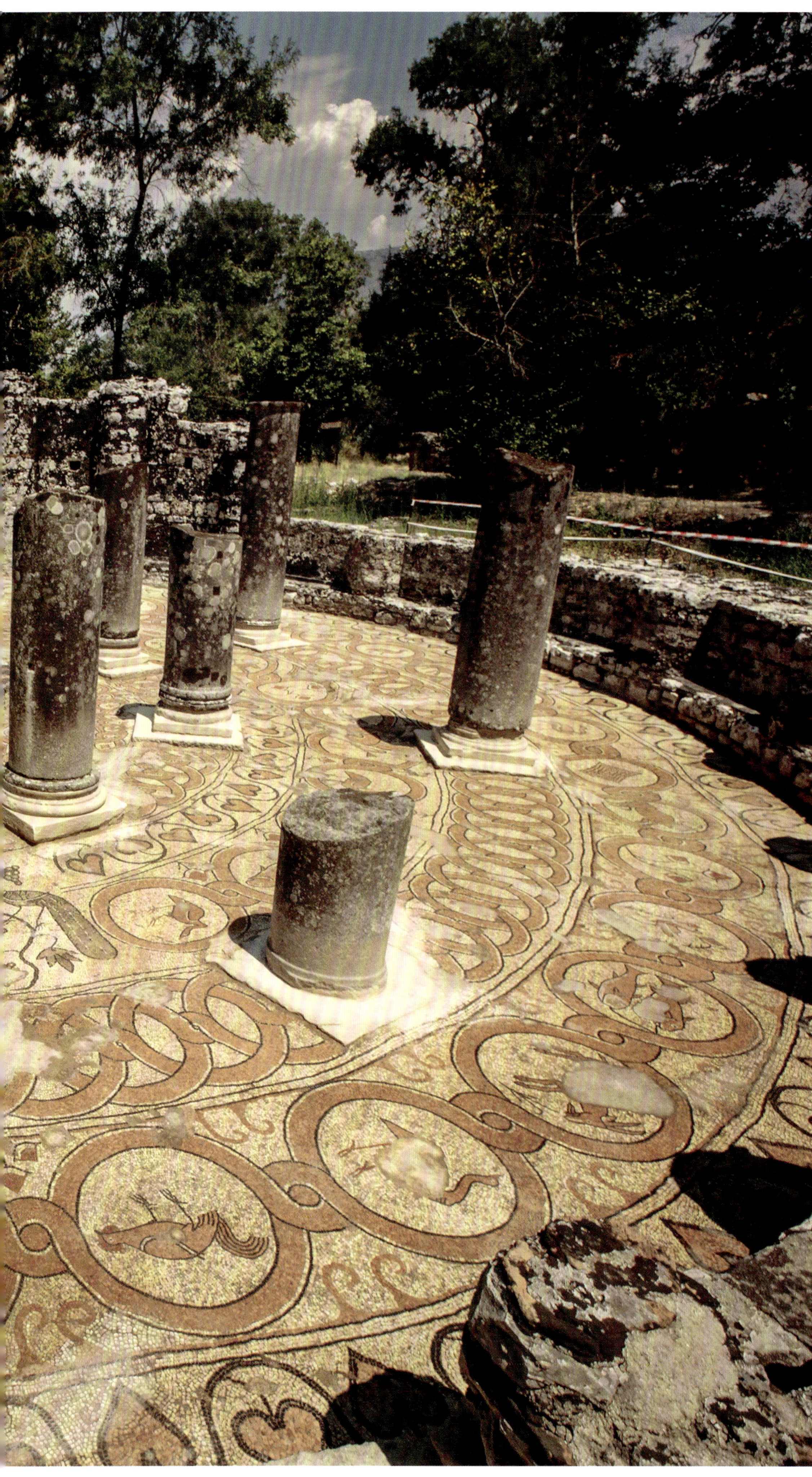

PREVIOUS PAGE:

Tomb of the Kings, Cyprus

Beautifully sculpted pillars frame this subterranean courtyard in the Tombs of the Kings. Here local rites co-existed with foreign deities, notably Aphrodite and Zeus. Despite the name, however, these tombs were for nobles, not kings, and were built between 300 BCE and 300 CE. Cyprus became a Roman province in 58 BCE after periods of independence and rule by Assyrians, Greeks and Persians. Cypriots later adopted Christianity, thus sealing the fate of pagan sites.

LEFT:

Baptistry, Butrint, Albania

A charming exemplar of early Romano-Christian architecture, the baptistery in Butrint arose when the area became a bishopric in the 6th century CE. Its mosaic pavement clearly blends Hellenistic with local aesthetics.

Butrint had first become a Roman colony in 44 BCE and the Byzantines revived it in the 9th century CE, after which Venetians, Angevin English and Ottoman Turks ruled the region. But the town was largely abandoned in the Middle Ages because of encroaching marshland.

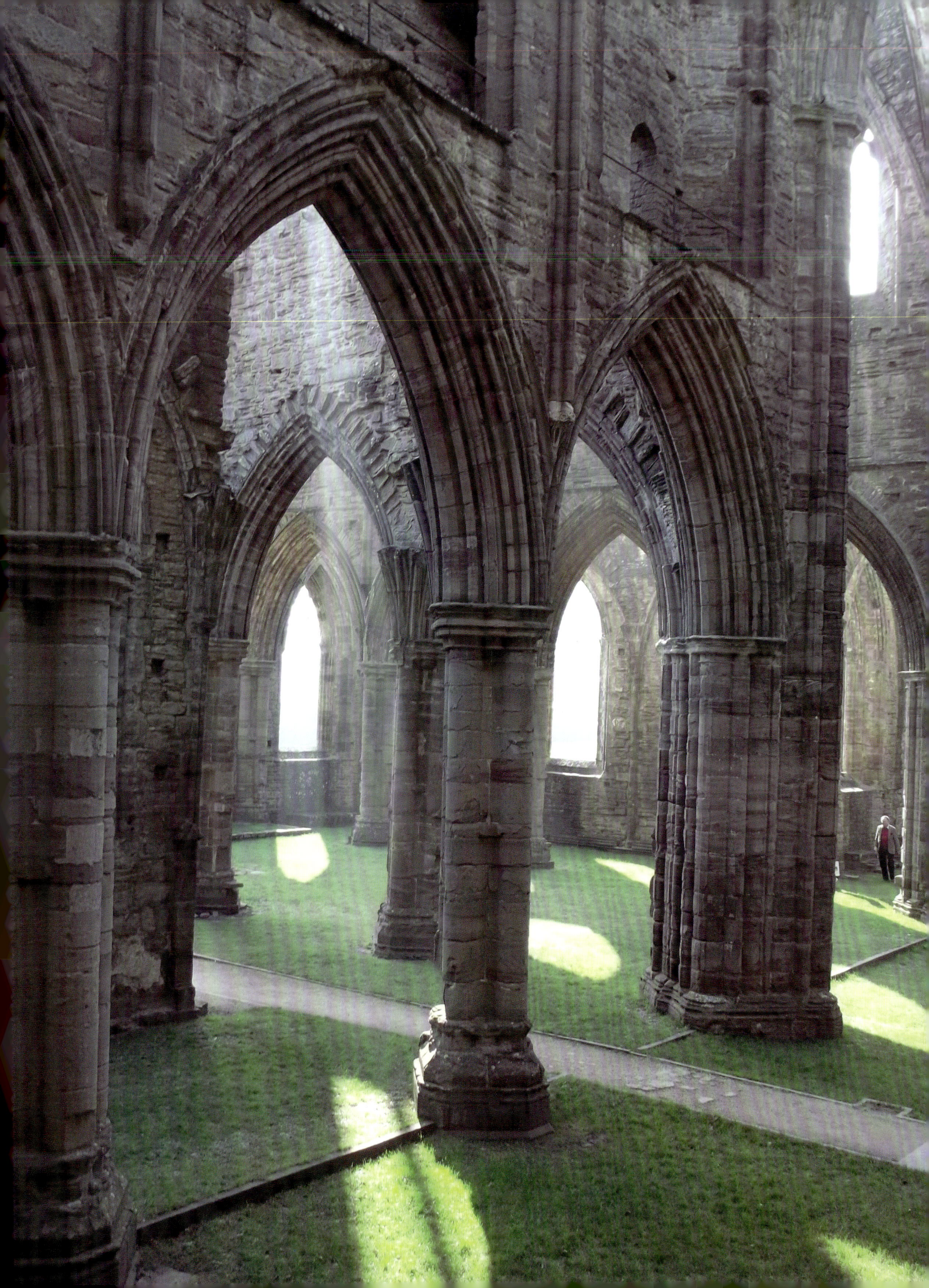

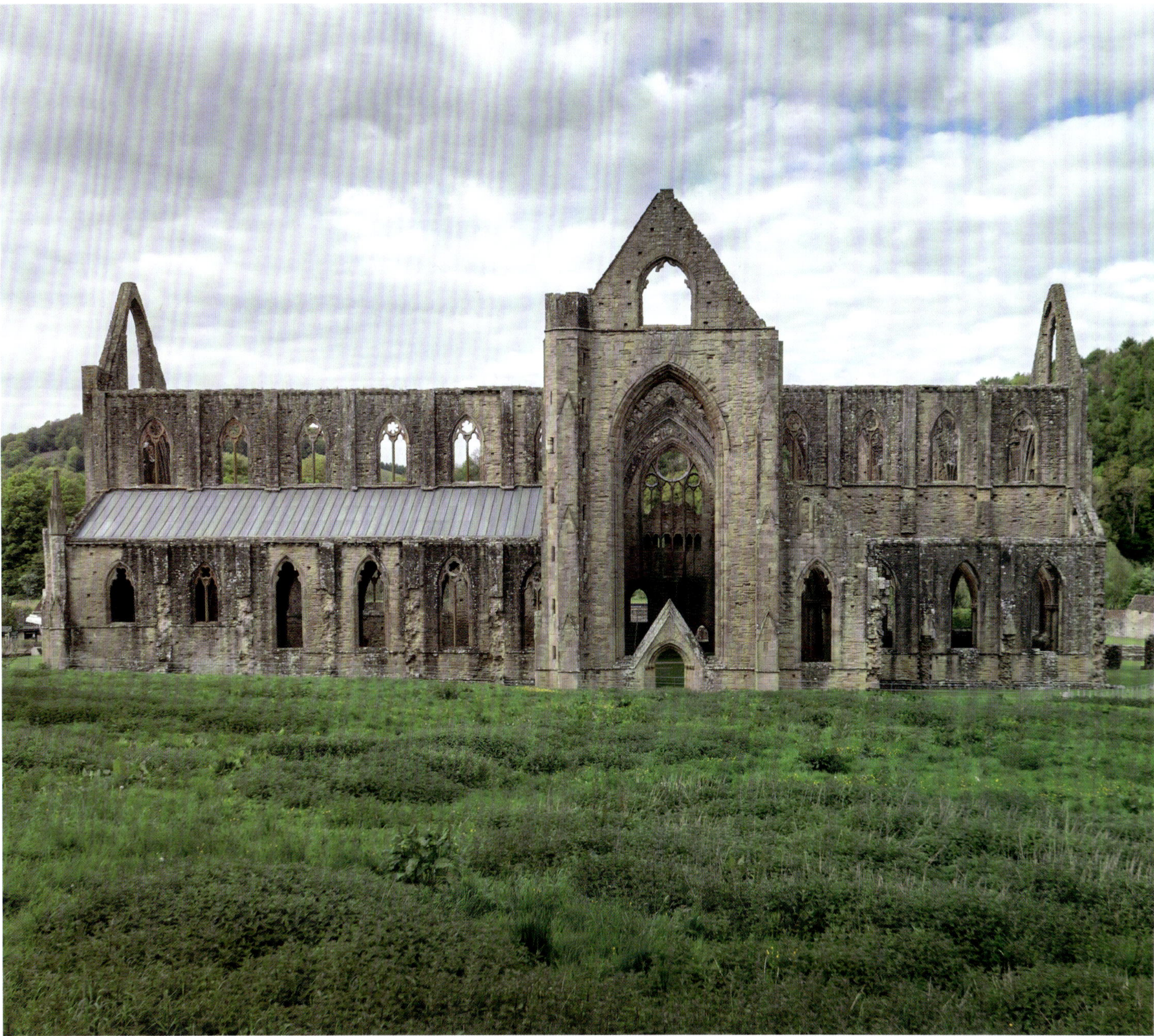

BOTH PHOTOGRAPHS:
Tintern Abbey, Monmouthshire, Wales
Tintern Abbey began life in 1131 as one of Britain's earliest Cistercian foundations. Lay brothers worked the surrounding lands, adding to riches already gained from endowments in neighbouring counties. The present structure was built between 1269–1301, complete with Gothic archways and cloisters.

In September 1536, however, Henry VIII forced both the abbey, associated monastery and small industries to close. This was two years after the Church of England officially broke with Rome. All told, the king dissolved around 900 Catholic religious houses – which served as a gift to the Crown as they had owned a quarter of England's landed wealth.

Interest in the ruin revived in the late 18th and early 19th centuries when the French Revolutionary and Napoleonic Wars cut off continental Europe to wealthy British folk who had previously enjoyed the fashionable European 'Grand Tour'.

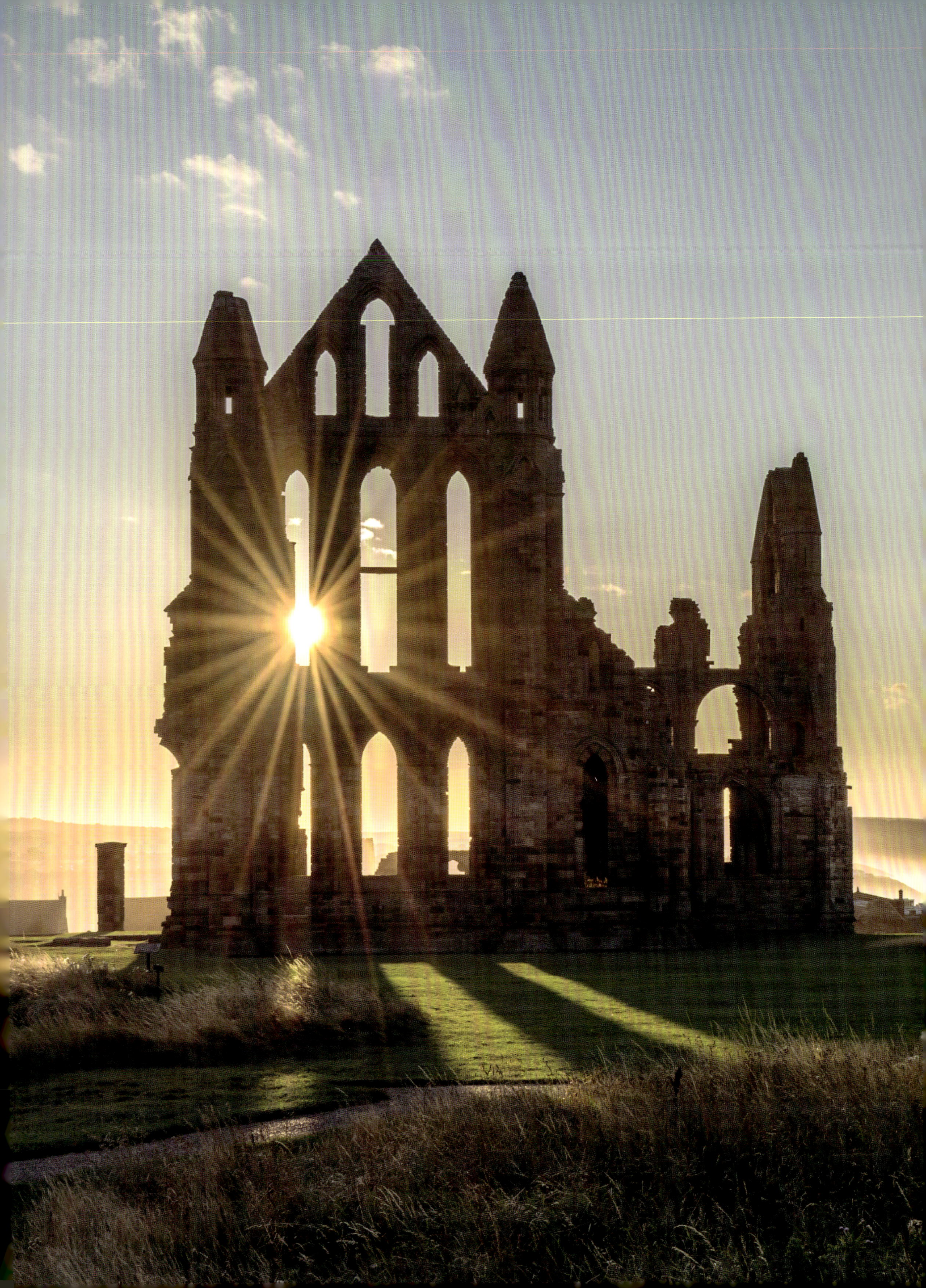

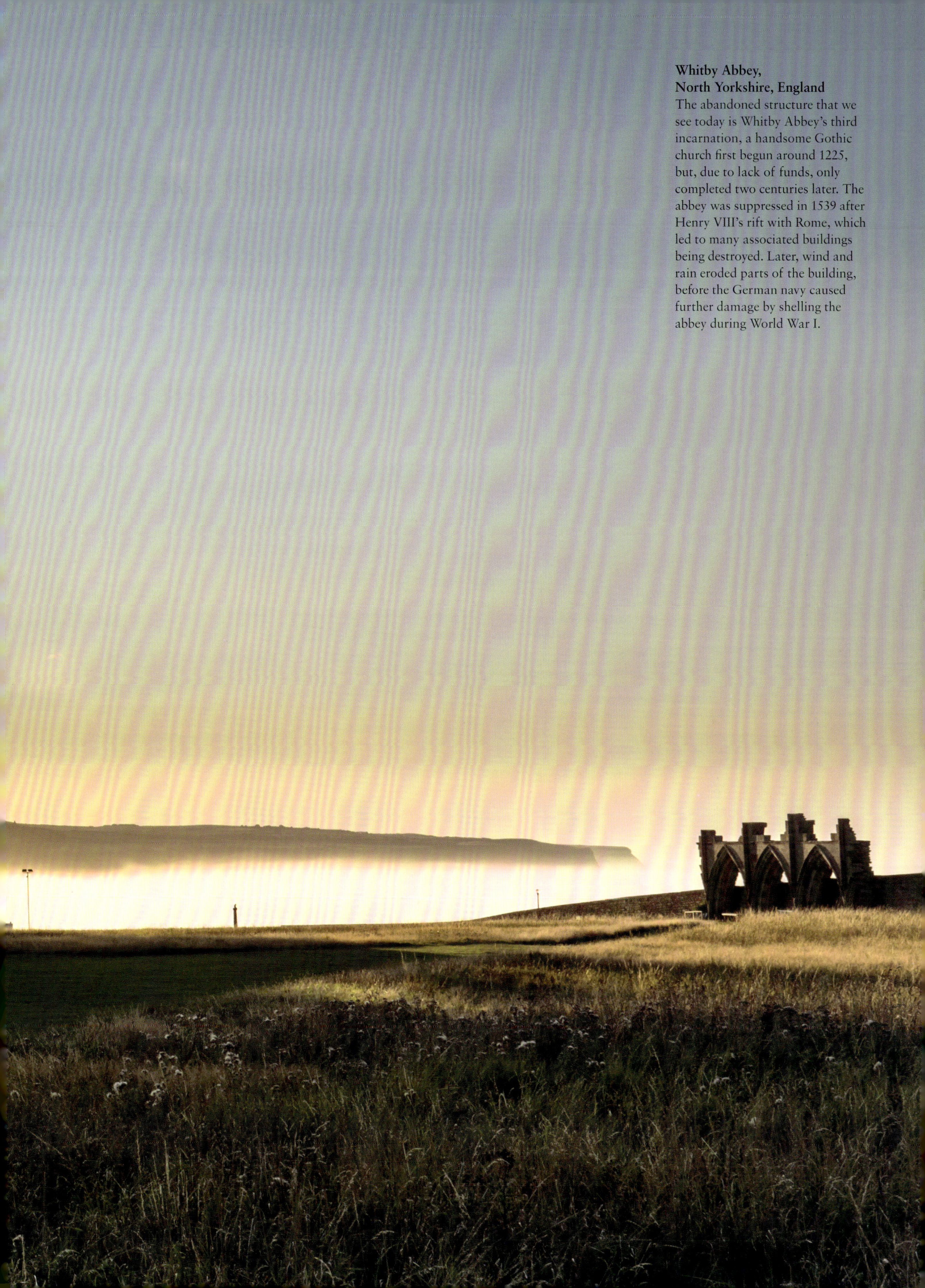

Whitby Abbey, North Yorkshire, England
The abandoned structure that we see today is Whitby Abbey's third incarnation, a handsome Gothic church first begun around 1225, but, due to lack of funds, only completed two centuries later. The abbey was suppressed in 1539 after Henry VIII's rift with Rome, which led to many associated buildings being destroyed. Later, wind and rain eroded parts of the building, before the German navy caused further damage by shelling the abbey during World War I.

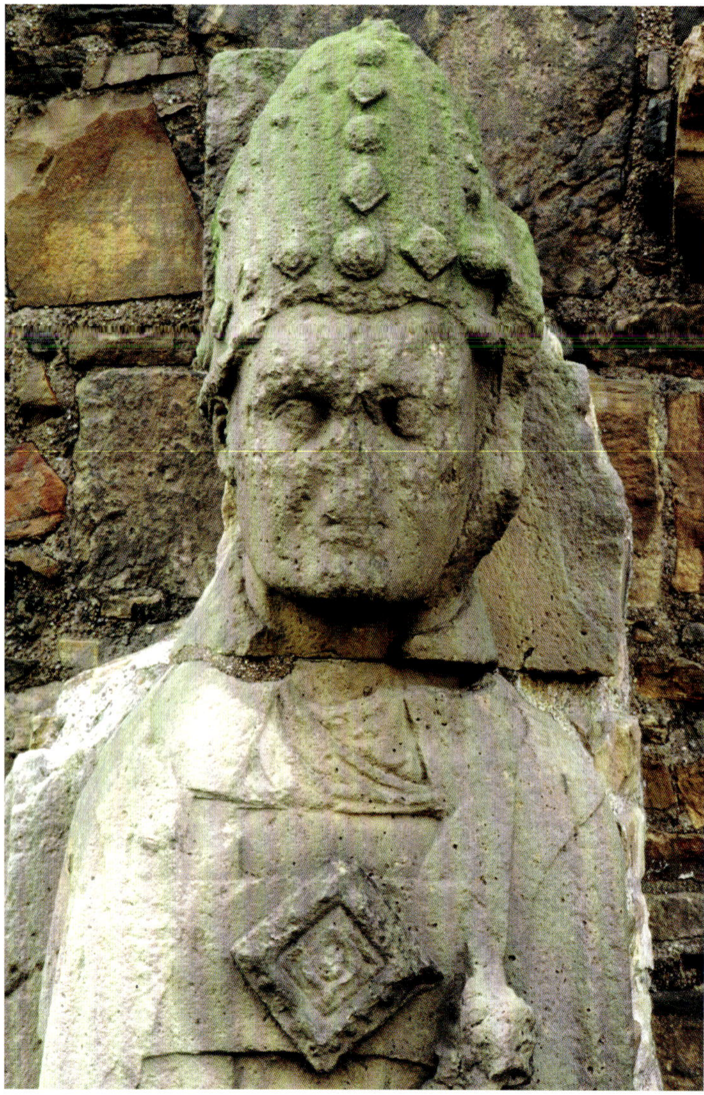

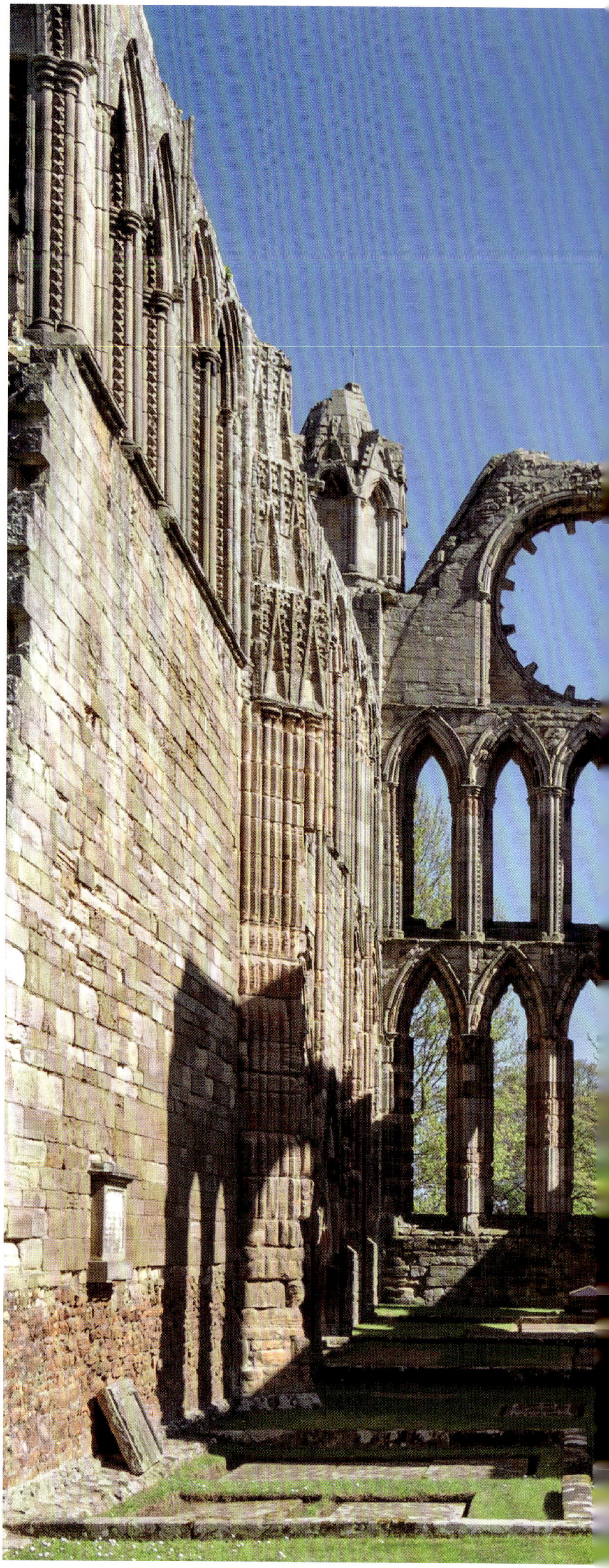

BOTH PHOTOGRAPHS:

Elgin Cathedral, Moray, Scotland

Described as 'the lantern of the north', Elgin Cathedral shows impressive window frames and columns in what remains of its choir and presbytery. Building began in 1224 with endowments from Scotland's Alexander II. Then, in 1390, Robert II's wayward son, Alexander Stewart, set Elgin on fire, probably in response to having been excommunicated.

After Scotland's Protestant Reformation of 1560, the cathedral lost its roof to rot, followed by its nave and central tower. In the 17th century, Puritan 'reformers' and Oliver Cromwell's troops looted icons and destroyed furnishings.

Since the 1800s, however, visitors have marvelled at its grand Gothic remains. Smaller, more human details include this carved stone bust of Bishop John de Innes (above), who had restored the cathedral after the Stewart raid.

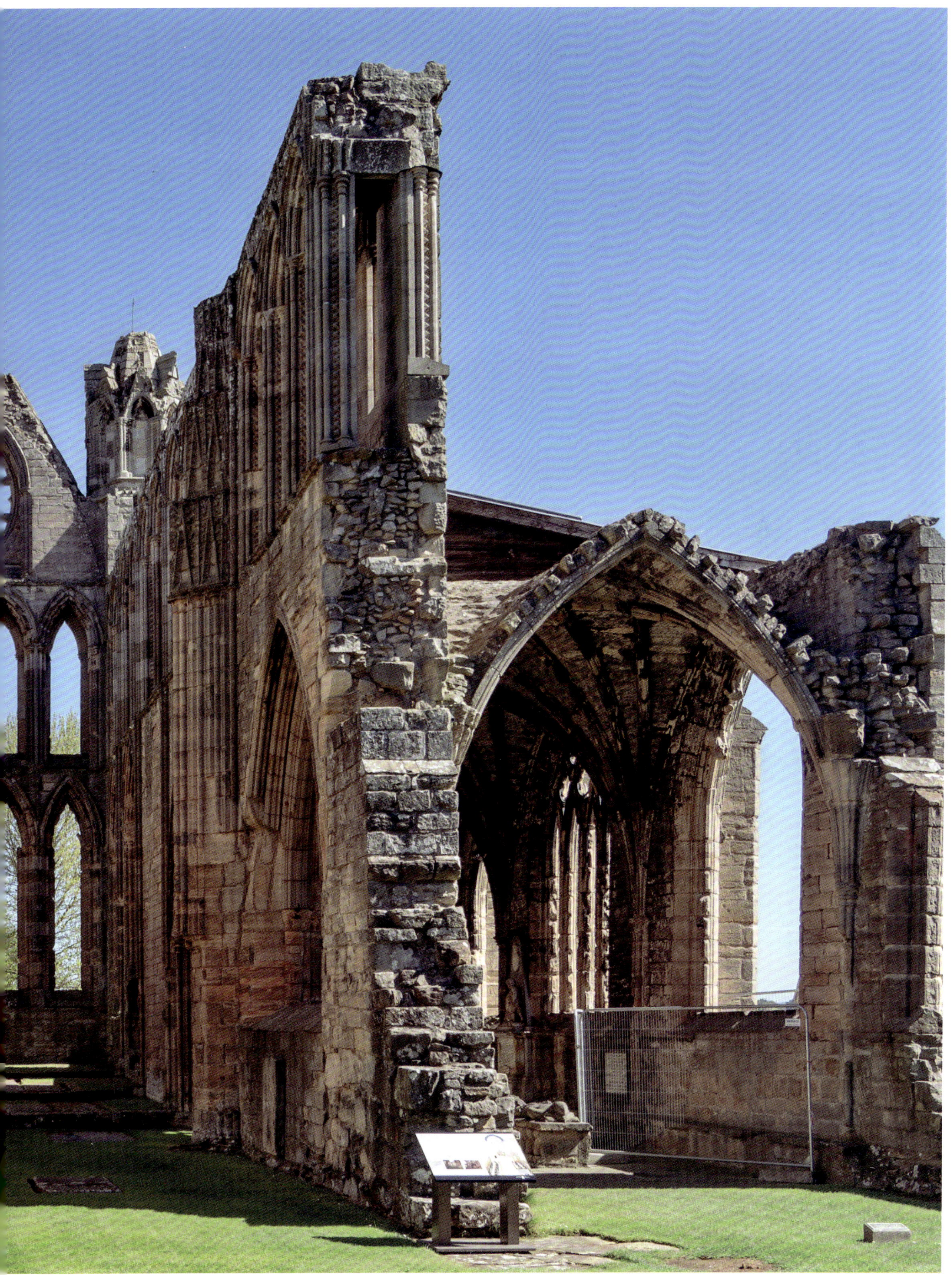

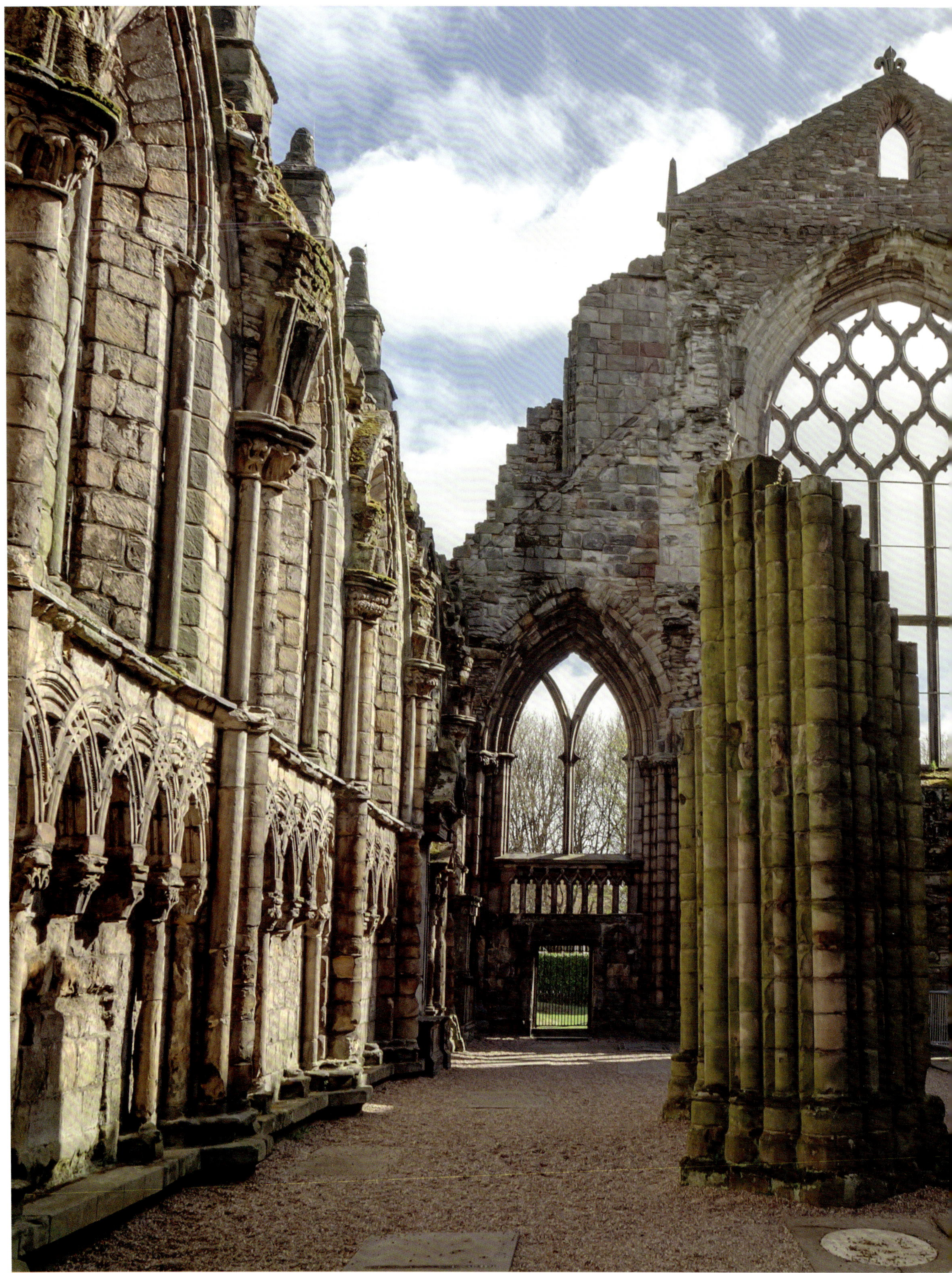

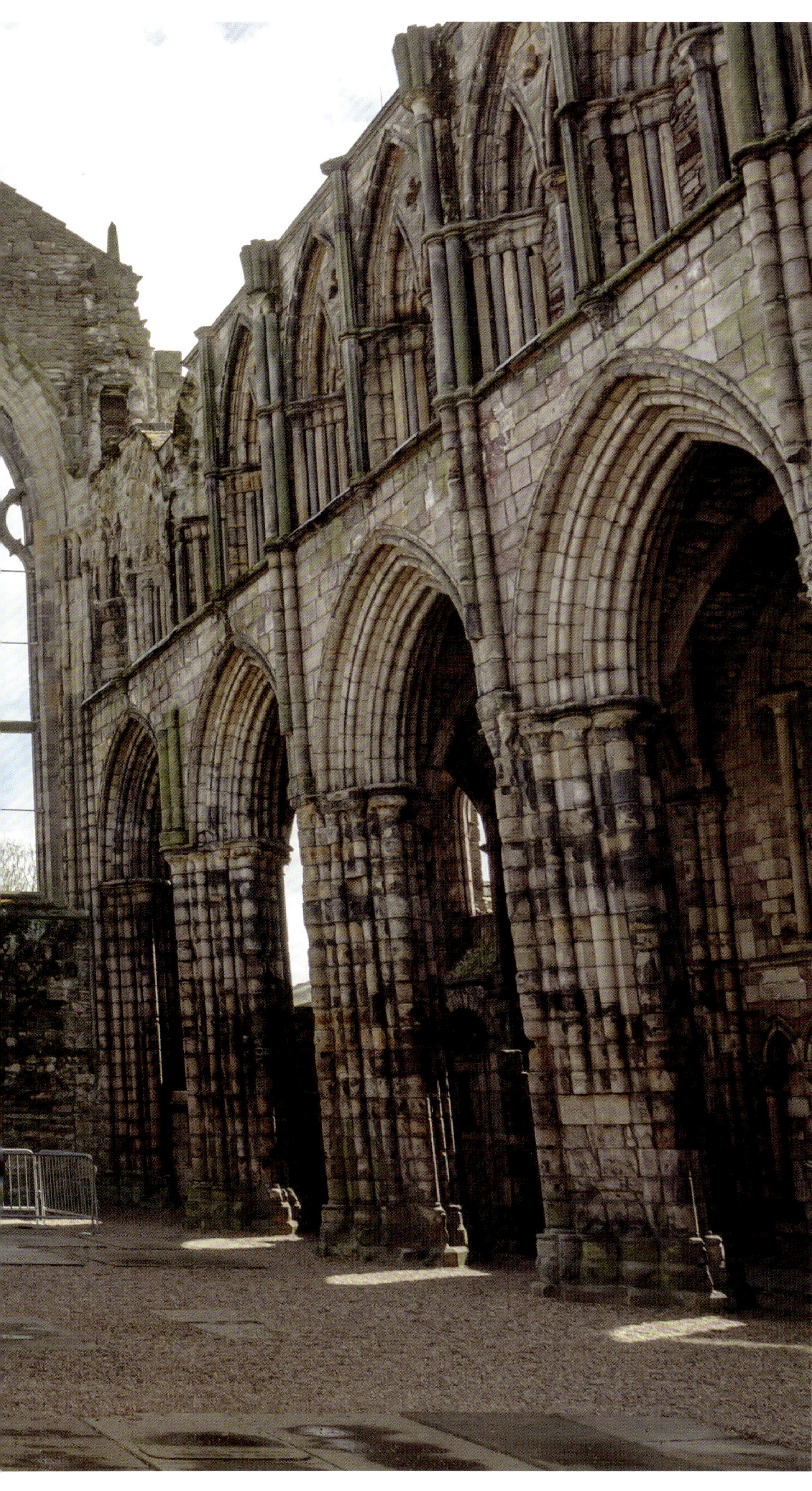

Holyrood Abbey, Edinburgh, Scotland

Founded in 1128 by King David of Scotland, Holyrood Abbey was intimately connected with Scottish royalty and national identity. James II of Scotland was born in an abbey guesthouse and crowned, married and buried in the abbey itself.

Built in increments, Holyrood traces architectural history from rounded Romanesque to soaring Gothic arches. Plainer worship replaced Catholic rites after the 1560 Protestant Reformation. With that political and religious change, all monks and monasteries were banned. As abbey outbuildings were demolished, Holyroodhouse – the adjoining castle – expanded. The abbey's surviving nave became a Protestant chapel until a storm destroyed its roof in 1768 and was deemed too costly to repair.

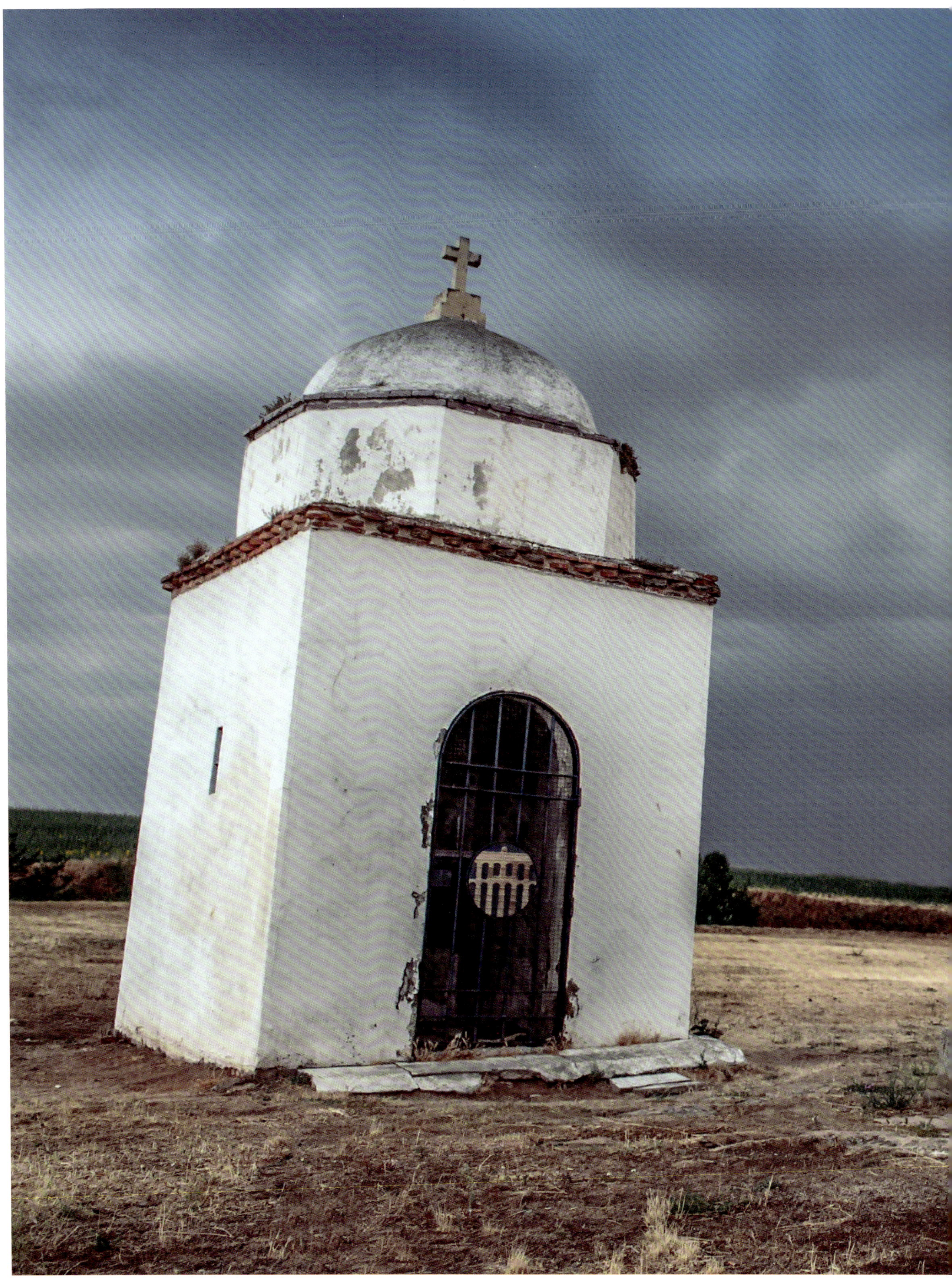

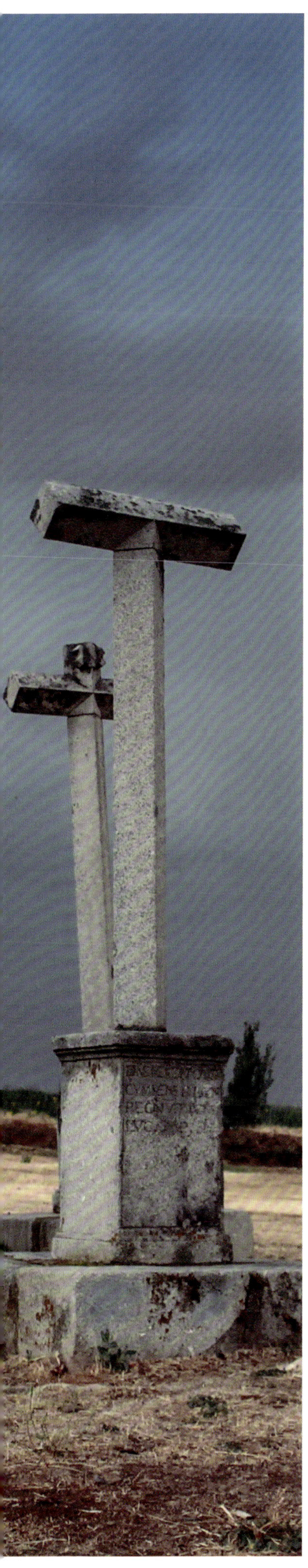

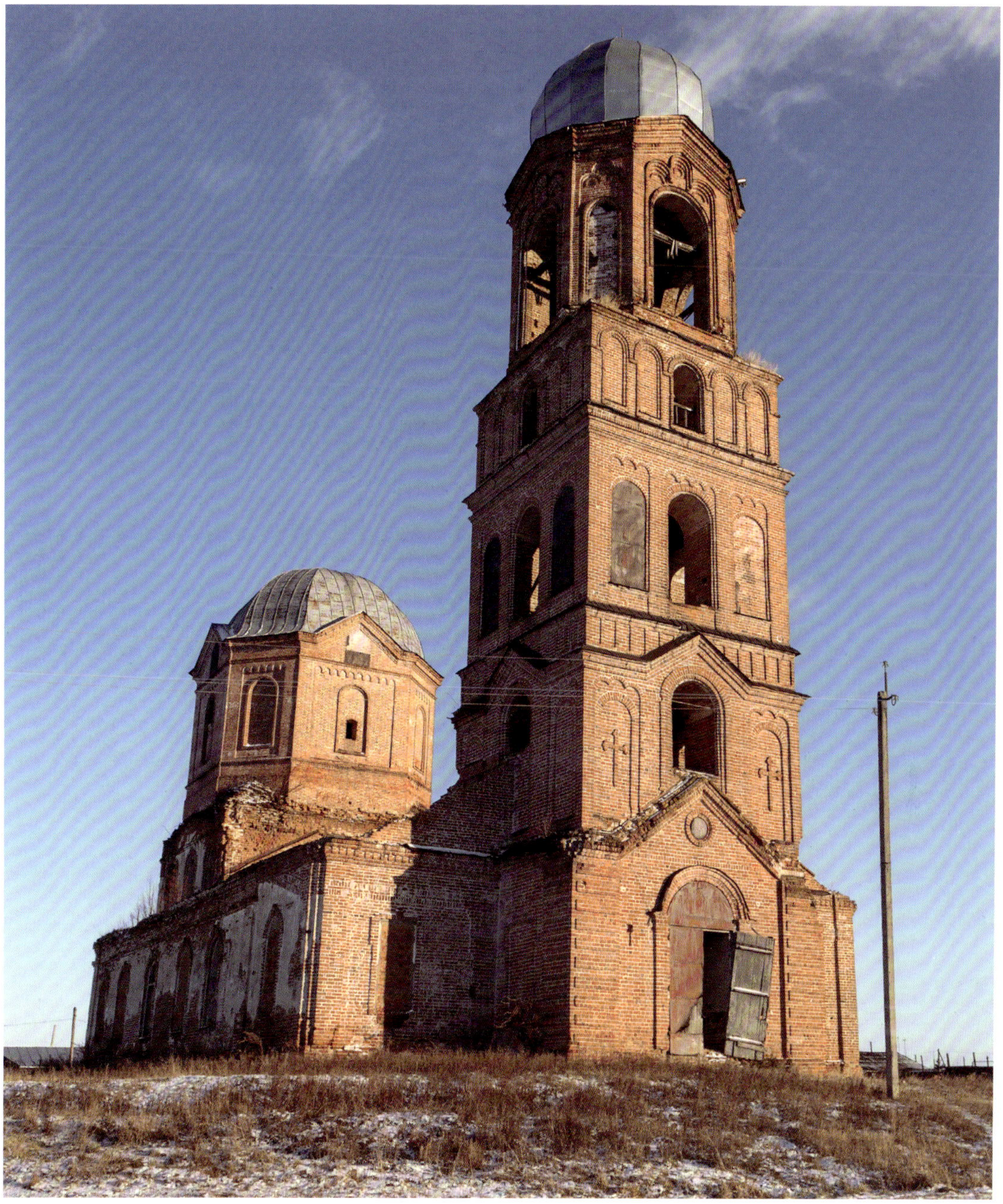

LEFT:

Chapel of Mercy, near Segovia, Castile and León, Spain

Segovia's oldest Way of the Cross procession stops at this chapel once a year during Holy Week. Other than that, the shrine lies derelict. Why? The answer is neither war, nature nor religious change, but bureaucracy – no one can agree who owns it. In the 15th century, Henry IV of Castile built a chapel here to thank the town for thwarting a plot to capture him. Four stone Calvary crucifixes were planted in 1679, and the current white-stucco chapel has occupied the hilltop overlooking Segovia since the late 1700s. Technically the chapel lies within the Parish of San Millán, but for centuries neither bishopric nor municipality has listed it in their records.

ABOVE:

Church of the Kazan Icon of the Virgin, Bogorodskoye, Penza region, Russia

First built in 1793 in a region previously held by Muslim khanates, the Orthodox Church of the Kazan Icon of the Virgin includes frescoes of John the Baptist and the prophet Elijah. As with a great many Orthodox churches in Russia during the 1930s, Stalin's anti-religious campaign closed it down. In recent years, restoration work has topped the tower with a round dome.

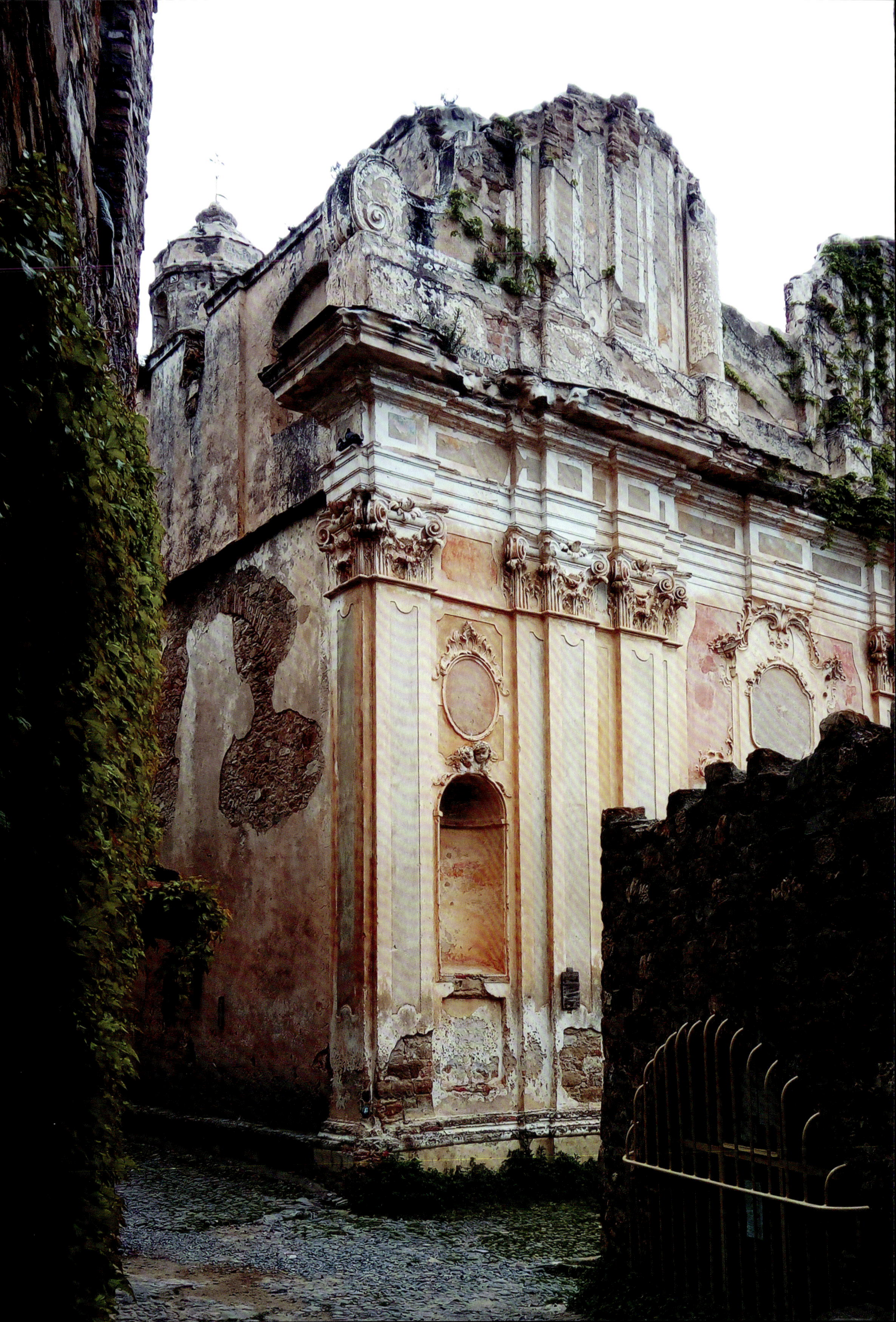

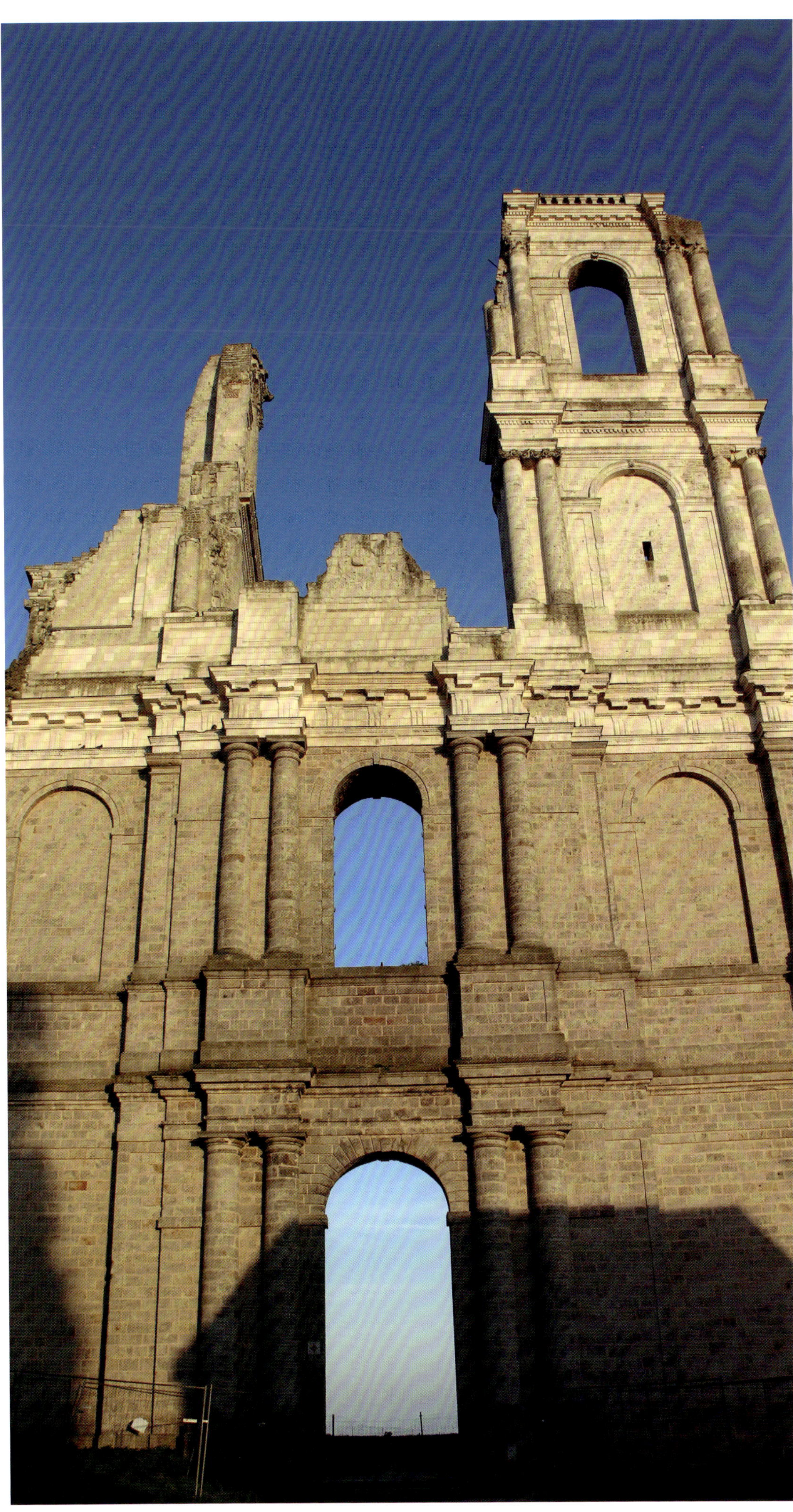

OPPOSITE:

Santa Maria della Grazie, Bussana Vecchia, Liguria, Italy

On Ash Wednesday morning in 1887, a massive earthquake struck the village of Bussana Vecchia, killing 2000 people. Seven years later, the village was abandoned along with this baroque church, built in 1652. Vegetation took over and after 1947 the local council threatened to detonate the church tower and other structures to deter illegal occupants. But times change: since the 1960s, a restored Bussana has thrived as an artists' colony.

LEFT:

Abbey, Mont-Saint-Eloi, Pas-de-Calais, France

The reputedly 7th century Abbey of Mont-Saint-Eloi led a thriving Catholic community during the Middle Ages. Yet subsequent politics spelled disaster. Looting during the French Revolution destroyed its walls, leaving just a porch and two limestone towers. Then, in 1915, the abbey came under shellfire from the Western Front after the German army discovered French spies using the towers as lookout posts.

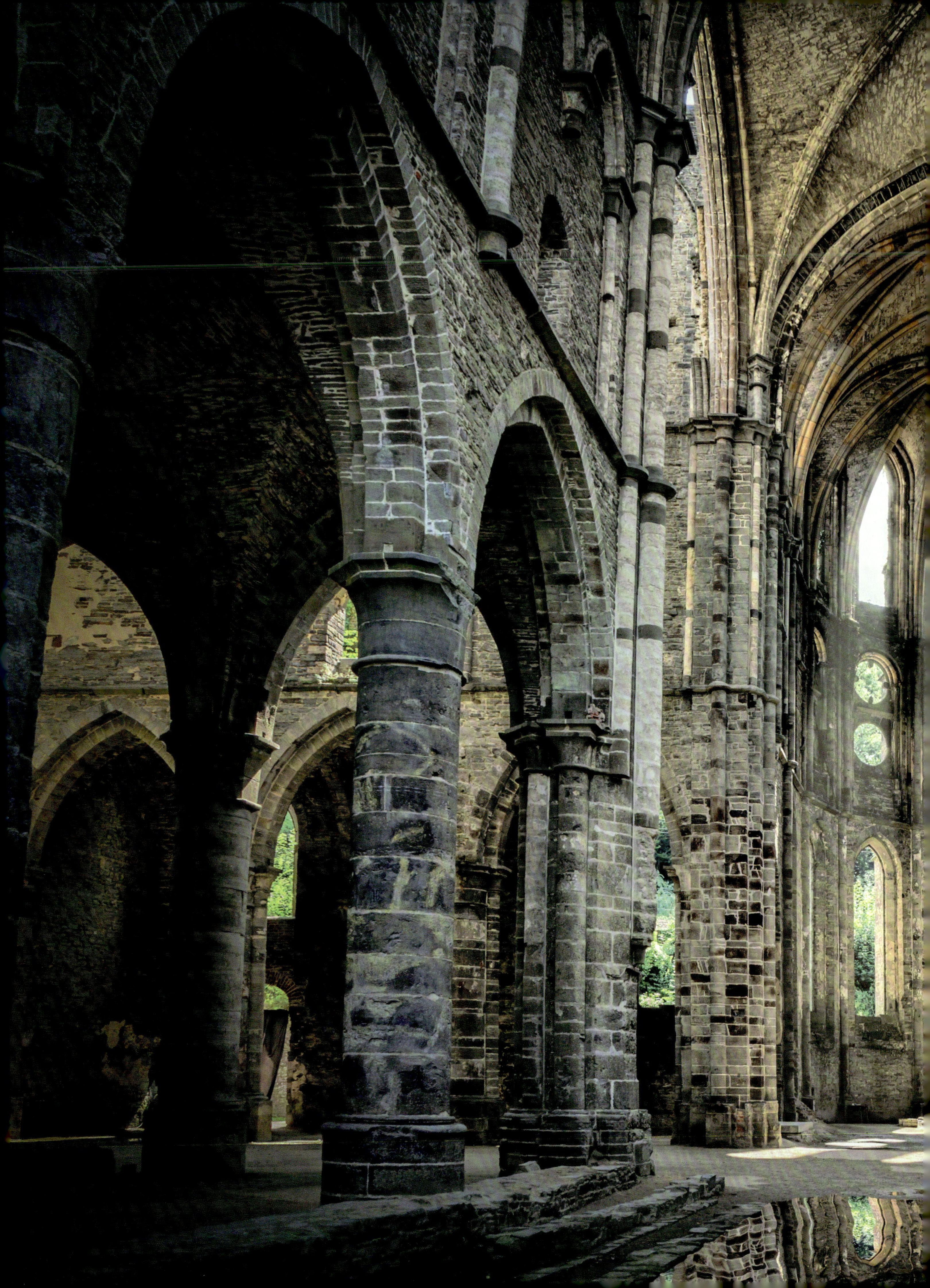

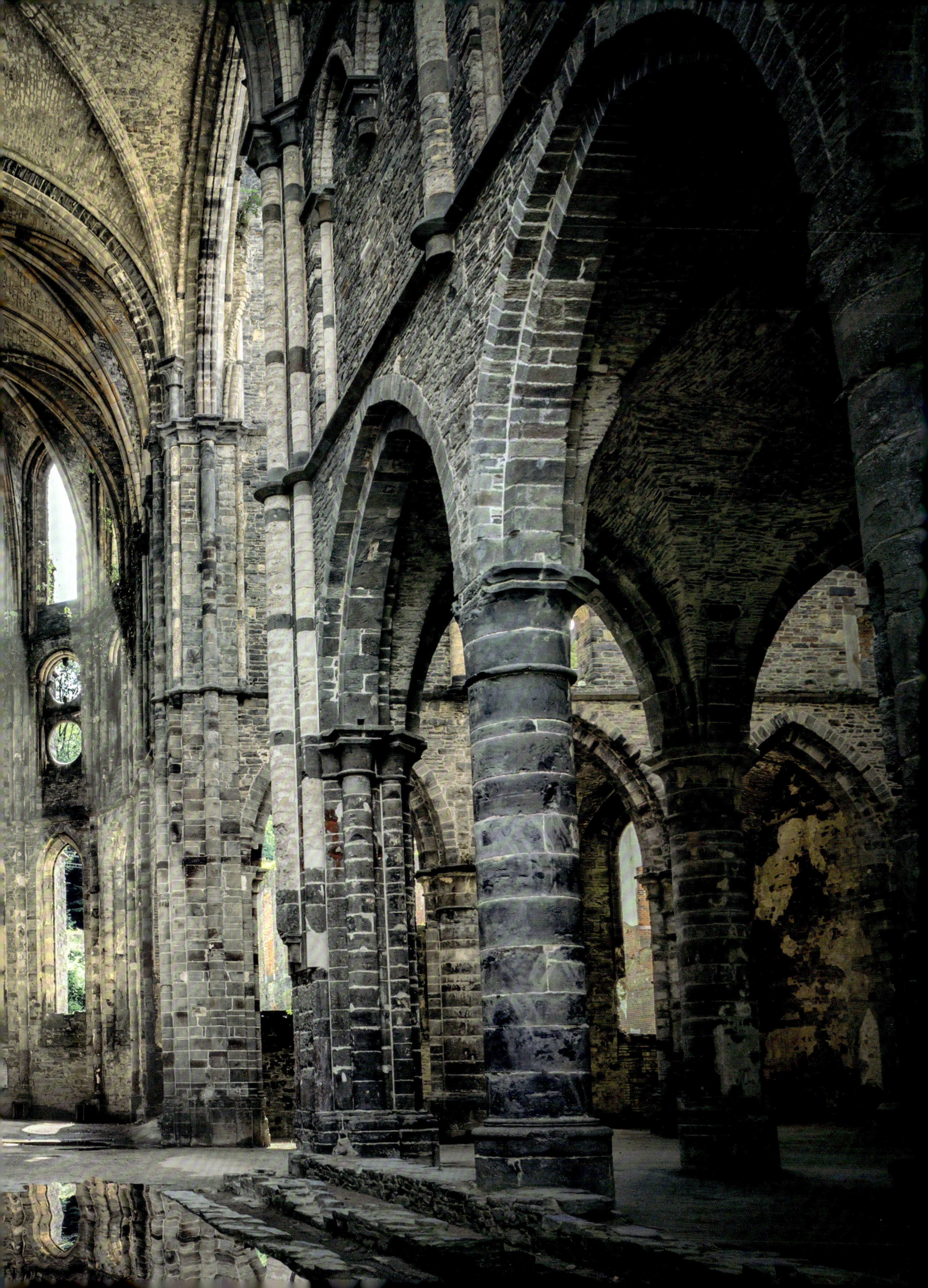

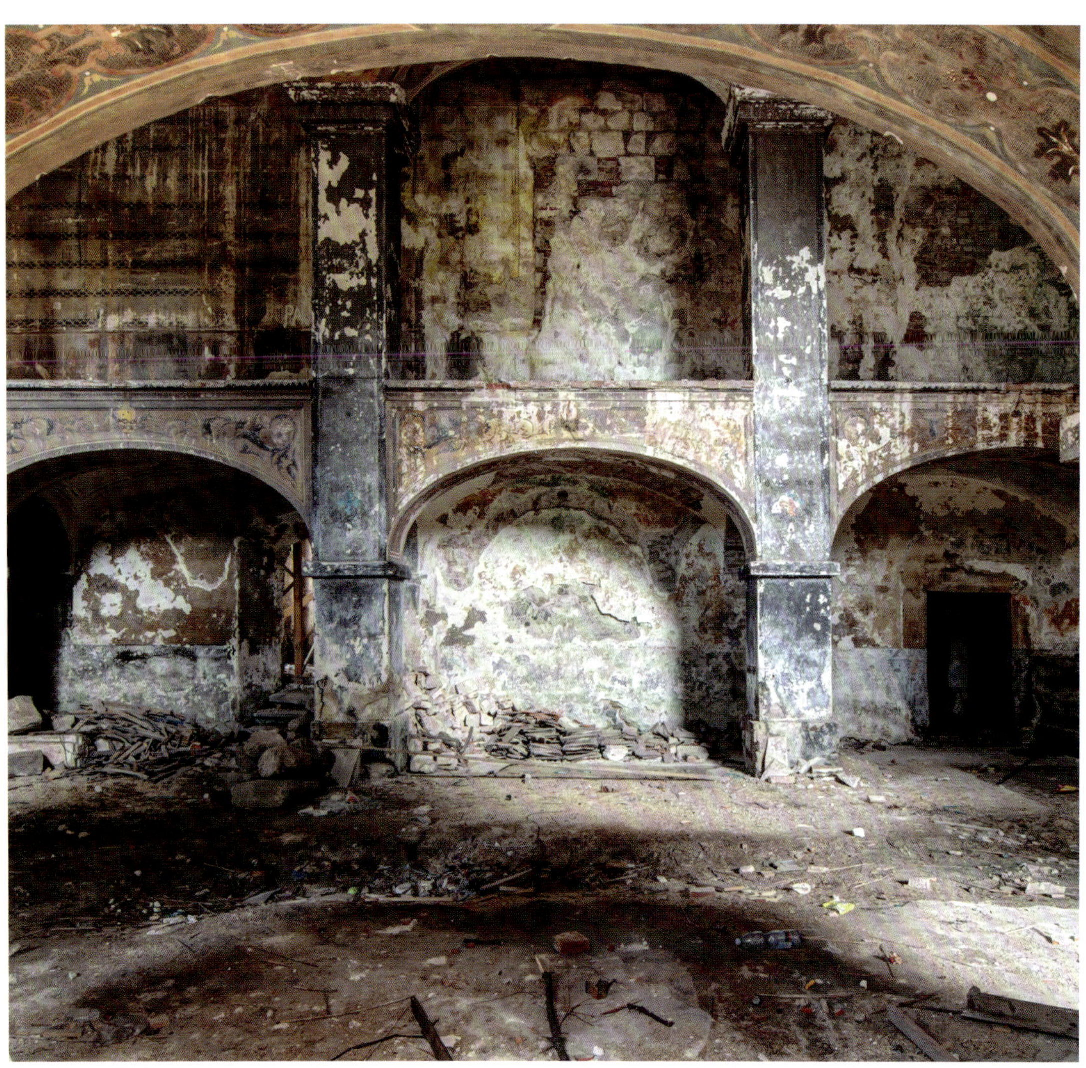

PREVIOUS PAGE:
Villers Abbey, Wallonia, Belgium
Rebuilt in the 13th century, the Cistercian abbey at Villers fell after attacks by republicans during the French Revolution.

LEFT:
All Saints Church, Stvolinky, Czech Republic
This 14th century church became a locus for Protestant preachers after 1554, but reverted to Catholicism in the 19th century. After World War II, it deteriorated under Czechoslovakia's restrictions on Christian worship.

BELOW:
Church, Chervonohorod, Nyrkiv, Ukraine
This Catholic church fell under the Kingdom of Poland until 1795, but declined when power passed to Orthodox Christians. In 1939, the Soviet Union annexed the area, later removing the settlement from maps.

OPPOSITE:
Church of the Holy Trinity, Novotroitskoye, Lipetsk, Russia
Erected in 1809–1819, this church stood little hope when Christianity was attacked after the 1917 October Revolution.

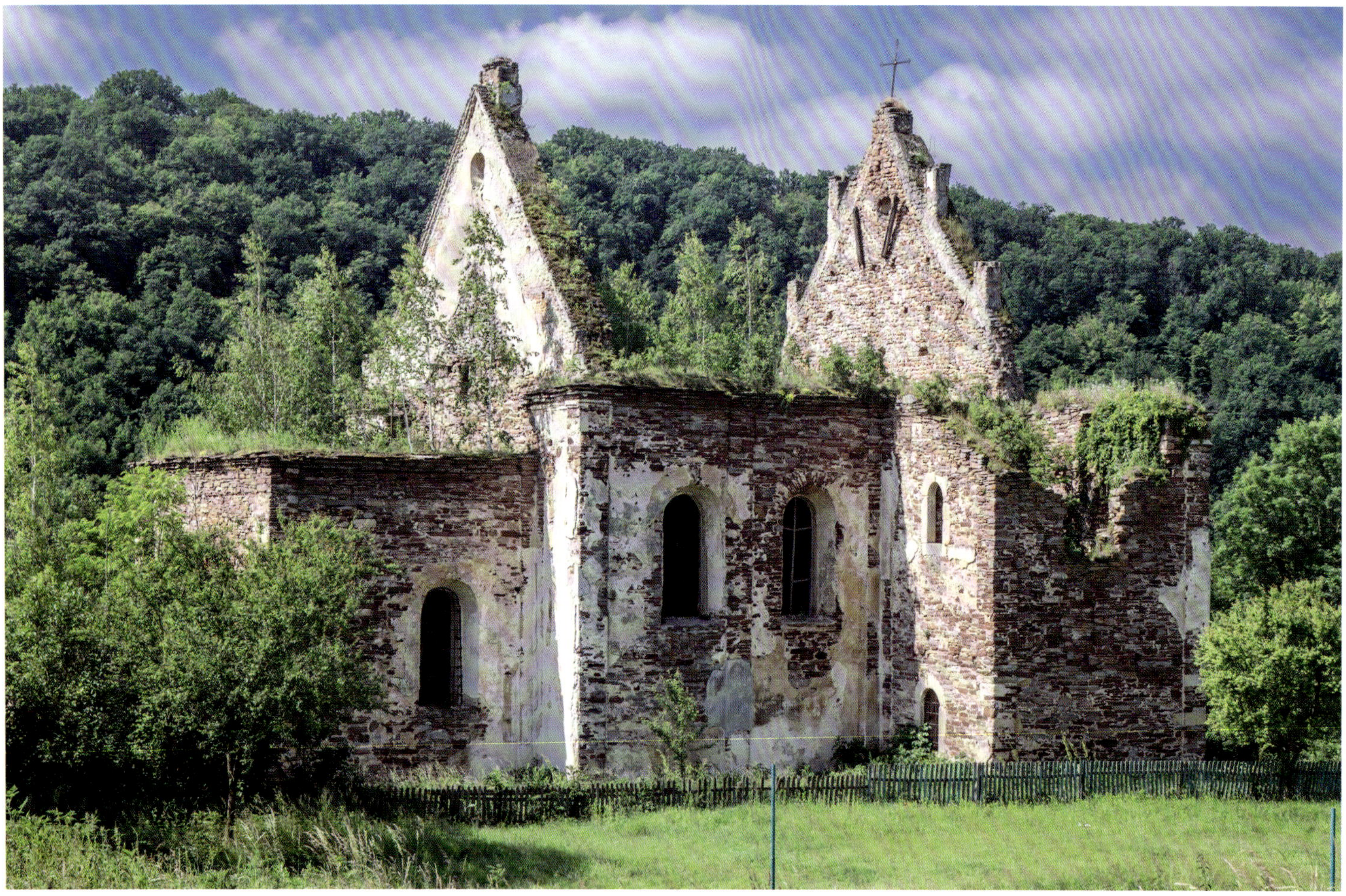

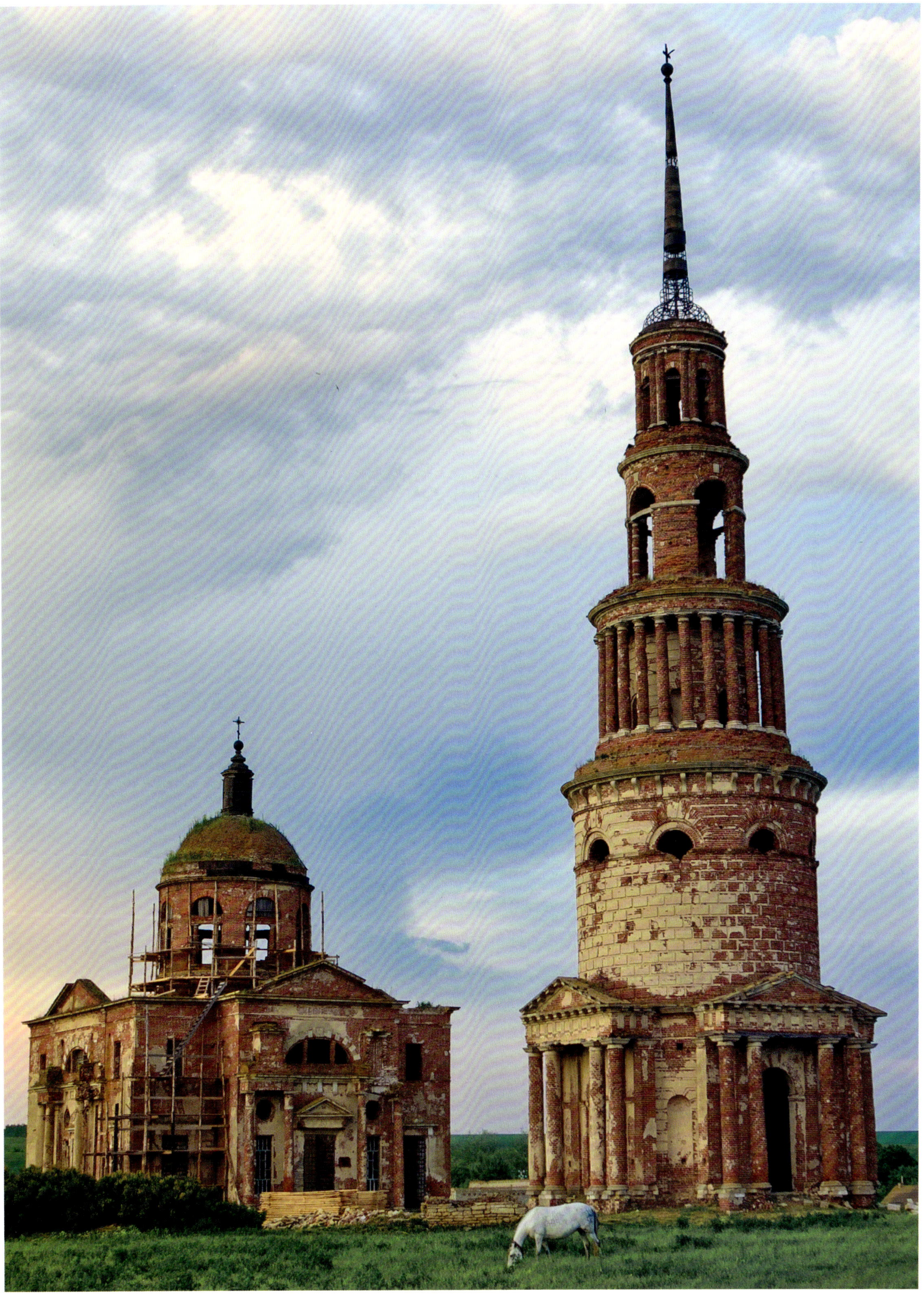

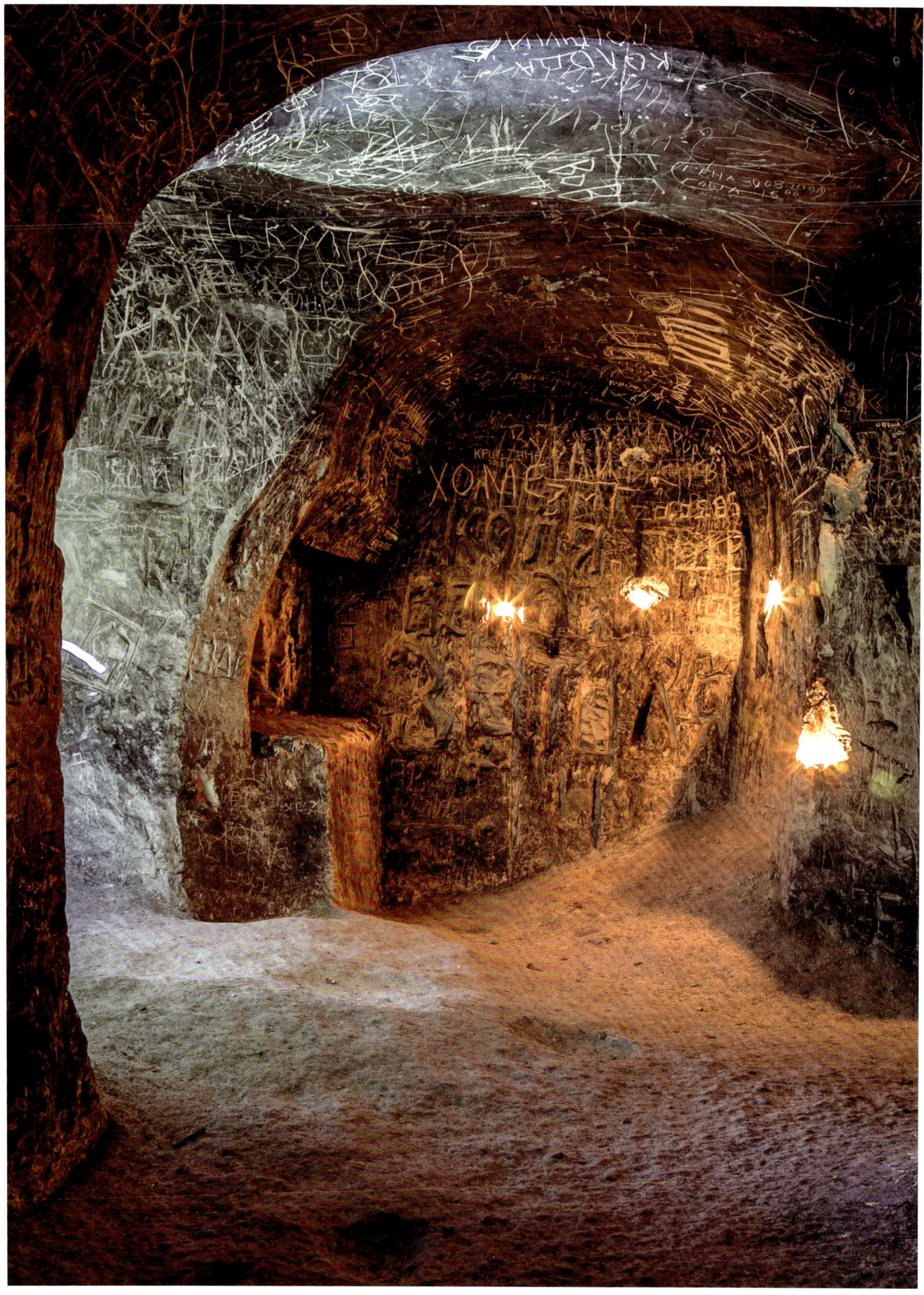

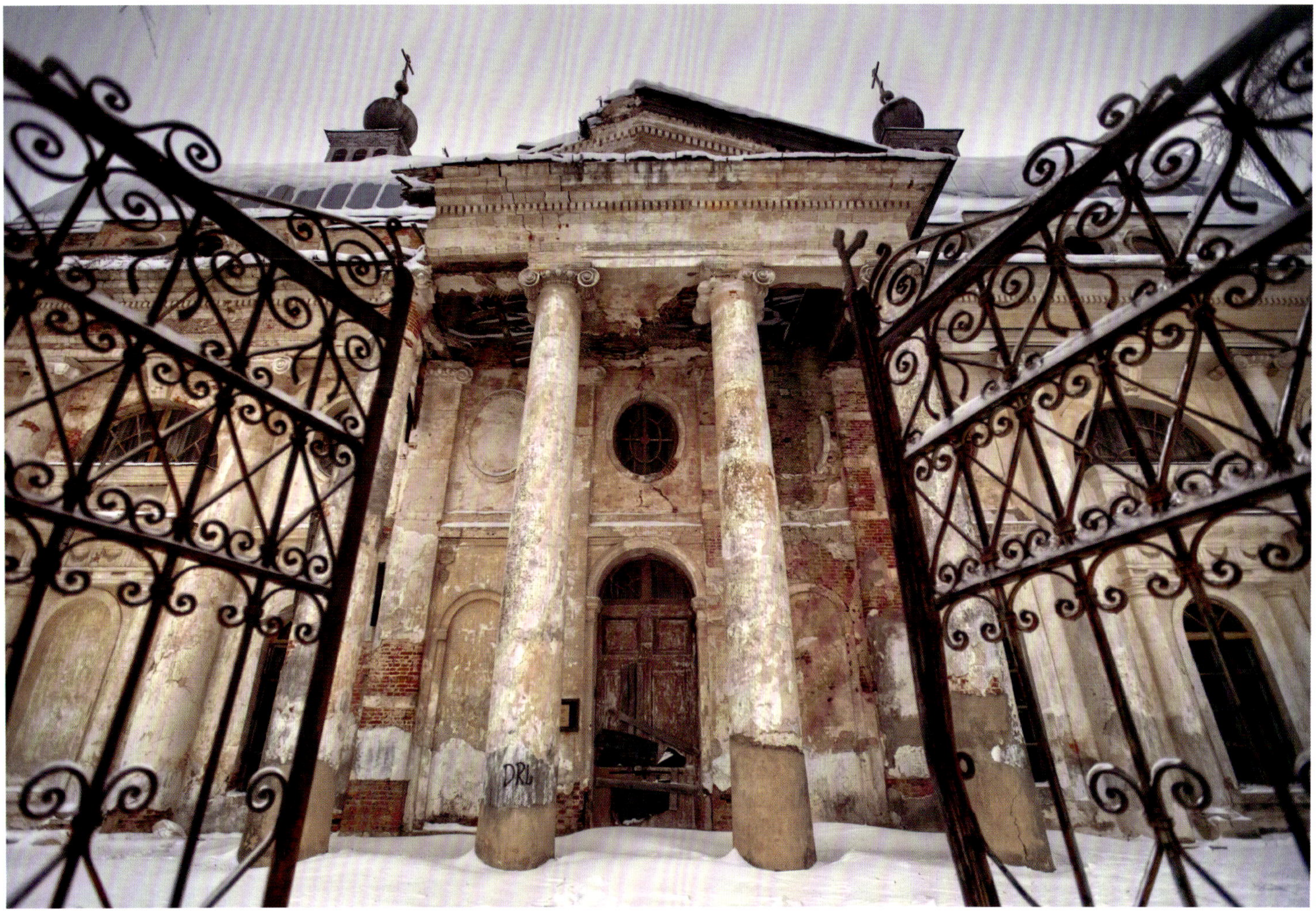

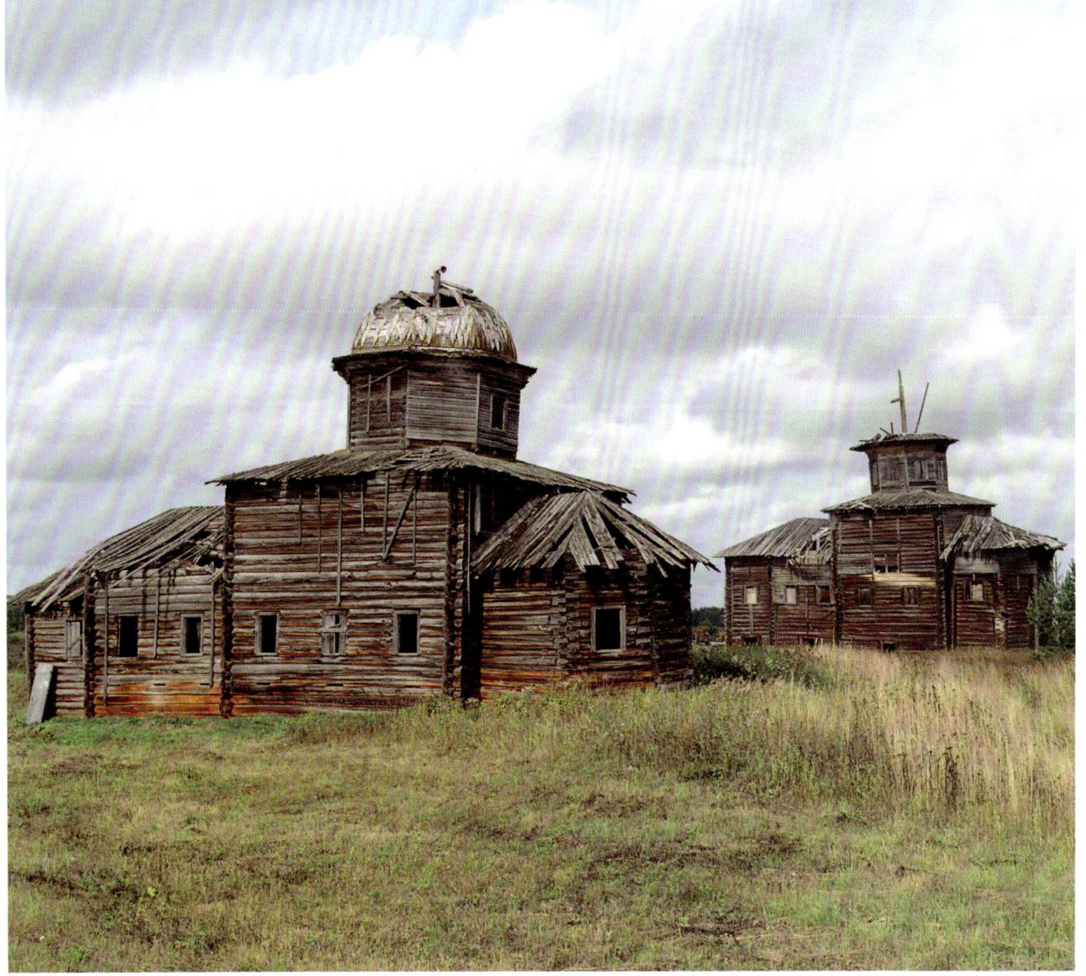

OPPOSITE:

Monastery near Kalach, Voronezh, Russia

Monks once worshipped at this unusual underground monastery. The maze-like 892-metre-long (2927ft) cave was dug out of chalky rock probably in the early 18th century. Long since abandoned, the cave had two churches and multiple levels linked by spiral staircases.

ABOVE:

Church of Our Lady of Kazan, Yaropolets, Volokolamsk, Russia

The Chernyshev family owned half the town of Yaropolets, including this church, for 200 years until the Bolsheviks seized their estate in 1917. Neglected thereafter, it was further damaged by German artillery during World War II.

LEFT:

Wooden Churches, Maslovskaya, Arkhangelsk Region, Russia

Coniferous forests provided the material for these wooden churches in Russia's frozen north. Interestingly, most were built without nails. Communist rule saw congregation numbers fall.

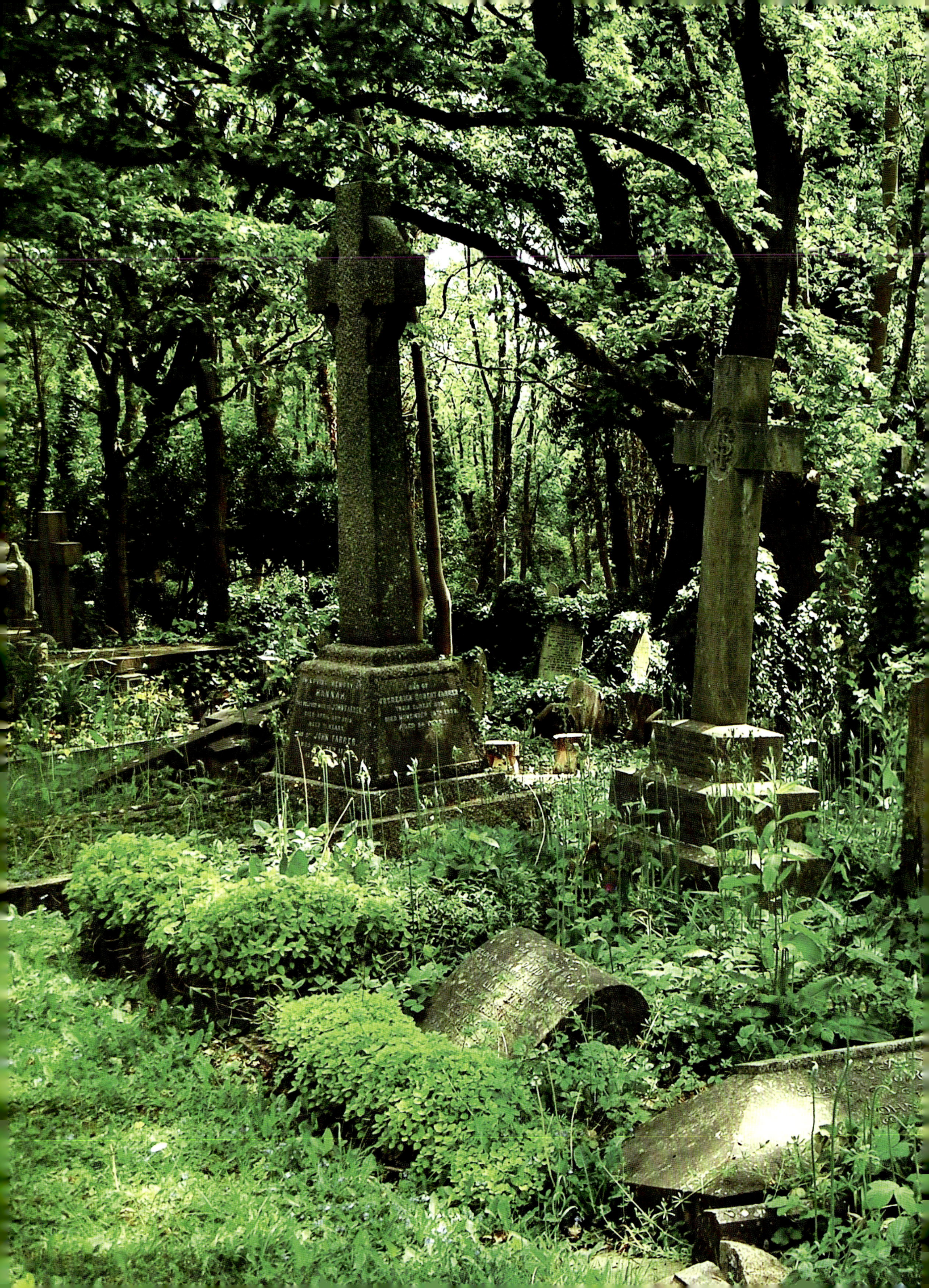
HANNAH
JOHN FARRER

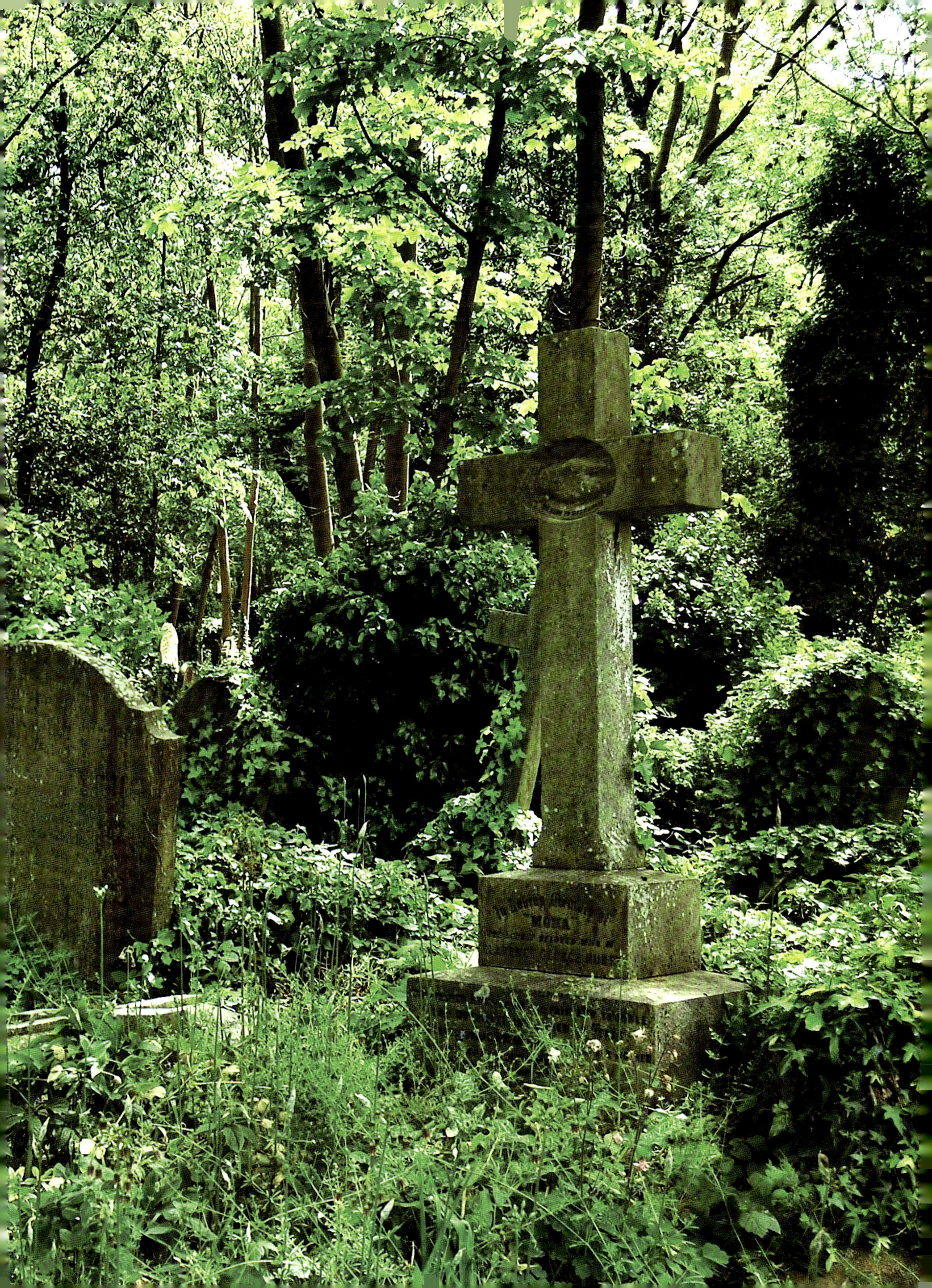
MONA

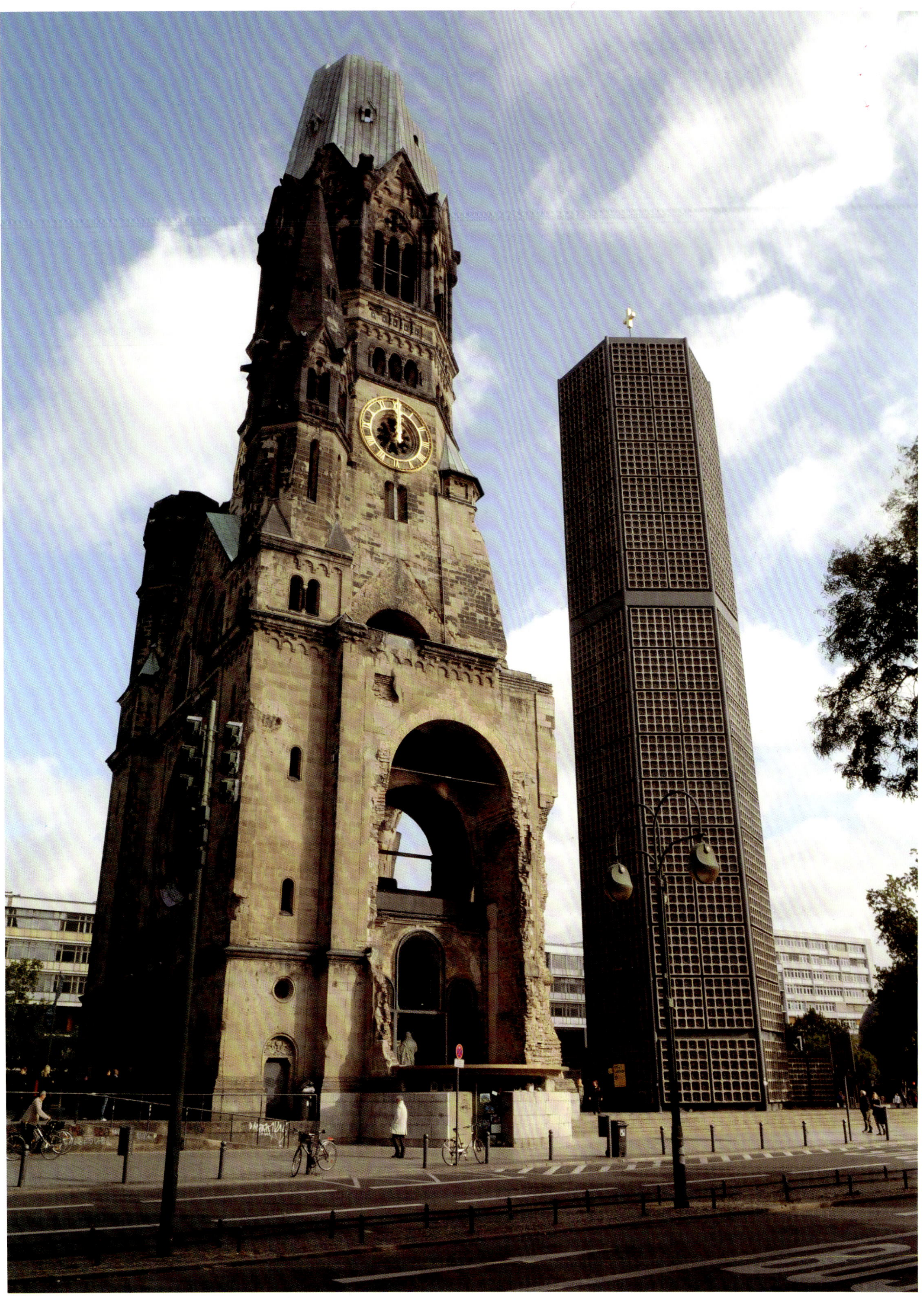

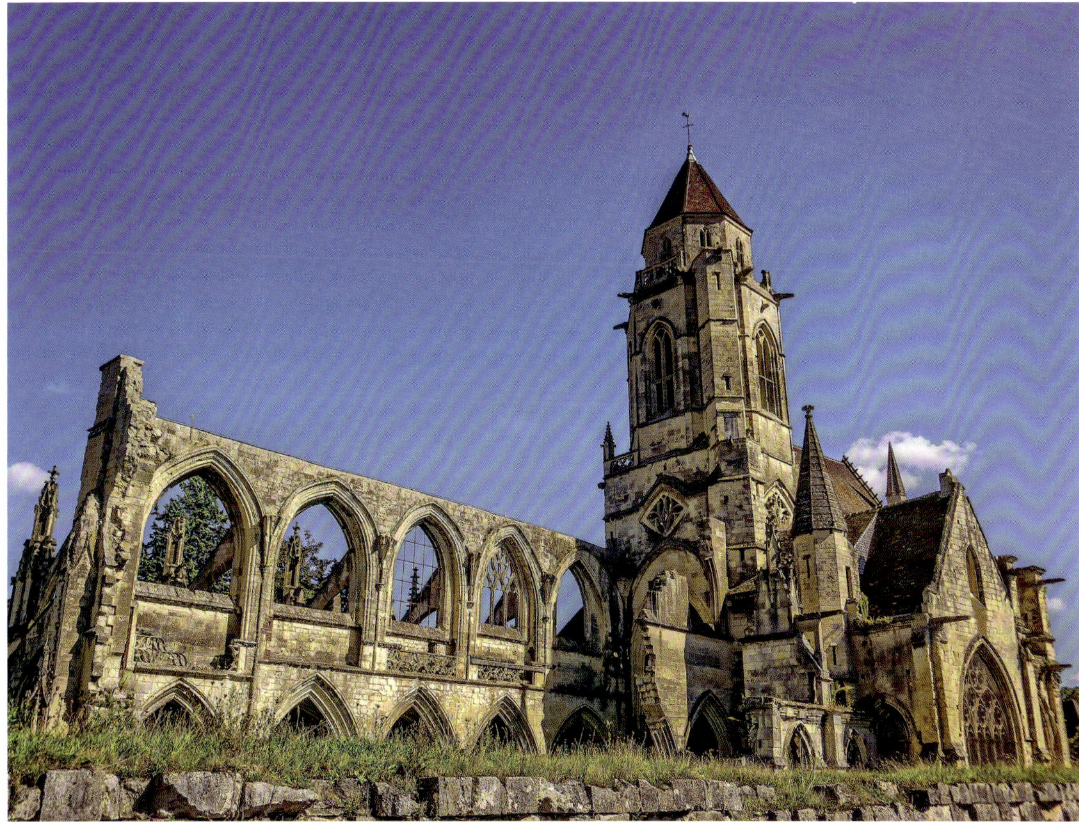

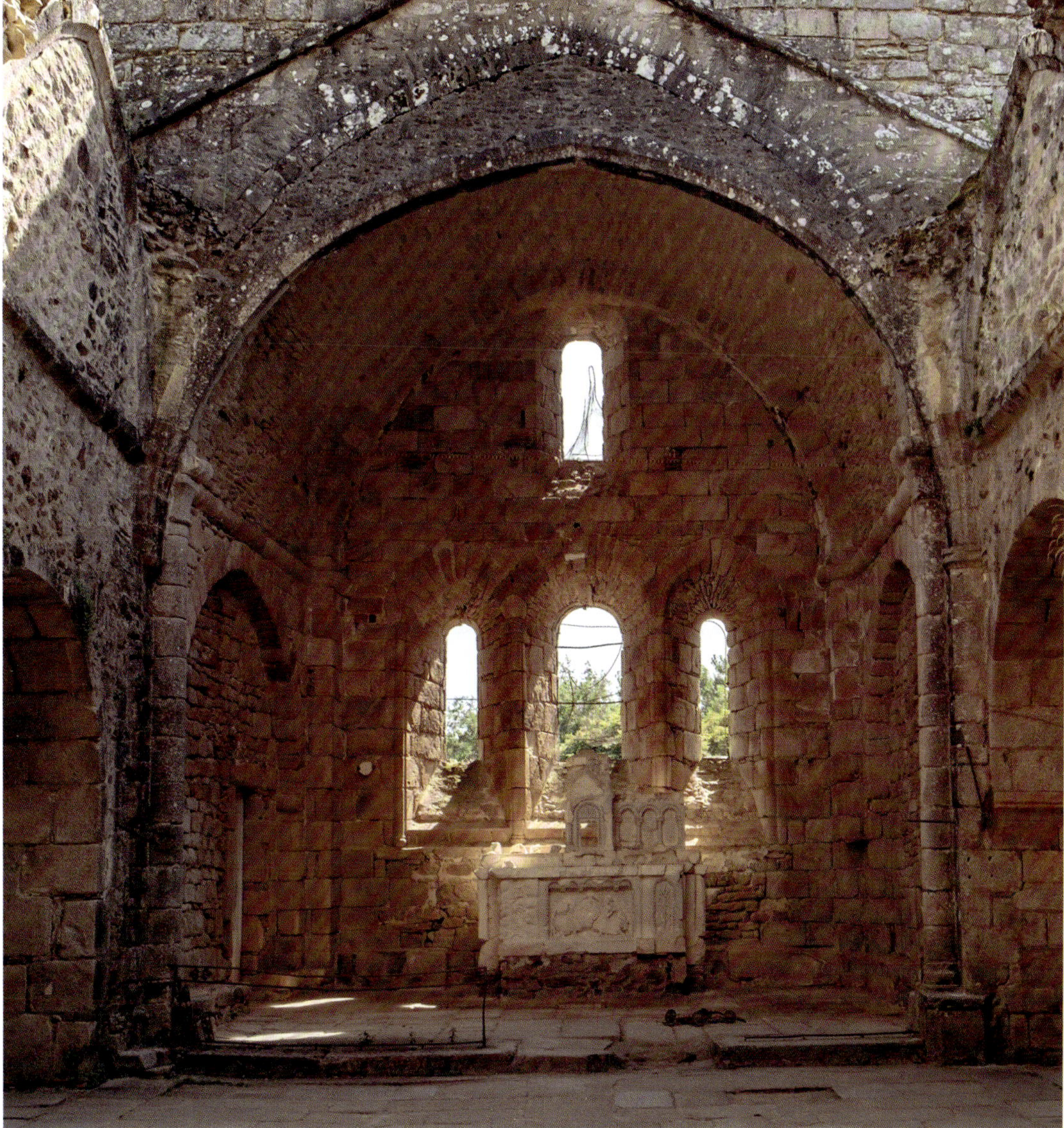

PREVIOUS PAGE:

West Cemetery, Highgate, London, England

First opened in 1839, Highgate Cemetery was one of seven private cemeteries authorized to cope with London's booming population. The necropolis fell into decline in the 1970s until a charity trust began leading tours and clearing weeds. Karl Marx is among many famous names buried in Highgate's still operating East Cemetery, but the derelict and overgrown West Cemetery boasts Egyptian-style catacombs and neo-Gothic mausoleums.

OPPOSITE:

Kaiser Wilhelm Memorial Church, Berlin, Germany

A double victim of World War II, Berlin's Kaiser Wilhelm Church was hit twice by Allied air raids. Only the 'hollow tooth' of its west tower remained. Today the church, built in 1891–1895, survives as a memorial to the war. The adjacent belfry, along with a new church, was completed in 1963.

ABOVE LEFT:

Church of St-Étienne-the-Old, Caen, Normandy, France

History has hardly been kind to the Romanesque Church of Saint-Étienne-the-Old. In June 1944, Allied troops fired at a German tank column, but hit the church instead, wrecking its nave. The 10th century building had already been damaged when Caen was besieged by the English in 1376 and 1417, and had served as a stable during the French Revolution. Decommissioned in 1793, it was narrowly saved from demolition in 1847.

LEFT:

Church, Oradour-sur-Glane, France

One of the most ghastly events of World War II occurred on 10 June 1944 in the west-central French village of Oradour-sur-Glane. On that day occupying German SS troops slaughtered 642 inhabitants, including most of the town's women and children who they corralled into this church, and then firebombed. By government edict, the burnt-out village remains as it was; at its entrance hangs a sign with these words: 'Souviens-Toi' – 'Remember'.

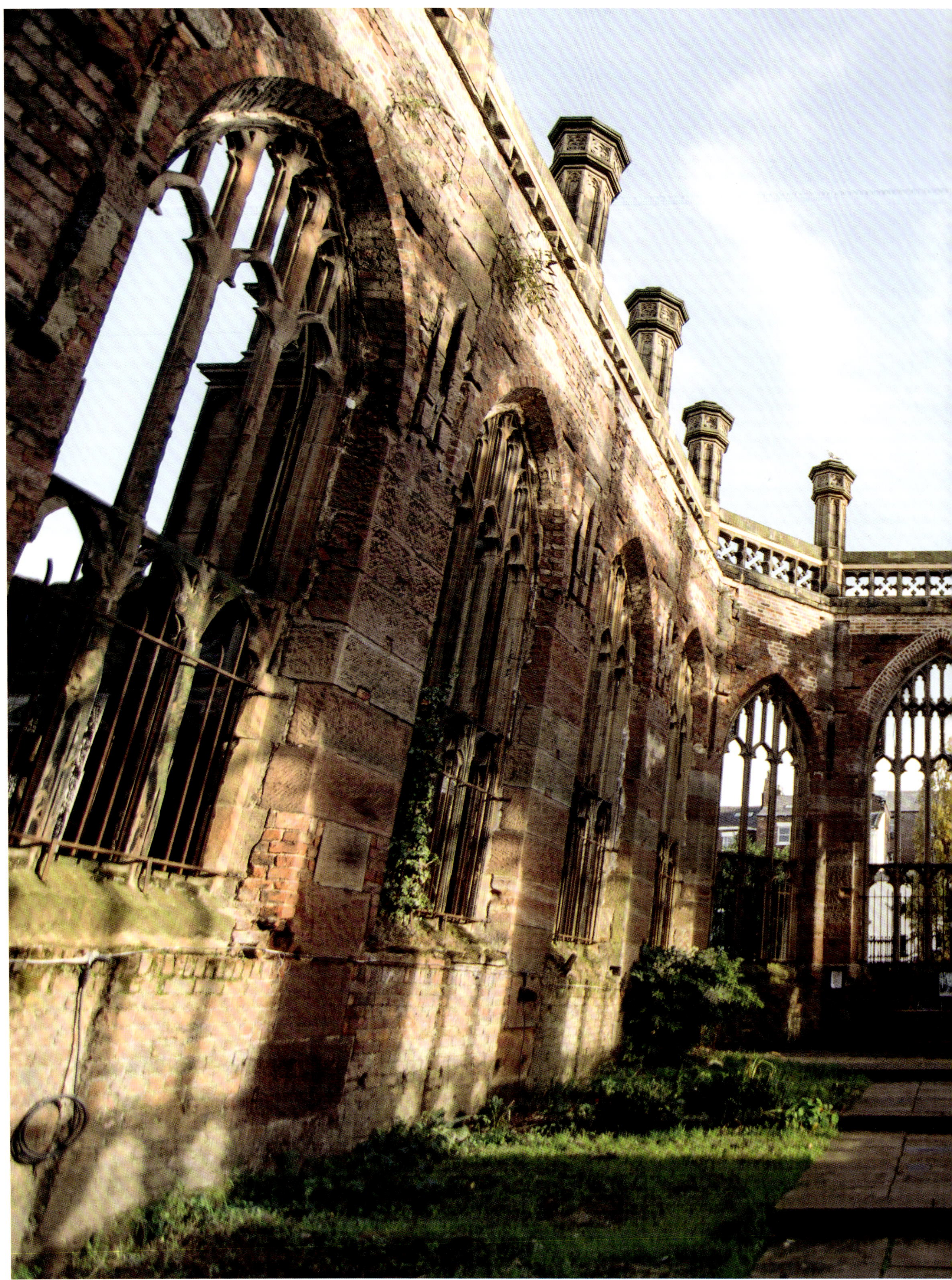

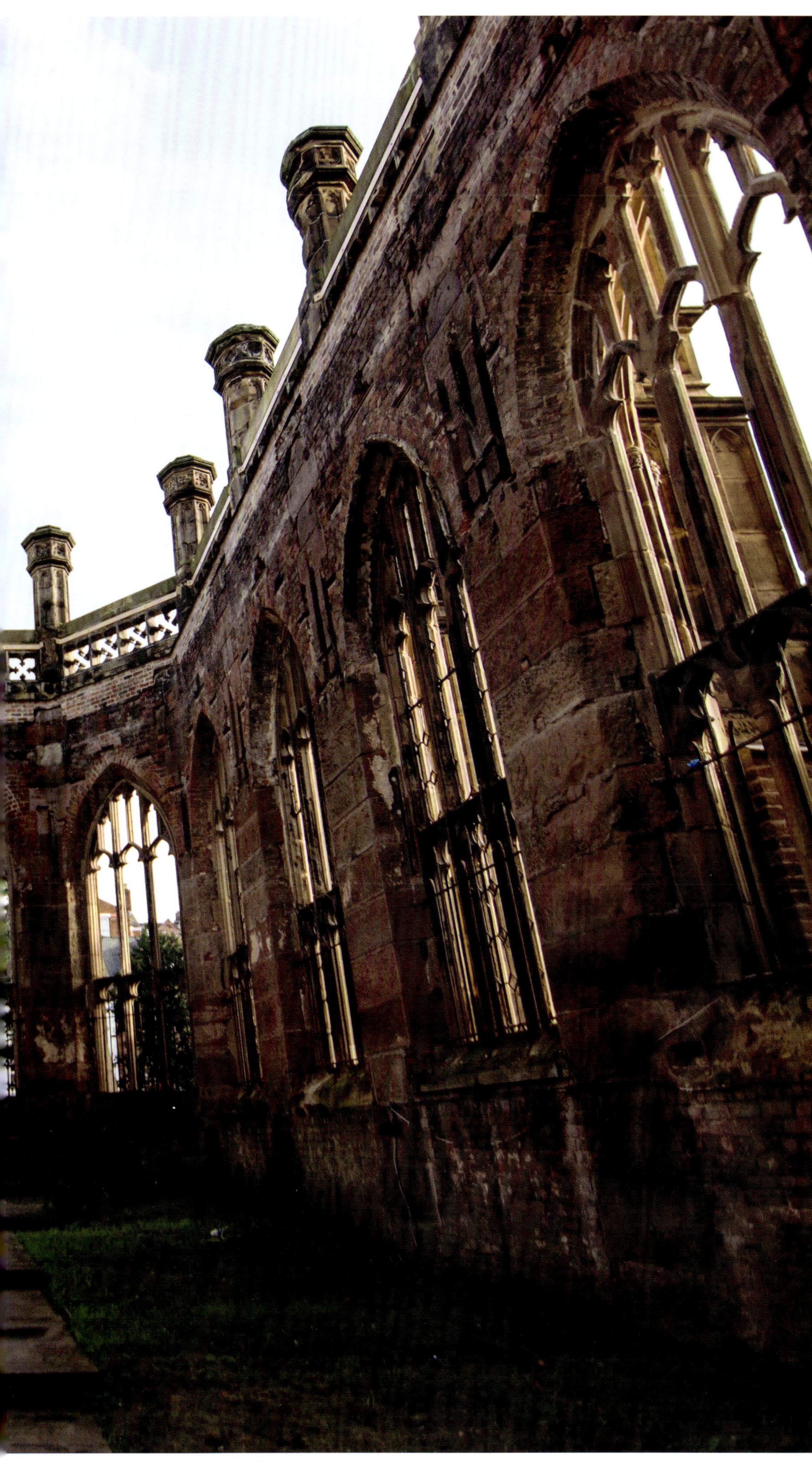

St Luke's Church, Liverpool, Merseyside, England

St Luke's Church symbolizes World War II's forgotten blitz. German bombers hit Liverpool, a strategically vital port, on 6 May 1941, setting the church ablaze just after midnight. St Luke's clock froze at 3.36 am, marking the moment flames reached the spire.

The Anglican parish church was built in stages from 1811–1832. Today its ruins are used for occasional exhibitions and events.

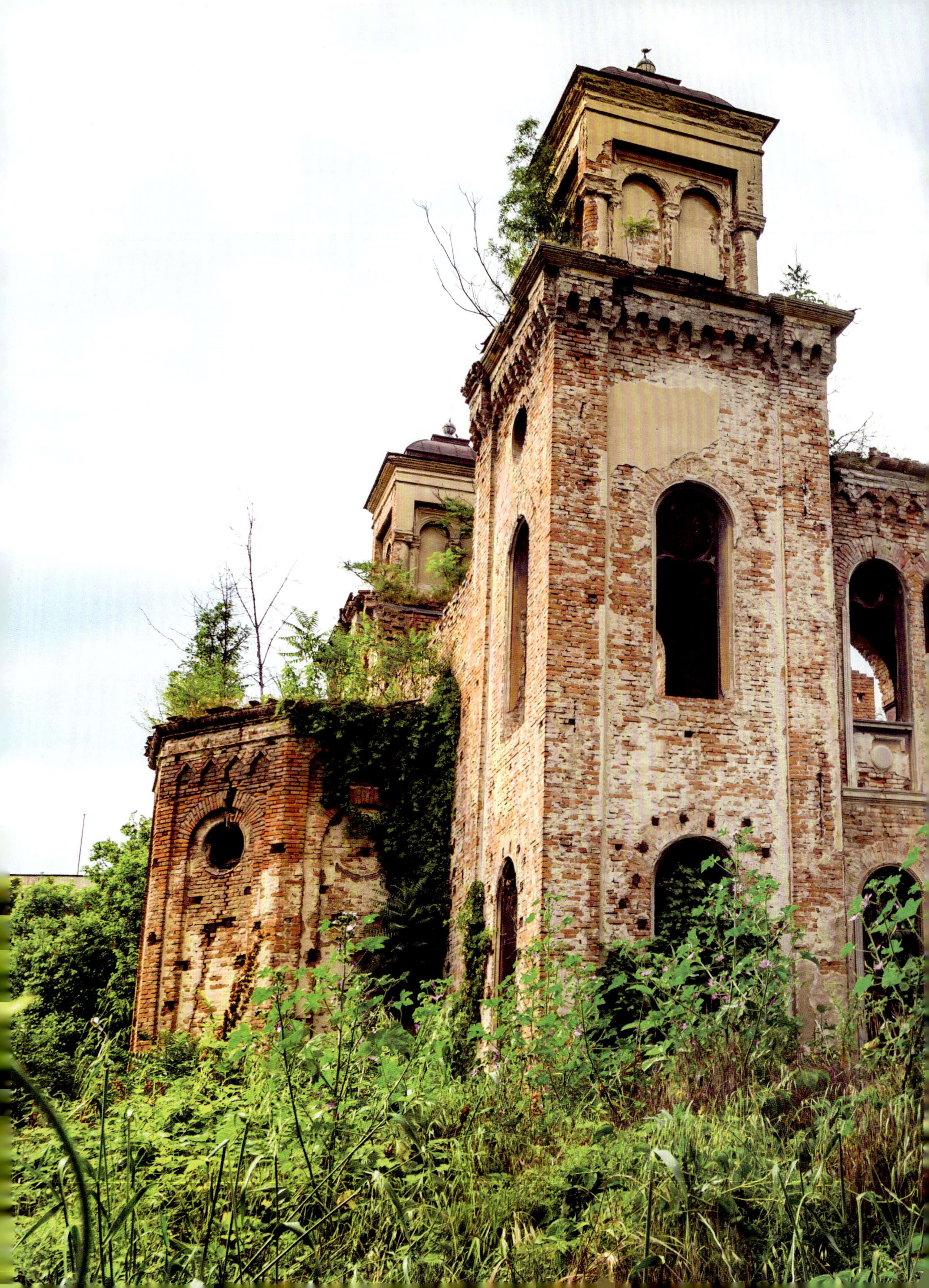

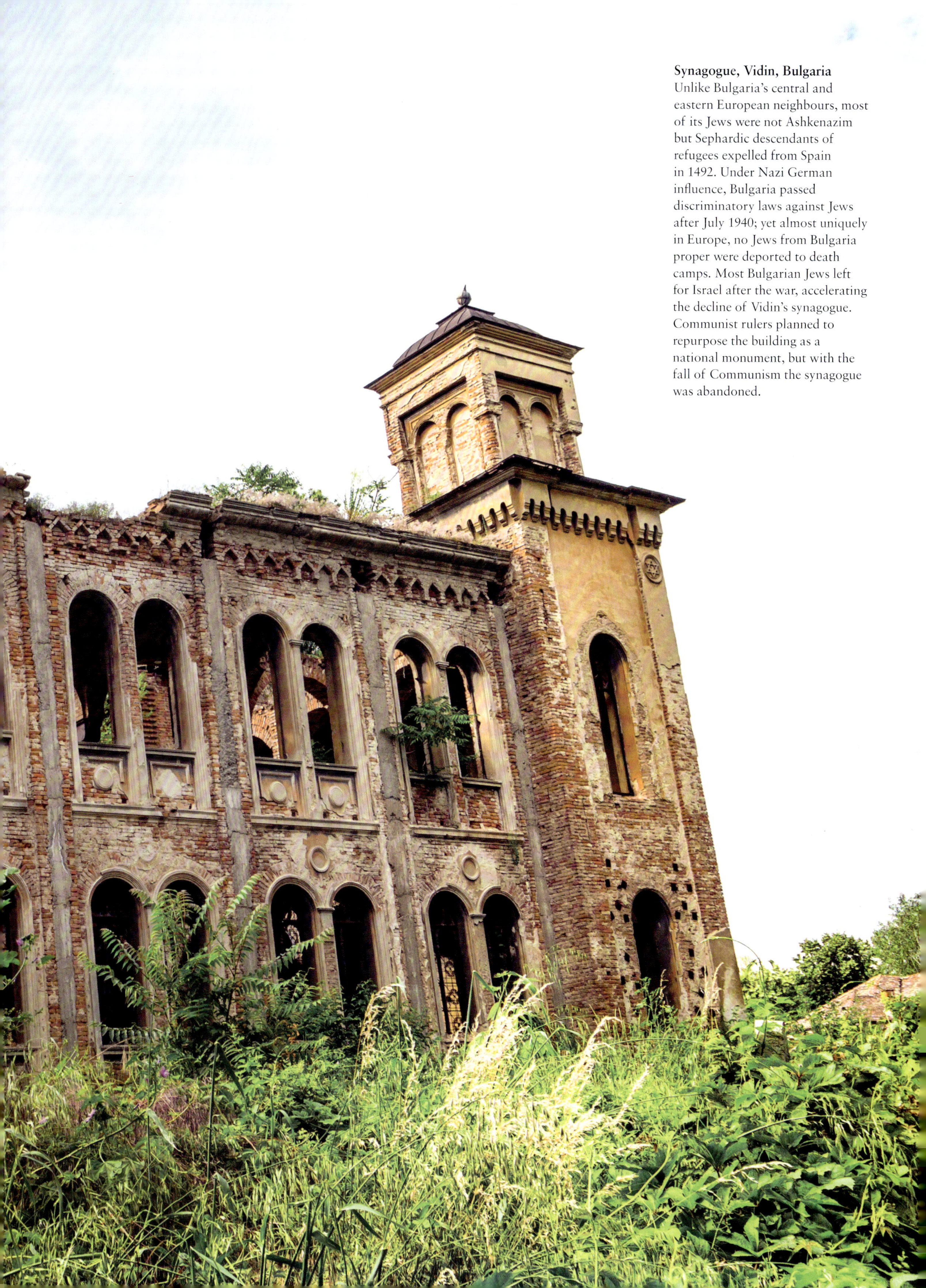

Synagogue, Vidin, Bulgaria
Unlike Bulgaria's central and eastern European neighbours, most of its Jews were not Ashkenazim but Sephardic descendants of refugees expelled from Spain in 1492. Under Nazi German influence, Bulgaria passed discriminatory laws against Jews after July 1940; yet almost uniquely in Europe, no Jews from Bulgaria proper were deported to death camps. Most Bulgarian Jews left for Israel after the war, accelerating the decline of Vidin's synagogue. Communist rulers planned to repurpose the building as a national monument, but with the fall of Communism the synagogue was abandoned.

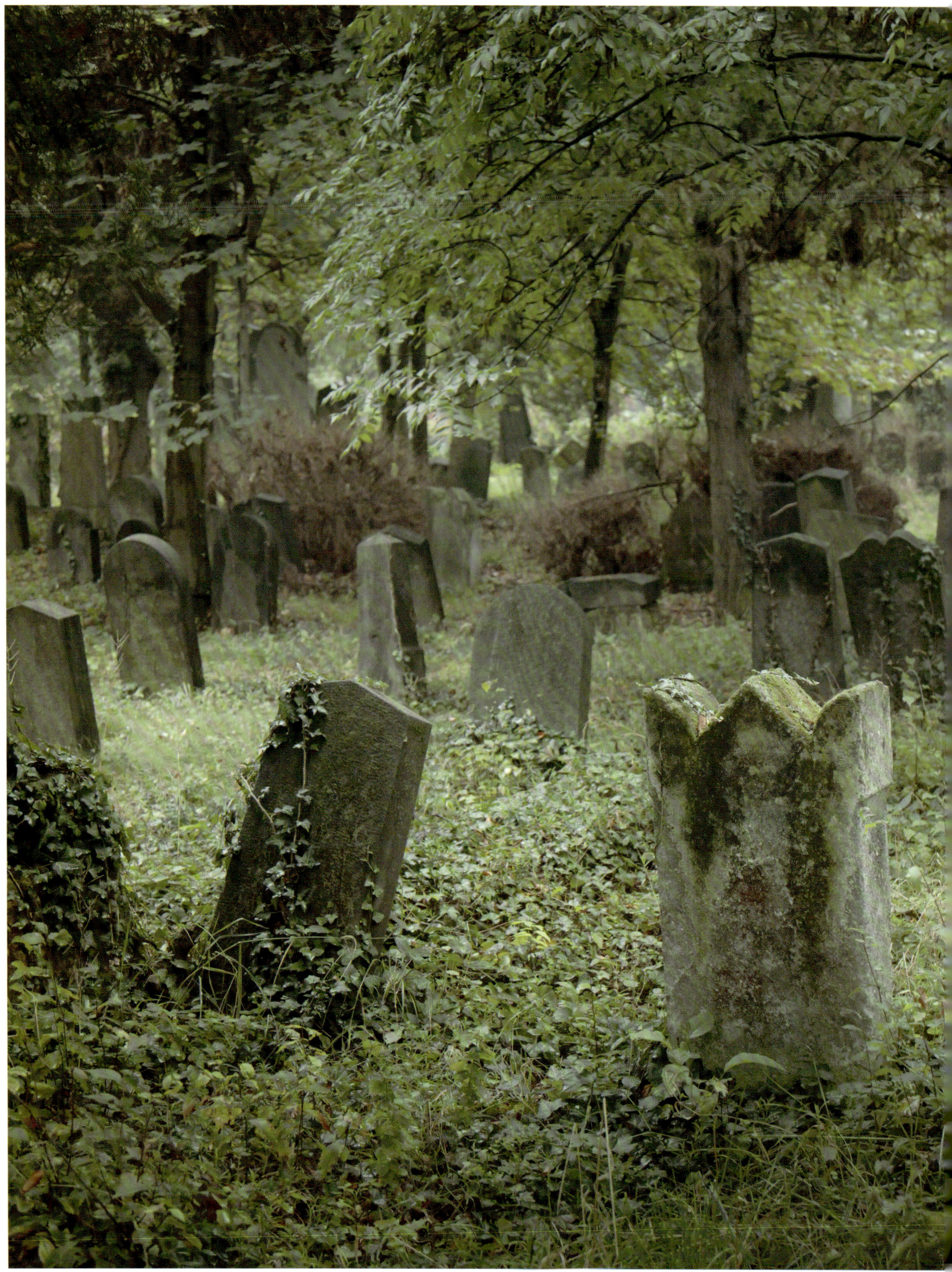

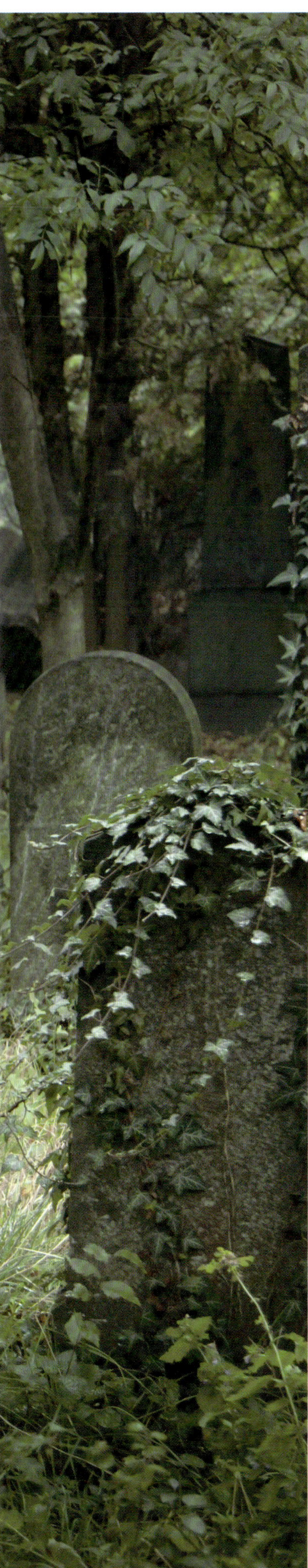

LEFT:
Old Jewish Cemetery, Vienna, Austria
Founded in 1540 but shut in 1784, the Old Jewish Cemetery hints at Jews' long heritage in Vienna. It also symbolizes an Austrian community reduced by emigration, deportation and death camp killings from 192,000 in 1938 to just 7000 by November 1942.

BELOW:
Old Jewish Cemetery, Wroclaw, Poland
Wroclaw's Old Jewish Cemetery recalls a once thriving community that was wiped out during World War II. Established in 1856 when Wroclaw was Breslau in German Silesia, it closed in 1942. By then all remaining Breslau Jews had been deported to Nazi camps, where most were murdered.

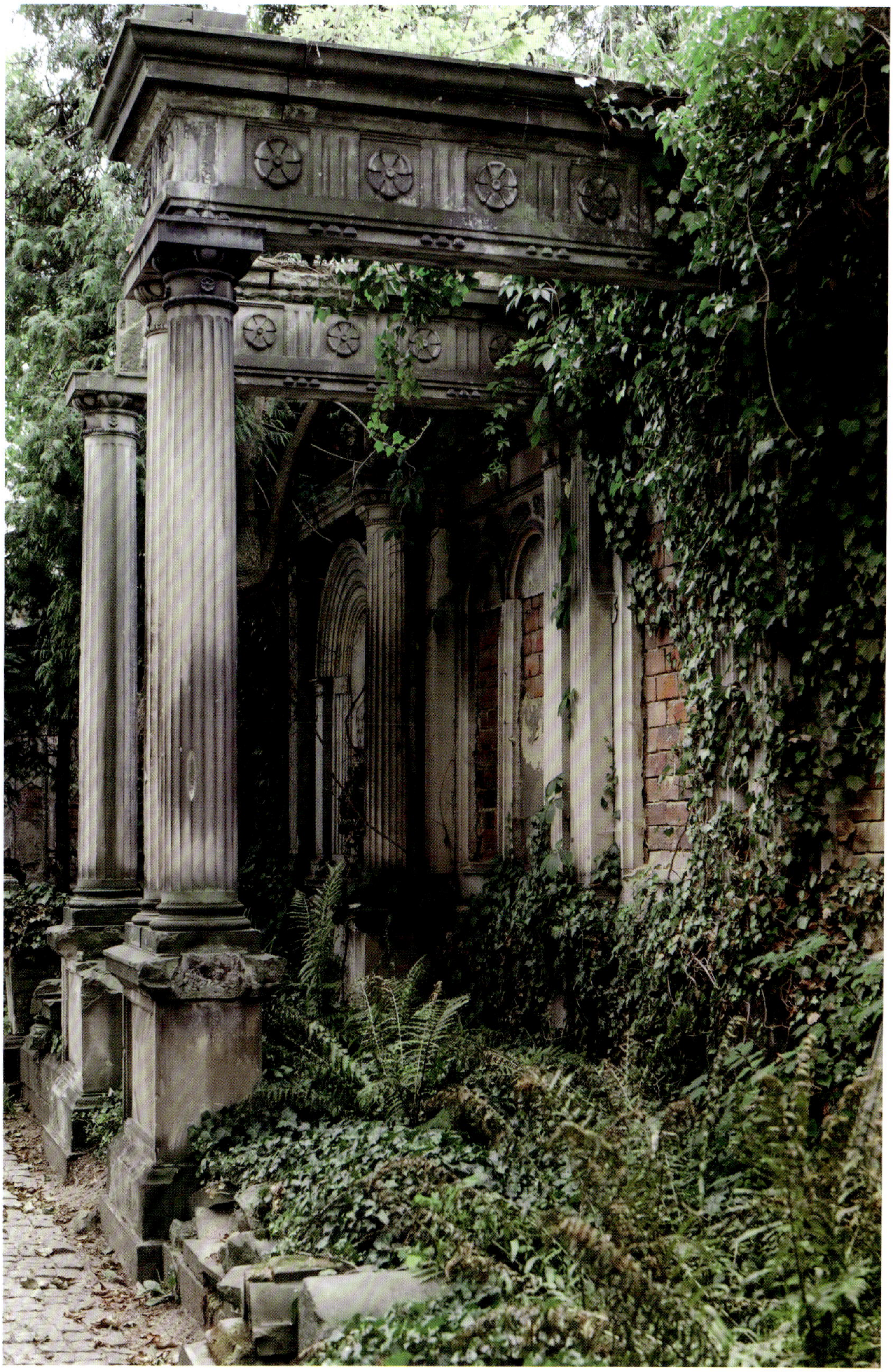

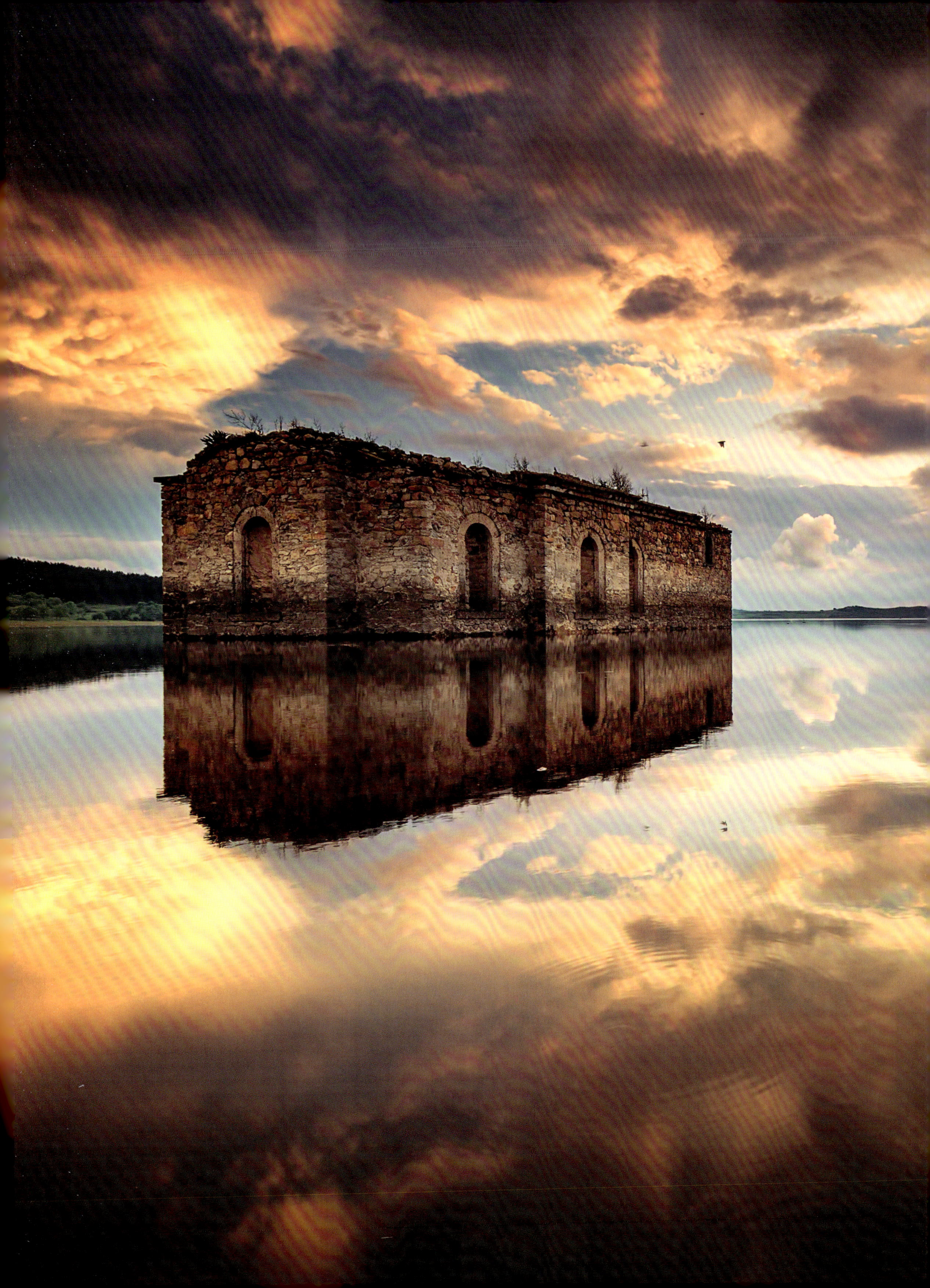

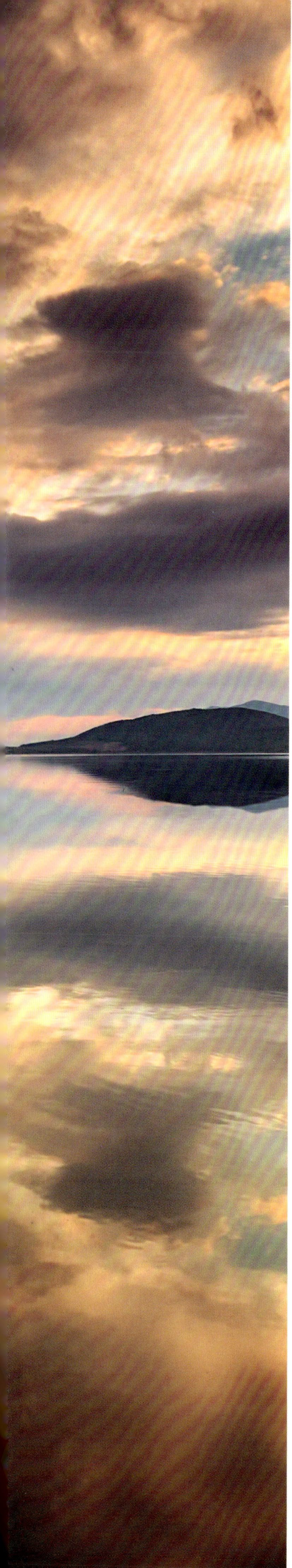

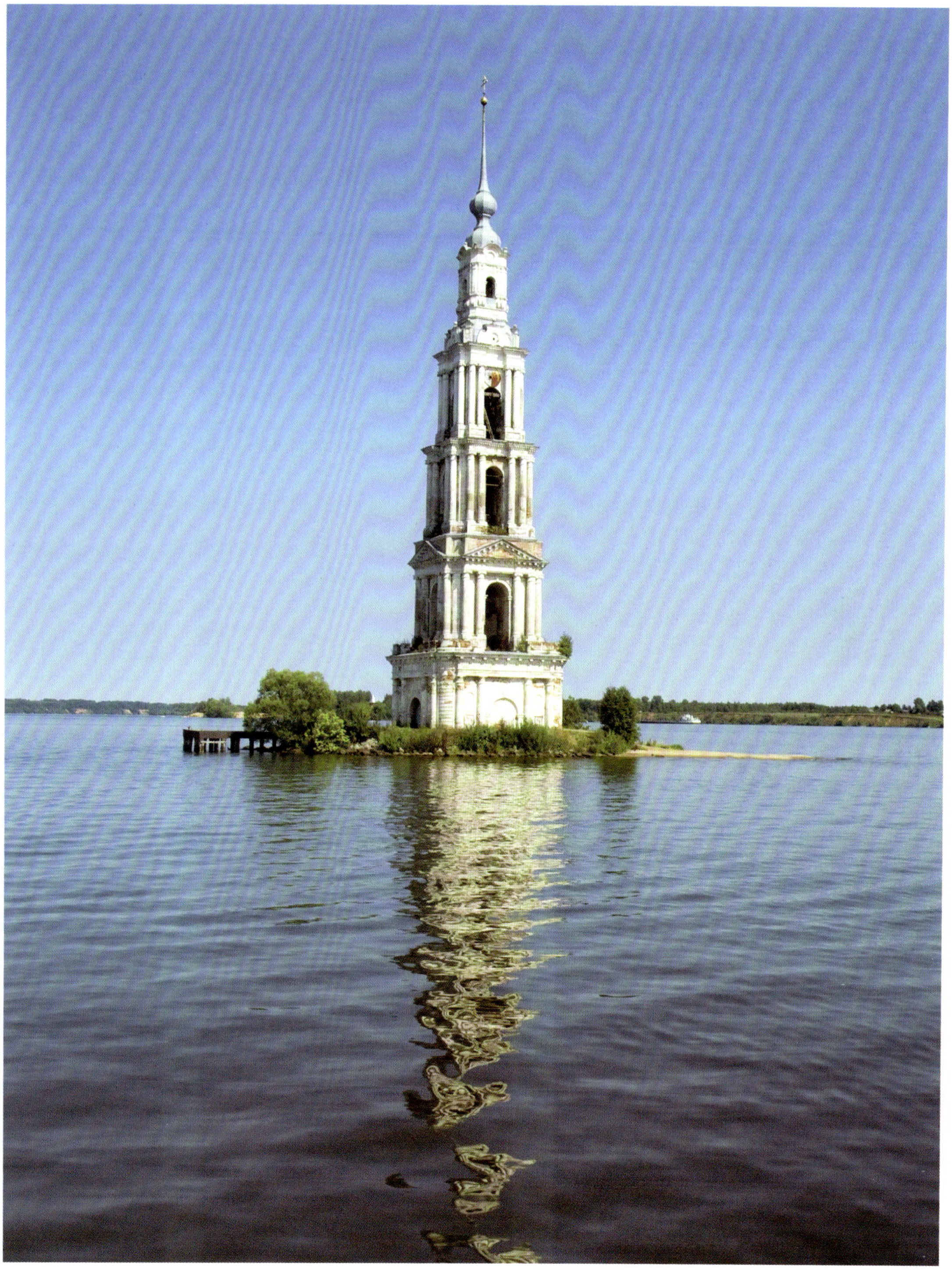

LEFT:

Church of St Ivan Rilski, Jrebchevo, Bulgaria

In summer, the 19th century Church of St Ivan Rilski stands two-thirds buried in water; in winter, the waters recede and anyone can walk inside. In 1965, Bulgaria's Communist rulers relocated residents from three villages to make way for the Jrebchevo Dam.

Mussel shells, mossy vegetation and river stones have replaced the church's icons and frescoes.

ABOVE:

Saint Nicholas Cathedral, Kalyazin, Russia

Little survives of the original old part of the town of Kalyazin apart from the tower of its otherwise submerged Saint Nicholas Cathedral. It rises above the Uglich reservoir, created when a hydroelectric plant was built across the Volga River in 1939–1940. Before the flooding, the cathedral was dismantled, the tower severed, emptied of its 12 bells and 'floated' on an artificial island.

Today some Orthodox believers still cross to the tower and hold unofficial services in the belfry.

Picture Credits

Alamy: 6 (Arcaid), 18 (Hemis), 29 (Greatstock), 35 (Luis Dafos), 45 (Blickwinkel), 48/49 (Marion Bull), 50 (Eddie Gerald), 51 (BibleLandPictures.com), 56 bottom (Mustafa Olgun), 70/71 (Robert Harding), 98/99 (Age Fotostock/Ioseba Egibar), 121 (Michal Knitl), 127 (David Pearson), 158 (Luc Novovitch), 159 (Leon Werdinger), 174 (Bart Pro), 187 (Robert Harding/Eleanor Scriven), 198 (Holmes Garden Photos), 199 (John Bracegirdle)

Dreamstime: 14 (Abrilla), 15 (Efesenko), 22 (Tom Wyness), 24 bottom (Meunierd), 30/31 (Blossfeldia), 32 (Witr), 52/53 (Pressc750), 54 (Igercelman), 55 top (Asafta), 58/59 (Katiekk), 90 (Leswrona), 91 (Tigerpike), 92/93 (Iaranik), 94 (Tinroma), 95 bottom (Nok6716), 96/97 (Mrallen), 106 (Radiokafka), 107 (Biggabig31), 108/109 (Zkruger), 117 (Mrallen), 148 top (Christopher Heil), 149 top (Leswrona), 151 (Diego Grandi), 166 (Sepavo), 173 (Ativ), 175 (Rchphoto), 178 (Prestonia), 182/183 (Albo), 192/193 (Klemenr), 196/197 (Davedt), 200/201 (Hanart), 202 (Photopress2), 206/207 (Bbsferrari), 208 top (Siloto), 208 bottom (Fotokon), 209 & 210 (Mulderphoto), 211 top (Juliasha), 218/219 (Kisamarkiza), 222 (Valio84sl)

Getty Images: 47 (De Agostini), 114/115 (S M Rafiq Photography), 167 (Corbis/Timothy Fadek), 168 (AFP/George Castellanos), 169 (Robert Harding/Peter Groenendijk)

iStock: 60/61 (Joel Carillet)

Shutterstock: 7 (Anton Ivanov), 8 (Lisa S), 10/11 (Dmitry Pichugin), 12/13 (Dan Breckwoldt), 16/17 (Niall O'Donoghue), 19 (Michele B), 20/21 (Anthon Jackson), 23 (Marcelo Alex), 24 top (Renee Vititoe), 25 (Anton Boldak), 26/27 (Anton Ivanov), 28 (Fazwick), 34 (Hakan Temucin), 36 (D D Coral), 37 (Huey Min), 38 & 39 (Cpaulfell), 40/41 (Ivan Goryachev), 42/43 (Ganna Glushakova), 44 (Milosk 50), 46 (Gorb Andrii), 55 bottom (Muratart), 56 top (Evren Kalinbacak), 57 (Mehmet O), 62 (Cristi Popescu), 64/65 (Massimiliano Lamagna), 66 (Elena Shchipkova), 67 (Mind Storm), 68 top (Emdadul Hoque Topu), 68 bottom (Pikoso.kz), 69 (Yongyut Kumsri), 72 (Arun Sambhu Mishra), 73 (W_Nakmet), 74 (Lana Kray), 75 (Mazur Travel), 76/77 (Saiko3p), 78/79 (Torsten Pursche), 80/81 (Pinkcandy), 82/83 (DR Travel Photo & Video), 84/85 (Manuel Ascario), 86 (Akedesign), 87 (Scott Biales), 88 (Tatsiana Tur), 89 (Akturer), 95 top (Pae Roengchai), 100/101 (Valery Shanin), 102 & 103 (Marcin Szymczak), 104/105 (Aleksandar Todorovic), 110 (iPhoto-Thailand), 111 (Phyman), 112 (Dmytro Gilitukha), 113 (Napoleonka), 116 (Catalin Lazar), 118/119 (Jimmy Tran), 120 (Antonina Polushkina), 122 & 123 (Vladimir Mulder), 124/125 (Henning Marquardt), 126 (Diy13), 128/129 (Michal Hlavica), 130 (Bernhard Klar), 132/133 (Mark Tucan), 134 (Paulo Afonso), 135 (SL-Photography), 136 (Robert CHG), 137 (Lenka Pribanova), 138/139 (Johnny Adolphson), 140/141 (Jorge Ivan Vasquez C), 142/143 (Rafal Kubiak), 144 (Lorena Huerta), 145 (Kohey), 146/147 (Jose Ignacio Soto), 148 bottom (Douglas Depies), 149 (Rafal Cichawa), 150 both (Elena Diego Photography), 152/153 (Fabio Lamanna), 154/155 (Milton Rodriguez), 156/157 (F11photo), 160 (Silent O), 161 (Tomas Nevesely), 162/163 (Sylvie Corriveau), 164 & 165 (Kevin Key), 170/171 (Jan Jerman), 172 (Natursports), 176/177 (Little Adventures), 180/181 (Cecilia Lim H M), 184 (PNIK), 185 (Pavle Marjanovic), 186 (Samot), 188/189 (Aleksandar Todorovic), 190/191 (Heracles Kritikos), 194 (Sarah1986), 195 (Tamas Gabor), 203 (Oleg Anisimov), 204 (Paola Balduzzi), 205 (Love Mountains), 211 bottom (Svic), 212/213 (Eclecticism), 214 (Bumble Dee), 215 top (Naturestock1), 215 bottom (Alfonso Cannavacciuolo), 216/217 (Joe Dunckley), 220 (Elena Schweitzer), 221 (Sherlesi), 223 (Irina Afonskaya)